HISTORY OF CIVILIZATION

The Classical Age of Greece

The Classical Age
of Greece

N. G. L. HAMMOND

Emeritus Professor of Greek in the University of Bristol

BARNES & NOBLE
BOOKS
10 East 53d St., New York 10022
(a division of Harper & Row Publishers, Inc.)

ISBN 0 06 492672 9

Published in the U.S.A. 1976 by
Harper & Row Publishers, Inc,
Barnes & Noble Import Division

To my wife

CONTENTS

ILLUSTRATIONS

Between pages 148 and 149

ACKNOWLEDGEMENTS

The author and publishers would like to thank the following for supplying photographs for use in this volume: British Museum, plates 8, 11, 12, 13, 14, 24, 25; Mansell Collection, plates 1, 2, 3, 4, 6, 7, 9, 10, 15, 19, 20, 21, 22, 23, 27; Museum of Art, Basle, plate 18.

MAPS

FOREWORD

This book is due to the initiative of Michael Grant, and I am grateful to him for the encouragement he has given me and for helpful advice. The bulk of the book was written in my last year of teaching at the University of Bristol, which extended every kindness to me during my eleven years there, and the last part was written in the congenial company of my colleagues at the Institute for Research in the Humanities, University of Wisconsin, where I was Johnston Professor for 1973–4. I am very grateful to Miss Rachel Lee of the Department of Classics at Bristol for her careful typing of my manuscript, and to my wife for her help, advice and typing at Madison, Wisconsin.

Part I

THE CREATION OF THE CLASSICAL WORLD
800–546

CHAPTER 1

THE SIGNIFICANCE OF THE POLIS IN GREEK CIVILIZATION

The hallmark of classical civilization was the *polis* or small independent state. The society of the polis was male-dominated, for free adult men alone had the political franchise. It was bound by race in the sense that the citizenship was hereditary, and the granting of the franchise to anyone outside the citizen family was almost unheard of. It was an élite which controlled the underprivileged class or classes within its territory, whether made up of serfs, slaves, resident aliens or mere aliens. These characteristics persisted in the society of citizens which constituted the state, no matter how successful it might be in its policies. They seem to have been as indestructible as the polis itself.

The scale of the polis was tiny. Even at the end of the classical period when great states were casting their shadows over Greece, Aristotle defined the optimum size of the citizenship of the polis as follows: 'A state consisting of too few people will not be self-sufficient, and one consisting of too many will not easily retain the quality of being a community of citizens, for who will address them unless he has the lungs of a Stentor? It is necessary for the citizens to be of such a number that they know each other's personal qualities and thus can elect their officials and judge their fellows in a court of law sensibly.'[1] On similar criteria Plato fixed the number of citizens in his ideal state at 5,040 adult males, remarking that 'the greatest advantage for any state is that the citizens are known to one another'.[2] In practice the great majority of Greek states had less than 5,000 citizens. It is doubtful if Plataea, for instance, had more than 2,000 citizens and Mycenae more than 600 citizens in 479. Size, or the lack of it, did not of itself qualify a state for particular esteem. The names of the thirty-one states, big and small, which defeated the Persian invasion, were inscribed side by side on the golden serpent of the tripod at Delphi, even though Sparta sent 5,000 citizen soldiers, Plataea 600 and Mycenae jointly with Tiryns 400 to the decisive battle at Plataea in 479.

The citizens of a polis knew one another to a degree which is possible nowadays only in a village community. Most of the citizens were related by blood; and family ties were strong in religious and secular contexts and were maintained in corporate ceremonies. As boys they grew up together in small year-classes, each numbering perhaps two hundred at Sparta in her heyday, sixty-five at Plataea and twenty at Mycenae. As men they served side by side in the armed forces; they debated and voted in the assembly; they elected one another and took their turn as elected magistrates; and they cast their votes as jurors for or against their fellows. Communal activities were numerous at all ages. Men engaged together in literary, musical and athletic contests and participated in religious processions and festivals not only as citizens but also as members of a clan or guild or family. Intimate knowledge of one's fellow citizens resulted not simply from the small numbers concerned but much more from the amazing extent to which they did things together. Even at Athens, the largest of all poleis with some 30,000 citizens, we see from the comedies of Aristophanes that an extraordinarily large number of individuals were well known to all the citizens.

In such close-knit societies the individual citizen was in no danger of feeling lost. He was directly involved in politics, justice, military service, religious ceremonies, intellectual discussion, artistic appreciation and so on. To opt out, to be inactive, to shirk responsibility was as rare in the individual as it was reprehensible in the eyes of society; thus at Athens, as Pericles said, the non-participating citizen was regarded 'not as easy-going but as useless,'[3] and at Sparta he was labelled 'an Inferior' and treated as such. The competitive spirit among the citizens was strong and general. Men and women had the desire to excel and to win the fame which in their belief alone survived death. During most of the classical period they sought to excel within their community and often in the service of that community.

Polis differed from polis, even in such details as the names of the months, and each polis preserved its entity and its own traditions. When Pindar wrote his odes honouring the victors in the games and the states to which they belonged, he drew upon an infinite variety of family and state traditions, each appropriate to the occasion and each overlaid with emotional associations. The past was very much a part of the present. When Tegea and Athens put forward rival claims to fight in a more honourable (and more dangerous) position in the line

4

of battle against the Persians, they referred not to their numbers and equipment or their recent exploits but to traditional honours won seven hundred and more years before.[4] Yet the past did not restrict the present. When a colony was planted, it inherited the traditions of its mother-city but it was from the outset a new, independent polis which set up its own laws and constitution. What we call the Greek world was the sum of many hundreds of independent, individual small states, of which no single one was a replica of another. It was a mosaic of very many colours and it had no national pattern at all.

The Greek world of poleis felt itself to be distinct from all contemporary civilizations. They noted the fact by calling all who did not live in poleis by a common name, 'barbarians'. Although the original meaning of the word *barbaros* was a speaker of gibberish, the difference of which the Greeks of the classical period were aware was not primarily one of language, for they applied the word not only to speakers of other languages but also to Greek-speaking peoples who were still at a tribal stage of development. Rather the difference lay in the fact that the polis was a self-governing community in which there was a direct dialogue and interplay between the electorate and the elected magistrates; whereas in the Oriental states of Persia, Lydia or Egypt, for instance, a gulf separated ruler and subject, and in the lesser tribal systems of Europe the authority of the chiefs was based upon the hereditary principle and feudal obligations. Indeed in a modern state how few of us know our rulers? To put it in another way, a member of a Greek state, a *polites*, recognized the authority of no man or number of men but only the authority of the laws which he and his fellow-citizens accepted or enacted as the framework of their community. When Demaratus, the exiled Spartan king, explained to Xerxes the difference between a Persian and a Spartan, he said of the Spartans: 'They are free, yet not altogether free because the law is their master. They fear the law much more than thy subjects fear thee, and they obey its orders which are always the same, not to yield in battle to the enemy, however numerous they may be.'[5]

The distinctive quality of the Greek of the classical world *vis-à-vis* all other men was his combination of courage and intelligence.[6] His courage was moral as well as physical, the courage to carry his convictions to their logical conclusions, as exemplified for instance in the lawgivers Lycurgus, Solon and Pericles and in the imagined characters of Sophocles' plays, Oedipus the king, Antigone and Electra. Courage, enterprise and determination planted colonies on the coasts of the Mediterranean Sea and introduced Greek civilization into Europe;

5

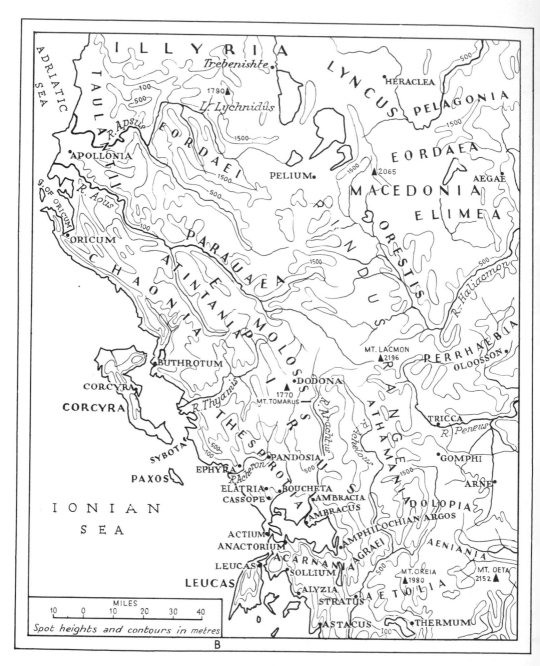

Map 1 Northwest Greece

6

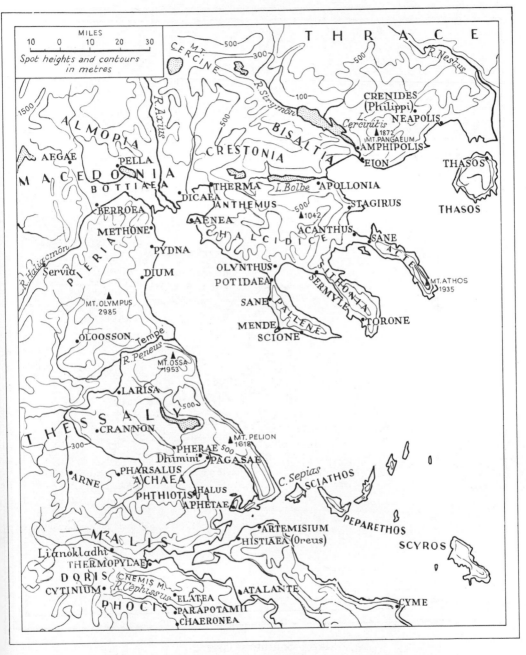

Map 2 Northeast Greece

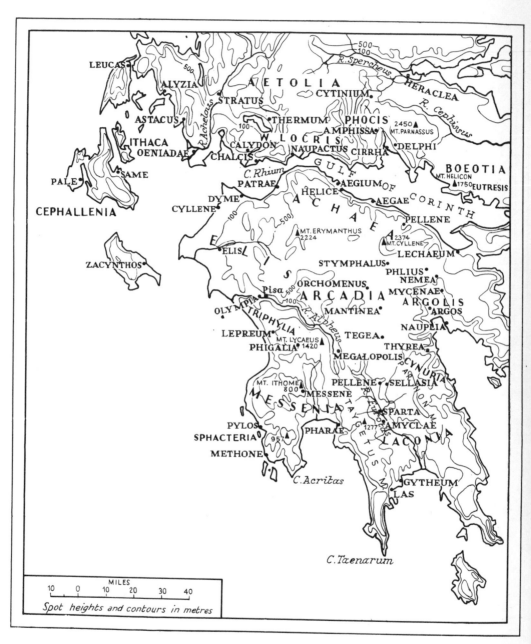

Map 3 Southwest Greece

Map 4 Southeast Greece

9

and the same qualities turned back the tide of Oriental despotism and saved Europe for the development of a distinctively European civilization. The intelligence of the Greek was an innate faculty, to which the Greek language itself bears witness; for no language surpasses it in clarity, subtlety, precision and flexibility. Greek intelligence was at the same time inquisitive and constructive; it asked questions and discovered principles, and on those principles it built castles of logical thought which have stood for two millennia. Here one thinks not only of the intellectual concepts which formed the foundations of metaphysical philosophy, physical science, atomic theory, mathematical logic or human biology, but also of such unrivalled products of the Greek mind as the democratic constitution of Athens and the proportions of the Parthenon.

In the earlier part of the classical period courage and intelligence were directed by a strong sense of what it was right for men to do in the eyes of the gods. We may rationalize this sense as a product of social conscience, traditional values and religious beliefs in a society which was still made up of closely united families and clans. But to the Greek of the polis the gods were immediate and real. They were of two kinds. The first, the Olympian gods, had courage and intelligence. These gods organized their own society on intelligent lines, just as a polis should be organized, and they achieved order and concord as long as they respected the lines on which they had made allocations of power and wealth. To a modern anthropologist these gods are anthropomorphic, but to a Greek of the polis it was rather man who was theomorphic. 'Men and gods are of one family,' wrote Pindar, 'and one mother gives us both the breath of life. What separates us is the sheer totality of power, so that the one is nothing and the other has his everlasting throne set firm in the brazen heavens. Yet we have some likeness to the gods in greatness of mind or in temperament.'[7] The other kind of gods were blind and impersonal. They enforced the laws of human existence and punished the breaches of natural order in human society without that consideration of individual motives which intelligence might seem to demand. Chief among them were the *Erinyes*, 'the Furies', who drove Orestes mad when he had murdered his mother. In facing these deities, which are unlike himself in his better moments, man has need of piety and understanding. As the chorus of Furies say to the Athenians in the *Oresteia*: 'I declare to you the sum of the matter. Respect the altar of Justice. Do not look to material gain and overturn her altar with impious feet; for retribution will follow.'[8]

In the later part of the classical period courage and intelligence continued to be characteristics of the Greeks, but the strong sense of what was right for men to do in the eyes of the gods had almost disappeared. When the Athenian Assembly wished to pass sentence collectively on the generals after the Battle of Arginusae in 406, Socrates was alone in protesting. We may rationalize the change by saying that the Greeks had now evolved to a stage where individual emancipation takes the place of social conscience ('No act is shameful unless the doers of the act think it so' said a character in a play by Euripides) and intellectual realism takes the place of religious belief. The more intelligent of the Greeks probed deeper than this. They saw that a sense of right and respect for the law were essential to the health of any community and especially of a community under a democratic system, and that under a variety of pressures the communal spirit of the polis was giving way to individualism and anarchy. The most dangerous forces were the greedy desire for more pay, power, possessions, etc., in individuals and in states, and a lack of judgement, discrimination and purpose in the political decisions of the majority.[9] Plato, Isocrates and Aristotle proposed ways and means of reforming the polis from within and of improving the relations between poleis. It is interesting that they put their faith primarily in education. But the re-education of a society takes time. As events proved, time was not on their side; for Philip and Alexander of Macedon, moving with stronger purpose and greater speed, took control of the Greek world.

Within the classical period we see the life-cycle of a distinctive political form. Alongside it and closely integrated with it there was a culture of unparalleled brilliance which underwent similar phases of development. In the earlier part of the period poetry predominated over prose in literature and idealism over realism in art, and it was at this time that a sense of right gave direction and purpose to the natural courage and intelligence of the Greeks. In the later part of the period poetry withered and prose flourished; in literature and in art it was an age more of reflection and realism than of creation and idealism. Politically it was a time not of decline but of increasing disintegration. We have much to learn from both parts of the classical period. The close-knit intimate society of the early polis generated an intellectual and artistic energy, a direct involvement of its citizens and a sense of purpose, which are generally lacking in the larger and looser structure of the national territorial state. A national crisis may generate such qualities in our own society, but only for a brief time; or, within the national complex smaller units such as universities, schools or regiments may achieve a similar ethos. Perhaps we are living in the last phase of the life-cycle of the national territorial state and of the civilization which we regard as distinctively European. Ours is certainly an age of prose rather than.poetry, an age of reflection and realism, in which the dangerous forces of material greed and faulty judgement threaten the traditional structure of society with disintegration. The historical analyst has incomparable material in the history of the polis in the classical period for the study of a society in miniature, brightly lit by the brilliance of its literature, art and thought, and precisely defined by its own specific qualities.

CHAPTER 2

THE GROWTH OF THE DORIAN STATES
800–546

A complete collapse of civilization is hard to imagine. Yet it certainly occurred on the Greek mainland and in the southern islands of the Aegean Sea towards the end of the second millenium. At first the new masters – Dorians, Boeotians, Thessalians and 'West Greeks', all originating from backward regions of northwestern Greece – took over the large Mycenaean kingdoms in which, for instance, Idomeneus had commanded all Cretans and Menelaus all inhabitants of Laconia. But large kingdoms need good communications and a literate executive. Both disappeared completely in the aftermath of the invasions, and masters and serfs alike in the conquered areas reverted to village existence, illiterate, ill-organized, living family by family on its own produce at subsistence standard. Hesiod is the poet of such a 'peasant economy' in *The Works and Days*. To him as a hill-farmer in Boeotia manual labour is no disgrace; honesty, industry and religious observance pay in the end. His concern is with truth and reality – how to cultivate the soil, propitiate the gods, avoid unlucky days, foretell the weather – and he is consciously didactic as he reproves his idle, good-for-nothing brother. Yet peasant as he is, he has the vision of the poet, transforming the particular into the universal. 'Pull your felt cap down to protect your ears; for dawn comes chill when the North Wind strikes.'[1] The originator of personal didactic poetry, Hesiod has few rivals in this genre in any language.

In the self-standing village the unit was the family. In the conquered areas the life of the masters was complicated by the fact that they belonged to rival clans and tribes, and this led often to strife, vendetta and warfare between family and family or clan and clan, so much so in Megaris that a man at work in the fields was by convention exempt from attack.[2] It was in an attempt to arrest this destructive dissension that the freemen of several villages first put aside their differences and combined into a single community. Thus the polis originated. 'The association of several villages', wrote Aristotle, 'is the full-grown polis, because it already possesses the dimensions of almost complete self-sufficiency. The polis came into existence for survival; it continues to exist for the good life.'[3]

Such poleis came into existence first in Crete, then at Sparta, Corinth and Megara on the mainland. The name 'polis' was probably adopted from the defensible point (later 'acropolis') round which the cluster of villages often formed. It should not be translated '*city*-state', for no urban centre or conurbation was involved in the association. The citizens continued to live in their villages or *obes*.

The polis was at once stronger than any single village. It lay within its power either to incorporate more villages, extend its citizenship and so create a larger state, or to subjugate its neighbours. The first poleis took the latter course, naming their subjects the *Perioeci* ('the neighbours'). For two or three centuries the polis proliferated as a political form of society, but the aggregation of poleis into a larger state did not occur. The process stopped at polis level. Within the Dorian poleis, which were the first to form, the Dorian masters held the descendants of the earlier population in serfdom. At first each family had its own serfs; then for the greater security of the society the legal ownership of the serfs passed from the families to the state itself. But whatever the terms of ownership, it was a racially exclusive élite which held a monopoly of power within the polis. In the Dorian form of state this élite had the tasks of controlling the state-owned serfs, keeping the Perioeci in subjection and dealing with neighbouring poleis.

The formation of a polis did not of itself put an end to dissension between families or clans. It was necessary to reorientate the citizens away from the family-clan-tribe complex and towards the concept of a common citizenship. The first successful reorientation was made at Lyttus in Crete. Sparta soon followed suit, and eventually the Dorian poleis of Crete, perhaps as many as a hundred in number, adopted the same methods as Lyttus, no doubt with local variations. The essential features of the new system were state education and state selection of citizen for state purposes.

At Lyttus boys of citizen birth on reaching the age of seventeen were organized in troops and subjected to a rigorous training under strict discipline. Two years later those who graduated successfully were considered for election to the men's clubs, in each of which the members fed together and campaigned together for the rest of their active life. The state maintained the troops for the boys and the clubs for the men from public funds, and the state granted the political franchise to those who graduated from the troops and were elected to the clubs. The fall-outs had lesser rights not only in politics but also at law. The state restricted the ownership of good land to citizen families and subsidized them with the labour of the state-owned serfs. The citizens, significantly called 'the warrior group', served the state in politics and in war, while the under-privileged, called 'the land-working group', provided the citizens with the means of subsistence. In this division of specialized functions the citizen class – 'the party', to use a modern term – was small, tight-knit, exclusive and dominant. Its position is expressed frankly in the words of a Cretan clubman's drinking song: 'My wealth is spear, sword and shield . . . with this I plough and reap and tread the sweet wine from the grape, I the master of the serfs.'[4]

Within 'the party' a stable constitution was essential. Ten men from certain families were elected by the citizens to hold office for a year as magistrates, superintending the state system of troops and clubs, commanding the army, and wielding strong executive powers. Policy was initiated and directed by a council of thirty elders who were recruited from the ex-magistrates by election, held office for life and were not answerable to the electorate. The citizens meeting in assembly elected the magistrates and the elders; they passed without question the unanimous proposals of the magistrates-and-elders; and they decided when rival proposals were brought before them. Thus the party line was generally imposed from above by an elected caucus, but the party-members *en masse* retained the basic rights of admitting new members, electing bosses and deciding in disputed matters.

The logical completeness of this Cretan system in organizing education, society and government for a clearly envisaged objective is of great interest because it foreshadows many subsequent systems of one-party rule. The effect of this system being adopted by so many poleis within Crete was that the island was throughout the classical period the arena of inter-state politics and often of inter-state warfare; as a whole it played little part in the history of Greece. It was a different matter when the system was adopted by Sparta. There it had a decisive effect upon world history.

The Spartan account was that one man, Lycurgus, passed a fundamental and multilateral reform based upon the Cretan model but incorporating some native features such as the dual monarchy. It may well be correct. The freemen of five villages or obes combined to form the new polis, 'Sparta', and the electoral system was based on residence in the obes at first and on heredity thereafter. State education was more thorough than in Crete. Boys left home at seven. They were organized in troops and played competitive team games. They underwent military training from eighteen to twenty, and they were billeted in barracks for ten years thereafter. At the age of thirty, if they were elected unanimously to a club, they became citizens and were entitled 'Equals' among themselves and 'Spartiates' to the outside world. The unsuccessful became 'Inferiors' as in Crete. There was state education for girls, who lived at home but were organized in troops. Boys and girls engaged together in basic subjects and in athletics, dancing and music. Relations between the sexes were more free than in other states, but after marriage (usually at thirty for the man) the husband fed in his club until the age of sixty and the wife stayed in the household. The state arranged for the 'Equals' a basic equality in land-holding and provided them with the labour of the state-owned serfs, called *Helots*, while the Equal had to contribute a fixed amount of produce to his club as a condition of retaining his citizenship.

The constitution accommodated the two kings by treating them as executive magistrates with defined powers. The kingships were restricted to members of two houses of the Heraclid clan, claiming descent from Heracles, which had led the Dorian conquerors into Laconia. The kings were elected usually in direct hereditary succession by the people and could be deposed by the people. As magistrates they commanded in war and conducted state ritual; their prestige and on the whole their competence safeguarded Sparta from *coups d'état* by colonels in what was inevitably a highly militarized state. Policy was initiated by a council of thirty elders. The council included the two kings, the other members being elected for life from the Equals of sixty or more years of age. The society of Equals in full assembly debated proposals which were made only by the council and decided upon them. They also elected the kings, the elders and the five *Ephors*, the last being aged over thirty and being elected for one year to superintend the state system of troops, barracks and clubs. At the time when the fundamental reform was carried, the Spartan constitution was more liberal than that of Lyttus in Crete which it had taken as a model. Throughout antiquity it was regarded as a mixed constitution, but the age and authority of the elders ensured a very conservative approach to policy.

The concept of statesmanship which we see at work at Lyttus and at Sparta is strange to us because we tend to see a modern government engaged primarily in devising expedients to restore a balance of payments, ease disputes between management and labour, and appease the multifarious demands of the citizens. The Greeks regarded statesmanship as the supreme creative art. As they saw it, the statesman consciously and deliberately moulded a fully-rounded society to a preconceived image, just as a sculptor shapes a fully-rounded statue, imposing his will upon nature's raw material. The point was emphasized by Plato.[5] The system of Lycurgus at Sparta, for instance, was not an expedient devised merely to hold down the Helots by military force. His aim was to achieve 'complete *arete*': to realize his ideal of man's full stature within the society of the polis. The ideal was austere, perhaps, and limited in our way of thinking, but it was artistic and satisfying. When political philosophers from Plato onwards tried to create a society on paper in the image of an ideal, they turned admiring eyes on Sparta rather than on Athens because Lycurgus had created such a society not in theory alone but in action.

It is a mistake to suppose that the Equals found the Spartan way of life repressive. Within it they enjoyed parity of education, training and opportunity, parity of basic income and parity of esteem; and equality among the privileged was as acceptable then as it is rare today. Spartans were probably predisposed by temperament as well as conditioned by training to an orderly, disciplined way of life. Thucydides described the salient characteristics of the Spartan national character as a sense of order and a sense of honour, the former producing a disciplined society which was obedient to the spirit and the letter of the constitution and the latter producing men who were courageous in war and sane in policy.[6] The Spartans themselves emphasized the orderliness of their life and their willing obedience to the state when they called the restructuring of their society by Lycurgus the *Eunomia*, the 'well-ordered government'; and Simonides expressed the Spartan spirit in the epitaph written for the men who fell at Thermopylae: 'Go, stranger, tell the Spartans that we lie here obedient to their word'.[7]

We may well be outraged by Sparta's treatment of the Helots and the Perioeci. But we should note that ancient societies were to a great extent based on slavery, and the Helot was better off than the slave. At Sparta certain rights were conceded to the Inferiors, the Perioeci and the Helots, in the interest no doubt of order and efficiency rather than of humanity. On many occasions Perioeci and Helots fought loyally with the Spartiates against other Greek states, and seven armed Helots fought alongside each Spartiate against the Persians at Plataea.

Whether the Eunomia was carried just before 800 as Thucydides said,[8] or some decades after 800 as some scholars maintain, the Spartans went on to conquer their neighbours in Laconia in 800–750. They left the Perioeci of each village community to administer their internal affairs but made them dependent on Sparta in matters of foreign policy and in military service. Perioecic troops served under the command of the kings who styled themselves 'kings of the Lacedaemonians'. Thus a larger state, 'the Lacedaemonians', was created. Within it the Spartiates had a monopoly of control, and the Perioecic communities had a restricted freedom such as that enjoyed by some Russian satellites. With her augmented forces Sparta attacked Messenia, a territory as large and as fertile as Laconia, and after twenty years of war, c. 740–720, incorporated it in the Lacedaemonian state. The Spartiates were given estates of the richest land and the previous possessors became state-owned serfs, 'toiling like asses under great burdens'[9] and paying half the produce to their masters. Thus the bulk of Messenia became analogous to a ranch run by slaves. The communities in the hills were given the status of Perioeci. Henceforth the only free Messenians were *émigrés*.

The annexation of Messenia by Sparta was an act of open aggrandizement, not unparalleled in modern European history. It doubled the resources and the commitments of Sparta, and it underlined the need for a firm and unwavering control of policy. Modifications in the constitution which had been made during the period of expansion became permanent. If the Council of Elders agreed on a proposal, that proposal was now automatically ratified; thus the right of the Assembly to decide came into play only when the Council put forward two or more rival proposals. The five Ephors were made into representatives of the citizens; they led the Assembly, attended meetings of the Council, negotiated with the kings at home and on campaign, and declared war each year on the Helots. Thus major decisions could be taken in cabinet, as it were, and the executive authority was concentrated in as few hands as possible. In a modern democratic state such modifications are made only in time of war, and in a sense Sparta was continually on a footing of war with the Helots, the Perioeci and other states, especially with the rival Dorian state, Argos. In 669 Sparta was defeated by Argos, and in 640 Messenia rose in revolt with the help of Argos; but Sparta won in the end, reducing the Messenians to bondage again by 620 and restoring her frontiers with Argos. During these critical years Sparta's poet, Tyrtaeus, wrote the marching songs which inspired the Spartiates in action. 'Forward, you sons of stalwart Sparta's citizens, forward with shield advanced on your left arm, with spearpoint poised courageously. Think not to save your life; that is not Sparta's way.'[10] In 546 Sparta defeated Argos decisively and annexed a frontier district. She was without any doubt the most powerful state in the Greek world.

Sparta's example was followed by other Dorian communities on the mainland in the course of the eighth century. Two examples will suffice. The freemen of eight villages combined to form the polis of Corinth. There are mentions of citizen estates, serfs and Perioeci in Corinthia, and the citizens prided themselves on their system, the Eunomia, which was evidently akin to that at Sparta. The constitution was different in that the members of an aristocratic clan had a monopoly of office and directed policy. This clan, the Bacchiadae, which claimed descent from Heracles, consisted of some two hundred households, and marriage was entirely within its own membership. It is an interesting example of a closed aristocratic oligarchy, that is of rule by the few, based on noble birth. The new state sided with Sparta against Argos. It also tried to annex some territory to the north and reduce the people there to serfdom and Perioecic status. But the neighbours of Corinth to the north, the Megarians, maintained their liberty. For they too had formed a polis: the peoples of five villages had coalesced to provide a new community of citizens. Here too the Dorian masters held dominion over the serfs and trained themselves in the art of war. The nature of Megara's constitution is not known to us.

The Dorian form of polis, which Sparta initiated on the mainland and other Dorian communities imitated, was particularly well suited to a closed and static agricultural economy. The Lacedaemonian state rested on such an economy throughout the classical period, and its constitution renamed the same. On the other hand, economic changes at Corinth and Megara led to changes in their political systems.

Corinth was strategically placed on the land-route which connected the Peloponnese and central Greece, and she was now strong enough to impose tolls on goods in transit through her territory. At the same time she lay at the junction of the sea-lanes which came from the west to the head of the Gulf of Corinth and from the east into the Saronic Gulf; she offered the best harbours for mariners on both gulfs and the shortest route for the porterage of goods across the narrow isthmus. A pioneer in the design and building of warships, she levied dues on the maritime trade which was attracted to her harbours and was safe-guarded by her navy. As her wealth and population increased, she planted very strong colonies at Oeniadae, Corcyra and Syracuse, and her fleet became the strongest in the western seas. Although the Bacchiadae and the citizens of Corinth were not traders themselves but exploiters of trade, new forms of wealth came into their hands and disrupted the solidarity of the state. The ranks of the Bacchiadae split, and a military commander, Cypselus, seized power by a *coup d'état*

c. 657. For seventy-five years Corinth was under 'one-man-rule', the very negation of the self-government which was the birthright of the polis. Disapproval is inherent in the Greek word *tyrannos*, which was applied particularly to an illegitimate ruler.

At Corinth the tyrants pursued a brilliantly successful policy, planting colonies at Potidaea in the northeast and at Leucas, Ambracia, Apollonia and Dyrrachium in the northwest, and constructing a paved way for transporting ships as well as cargoes across the isthmus. Prosperity reached a new level, alliances were made far afield, and a naval presence was maintained in the Aegean Sea. The tyrants tried to improve the image of the state and themselves by encouraging art, literature, athletics, full employment and high wages. But the desire for liberty remained strong. The last of the line was assassinated c. 582. The Dorians took control again, organizing themselves under the Eunomia and establishing an oligarchic form of constitution.

Megara, like Corinth, was on the land-route through the isthmus and had harbours on both gulfs, but she had a less favourable position than Corinth and did not reach such a high level of prosperity. She too founded colonies, some in Sicily but the most successful on the shores of the Sea of Marmara and the Black Sea. Byzantium, Chalcedon and Mesembria became the most distinguished of her daughters. The influx of new forms of wealth split the ruling class and resulted, in the words of the Megarian poet, Theognis, in 'party faction, civil war and one-man-rule'. Tyranny was short-lived at Megara, and the Dorian oligarchy returned to power. But the fabric of the Dorian system had been shaken. A democratic revolution ensued, and the democrats threw out the oligarchs and enfranchised the serfs, who hitherto had lived 'like deer outside the city walls'. An internal struggle between Dorian and non-Dorian, between oligarch and democrat, soon became a class struggle between rich and poor which Theognis regarded with horror. 'Gone is Faith, goddess supreme, gone Moderation from mankind, and the Graces have deserted our land, my friend. Among men solemn oaths are no longer respected, and no one reveres the immortal gods.'[11]

The political troubles which overtook some of the Dorian states – in particular Corinth, Megara, Sicyon and Epidaurus – were watched by Sparta, whose political stability and agricultural economy continued unperturbed. She declared herself the enemy of tyranny, enlisted the support of the priests at Delphi and helped in the final liberation of Corinth and Sicyon from tyranny. While Argos claimed to be the leader of the Dorians and pursued a narrowly aggressive policy, Sparta proclaimed herself the protector of all Peloponnesians of whatever racial origin against the aggression of Argos. She then initiated the first large-scale military coalition in the history of the Greek states.

The basis was a defensive alliance made between Sparta and a single state, such as Tegea in Arcadia or Corinth or Megara. These states were not necessarily in alliance with one another. Thus a coalition came into existence which, like a spoked but rimless wheel, had Sparta as the hub and centre. Let us suppose that Argos attacked Corinth. Corinth could then invoke the help of Sparta, and Sparta, if she wished, could invoke the aid of her other allies. Thus Sparta, and Sparta alone, could call out the forces of all her allies against an aggressor. Such a coalition proved very attractive. By 550 all Peloponnesian states except Argos had treaties of alliance with her.

It is probable that each treaty of defensive alliance had two clauses which benefited Sparta: the first that Messenian *émigrés* would be expelled, and the second that the Spartan kings or their deputies would command the allied forces in the field. Thus Sparta created for herself a protective shield of allies, put Messenian *émigrés* at a safe distance from her frontiers, and increased very greatly the military forces of which the kings would take command in a crisis. At the same time each ally received the guarantee that it would be given the most powerful protection possible against any aggressor at what seemed a very small price. Yet the preponderance of Sparta in the military field had political consequences which she may well have foreseen, namely the supremacy of the oligarchs in the member-states of the coalition, which we shall call more appropriately 'the Spartan Alliance' than 'the Peloponnesian League'. The Alliance was to hold firm for almost two hundred years. Statesmanship in Europe has not since devised any coalition against aggression which has proved so long-lived and so effective.

Another important development took place in central Greece at about the same time. There Thebes had become a polis on the Dorian model in the latter part of the eighth century. At first she incorporated the peoples of some nearby villages on equal terms, but then she made them tributary. Meanwhile a considerable number of other poleis developed in the plains north and south of Thebes, some being Dorian in dialect and others Aeolian. Shortly before 550 a federation was formed by Thebes and most but not all of these poleis, and the citizens of the federal state were named 'The Boeotians'. Thus there came into being a double citizenship; for one was both a Theban (or a Thespian) and a Boeotian. This double citizenship is the mark of what we shall call a *League*, in this case 'The Boeotian League'. The close degree of integration within the federation was indicated by, for example, its federal army under federal commanders, its federal coinage, and its common religious symbol, the shield of Athena.

The administrative centre of the Boeotian League was at the geographical centre of Boeotia, Thebes, which was destined to dominate the League not by any treaty right but by virtue of her strength and ability. Throughout the history of the League any political developments at Thebes tended to be reflected in the other member-states. In the early days of the League a narrow oligarchy ruled over Thebes, and similar oligarchies took power in the member-states. Ideologically there was a natural affinity of outlook between the Boeotian League and the Spartan Alliance. If Boeotia were to be attacked by her northern neighbours, Thessaly and Phocis, where less advanced forms of federal union were in being, or by her southern neighbour Athens, it was likely that the Boeotian League would seek and obtain aid from the Spartan Alliance.

CHAPTER 3

THE CONTRIBUTION OF THE DORIAN STATES TO EARLY GREEK CULTURE

After the collapse of the Mycenaean world the first revival of culture within Greece was at Athens, almost the only Mycenaean kingdom which had not been overrun. There the 'Protogeometric' style of pottery arose in which painted geometric patterns, sparingly used at first, emphasized the structure of the vase in an austere and mathematical manner. Its successor c. 950, 'Geometric', continued the tradition but admitted more patterns on the surface of the vase and added stylized human and animal figures to the patterns. When Dorian poleis were formed early in the eighth century, they adopted the Athenian Geometric style and developed independent and fine local schools, for instance in Boeotia, Corinth, Argos, Sparta, Crete and Rhodes. It is evident that the austere symmetry of the style appealed alike to the Ionians of Athens and the Dorians of the mainland.

However, the revival of culture was due in general to influences which came to the Peloponnese and Athens from the more developed countries of the Near East – Syria, Phoenicia and Egypt. The main route at first was via Rhodes and Crete. An early arrival around 800 was the Phoenician alphabet, which was brilliantly adapted by the Greeks to provide a symbol for each vowel as well as for each consonant in the Greek language. The adaptation was done in different ways in different states; the earliest forms have been found in the Dorian communities of the islands of Crete, Thera and Melos. Carved ivories of Phoenician and Syrian origin were imported into Rhodes, Crete, Sparta, Corinth and Athens, where Greek craftsmen soon mastered the new media. Clay masks at Sparta showed Phoenician influence. In the latter part of the eighth century Geometric pottery was replaced by 'Orientalizing' pottery. This was a revolutionary change for Orientalizing pottery was rich in colours and in designs, being inspired by acquaintance with eastern rugs and tapestries. It developed first in

Crete, Corinth and Laconia, and it was at this time that the leadership in pottery and in the goods it contained passed from Athens to the Dorian states of the islands and the mainland. Crete led c. 750–650 in the Aegean, and then Rhodes. Corinth led on the mainland, and her pottery was supreme among the Greeks of the West c.700–550. Laconian pottery, second only to Corinthian in quality, reached most parts of the mainland and was exported to Sparta's colony Taras (Taranto), Etruria, Cyrene, Egypt and Samos. Similar developments took place in the working of gold and bronze. Corinth excelled in the making of bronze cauldrons with animal heads projecting, like handles, from the rim; conspicuous among these were the heads of griffins, fantastic in the East but beautifully stylized by the Greek craftsman.

In adopting artistic forms from the East the Greeks showed discrimination and taste, reducing excessive ornamentation to a level which suited their sense of order and composition. In statuary and architecture they had their own tradition of working in wood. What they learnt from the East was the use of bronze and stone. The earliest bronze statuettes combine strength with poise, for instance in the representation of young men, naked except for a belt or a helmet; Crete and the Peloponnese were outstanding in this field. The Greeks had had long experience of building in wood. The expertise they had acquired lay behind the rapid development of the Doric order of architecture in stone, which was established late in the seventh century and thereafter underwent little change. The earliest surviving temples of the Doric order are the temple of Apollo at Corinth with its monolithic columns, imitative of wooden columns, and the temple of Hera at Posidonia (Paestum) in south Italy. The order is remarkable for strength and simplicity, two qualities which recur in Norman church architecture, and it expresses the orderliness and the austerity of the Dorian outlook. The grasp of proportion and perspective is amazing when we remember that the tradition of working in stone was just beginning.

The Dorian states were deeply religious. The Spartans, for instance, believed that Zeus had given Laconia to the Heraclid kings, Apollo himself had inspired the Eunomia, and Zeus and Athena were protectors of the state. The first words of the charter of their newly-founded polis were these: 'Found a temple of Zeus Syllanius and Athena Syllania'.[1] The community of citizens expressed its devotion and gratitude to the gods in numerous ceremonies, festivals and competitions, and in music, dance and song. Religious expression in the Dorian states was communal rather than individual. The Dorians excelled in the choric dance, and the music to which it was set, 'the Doric mode', was held to be serious and manly. Their lyric poetry too was composed not for the single voice but for choral performance. Only a few pieces of this poetry survive, but we can recapture something of its beauty from a fragment written by Alcman for a choir of Spartan girls. As they carried the sacred robe to the temple of Artemis Orthia in the twilight between moonset and sunrise, the choir divided into two groups and sang of the charm and quality of their leaders in antiphony.[2] The Greeks were much more conscious than we are of the moral import and influence of music, dance and song. Certainly the Dorian forms of art reflected and encouraged the corporate spirit of the Dorian community in the polis.

Sparta was a centre of art and literature. Competitions, similar to those of an Eisteddfod, were held there. Poets came to it from overseas; Terpander, for instance, came from Lesbos and stayed on at Sparta in the middle of the seventh century. He wrote of Sparta as the place 'where the spear of the young man and the clear-toned Muse flourish, and orderliness, defender of honourable actions, walks in her streets'. Corinth too was famous as the home of the war-god Ares and 'the gentle-voiced Muse'. Her poet Eumelus wrote epic and lyric poetry c. 730, and the court of her tyrant Periander was visited c. 600 by Arion, who first brought to the mainland the *dithyramb*, a form of choral dance which was set to music and accompanied by songs for which there was a metrical lyric script. Sicyon was famous for her 'tragic choruses', which honoured a local hero Adrastus; and when the god Dionysus became the object of their worship, about 590, Sicyon led the way towards the development of what was to be known later as tragedy (*tragōdia*). Megara was represented by the poet Theognis and claimed to have been in some sense the originator of comedy. It was indeed the springtime of Greek poetry when so many new forms were being invented, and in some cases perfected, and when choral lyric was expressing the religious faith and the creative excitement of the age.

During this period the Dorian element on the mainland was the most progressive part of the Greek world. It provided the framework for the classical period by creating the polis and by inventing the particular type of coalition with one commanding state, which we call 'The Spartan Alliance'. It planted many of the most powerful colonies, e.g. Syracuse, Taras, Apollonia, Corcyra, Ambracia, Potidaea, Chalcedon and Byzantium, and it developed maritime commerce and naval power, especially in the West. Its leadership in art, music, literature and architecture was partly due to its own abilities and partly to the fact that its prosperity attracted artists to the Peloponnese. In the same way the abilities and the prosperity of Athens were to attract artists and thinkers to Athens in the fifth century. The Dorians created the first Panhellenic centre, which soon drew people from all parts of the Greek world. This was established in the Peloponnese at Olympia, where Zeus and Hera were worshipped, and here the Olympic games were held every fourth year from 776 onwards. At first it was a Peloponnesian gathering and Spartan competitors won most of the prizes. Later in the seventh century it became a truly international festival. Two more such festivals were organized early in the sixth century, one at Nemea and the other at the Isthmus of Corinth; and another, on the initiative of the Thessalians, at Delphi in honour of Pythian Apollo, the particular god of the Dorians. Athletics were an important part of Greek life.

The sense of Greek civilization as an independent entity distinct from Phoenician or Egyptian civilization grew stronger in the century 650–550, partly as a reflex of the colonizing movement, partly through the unifying influence of the centres of Greek religion at Delphi, Olympia and Dodona, and partly through attendance at the great festivals. This sense did not, of course, diminish the difference between Argos and Sparta or between Dorian and Ionian, any more than the concept of European civilization, which has grown from similar sources, has blurred the distinction between France and Germany or between Teuton and Slav. But the growing sense among the Greek states that they belonged to a common culture was to be of capital importance when the Greek world was threatened with invasion from the East and from the West.

CHAPTER 4

THE STAGNATION OF ATHENS AND ITS
REVIVAL THROUGH SOLON

In ancient times the direct route between northern Greece and the Peloponnese ran from Thebes through the Megarid to Corinth (see Map 4). It left to one side the peninsula which is called Attica. It was this geographical fact which saved the Mycenaean kingdom of Athens when the first great waves of the Dorian invasion broke against the entry to the Peloponnese. A trial of strength came later, c. 1050. By then Athens was stronger, having received an influx of refugees from other parts of the Mycenaean world, and by then the original impetus of the Dorian invasion had almost died away. Victory went to Athens. Thus the Mycenaean state of Athens was preserved, though in a sadly impoverished world, and it was there that the old traditions were fostered, and there that the first revival of culture occurred.

Tradition relates that Athens owed her victory to her king, Codrus. He was a member of a refugee family, the Neleidae, which had fled from Pylus in Messenia and became the ruling house at Athens. Members of this family promoted and led a great migration which was launched from 'Ionian' Attica and resulted in the foundation of many 'Ionian' states on islands of the Aegean basin and on part of the coast of Asia Minor (see p. 41, below). The name 'Ionian' was both a tribute to Athens as foundress and a mark of differentiation from the Dorian group. Those who went overseas as settlers were not native Athenians but refugees from many parts of the mainland. The migration continued during several generations, from c. 1050 to 900. But in the succeeding centuries Athens lost her momentum. When colonization began in the eighth century the pioneering states were Chalcis and Eretria in Euboea on the one hand, and Corinth and Megara on the other. The primacy in commerce and in art passed to Corinth, and innovations in literature and in architecture were associated not with Athens but with the Dorian states, at least as far as the mainland was concerned. Even in the first half of the sixth century, when Sparta formed the Spartan alliance and the Boeotians formed the Boeotian League, Athens made no contribution to inter-state politics.

The decline of Athens is something of an enigma to historians. Her territory was considerably larger than the territories of Megara and Corinth put together, and her free population was three or four times greater than that of Sparta in the sixth century. It seems to the author that the reason for Athens' plight is to be found in the fact that, whereas her Dorian neighbours had restructured their society and formed the tightly-knit polis, Athens had not done so and therefore suffered still from the internal divisions which were inherent in a racially organized society. We owe our knowledge of Athens at this time mainly to Aristotle. 'The whole population', he wrote, 'was in four tribes, and in each tribe there were three divisions, called Thirds or *Phratries*.'[1] He goes on to explain that a *phratry* was a group of clans (*gene*) and that a clan was made up of a number of families (*oikoi*). Such a pattern of blood-related groups is familiar in primitive Indo-European societies. The division into four tribes recurs with the same names in other Ionian societies; indeed they are generic to the Ionian branch of the Greek-speaking peoples. The phratry, being a group of related clans, was a more compact entity than the tribe, and its internal affairs were managed by the adult male *phrateres* or 'brothers' (the word being of the same root as *fratres* in Latin). The head of the phratry was a *phratriarch*. A clan being a group of related families, was more compact still. Its affairs were in the hands of the adult male clansmen (*gennetai*). At the end of the line the family was the basic unit, and it was represented in the clan by its adult male members only (*oikeioi*). The actual running of affairs within the racial units might be oligarchic or democratic; for instance, the phrateres who ran the affairs of a phratry might be either the oldest only or all adult male members, and a genos might be run by or be represented by a small number of gennetai.

The 'thirds' were units of territory, and it is clear that a given third was inhabited by a given phratry, that is by a phratry's constituent clans and families. We may assume from analogies in the Dorian areas and in some Ionian areas that the division of the land into thirds had happened in the very distant past and that it had been made only in respect of the good arable land, which in Attica was the land in the plains, quite a small proportion of the surface area. To which level in the racial structure was the possession of this land attributed? The answer is given by Plutarch when he says that at the time when Solon legislated, 'the property and the house had to stay in the genos'.[2] In other words, the genos or clan as a whole was the possessor, and land of this kind could not be alienated by any family or any individual member of the clan.

We have seen that the population of Attica was greatly increased in the eleventh century by the influx of refugees, and Thucydides tells us that the refugees were made citizens. How were these new citizens grafted onto the racial tree of Athenian society? It appears that the new citizens were organized in guilds and called guildsmen (*orgeones*) and that the state 'required the phrateres to accept not only the gennetai but also the orgeones' into its membership.[3] Thus the grafting was done at the level of the phratry. Long after the time of Solon, when other qualifications for admission to the citizenship were required, an aspirant had still to be admitted to a phratry either as a clansman or as a guildsman. Admission did not necessarily mean equality. For example, a guildsman's family not being a part of a clan could not obtain the use of good arable land in the plains.

In a state organized in this manner the chances of dissension were very great. Rivalries between clans, leading to strife and vendettas, were certainly as rife in early Attica as they were later in Scotland and, until recently, in Albania. Even within the clan there were rivalries; for some families regarded themselves (and were sometimes regarded by others) as the leading houses of a clan. Jurisdiction over the clans was in the hands of the phratry which administered justice and regulated religious ceremonials as well as admitting new members. Even phratries might enter into conflict with one another; then it was the four tribal kings who administered justice, each within his own tribe. The inherent rift in society between the clansmen and the guildsmen was also full of danger for the unity of the state.

Bloodshed raises special problems in a community of this kind. In Albania, for instance, the settlement of a vendetta depended on the voluntary consent of the two families involved and the observance of certain rules which had been laid down at a meeting of tribal elders. The central government took no part, except that from time to time it announced its support of the rules. We know of two cases at Athens in the late seventh century which concerned killings. In the first instance, in 632 some men of the Alcmeonid clan killed a number of citizens who had taken part in an unsuccessful attempt to seize power, when they were suppliants at the altar of Athena. Many years later a state court decided that sacrilege had been committed and passed sentence of banishment on the entire Alcmeonid clan; the bones of those who had died since the killing were exhumed and cast outside Attica. The state court was composed of 300 judges elected on the qualification of birth (*aristinden*). In the second instance, in 621 Draco published a state law establishing a court of appeal in matters of homicide. Fifty-one judges were elected, on the qualification of birth, to serve on the court. If they found a man guilty of unintentional homicide, he was exiled for life. However, provision was made for a 'pardon' (corresponding to a settlement in Albania). A pardon could be granted only on the *unanimous* agreement of the dead person's immediate male relatives; or, failing these, of male relatives to the degree of cousin. If there were none extant (i.e. no *oikeioi*), the right of pardon passed to ten phratores elected on the qualification of birth. Prosecution too was vested in the same way in blood-related groups of the dead person.[4]

In the first case we see that it is not the individual killers or even the families of the individual killers but the entire clan that was held responsible. In this matter, as in the tenure of good arable land, the clan is the significant unit. In the second case the state does not prosecute or fix the sentence or grant pardon; it is concerned to see only that the correct procedures are being observed. Here the blood-related group in its entirety on the male side (prolonged to the level of ten phrateres, if necessary) is the significant unit, and it has to act as a unit. Moreover, the court is a court only of appeal; we may assume that most cases were tried and settled in a primary court which was not a state court but a tribal or a phratry court. Thus we see that in certain matters the state was dealing not with individual citizens but with racial groups of citizens, whether phratries or clans, and that each phratry and each clan was a state within the state. This was very far removed from the contemporary situation at Sparta.

Election on the qualification of birth (*aristinden*) has been interpreted in various ways. Some have supposed that there was a blue-blooded group in each phratry and so twelve blue-blooded groups in the state, and that the members of these groups alone were entitled to represent the phratry and serve as judges within the state. There is however no indication that there was anything like a peerage or an aristocracy or a patrician class within Attic society. All who were racially Athenian seem to have been equally so in tribe, phratry, clan and family. The only distinction which was made was in regard to some priestly offices which were reserved to members of certain clans. One might, I suppose, call these persons a religious aristocracy; but holders of religious offices had no privileges outside the religious sphere, and they were in fact debarred on religious grounds from judging in matters of bloodshed. It seems then that the only distinction by birth was that between those who were citizens by racial descent and those who were citizens by adoption, that is between clansmen and guildsmen. Thus if a guildsman were killed and he had no male relatives alive, he was represented by ten phrateres who were elected *aristinden*, that is from those who were phrateres by racial descent and not from those who were phrateres by adoption. Similarly at the state level the judges were drawn from clansmen only and not from guildsmen. This then seems to be the meaning of *aristinden* in these contexts. We shall come to it again in a political context.

We can reconstruct Draco's laws of debt from the poems of Solon (who changed the laws) and from ancient commentaries on the laws. The reconstruction is controversial, but the following version seems the most probable. Bankrupt debtors 'either worked the land paying a sixth of the produce to the rich [creditors]', writes Plutarch, 'or were liable to be seized by their creditors as they had made their persons security for the loan'.[5] It is apparent that we have one law for a family of clansmen which, when bankrupt, could not sell the land and could not be deprived of it, because it belonged inalienably to the clan, and another law for a family of guildsmen, which, when bankrupt, could be seized and sold in the slave market. The law, in fact, was less severe for the clansman than for the guildsman, for it was better to be forced to stay on the land and pay one-sixth of the produce, being as it were a serf or tied tenant, than to be sold as a slave; or, if we may express it in another way, it was better to put the good arable land under bondage (for a marker was put upon the land) than to put a human being under bondage. In 594 Solon revoked both laws with retrospective effect, and described his act of liberation in these words: 'I took up the markers which were fixed in the black earth in many places, and the earth hitherto in bondage is now free. I brought many persons back to Athens, their fatherland, who had been sold abroad or enslaved at home.'[6] The two groups which he set free were the clansmen tied to the land and the guildsmen sold into slavery.

The action of Solon was a turning point in Athens' history. For many years there had been strife and civil war due to the hostility of clan towards clan; there had been attempts to seize power, victimization of guildsmen and exploitation of the poor by the rich. The state was already on the verge of disintegration. When Solon was appointed to act as 'reconciler' with full legislative powers, it was admitted that the normal machinery of government had failed. Solon cut the Gordian knot by cancelling all debts, freeing all debtors and passing new laws of debt under which no distinction was made between clansmen and guildsmen and no Athenian citizen could be enslaved. His own words declare his purpose: 'I passed laws which did not differentiate between low-born and high-born and I accorded straightforward justice to each.'[7] Henceforward all Athenians were to be equal before the law in matters of debt and in the freedom of the person on the principle of *habeas corpus*. In addition he passed a law of amnesty, putting an end to past animosities and proclaiming a new start in politics.

The immediate result was an economic crisis. Yet state funds were found to buy the liberty of those Athenians who were in slavery abroad. All foodstuffs except olive oil, of which there was a surplus, were kept in the country to feed the hungry. More important were his economic measures for the future. At the time the basis of Athens' economy was agriculture. But the economy had been upset by the influx of new forms of wealth, and there were two systems of exchange, based upon barter and upon coined money, which had been only recently introduced. Solon saw that full employment was possible in the future only if Athens was able to enter the field of maritime commerce and join the market of the maritime states. With this in view he changed the currency of Athens. His new coinage fitted conveniently into the maritime area in which Corinth set the standard. At the same time he tried to increase the pool of skilled craftsmen by offering citizenship to any craftsmen who would come from abroad to work in Athens, and he encouraged Athenians to teach their sons a handicraft. By these measures he hoped to make Athens more competitive in her new markets.

When the storm of criticism died down, Solon was commissioned again, probably in 592, to modernize the constitution. Under the existing system the initiative in policy and the executive power were in the hands of the clansmen element in society, as they had been for many centuries. The three chief magistrates and the six 'recorders', all holding office for one year at a time, were elected on the double qualification of wealth and birth (*aristinden kai ploutinden*). In other words they could attain office only if they were wealthy clansmen. Solon deleted the first part of the qualification. He thereby opened the possibility of office to the guildsmen. Next, he related candidature for all offices of state to categories of income, assessed primarily in terms of agricultural produce; thus candidates for the chief offices had to be in the first two categories, and candidates for the minor offices had to be in the first three categories. Taxation was on a sliding scale, related to the categories. A member of the lowest category was eligible for no office and paid no tax. The differential between the annual wage of a man in the lowest category and a man in the top category was between one and sixty.

The initiation of policy and the direction of state affairs were in the hands of the Council of the Areopagus ('the Council of Ares' Hill'). The members were recruited only from those who had held the highest offices of state; they were Areopagites for life, and they were answerable to the Areopagus alone. The Council of the Areopagus had very extensive administrative, judicial and discretionary powers, and it alone initiated policy in the Assembly. In the past and for some years to come its bias was entirely on the side of the clansmen. Solon therefore instituted a second council, to which he nominated 400 men, 100 from each tribe, to hold office probably for life. If we understand Solon's purpose correctly, the ethos of the new council was liberal and moderate, whereas that of the Areopagus remained inevitably conservative and perhaps extremely conservative. The new council took over from the Areopagus the initiation of policy in the Assembly. It was known as the Council of the Four Hundred.

That the Assembly of all citizens (*ecclesia*) had had little influence hitherto is apparent from the plight of the lower class under Draco's laws of debt; for the lower class certainly was a majority in the state and yet it had been unable to resist the implementation of Draco's laws. Solon gave to this class a guarantee of personal freedom and the hope of a better economic position in the future, but he had no desire to give it political power. He regarded the two Councils as checks upon the Assembly: 'The ship of state, riding upon two anchors, will pitch less in the surf and make the people less turbulent.' The Council of the Four Hundred drew up the agenda and appended a draft resolution to each agendum for each meeting. Then the Assembly decided by voting for or against a resolution. The Assembly could not frame a new resolution. The screening of resolutions by the Council of the Four Hundred was fortified by a screening of the Assembly's decisions; for the Council of the Areopagus, being 'guardian of the constitution', could refuse to implement a decision of the Assembly on the grounds that it was unconstitutional. The House of Lords still has vestiges of such power in considering a decision by the House of Commons. As an elective body the Assembly elected the magistrates. But the elected persons were then screened by the Areopagus, and any of them could be rejected by that body as unfit for office.

Hitherto the individual citizen had had the right of appeal against a decision by a phratry court or a tribal court or an officer of state, but only to the Areopagus which had a bias in favour of these courts and of the officers of state. Solon instituted a new right of appeal. This was to the people or to a section of the people selected by lot, sitting as a court of justice, called the *Heliaea*. This right of appeal was extended later and resulted in a standing procedure of audit under which a magistrate was held to account for his acts while in office. However, there was still no appeal from an act of the Areopagus. Finally, Solon established for the first time the right of any citizen to initiate proceedings at law as an individual, except in some cases of bloodshed (see p. 30 above); his aim was to emancipate the individual from control by a group, whether phratry, clan or family. He made a complete legal code, which was new except in matters of bloodshed. All his enactments were published on wooden boards and his legal code was inscribed on stone columns for all men to read. Every citizen took an oath to obey the laws and Solon retired from public life.

What Lycurgus had done for Sparta, Solon did for Athens. He reorientated the state away from the agricultural oligarchy under which it had been labouring and towards a balanced constitution in which the powers of the wealthy were modified and the basic rights of the poor were protected. He laid the foundations of a balanced economy in which agriculture remained important but commercial development was facilitated. Solon too was consciously moulding Athenian society to a preconceived image. What he had in view was a just society in which the various classes had powers appropriate to their stage of develop-ment. The right of all citizens to freedom and justice was guaranteed. The traditional bonds of society both religious and secular which resided in the Areopagus, the priesthoods and the corporate bodies – phratries, clans and guilds – were not broken but were strengthened by some timely modifications. Solon's reform was as comprehensive as that of Lycurgus, but its effect was very different. Whereas Lycurgus produced, largely by state education, a static society with a closed agricultural economy, Solon gave the promise of a liberal, evolving society in which the powers of the classes would change as the classes developed, and of an open and developing economy in which Athens would draw upon the skill of imported craftsmen and the commercial prosperity of the Greek world.

In modern times a radical reorientation of society has come about either by violent revolution, as in France in 1789 or in Russia in 1917, or by sectional movements of a generally non-violent character, such as the suffragette movement or the trade union movement, which produce a reorientation by gradual degrees. At Sparta and at Athens a radical reorientation was achieved through the intellectual insight and imaginative ability of one man and through the willingness of society to put its future in his hands. This difference implies a belief in the intellect and in the outstanding individual, a belief which is largely lacking in modern societies except when they are faced by the desperate problem of survival in the stress of war.

CHAPTER 5

THE RELIGIOUS VIEWS OF SOLON AND THEIR INFLUENCE ON ATHENS

In order to understand an ancient religion, it is essential to lay aside our modern concepts about God: that he preceded matter, was and is absolute in power and love, and was and is a single being. Greek religion began with the almost opposite tenets. In the beginning there was matter, which separated out of its own volition into earth and sky and underworld, land and sea, day and night, etc., and so became the orderly universe, continuing to exist because the material elements have respect for order. But if the elements encroach on one another, the equipoise or balance or pattern of the universe will be disrupted and the whole will revert to chaos. To us this may appear to be science rather than religion, but to the Greek, one concern of religion was to explain the universe by observation and deduction and above all not by emotional or wishful thinking. The principles which maintain the ordered universe were personified as gods and goddesses in the Greek idiom: such were the *Moirai* (Apportioners), *Chronos* (Time), *Eros* (Sexual Power), *Dike* (Order, the way things are in the orderly universe), *Thanatos* (Death) and so on: impersonal, unseeing, perhaps unthinking deities, like science's laws of matter. Next in time came the children of Earth and Sky, namely the Olympian gods and goddesses: personal and seeing and thinking deities who 'divided their wealth and shared out their powers' and achieved a fairly orderly society. But it took them time to learn. A change or two of kings was required (the contemporary king was Zeus), for these gods had to operate within the material universe and they had to learn and accept its principles. Thus Zeus learnt that he could not abolish the Moirai or Thanatos. Indeed each of the primaeval principles or powers within its own sphere of operation was stronger than Zeus.

The Olympian gods were in existence when man was created, like them, from the Earth; gods and men being thus of one mother were and are to some extent alike in intelligence and temperament (see p. 10, above). While the Olympian gods are subject to the principles of the material universe, man is subject not only to those principles – Chronos, Eros, Dike, Thanatos, etc. – but also to the Olympian gods who have much greater power than he. The religious problem for man is to recognize those principles, which impose limiting conditions upon man within the universe, and to understand and placate the Olympian gods and goddesses, who have perhaps understandable intelligence, temperament and will.

The ideas which I have outlined formed the general background to Hesiod's poems, *The Work and Days* (see p. 13 above) and *The Theogony*. He expressed the simple, perhaps pietistic belief that the justice which Zeus deals out to man is in accordance with man's own sense of justice, in terms both of an individual man and of a group of men. If a man is honest, industrious, just and godfearing, success will come his way; and if a state is so, it will not suffer war or famine. It is the unjust state which will be overwhelmed by disaster. But by the time of Solon man had learnt from bitter experience that Hesiod's beliefs did not fit the facts. Religion therefore had to frame new beliefs and Solon was one of the first Athenians to do this. Through his poems, of which only a few survive today, he had a profound influence on Athens; indeed his poems were to the Athenian more or less what the Bible was to the Victorian.

In one poem[1] Solon begins with his personal prayer as an individual that the gods may grant him success and that he may win the regard of all men for ever. Now the success which the gods grant a man is firmly based, but the success which men acquire by committing outrage does not come in accordance with order and justice. Such success contains the seeds of disaster, and justice always asserts itself later. The fact is that what man achieves by outrageous methods does not last; Zeus oversees the final stage of everything. Yet the retribution sent by Zeus is as unexpected as a wind in spring which wreaks havoc and is gone, leaving a clear sky. Again, Zeus is not quick in anger, like a man, against the individual. 'One wrongdoer pays at once, another later; and when the wrongdoers themselves escape, when what is coming from the gods does not overtake them, it comes all the same: their innocent children or their descendants thereafter pay the penalty for their acts.'

In this part of his prayer Solon is not trying to justify or rationalize the ways of the gods towards men by any human standards. He is simply observing and recording the facts. To take an example familiar to Solon, the gross acts of Laius in disregarding a divine warning and in maiming and exposing his child brought retribution in the end, not at

37

once nor mainly upon him but upon Oedipus, Iocasta, Eteocles, Polynices and Antigone; and the spring wind which struck Antigone destroyed others in its train.

In the second part of the prayer Solon observes that all men hope to win the regard of other men which attends success. Indeed we go on hoping – the coward to be brave, the sick to be well, the ugly to be handsome, the poor to be rich and so on – until we suffer some failure; then we weep. Still we go on striving. Yet success is not at all correlated to our efforts; an excellent worker may fall into unforeseen and utter disaster, while a bad worker may be given by god a good outcome. For all our hopes and efforts it is not we who command success. 'Success and failure are accorded to men by Moira [apportionment], and what the gods give us cannot be averted.'

Here Solon is asking us to see the conditions of life clearly and not through rosy spectacles. To take an example from the same legends, Oedipus hoped and strove to win safety for his people and himself, but he could not command success; what the gods gave could not be averted. Again, Solon is not protesting. He accepts the ways of the gods as facts, and he wants man to act in awareness of those facts.

Solon saw the problems of Athens from a religious standpoint, which he reveals to us in another poem.[2] He divided the experiences of a community into two parts: outer events which we do not control and inner relations which we do control. As regards the former he told the Athenians to put their trust in their guardian goddess, Athena, the daughter of Zeus, but as regards the latter to blame themselves. 'It is the citizens themselves who choose to destroy the greatness of their country by their stupidity, and their motive is financial gain.' He censured the leading men for their disregard of justice and their un-restrained greed in acquiring wealth. Their actions had destroyed the health of the whole community, bringing enslavement, strife and civil war from which no one could escape by hiding in an inner room. These troubles were due mainly to a spirit of lawlessness. They could be stopped only by returning to a respect for order (eunomia), which puts human relations on a sane and harmonious basis.

We can see from this poem why Solon made each citizen swear to obey the laws which he had enacted. 'The citizens themselves' had to choose whether to destroy or save their city. Solon put before them the blue-print of a society in which a fair deal for all classes would be the basis of an internal harmony. Whereas Lycurgus introduced state education to change the ways of the citizens, Solon made his own religious and spiritual appeal to each citizen individually to change his outlook.

In his personal life Solon may have faced the same choice. Many 'reconcilers' in the past had seized power, and many men criticized him now for not making himself tyrant. To them he replied in a poem of which a fragment survives. 'Wealth comes to many bad men, and poverty to many good men; but we shall not exchange our self-respect (*arete*) for their wealth, because self-respect is constant always but wealth changes hands.'[3] His own example was a lesson to the Athenians that self-respect and respect for order in a society were more valuable than grasping after greater profits or higher returns at the expense of the community.

The effects of Solon's reforms must have seemed disappointing to a superficial observer. While it is true that the reduction of impoverished citizens to serfdom or slavery was ended, the internal struggles continued intermittently between clan and clan and between the sectional interests of the plain-land, the hill-country and the class which was engaged in handicrafts, production and commerce. When constitutional government broke down Solon blamed the leading men for destroying society and the people for their lack of intelligence. One of the leading men, Peisistratus, seized power twice for short periods, and in 546 he was laying plans abroad for another attempt to take control of Athens. But on the economic side the plans of Solon succeeded. Craftsmen from abroad settled in Athens, a beautiful black-figure pottery was produced and by 550 Athens was beginning to take the lead in the world of Greek commerce. The priority which Solon had asked the citizens to give to the State was realized in the inauguration of the Panathenaic Festival in honour of Athena in 566, and in the institution of games at Eleusis; for Athens thus became one of the leading states which were in a position to organize international events. The spiritual appeal of Solon bore fruit more noticeably after 550 when a new concept of the state began to emerge and led eventually to remarkable achievements.

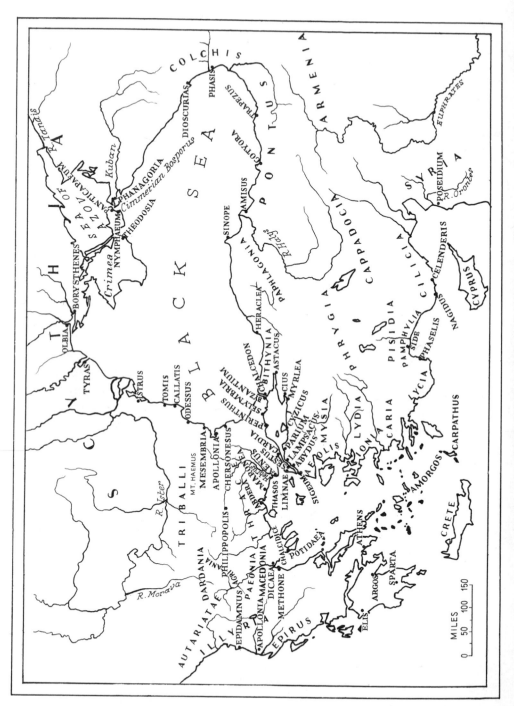

Map 5 The eastern Mediterranean and the Black Sea

CHAPTER 6

THE OUTER GREEK WORLD FROM 800 TO 546

The Greek expansion, like the European expansion, was a very lengthy process. It operated partly through migration, when a tribe left one habitat for another, and partly through colonization, when a state sent some only of its citizens to found a colony. The first phase, completed before 850, was mainly migratory. At the end of it the Aegean islands, parts of Cyprus and most of the west coast of Asia Minor were Greek-speaking, and the whole area remained so until the exchange of the Greek and the Turkish populations in 1923. The Greeks of the first phase settled in zones which were distinguished by differences of dialect. Thus the Aeolians occupied Tenedos and Lesbos and the northern part of the western Asiatic coast; the Ionians, the islands across the central Aegean and the central sector of the same coast; and the Dorians, the southern Aegean islands and Halicarnassus and Cnidus on the southern sector of the same coast. To the southeast the Arcadians and others who had a Mycenaean background in common took possession of many parts of Cyprus. The settlers won their lands by hard fighting. They usually exterminated or expelled the previous occupants. There were clashes too between rival bands of settlers. The margins of power were very narrow and life was hazardous and exacting. An Ionian poet, Mimnermus, shows their buccaneering spirit. 'We are they who left Pylus, the city of Neleus, and came in our ships to lovely Asia; with overmastering might we settled at beloved Colophon, we the pioneers of boisterous violence, and thence . . . by the grace of the gods we captured Aeolian Smyrna.'[1]

The settlers of any one site came often from several parts of the Greek mainland. They were fused together into a community not by racial kinship but by common danger and common interest. They preferred sites – especially those on the Asiatic coast – which were small and defensible with open access to the sea, peninsular knobs being particularly suitable. Separated from one another by hostile peoples and often by mountain ranges, they communicated with one another mainly by sea and they formed only spasmodic associations at first. As the population increased, the settlers on the coast acquired considerable areas of land and native labourers by conquest; Ephesus and Miletus, for instance, advanced their grip some thirty miles inland up the river valleys. Individual settlements became closer to one another. By 800 the Ionians of the coast and the Ionians of Chios and Samos met regularly together at the Panionium on Cape Mycale, where they worshipped Poseidon. The islanders of the central Aegean held a festival at Delos in honour of Apollo at which there were contests in music, poetry and athletics. Memories of the glorious Mycenaean age were strong for the epic tradition had been brought over from the mainland during the migrations. Greek epic attained its highest level in the *Iliad* and the *Odyssey*, which reached their Homeric form in the Ionian milieu probably within the period of 850 to 750.

The states of the Ionian and Aeolian Greeks in the east were less powerful in general than those of the Greek mainland, partly because they were often smaller and mainly because they were racially mixed and less tightly organized. They too were called 'poleis'. The translation 'city-state' and the urban connotation which it suggests are more appropriate here since the settlers chose a defensible site at the outset and the houses were set from early on within a defensive wall, as for instance at Smyrna. The initial settlements were small, and amalgamation of settlements was rare; for example, the island of Lesbos had five settlements which became separate and independent poleis. One of these, Mitylene, played some part in Greek history; the other Aeolian settlements were of little significance. The Dorians in the southeast were better seamen than the Aeolians and they showed themselves to be more vigorous and enterprising. Rhodes, in which there were three poleis, joined with Dorian Crete in founding Phaselis on the south coast of Asia Minor and Gela in Sicily, while Cnidus founded Lipara beyond the Straits of Messina. Rhodes, Cnidus, Cos and for a time Halicarnassus joined together in a common worship of Apollo and held a festival with athletic events at Triopium on the Cnidian peninsula.

The Ionian settlements were the most numerous. They were also the most successful in expanding their territories in Asia inland; moreover, their situation made them the terminals of important trade routes from the Asiatic hinterland. Miletus attained prosperity early. She led the way in colonization. She planted Sinope on the south coast of the Black Sea and Cyzicus on the Asiatic coast of the Sea of Marmara before 750, and in the next two hundred years she founded a huge number of colonies. Pliny credited her with seventy-five colonies in the Crimea and on the shores of the Black Sea and the Sea of Marmara. The abundance of east Greek pottery in these regions shows that Miletus and her Ionian associates held a dominant position there in the extensive trade which brought wheat, salted fish, hides and ship-timber to the increasing population of the Aegean basin. A much smaller Ionian state, Phocaea, showed remarkable enterprise. She joined Miletus in founding Amisus (Samsun) and Apollonia Pontica in the Black Sea; she founded also Massilia (Marseilles), which in its turn planted colonies on the south coasts of France and Spain, and she planted a colony at Alalia in Corsica. Phocaean warships passed through the Pillars of Heracles (the Straits of Gibraltar) and traded with Tartessus (near Cadiz), where they obtained precious metals, while Euthymenes of Massilia sailed to the mouth of the Senegal river in west Africa about 550.

Ionia prospered greatly from these colonial and commercial developments. Moreover in the period 590–546 there was a marked increase in trade with the interior of Asia Minor. Great temples were built and planned at this time at Samos and Ephesus. The earliest ones were constructed of timber and mud-brick; the later ones of stone. The Ionic order of architecture became established as the norm in Ionia. As compared with the Dorian order it was much less strict and austere, more inventive, and more interested in decorative elements, such as the leaf capital and the volute capital. Samos rivalled Corinth in bronze-work, especially in the making of cauldrons with griffin heads (see p. 24 above), but in the minor arts in general Ionia followed rather belatedly in the wake of the fashions which had been initiated on the mainland. Orientalizing pottery, for instance, developed late in Ionia and was not outstanding. In this respect Dorian Rhodes was far ahead.

The originality of the Ionians and the Aeolians in east Greece was most marked in literature. Ionia continued to be the centre of the epic tradition; fine poems were composed but they did not come up to the standard set by the *Iliad* and the *Odyssey*. Ionian poets developed a new form of hexameter verse in the shape of hymns honouring a god, which were sung at festivals. These hymns have none of the didactic purpose or cosmological interest of Hesiod's hexameter poems (see p. 13, above); their excellence lies in charm of expression, *joie de vivre* and a sense of beauty, and they express an uncomplicated worship of anthropomorphic gods and goddesses. Such are their descriptions of Hermes and Pan:

Map 6 Sicily and Magna Graecia

44

Born at dawn he played the lyre at noon and stole the cattle of the unerring archer Apollo that evening.

Nor is Pan surpassed in melody by the nightingale which pours forth her trills amid the blossoms of all-flowery spring and grieves in honey-noted song.

Another new form was personal lyric poetry, established in Lesbos by Terpander and Arion alongside choral lyric (see p. 25, above). It reached its zenith about 600 in the lyrics of Alcaeus and Sappho, the former writing with directness on politics, love and wine, and the latter expressing her mystical adoration of Aphrodite and her love of the girls who shared with her the cult of Aphrodite, the Graces and the Muses. Ionian poets of Ephesus and Smyrna wrote camp-songs, love-songs and political catches in the elegiac metre. Others used the iambic metre in satire and controversy.

We see here the extraordinary creativeness of the Greek mind. A galaxy of metres was invented, each with its own special accompaniment of music, dance and diction, the last often in a local dialect. The metres alone set their stamp upon later poetry, whether Greek, Latin or European. A common feature of the Aeolian and the Ionian poets is that they were inspired not by the communal feeling of a group but by personal emotions, especially by love and hate. Sappho wrote of a girl who was leaving her to be married. 'I would rather see her lovely walk and the shining sparkle of her eyes than the chariots of Lydia and the soldiers on parade.'[2] Archilochus wrote of an unfaithful friend: 'May the top-knotted Thracians take him, stripped of his kindly friends, where he will eat the bread of slavery and fill his cup with many ills. May they take him frozen stiff and strung with seaweed from the surge, his teeth chattering, his lips spewing the brine, his body sprawling dog-like on his face by the edge of the surf.'[3]

The growing emancipation from traditional and communal beliefs which we see in the later Ionian poets helped to bring about a revolution in thought. The new thinking was associated with the names of Thales and Anaximander, both citizens of Miletus. They looked at the physical universe with a reliance on the intellect and with a faith in scientific inquiry which were to be paralleled almost two millennia later by Leonardo da Vinci. They first asked the question of how the physical universe evolved, and thereby assumed the ability of the human mind to find an answer. Thales supposed that it evolved from water, as water is a substance possessing life and motion. Anaximander began with 'the unlimited', i.e. matter unlimited and undifferentiated in the quantity and the quality of its ingredients, from which the universe or universes have emerged and into which the universe or universes will return, disintegrating in accordance with the rule of time. The creation and the emergence of a universe were due to the action of opposite elements – hot and cold, wet and dry – within the unlimited. The cold elements and the wet elements, for instance, coalesced into earth enwrapped in mist, while the hot elements and the dry elements formed into an outer sphere of flame. As the earth was dried by the heat of the outer fire land became differentiated from water and life arose from the warmed slime; the first living things were fishlike, and from them animals and men evolved. The outer sphere revolved throwing off wheels of fire, visible to us through the mist as sun, moon and stars. The earth, cylindrical in shape and centrally placed within the sphere, was stationary because it was in equipoise. Anaximander based his hypotheses upon phenomena which he himself observed in the fields of geography, biology and physics.

The two Milesian philosophers became more mathematical in their approach when they turned to practical problems. They helped navigators to determine their course and their position at sea and they calculated the height of a pyramid from its shadow. At a time when most men regarded an eclipse as due to the anger of a god or goddess, Thales startled his contemporaries by predicting correctly a total eclipse of the sun. The eclipse occurred probably in May 585. As logic needed a form of expression more precise than poetry Anaximander wrote a work in prose, the first in Greek as far as we know, c. 546. Inspired by the Greek voyages of discovery which we have mentioned he constructed a map – perhaps the first ever – of 'the inhabited earth', that is of the circular surface on the top of the cylinder. There is no doubt that Thales and Anaximander took decisive steps forward in the development of man as an intelligent being.

The Greek colonizing movement lasted continuously from about 750 to 550. It resulted in the planting of small Greek states on the coasts of the Sea of Marmara, the Black Sea, the north Aegean, the Ionian Sea, the Sicilian Sea, parts of eastern Italy, southern France, southeastern Spain and Libya. Meanwhile the Phoenicians were planting colonies in Morocco and Algeria, of which Carthage became the most famous, and in western Sicily and southwestern Spain; and the Etruscans, themselves, also a people of east Mediterranean origin, were gaining control of northern Italy and trading especially in the western seas. The resulting pattern of peoples on the coasts of the Mediterranean sea persisted until the breakdown of the Roman Empire. Of the three colonizing powers the Greeks were destined to exert the greatest influence upon the culture of the ancient world and its aftermath, the Byzantine Empire.

The account of Thera (Santorin) colonizing Cyrene may be cited as an example.[4] On a visit to Delphi the King of Thera was ordered by the priestess of Apollo to found a city in Libya. He did not do so. Seven years of drought ensued at Thera and the order was repeated. The Theraeans decided now to reconnoitre. A few went to an island offshore, called Platea (Bomba). They took with them a Cretan sailor who had been driven there on a previous occasion by adverse winds. While they went home to report, the Cretan stayed. His provisions were running out when a Samian captain, called Colaeus, gave him supplies for a year. (Colaeus was *en route* for Egypt, but adverse winds drove him out into the Atlantic, where he put in at Tartessus [Cadiz]. He returned home with a cargo of record value.) The Theraeans, led by one Battus, came back to Platea with two longboats and rejoined the Cretan. After a difficult and unhappy two years they settled on the coast nearby. Six years later they moved to a better site, Cyrene, with the co-operation of the Libyans, and built their city there.

The Assembly at Thera then made a sworn agreement with the founders of Cyrene. The gist of the first part is as follows:

Apollo having of his own accord told Battus and the Theraeans to colonize Cyrene, the Assembly resolves to send Battus as leader and king and the Theraeans as his companions to Libya. They are to go on terms of complete equality, being selected by family, there being one son in the prime of life from each family. The penalty for disobedience is death. Also any freeman of Thera may volunteer to go. If the colony succeeds, any kinsman of the colonists who sails to Libya shall receive citizenship with all its privileges, and he shall receive an allocation of land which is not in private ownership. If the colonists do not succeed and Thera cannot come to their help and they endure their hardships for five years, they may return with impunity to Thera and resume their property and their citizenship.[5]

In the early days at Platea or on the coast some of the colonists did sail home, only to be driven off by missiles. Others asked Delphi to release them from the divine order, whereupon the god replied through his priestess, 'Do you know sheep-rearing Libya better than I do?' So the settlers stayed where they were, and the colony was established. Sixty years later the citizenship of Cyrene was opened to any Greeks who wished to settle. Many came from the Peloponnese, Crete and the islands, and they were given land at the expense of the native Libyans. When the Libyans invoked the Egyptians, a combined force of Libyans and Egyptians was defeated by the Cyrenaeans. Thereafter several colonies were planted by Cyrene along the Libyan coast. The Greek hold was now firmly established. It lasted until the coming of the Arabs.

Many features of Greek colonization are illustrated by this story. It was seaborne, and it began after voyages of exploration. Over-population at home often provided the chief motive, and Delphi usually gave instructions and advice. The colonizing state organized the initial expedition. The colony was a separate state with its own citizenship from the outset; and if it planted a colony in turn, that colony was a separate state. There was no example of a single citizen-ship embracing homelanders and colonials, as British citizenship has done. The Greek states proliferated. They made no attempts to combine under a common flag. The tiny scale of the first stage at Platea was not unusual (for instance, we hear of 200 men of Corinth founding Apollonia Illyrica), and when a further wave or further waves of colonists arrived expansion was very common. Co-operation with the natives was often followed by exploitation and oppression, but native resistance was usually too late to succeed. When a Greek colony was destroyed, it was not the natives but more often another Greek state which was to blame.

As a Greek colony intended to start an independent life from the outset, it needed arable land to support its citizens; indeed arrangements were made in advance for the distribution of land in equal lots among the colonists, and it was assumed that such land would be acquired by agreement with the natives or be taken by force from the natives. This basic desideratum could be met at a great many sites. Sometimes good land was enough in itself, as at Croton in south Italy, but good land was often combined with a good harbour and trade-routes inland, as at Taras near Croton. It is clear that the colonizing states varied in their choice of sites. Miletus had trade in mind when she planted colonies at Sinope, which was the southern terminal for ships crossing the Black Sea from the Crimea, and at the mouths of the great Russian rivers. On the other hand the first states to colonize in the west, Chalcis and Eretria, which controlled the narrow straits of Euboea, sent settlers to Pithecusae (Ischia) and Cumae, which have a strait between them, and Rhegium and Naxus (and later Zancle) on either side of the straits of Messina. Achaeans, Eleans and Aeolians preferred sites which were primarily agricultural; they settled respectively in south Italy, in Epirus and in the northeastern Aegean. Three Dorian states – Sparta, Corinth and Megara – preferred sites which had splendid harbours and good stra-tegic position such as Taras, Syracuse, Corcyra, Potidaea and Byzantium.

The Greeks were able to plant so many small colonies for two reasons:

the lack of organized states on the coasts they colonized and the superior arms of the Greeks. It was the same when Europeans colonized America, Africa and Australia. Native canoe and club were no match at first for the Greek longboat of thirty oars or fifty oars with an underwater ram and for the Greek weapons and protective armour of metal. By the time that native resistance became organized, e.g. against Cyrene, the Greeks had developed a very efficient form of warfare in which closely packed lines of infantrymen, wearing full protective armour of bronze and carrying a metal shield, fought at close quarters with thrusting spear and sword; indeed these 'men of bronze' were superior to any infantry anywhere in the world until the middle of the fourth century BC.

The Greeks had much to offer the natives: wine, oil, pottery, clothing, jewellery, weapons and *objets d'art*, which travelled far inland up the great rivers of Europe, Asia and Africa. They brought literacy in the form of an adaptable Graecized Phoenician alphabet (which has not been superseded in our modern world) and literature both in verse and prose; a flow of ideas which proved particularly stimulating to the peoples of Europe; and a form of capitalism, based on maritime commerce, which is still the practice of most of the western world. They had no intention of imposing their own religious views or of teaching the native to ape Greek manners. On the other hand there is no indication that their influence corrupted or undermined or destroyed native cultures for, unlike the Romans and the British, they did not have the urge to conquer and administer vast areas of land.

A Greek colony perpetuated the characteristics of its foundress. As one of them was exclusiveness in race and in citizenship, natives were rarely absorbed, except as serfs or slaves. Among the citizens of a colonial state the families of the original settlers had special status and sometimes lasting privileges in politics. Colonial aristocracies grew up quickly in the outer Greek world, reflecting those of the homeland and often retaining power for longer. They became extremely wealthy and competed successfully in the most expensive events at the Olympic and other games. Some colonial states were proverbially rich, e.g. Sybaris, and they used their wealth to build magnificent temples such as we can see today at Acragas (Agrigento) and Posidonia (Paestum). Except in the humble art of terracotta figurines the colonial states showed little originality in art; they tended rather to follow the schools of the homeland, e.g. Selinus following the Peloponnesian school in the sculpture on the metopes of her temples. The same is true of literature and thought in the colonizing period.

The effect of the colonial expansion upon the Greek world was immense. The range and scale of Greek commerce changed enormously, and its markets were constantly expanding. The flow of commerce from the Black Sea and its European and Asiatic hinterlands, from Asia Minor and the Near East, and from the southwestern Mediterranean littoral brought great prosperity to Ionia, its offshore islands and Rhodes. The flow of trade between the eastern world and the western world reached points of concentration in the Saronic Gulf and the nearby states of the Corinthian Gulf, on either side of the Isthmus. In consequence Corinth, Megara and Aegina and subsequently Athens became very rich. The colonies of the west had their own commercial sphere: they traded with the Phoenicians and the Etruscans as well as with the native peoples of Europe and Africa.

Commercial exchange was accelerated by the use of coined money. The credit for inventing coinage goes to the royal house of Lydia in Asia Minor, but it was quickly adopted from Lydia by Miletus and Ephesus. The use of coinage spread to the west by 550. It was used at first for large-scale transactions rather than for internal retail. As capital became more mobile, monetary wealth tended to gravitate towards the richer states and the richer families. The ownership of slaves as a form of capital investment increased greatly, and the hiring of mercenaries became possible. Although a few states such as Sparta, Crete and Byzantium resisted the tide, the world of the Greek states was already launched by 550 on the flow of capitalism with all that it meant in terms of financial, military and political power for the next two and half millennia. It is true to say that the first phase of the classical period, c. 800–546, laid the foundations upon which not only the Greco-Roman world but also the European world were to be built.

Part II

THE TRIUMPHS OF THE GREEKS AND THE
ADVANCE OF ATHENS, 546–466

CHAPTER 7

DICTATORSHIP AND DEMOCRACY AT ATHENS
546–500

Although Solon had been successful in changing the economic course of Athens and in advocating the principles of a just society, he had not healed the political weaknesses of a state which was still organized on a racial system (see p. 39, above). Thus the rivalry between clan and clan continued, and it was still the clan leaders who took control of political factions and were elected to the archonships which were analogous to our Ministries of State. Equally harmful to the unity of the state was the division between the clansmen and the guildsmen; for the latter did not forget the oppression, disfranchisement and enslavement which they had suffered under Draco's laws of debt (see p. 31, above). In addition the changing economy of Athens and the mobility of capital intensified the struggle between rich and poor which, like a ground swell running across a stormy sea, complicated the task of government. There was one encouraging feature in Athens' situation: her productivity had been steadily increasing and she was now about to take a leading place in the expanding markets of the Greek world.

The political stresses at Athens led on several occasions to a breakdown of constitutional government – to what the Greeks called *anarchia*, though the word 'anarchy' may have for us a wider connotation – and to the short-lived seizures of power by clan-leaders between 590 and 550. These symptoms of political disintegration are familiar to the modern world, particularly in some western democracies and in some states of Latin America, and our experience over the last forty years does not point to any one form of settlement which reverses the process of disintegration in a decisive and lasting manner. It is therefore interesting to study the case of Athens where the process of disintegration was completely reversed within the period 546–500 by a long-lasting authoritarian régime followed by a democratic realignment of the state. It is likely that neither the one nor the other alone would have

53

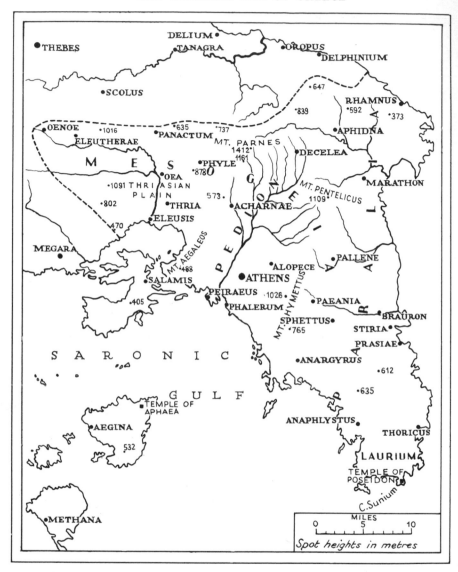

Map 7 Attica

achieved this result; it was rather the combination of the two which was significant.

Solon lived long enough to pass judgement on at least the first of the three occasions when Peisistratus seized power. 'Clouds shed thick snow, bright lightning is accompanied by thunder; so the leading men destroy the state and the people in their folly fall into slavery under one-man-rule. It is difficult for one who sails far out to come inshore again; one

54

should think of all things in good time.'[1] He saw that new attitudes and new initiatives were needed both in the leading men and in the people; if they were not forthcoming and the overcast situation continued, one-man-rule and the loss of political freedom would ensue.

The third seizure of power came about through the collusion of two rivals, Peisistratus and Megacles. A *mariage de convenance* was arranged between Peisistratus and the daughter of Megacles. Peisistratus had the support of the cultivators of poor land, of all impoverished persons and of those naturalized citizens who had come to Athens since 594. His programme was left-wing. On the other hand Megacles, head of the powerful Alcmeonid clan, had the support of those who were engaged in the various trades and in commercial activities. They stood for a liberal and moderate policy. The only bond between Peisistratus and Megacles was a detestation of the reactionary conservative party, that is, the bulk of clansmen who cultivated the good land and were the chief possessors of capital; this party was led by Lycurgus, the head of a prominent clan. But when Peisistratus double-crossed Megacles and in particular did not consummate his marriage with Megacles' daughter, even this bond snapped and Megacles made common cause with Lycurgus.

Peisistratus fled to the north, taking his money and his close supporters with him. He probably offered his services to the King of Macedon and obtained as his reward the control of a rich region on the eastern shore of the Thermaic Gulf; later he acquired territory in the Strymon valley and made a fortune by exploiting the resources of the district in silver and timber. He minted coins on which he coolly placed the name of Athens, built warships, hired mercenaries, and bought political support from several states. In 546 he landed in strength at Marathon on the west coast of Attica. He defeated the government's forces, seized the Acropolis of Athens, arrested the sons of the leading families and held them as hostages for their good conduct. He then proceeded to disarm the entire population. He showed in an exemplary manner how an able and unscrupulous *émigré* can seize and retain power. He was to have many successors in the course of history.

Peisistratus and after his death his son Hippias ruled Athens for thirty-six years. There was no rising within the state, and there is no doubt that under their régime Athens grew immensely in power, prosperity and enlightenment. To call Peisistratus and his son tyrants is for us, as for the later Greeks, to use a loaded word. 'Dictator' is less distasteful because a gallery of those who have usurped power in modern times from Mussolini to Nasser includes not only villains but also national heroes and many betwixt and between. Even so no régime inaugurated by dictators in this century has lasted as long as that of the Peisistratid family.

We must recognize the fact that Peisistratus and Hippias received very considerable support from the Athenian people, and to that extent, but not by democratic election, legitimized their régime. So too have some modern dictators, especially when they are resisting a threat of exploitation or invasion by foreigners. Again, if the contrast is between an inefficient oligarchy – or for that matter between an inefficient democracy, that is one in which anarchy disruptive of order, business and government is recurrent – and an efficient dictatorship, there will always be those who are grateful for the move from a slump to a boom. This was no doubt the meaning of those individuals who, having experienced the freedoms of the pre-Peisistratus situation, called his régime 'the golden age',[2] presumably because it gave them freedom from anarchy, fear and want as long as they themselves abstained from revolutionary activities.

Yet one-man-rule, like one-party-rule, without democratic election, however efficient it may be, deprives the citizens of the possibility of developing by experience that sense of personal responsibility in politics which enables a state to act with corporate solidarity in a crisis. Peisistratus was described by later Greek writers as an almost constitutional dictator. This no doubt was the impression he sought to create. The Solonian constitution was kept in operation and the judicial system was even improved by the addition of state judges who tried cases not at Athens but at local centres. Peisistratus himself stood trial on a charge of homicide before the Council of the Areopagus, sitting as a court. The main deviation from constitutionalism, and it was a decisive deviation, was that Peisistratus' men were elected to the top posts and Peisistratus' policies were adopted and implemented; for behind the constitutional façade Peisistratus (like Augustus or any modern dictator) controlled the means to power – armed forces, warships, weapons, revenues and executive posts.

He tried to identify his image with that of the state. His coins bore the head of the state-goddess, Athena. Under his patronage the state festivals were celebrated with distinction, the Dionysia was improved by the addition of a competition in tragic drama, and altars and temples were dedicated by the state to the leading Olympian gods. Peisistratus and his sons set an example in holding priestly offices themselves and in sacrificing in person on state occasions. Peisistratus was indeed concerned to advance the claims of the state on the citizens' loyalty as against the claims of the clan, for the clan-leaders and the clansmen constituted the only internal threat to his position. The long rule of Peisistratus and Hippias, during which the clan system was weakened decisively in political life, shifted the centre of gravity in politics from the clan to the state, the polis of Athena.

Dictatorships win support by material success. Peisistratus began as the champion of the poor and the naturalized citizens, but he was not an example of the revolutionary type of dictator who reverses the capitalist order in the interest of the poor. He did not dispossess the clansmen or even confiscate the estates of his opponents. He relied rather upon his economic policy to bring prosperity to all levels of society. With peace and full employment at home, and with the coming of further craftsmen to Athens, the volume of trade increased so that Athens outdistanced Corinth and Athenian pottery took the lead in the East and the West. In the past Athens had been unsuccessful in planting of colonies and an isolationist in mainland politics. Peisistratus now brought her some overseas possessions, which provided ports of call on the trade route to the Black Sea: his own winnings in the Thermaic Gulf and the Strymon valley, the Thracian Chersonese (the Gallipoli peninsula) and Sigeum on the Asiatic side of the mouth of the Dardanelles. And he resuscitated the sentimental attachment between Athens and the Ionians (see p. 27, above) by purifying the island of Delos as the religious centre of the Ionians and by accepting Ionian refugees who had fled from Persian rule.

His policy and that of Hippias led to a short-lived Ionian phase in the culture of Athens. A great temple of Olympian Zeus with a double peristyle in the Ionic order was planned, but never completed (some columns are still standing). Ionian dress and Ionian hair-styles were adopted, and the recitation of the Homeric poems was made an integral part of the Panathenaic festival. Life in the city of Peisistratus and Hippias and his brother Hipparchus, a patron of the arts, offered many pleasures and graces which had been unknown to the strife-torn Athens of the preceding generation.

The position of Hippias was undermined by the advance of Persia in the east Aegean and the entry of Persia into Europe in 513. His chief supporters, the fellow-dictators Polycrates of Samos and Lygdamis of Nazos, were overthrown; Athens lost the Chersonese and other possessions overseas and the number of refugees entering Attica increased. In the full publicity of the Panathenaic festival of 514 Hipparchus was assassinated by Harmodius and Aristogeiton for personal reasons, arising from a homosexual love affair. Hippias and his associates became nervous and Peisistratid rule began at last to be oppressive. The number of *émigrés* from Athens increased rapidly. Soon some aristocratic partisans crossed the frontier of Attica and made a base at Leipsydrium, hoping to raise the people against Hippias. The attempt failed. Their defeat was mourned in a drinking song of the day. 'Alas, partisan-betraying Leipsydrium, how you destroyed our heroes, brave in battle, noble in blood. They showed the stuff their fathers were made of.'[3] The *émigrés* found a centre for their plotting at Delphi, where the wealthy and prestigious Alcmeonid clan had obtained a lucrative contract to rebuild Apollo's temple. The Alcmeonid leader at the time was probably Cleisthenes, who had held the leading ministerial post under Hippias in 525 but was now his mortal enemy. He and others enlisted the sympathy of the priests. Whenever Spartan envoys asked the oracle for advice on their own affairs, they were told to free Athens first.

The Spartans did not find the monotonous order of the god distasteful. It suited their book as they claimed to be 'liberators'. Indeed they owed much of their influence at this time to their deposition of tyrants in other states and to their support of the oligarchic régimes which usually succeeded the tyrannies. The moment for intervention at Athens seemed to have come. A sea-borne landing by a Spartan force was made at Phalerum. It was unsuccessful. In 510 a Spartan army, commanded by the king Cleomenes and aided by the *émigrés* and their local supporters, forced Hippias to capitulate on terms: he and his family were given safe passage to Sigeum where he hoped to enlist the support of Persia.

Athens was free at last thanks to Sparta. The restored nobles took the customary step of allying themselves with Sparta, thus bringing Athens into the membership of the Spartan Alliance (see p. 20 ff, above). Later generations did not relish this fact. They attributed their liberation not to Sparta but to Harmodius and Aristogeiton, whose names were celebrated in the democratic drinking-song: 'I shall carry my sword in a myrtle branch, as did Harmodius and Aristogeiton, when they slew the tyrant and made Athens the land of equal rights.'[4]

Sparta's intervention at Athens was prompted in part by her fear of Persia, which had given support to tyrants in the east Aegean and might use Athens under Hippias as a base of operations. The Persian colossus was already an immediate neighbour. One hand stretched out over Cyrene and the other over Macedonia, while her navy controlled Ionia and the approaches to the Dardanelles. As a committed enemy of Persia, Sparta saw that resistance in Europe would have to be based

upon the Spartan Alliance. She had therefore taken every opportunity
to extend the membership of the Alliance beyond the limits of the
Peloponnese. By the end of 510 she had obtained the accession of
Athens, the Boeotian League and Phocis, and at sea Aegina and
probably Chalcis. Further north Thessaly was hostile; but during the
liberation of Athens the Spartan army had defeated the Thessalian
cavalry force which had come into action in support of Hippias. It
looked as if Sparta might bring all the Greek states of the mainland
except Argos and Thessaly into a lasting coalition which was prepared
to oppose Persia.

The first reactions in liberated Athens seemed to favour Sparta's
hopes. The political clubs through which the clan leaders operated
were fully in control of the city. Putting the oligarchic principle of the
pre-Peisistratus period into practice, they disfranchised many who had
recently been naturalized. Then they fell out among themselves. In a
trial of strength the leader of the largest oligarchic group, Isagoras,
came out on top; in addition he held what appeared to be the trump
card, the friendship of the Spartan King Cleomenes. The leader of the
lesser oligarchic group, the Alcmeonid Cleisthenes, broke the rules of
the oligarchic game by canvassing the support of the common people.
He even promised to give them political power. Nor was this a desperate
gamble, for having been a leading minister under the dictatorship he
realized that the common people were no longer the downtrodden and
gullible victims of the oligarchs that they had been before Peisistratus'
seizure of power but had become a capable and prosperous group in
the liberated state.

Isagoras did not underestimate the danger. He invoked Cleomenes,
whose order that Cleisthenes and others should be banished was
instantly obeyed. Not content with this, Cleomenes appeared at the
head of a small force, banished seven hundred households on the
ground that they were involved in the pollution which had been
incurred a century before by the Alcmeonid clan (see p. 29), and
proposed to disband the Areopagus Council, of which the members
were ex-magistrates who had served under the dictatorship, and to put
Isagoras and three hundred of his supporters in control of the state. His
intention was that Athens should become a satellite of Sparta, governed
by a narrow pro-Spartan oligarchy.

When it came to armed intervention the mood of the Areopagus
Council and the common people was not, as Cleomenes and Isagoras
had supposed, one of acceptance. The Council resisted, the people rose
in their support, and Cleomenes found himself cut off on the Acropolis.

On the third day Cleomenes came to terms. A safe conduct was granted to Cleomenes and to the Spartans in his force (Isagoras was smuggled out among them). All other supporters of the oligarchy were handed over to the Athenians. They were executed on the spot. The rift with Sparta was now complete. The disfranchised and the exiles were reinstated and Cleisthenes was empowered to carry out a radical reform. Athenian envoys sought an alliance with Persia; it was granted on condition that Athens recognized the suzerainty of the King of Persia. The envoys fulfilled the condition, but only because an attack by Sparta was expected and Persia was an enemy of Sparta. In the event the attack failed and Athens disowned the alliance.

In order to understand Cleisthenes' reform we need to go back to the beginnings of the Athenian state (which are described on page 28). The social system of tribes, phratries, clans (*gene*) and families (*oikoi*) was still in operation, and the members of a phratry still lived within a district, known as a 'third' (*trittys*) and divided into four wards (called *naukrariai*). It was upon these divisions that the systems of local government and of election to state offices were still based. Thus within a third the great majority of the residents were clansmen working the land as farmers (*georgoi*) and there were only a few resident craftsmen and traders (*demiourgoi*), who might work and live elsewhere much of the time. The centre of local government within a third was inevitably placed in an arable area where it suited the convenience of the clansmen-farmers. At these centres throughout Attica the clan-leaders had great influence, and they were able to sway the results of the elections to state offices. As the thirds were more or less uniform in geographical extent and in the nature of their population, the system of thirds was appropriate to a racially organized and agriculturally based community.

There was, however, an ever-increasing number of naturalized citizens who had been attracted from abroad by Solon and Peisistratus. For electoral purposes in particular they were allocated to wards within the thirds. Here they were not only unorganized as compared with the clansmen, but they often lived at a considerable distance from their ward centre, perhaps even outside the area of their third. Thus in proportion to their numbers the naturalized citizens and their descendants were underprivileged in local politics and in elections to state offices; as at Rome in 89, the voting power of the new citizens was 'inferior to that of the older citizens'.[5] Moreover shifts of population towards Athens, Phalerum and the hill country at Laurium (the area called Paralia) which resulted from the growth of trade and maritime commerce, had upset the earlier uniformity of the thirds. Thus the whole system of thirds and wards was out of gear with contemporary conditions, just as in England the borough system became outmoded after the industrial revolution.

Cleisthenes redrew the electoral map of Attica from bottom to top. He replaced the forty-eight old wards with about three times as many new small wards, called *demes*, some already in existence and others newly created in areas where there had been large increases of population. Every citizen resident in a deme, whether clansman or guildsman or recently re-enfranchized *émigré*, was registered as a member of his deme on equal footing, no patronymic being added. Membership of a deme was thereafter to be hereditary. Thus the naturalized citizens, whom their opponents scornfully called aliens and slaves, and the descendants of such citizens, were inextricably mingled in the membership of a deme. The deme now became the unit of local government for financial, electoral and religious purposes. It had its own assembly and officers.

Cleisthenes then divided Attica into three regions of approximately equal population: (i) greater Athens, with a generous surround of coast and plain; (ii) the Paralia (the eastern coastal region); and (iii) the Mesogeia (the interior). Within each region he made ten packets of demes. The demes in any one packet were not necessarily contiguous with each other, but the aggregate of their territories was called by the old name, a 'third'. He now had thirty 'thirds' at his disposal. Next, he selected one 'third' from each region by lot and made these three 'thirds' into a single tribe. He now had ten tribes in place of the previous four. The members of any one of the new tribes came from all three regions and from a random scatter of demes. Consequently each tribe was more or less a cross-section of the whole community of farmers, artisans, traders, fishermen, etc. Membership of the tribe, being based on membership of the deme, was determined by residence in 507 and by heredity thereafter. The tribe had its own assembly and elected officers, and it performed financial, electoral, religious and military functions. Its members fought side by side in the tribal regiment.

The new system of demes, thirds and tribes cut clean across the old system. For example, the phratry-members of an old third in the central plain in which the clan members had been a decisive pressure-group found themselves dispersed over several demes and over several tribes; and the members of the Eumolpidae, a strong clan, were now members of some ten demes and several tribes. Moreover, more people were admitted to the franchise than under Isagoras, and there was no distinction between old citizens and new citizens in registration, voting and candidature for office. Thus Cleisthenes brought into effect an equality of rights in these respects which matched the equality before the law that had been introduced by Solon.

The chief step which Cleisthenes took towards making the common people more influential in the constitution was the setting up of the Council of Five Hundred, which replaced Solon's nominated Council of Four Hundred. Its members were elected as follows: the demesmen of each deme elected a number of candidates, the number being fixed in proportion to the population of the deme, from those who were over thirty years of age and belonged to the middle or upper property-groups (see p. 32). The officers of each tribe then drew fifty names by lot from the candidates elected by its demes. The resulting five hundred names were then submitted to a final screening by the retiring councillors. There was no appeal from their decision.

The councillors held office for one year only. On entering the Council they swore 'to advise what is best for the state'. The councillors from one tribe sat continually for one-tenth of the year as a committee of the Council. They elected their own secretary for that period, and they drew a chairman by lot each day. The committee dealt with the day-to-day business of the state and decided whether a special meeting of the Council should be convened. The full Council met on statutory occasions throughout the year. Its chief function was to draw up the agenda for the Assembly and to attach its own recommendation to each agendum. Like its predecessor (see p. 33), the Council of Five Hundred acted as a brake on the Assembly, but it was more likely than its predecessor to reflect the mood of the people in that its members were chosen by election and selection and not by nomination.

If we compare the procedures for returning members of Council at Athens and Members of Parliament in the United Kingdom, we may notice at Athens the age-bar, the property-qualification and the final screening for moral dependability which are not required for Parliamentary candidature, and the lack of any party affiliation, which rates so high in the British Parliamentary system. The first stage of the procedure, election, is the same, and British wards provide in the same way for proportional representation. The second stage, selection by lot, was intended to diminish the chances of personal influence gaining a seat for a clan-leader or an employer. The Council sat without any recess, acting either in committee or in full; the councillor received no salary, and board and lodging were supplied only when his committee was sitting; loyalty was not to a party but under oath to the state.

There was also an important element of rotation. No one could be a member of Council more than twice. If he were a member twice, it would not be in consecutive years. And no one could be chairman of his committee more than once. The object of this was to give political experience to as many men as possible. Athens needed a politically educated public because the majority of the citizens meeting in the Assembly took all the final decisions of state.

The nine chief magistrates were elected by the Assembly to hold office for one year, as in the past. The higher command of Athens' forces was reorganized in 501. Each tribal assembly elected a brigadier to command its own tribal regiment, and the Assembly of the state elected ten generals, one from each tribe, to deal with the armed forces, defences, garrisons, etc., and take operational command in the field. In each case tenure of office was for one year. Consecutive tenures were permitted. We shall see this system of command, so unlike our own, in operation during the campaign of Marathon (p. 79, below).

It should be noted that the chief magistrates and the generals were appointed by direct election. In practice the Assembly nearly always chose members of the leading clans to fill these offices. Greek political theorists therefore came to regard direct election by the Assembly as an aristocratic feature in a constitution. Cleisthenes may have invented also the procedure known as ostracism. Under it the Assembly was able to expel a leading statesman for ten years and in effect to commit itself to a particular line of policy. We shall discuss this procedure when we first find it in use (p. 81, below). Thus the Assembly was given full power to decide who should administer state affairs, who should command its forces, and on occasion who should advocate its policy.

In general we may regard the constitution of Cleisthenes as a balanced constitution in which the Areopagus Council and the election of the chief officers of state were still aristocratic features and the Council of Five Hundred and the new electoral system were democratic. At the same time all the innovations pointed towards democracy: the electoral reform in particular established the equal rights of all citizens, regardless of birth and origin, which formed one of the bases of the full democracy. The Council of Five Hundred was to be another basis. But the constitution of Cleisthenes was not yet full democracy in the Greek sense, in which the majority's rule was direct and untrammeled. We must remember what Cleisthenes did not do. He left the Areopagus Council intact, he did not disturb the property qualifications for tenure of office, and he did not modify a method of election for the chief officers of state which favoured the leaders of large clans.

He did not abolish the racial system of tribes, phratries, clans and priesthoods with their own thirds and wards; for it was integral to the religious and moral structure of Attic society, which was still very traditional.

Thus Cleisthenes managed to reorientate the political development of Athens. He turned away from autocracy and oligarchy and towards democracy but without weakening the religious and social bonds of the state. Indeed he created a vision of Athens as a united state with equal rights for all citizens, which was to preserve her during the dangers of the next decades.

The first test of the Cleisthenic state came immediately. In 506 the forces of the Spartan Alliance, recruited from all states in the Peloponnese except Argos, were led into southwestern Attica by Cleomenes and Demaratus, the two Spartan kings. At the same time Sparta's Boeotian allies invaded northwestern Attica hoping to punish Athens because Athens had helped Plataea to resist incorporation in the Boeotian League, and the army of Chalcis crossed over from Euboea and ravaged northwestern Attica. The tripartite attack was well-planned and effected. The Athenian army, although outnumbered heavily, lay at Eleusis, prepared to fight a decisive battle. At this moment the forces of the Spartan Alliance departed in some confusion. The reason was that Cleomenes had concealed the purpose of the campaign, namely to put Isagoras in charge at Athens, until the army was in position in Attica. As soon as it was known, the Corinthian contingent withdrew in protest; the other Spartan king, Demaratus, took the troops under his command out of the line, and the remaining allied contingents followed suit.

When the Peloponnesians had gone the Athenian army trounced the Boeotians and the Chalcidians separately and confiscated the richest land of Chalcis. On this land she settled 4,000 Athenians of military age; they became owners of estates or *cleruchs*. While the defeated Chalcidians worked the estates, the 4,000 Athenians held Chalcis in subjection and raided the coast of Boeotia. The Boeotian League was now hard pressed and obtained help from Aegina, which raided the coast of Attica. But Athens had tempered her resolve in the furnace of war and she was prepared to stand up to any Greek state or any combination of Greek states.

CHAPTER 8

THE EXPANSION OF PERSIA AND THE REACTIONS OF THE GREEK STATES, 546–490

The Medes and Persians of Iran spoke like the Greeks an Indo-European language and were a vigorous, warlike and intelligent people. They were still at a feudal stage of development when a brilliant member of the Achaemenid house, Cyrus II, inherited the throne in 559. Thirty years later he left to his son and successor, Cambyses, an empire which stretched from the Caspian Sea to the Dardanelles and southwards to the Persian Gulf and the borders of Egypt. Cambyses conquered Egypt and received the submission of Cyrene. Darius (522–486) added Pakistan and invaded Europe; he put down numerous revolts and organized the empire in a form which lasted until the conquests of Alexander.

In many parts of Asia the Persians appeared as liberators, for instance in overthrowing the oppressive power of Assyria, and they were tolerant in matters of religion and social organization. Indeed they were successful in using the military and naval forces of recently subjected peoples; the Phoenician fleet, for instance, played an important part in the conquest of Egypt. On the other hand revolt was punished by massacre or deportation. 'The King of the lands of all peoples' as the Persian monarch styled himself, 'The Great King' or just 'The King' as the Greeks called him, held his court at Susa in southern Iran and governed his vast empire through the Persian rulers or 'satraps' of twenty large provinces, who had full military and civil powers, raised and trained troops locally and paid tribute in specie and in kind to the royal treasury. Darius minted gold coins (*darics*) and silver coins (*sigloi*, whence shekels), which were current from India to Sicily. He developed maritime commerce by driving a canal from the Nile to the Red Sea and by promoting a voyage of discovery from India to the Red Sea in which a Greek called Scylax took part and wrote a record. But the Persians themselves did not engage in commerce and all surplus revenue was hoarded.

The élite forces of the Great King were the heavy-armed cavalry, in which the Persian aristocracy served, and the heavy-armed Persian infantry, which included the guards or 'Immortals' of the King. The subject peoples provided large numbers of heavy-armed and light-armed cavalry, a variety of infantry which included 'the bronze men' of the Greek states in Asia, the experienced fleets of Phoenicia, Cyprus, Egypt and Ionia, and the siegecraft which had been a speciality of the Assyrians. Thus Persia had almost unlimited resources for war, and the mobility of her forces was increased not only by developing sea communications but also by building a network of roads, radiating from Susa and leading for instance to the Aegean coast near Ephesus.

While the Great King was constitutional monarch of Persia, he was ruler of the empire by divine right and his authority over his subjects was absolute. To the Greek mind he was the supreme example of one-man rule, which was the negation of freedom and self-government and therefore incompatible with the concept of the polis. The contrast was even sharper than the contrast today between a one-party centralized union of states and a group of autonomous national states lacking any central organization. The contrast in scale of material power between Persia and the Greeks was on the face of it very marked.

Persia reached the threshold of the Greek world in 546, when Cyrus defeated Croesus, King of Lydia and overlord of the Greek states in Asia, who had made alliance with Babylon, Egypt and Sparta but too late to receive any help. Next Cyrus demanded the submission of the Greek states in Asia, except Miletus with which he had made a separate treaty. The Ionians met at Panionium (see p. 42), and they and the Aeolians asked Sparta for help. The Spartans professed themselves unable to provide any troops, but they sent envoys who warned Cyrus that Sparta would not tolerate the molestation of any Greek state by Cyrus. As Herodotus tells the story, Cyrus asked some bystanders who these Spartans were to give him orders, and his commanders then proceeded to capture the cities one by one.[1] Most of the population of Phocaea and Teus sailed away to find new homes overseas. But the other cities submitted and provided Cyrus with troops which helped to reduce the peoples of Asia Minor, the Dorians included.

The statement by the Spartan envoys seemed to have been an empty threat. Yet the clear declaration by Sparta, and the belief of others that she would keep her word, to resist Persia to the death in the cause of Greek freedom, was of the greatest importance in encouraging the Greek states in general to resist the advance of Persia.

The next conquests of Persia were Babylonia in 539 and Egypt in 525.

Because Persia favoured tyrants as governors of the Greek states in Asia Minor, it was easy for tyrants elsewhere to collaborate with Persia and batten on her success. One such was Polycrates, who had made himself tyrant of Samos and now had the strongest fleet in the east Aegean. He undertook to help Cambyses in the invasion of Egypt, and it was apparently as a vassal of Persia that he sent forty ships. However, the ships' companies mutinied. Eventually they reached Laconia, where they appealed to Sparta. At that time Cambyses was about to invade Egypt with large forces by land and sea, and it was obvious that the same forces might be used for an advance across the Aegean; in that event Samos would be a valuable base for Cambyses.

Sparta and Corinth made a determined effort to capture Samos first; they failed only because they lacked skill in siegecraft and the mercenary army of Polycrates remained loyal to him. This action by Sparta and Corinth was regarded by Persia as an act of war, and Sparta must have intended it as such. Whatever the reason, Cambyses did not follow up his conquest of Egypt by advancing westwards. Samos was still subject to Persia in 518, when Syloson was installed as tyrant and Persian puppet.

Darius was not a descendant of Cyrus: he was an Achaemenid who had taken part in a palace revolution and had been chosen by his accomplices to take the throne. Young, vigorous and ruthless, he stamped out a large number of revolts and impaled any pretenders. When order was restored, he recruited the forces of the empire and led them to the East. His predecessors had reached the northwestern frontier of India and the southern slopes of the Hindu-Kush, but he crossed the Hindu-Kush and conquered the entire Indus valley, a spectacular achievement which required a planning ability and a trained army such as were found later in Alexander and his Macedonians. He turned next to Europe. Having sent ships and agents ahead to obtain information, he made the crossing from Asia to Europe by the northern route, using his fleet to form a pontoon bridge between Chalcedon and Byzantium. This choice of route committed him to the conquest of the great plains which extend from the coast of the Black Sea into central Bulgaria, for unless he held the plains his bridgehead in Europe would be vulnerable. Strategic considerations moved him, as they did Alexander later, to carry his control up to the Danube. The Thracian tribes who occupied most of what is now Bulgaria submitted, but as he drew near the Danube he met resistance from the strongest local tribe, the Getae, whom he defeated and conscripted for the next stage of his campaign.

It was possible for Darius to advance with his army and his navy in close co-operation either through western Thrace and Macedonia into Greece or along the coast of the Black Sea into the land of the Scythians. He preferred the latter course. The navy had already been ordered to meet him near the mouth of the Danube and to make a pontoon bridge across the river. His army crossed the river, probably in the year 513, and disappeared into the Ukraine where the Scythians withdrew before him, sending their families and cattle to the north. The fleet waited at the mouth of the Danube. The news that Darius was retreating was given to the ship's captains by some Scythians who rode up and asked them to destroy the pontoon bridge. But the captains of the fleet, the Greeks included, remained loyal to Darius. Some days later Darius and his army crossed back into Thrace, having abandoned their sick and wounded. Darius had neither forced a decisive battle nor annexed any territory. He wisely turned his back on the steppes of Russia. While he returned to Asia, his deputy as commander advanced to the border of Macedonia and received the formal submission of Amyntas, King of Macedon, who gave his daughter in marriage to a son of the commander. A new satrapy was now formed in Europe. It was called *Skudra*, probably a Phrygian word, which recalled the presence of Phrygians there before they crossed into Asia. The satrapy included all Thrace and Macedonia. The campaign had added a large satrapy to the empire and Persian forces were now stationed in the immediate neighbourhood of the Greek mainland.

There the concern of Sparta was to extend the Spartan Alliance into central Greece and to unite as many Greek states as possible under her leadership. Her opposition to tyrants was now in line with her opposition to Persia. She gained the adherence of Phocis by helping to expel a local tyrant, and she avoided any friction with the Boeotian League when Plataea asked Sparta for aid against Thebes in 519. The chief danger to Sparta's cause appeared to be the tyrants of Athens, who were in touch with Persia both at Sigeum on the Asiatic coast and in the Gallipoli peninsula, where their friend Miltiades was ruler. When Darius returned from Scythia in 513, the Scythians sent to Sparta some envoys who taught Cleomenes the art of hard drinking and persuaded the Spartans to make an alliance against Persia. In 511 the Scythians raided the Persian satrapy in Europe as far as the Gallipoli peninsula and raised a number of Greek states in revolt, in particular Byzantium and Chalcedon, which controlled the crossing of the Bosporus. Sparta made no move and the Scythians withdrew. In this year Sparta made her first attack on Hippias, the tyrant of Athens, and in midsummer 510 she liberated Athens and brought her into the Spartan Alliance. She had chosen her time well for Persia was engaged in reasserting her authority over the Bosporus and Thrace. In 509 Persia annexed the islands of Imbros and Lemnos off the Dardanelles. During these operations the Athenian settlers and their leader Miltiades fled from the Gallipoli peninsula, because Athens was at the time in alliance with Sparta.

Darius abandoned the advance in Europe for the time being. This was fortunate for Sparta, because the conflict between Sparta and Athens split the Spartan Alliance. At the centre of the conflict was the personality of Cleomenes. An energetic and ambitious king, he seems to have acted on his own authority whenever he was in command of a Spartan force outside Laconia. His methods during his second intervention at Athens – sending orders ahead, pronouncing wholesale banishments, and deposing the Council of the Areopagus (p. 59, above) – were an outrage to the libertarian spirit of the Athenians and drove them to seek alliance with Persia. When the campaign against Athens was being planned in 506, the Spartan authorities sent both kings as commanders, but it appears that the secret orders which required exact timing with the commanders of the Boeotian and Chalcidian forces were divulged to Cleomenes only. This proved to be a fatal mistake. Cleomenes concealed the objective of the expedition until he was already on Attic soil. Thereupon the other king, Demaratus, was naturally annoyed; he played a leading part in the disagreement which ended in the disbanding of the allied forces. The Spartan Alliance had shown itself to be an inefficient machine.

In 505 Sparta asked the members of the Spartan Alliance to send representatives to a meeting. She told them that she wanted to intervene at Athens and reinstate Hippias, who was now out of favour with Persia and had come to Sparta. The representative of Corinth spoke in opposition. He was supported by the other representatives. Sparta had the good sense not only to drop the proposal but also to stand aside and not help Aegina and Boeotia which were at war with Athens. This policy brought important gains. Having failed to get help from Sparta, Hippias turned once again to Persia and this time the Persian satrap Artaphernes ordered Athens to take Hippias back as ruler. This order drove Athens into the anti-Persian camp. Reconciliation with Sparta was now possible. Meanwhile the war between Athens and her enemies developed into a stalemate when Sparta decided to stay out of it. Neither side was in any danger of being crippled.

The most important result was that Sparta and her allies adopted the procedure which they had used in 505 as a permanent feature of the

Spartan Alliance. In effect two deliberative bodies considered policy: the Spartan Assembly and the Congress of Allies. If the Spartan Assembly agreed to propose a policy as it did in 505, the proposal went to the Congress of Allies. There the representatives of the allies discussed the proposal and decided to accept or reject it in accordance with the majority of their votes (each state, whether large or small, having one vote). If the Congress of Allies sent a proposal to the Spartan Assembly, it was accepted or rejected there by a majority vote of the Spartiates. Thus no policy could be put into action unless it commanded a majority of the votes in each of the deliberative bodies. Under this system Sparta's influence in the making of policy was equal to that of the sum of the allies; similarly Sparta and the Congress had equal powers of veto.

This situation corresponded to the central position which Sparta held in the web of alliance and to Sparta's supreme command of the allied troops in the field which the allies individually had conceded in their treaties of alliance. The machinery of the coalition corresponded to the realities of the military situation. In practice it proved preferable to the alternative system under which there would have been one deliberative body and Sparta would have had in it a single vote like any other state.

The organization of a large coalition under this system, which could be called the bicameral system, is not practised in the modern world. Yet one can see that it might have advantages. If Britain and her allies in Europe had organized themselves in this way at the time when Hitler was laying hands upon his neighbours, there is little doubt that they would have formed an agreed policy, and that their forces under British command would have stopped him. Again Britain has no formal machinery for activating the theoretical alliance which exists between members of the Commonwealth and commanding its forces in the field. Where a large coalition exists, as in NATO, the largest state on which the organization depends for its efficacy has no more say in the forming of policy than the smallest state. On the other hand, to invest a power of veto in four states, as has been done in UNO, is likely to prove fatal to the organization. The problem, in short, is to devise an effective machinery and to convince all concerned to adopt it. This is what Sparta and her allies achieved, and the machinery worked efficiently for more than a century.

The Greek states of the east Aegean suffered a recession of prosperity during the establishment and the expansion of the Persian Empire. The centre of economic gravity was now at Susa and the wealthiest province was Pakistan. For a time Ionia was on the periphery of the empire. Then the advance into the Black Sea and into Europe and the effect of

Darius' furtherance of maritime commerce created a much more favourable climate. As trade between the east and the west began to recover, the Greek states under Persian rule became prosperous again. The island of Naxos, which lay just outside the Persian sphere, became an important centre of exchange. Pro-Persian tyrants cast envious eyes upon it. Some émigrés who had been exiled by the democratic régime of Naxos obtained the backing of the Persian satrap and of a puppet-tyrant of Miletus, called Aristagoras. In 499 they made an attack in force on Naxos. The landing was successful, but the attempt on the city failed. The Persians and their friends withdrew disconcerted and Aristagoras found himself in disfavour with the satrap. He set about organizing a revolt, which would keep him in a position of power for the moment.

Revolts were almost endemic in the Persian Empire. The loose structure of government made it easy enough for a state or a satrap to start a revolt, but the vast military resources on which the Great King could call made ultimate success very unlikely. In this case Aristagoras and his fellow-conspirators in the Ionian states had the advantage of being on the fringe of the empire and of having the Greeks of the mainland as potential allies. What should their strategy be? Hecataeus, the Milesian geographer (see p. 129, below), advised them to co-operate with the free Greek states and win the mastery of the seas. It was indeed conceivable that a combined fleet of all Greeks might be able to defeat the fleets of Phoenicia, Cyprus and Egypt under Persian command, but no one knew how far the free Greek states would commit themselves to the cause. On land the Greeks of Asia Minor had neither sufficient territory for manoeuvre nor the numbers of cavalry and infantry on which to base a campaign of liberation; their only hope was to raise their Asiatic neighbours in revolt. In any case the risks of defeat, leading to massacre or deportation, were very great; and even if revolt succeeded it would probably result in the weakening of Ionian trade. Nevertheless, when the conspirators attacked the pro-Persian tyrants and proclaimed the setting up of fair government (*isonomia*), the population rose in their support and the so-called Ionian Revolt was launched in autumn 499 without any previous sounding of the free Greek states.

During the winter Aristagoras sought help from the free Greek states. Sparta refused, rightly perhaps, because she was a military power and any addition she might make to the Ionian infantry force was not going to swing the balance on land against the Persian armies. Athens accepted, sending twenty ships to augment the Ionian fleet; it was a brave decision, committing Athens to war with Persia, and also, as it proved, a politic one in that it strengthened the bond between Athens and the Ionian states. Eretria, a state on friendly terms with Miletus, sent five ships. The lack of response from most of the free states left the Ionians in a desperate situation, but it did not deter them from striking the first blow, a raid inland which resulted in the burning of Sardis in Lydia, where the satrap Artaphernes had his headquarters. This spectacular start alienated the Lydians, but it raised in revolt most of the Carians, who were a warlike people, and the Greek states under Persian rule which were situated in the Bosporus, the Sea of Marmara and Cyprus. The chief problem now was one of co-ordination over so wide an area.

The nine Ionian states in revolt had their own traditional meeting place at the Panionium (see p. 42, above). They now sent delegates there and formed a political union of their own to which they contributed men, money and ships. The council of delegates decided the policy of the Ionian Union without referring back to the governments of the member-states, issued an Ionian coinage, and gave strategic directives to 'the generals of the Ionians', evidently a committee of higher command such as we have seen at Athens (p. 63, above). The contingent of each member-state was under the command of one or more of its own generals. The degree of political co-operation, which made rapid and final decisions possible, is impressive. But the system of command in operational matters was complicated and clumsy, for the committee of higher command was entirely separate from the contingent-commanders of each national contingent. Worse still, however, was the failure of the Ionians to invent any machinery of co-ordination with their numerous allies. They seem to have adopted an entirely *ad hoc*, opportunist attitude towards them.

Darius sent three army groups into action. They acted singly or in combination, splitting up the enemy and capturing cities now in the Hellespont and now in Cyprus. The Ionian fleet fought well off Cyprus, and the Carians fought well on land. But their efforts were sporadic and unorganized. By the end of 496 the Ionians were almost the only people still in revolt. They decided to give up the struggle on land, and they concentrated all their resources at sea. They stationed their fleet at the island of Lade off Miletus and waited for a decisive battle. The Ionians and the Aeolians of Lesbos had 353 warships – more than the Greeks were to have later at the beginning of the Battle of Salamis – but they failed to solve the problem of an overall command. At one stage the Ionian contingents agreed among themselves to put Dionysius of

Phocaea in command. He began to train the fleet in the tactics which he intended to employ but the crews went on strike, preferring to sit in the shade. When the Persian fleet came up and engaged, each contingent acted under the direction of its own command. Many Greek ships sailed away without fighting at all. Utter defeat followed. Miletus fell after a short siege in 494, and the revolt came to an end in 493.

The Ionian Revolt failed through lack of organization among the rebels, inability to accept a unified command and the discipline it entailed, and disunity in the face of the enemy. Persia's conduct of the campaign was far superior: its fleet, consisting of national contingents from Phoenicia, Cyprus and Egypt but directed by a unified Persian command and supported by an army advancing along the coast, gained a resounding victory. Persia punished the rebellious Greeks by looting and burning towns and temples alike, deporting part of the population of Miletus to the Persian Gulf, and sending a selection of boys and girls to become eunuchs and slaves at the court of Darius. Thereafter Persia made a sensible settlement. Tribute was re-assessed on a fair and moderate basis, the states were permitted to have democratic govern-ments, and young men were called up for service in the Persian forces.

In 492 Mardonius, a son-in-law of Darius, crossed into Europe with a large army and navy. He advanced as far as Macedonia driving out any Greek adventurers who had established themselves on the coast, among them the Athenian Miltiades who had returned to the Gallipoli peninsula. While Mardonius was marching into central Macedonia, his fleet was wrecked off Mt Athos with very heavy losses. But on land Persia's power was vindicated and the European satrapy was formed once more. In summer 491 Darius ordered his subjects on the Medi-terranean coast to build transports and equip a fleet. His purpose was clear; for he sent envoys to the Greek states of the Aegean islands and the Greek mainland demanding the tokens of submission, 'earth and water'. The demand was accepted by many states, including Aegina, a strong naval state, then at war with Athens. Without doubt Darius intended to invade the Greek mainland in the course of the following year, 490.

During the Ionian Revolt Athens' policy had vacillated. At the end of the first campaigning season she withdrew her fleet from Ionia; then when Miltiades came home in 493 he was put on trial, perhaps by those who wished to appease Persia. But Miltiades was acquitted, and an advocate of resistance called Themistocles was elected to the chief archonship in that year and began to fortify and develop the natural harbours of the Peiraeus. Thus Athens' intention was to resist Persia.

When Aegina submitted to Persia, Athens took the logical step: she asked Sparta to intervene. Although Sparta had refused the Ionian request for help, she had struck an important blow for Greek freedom when she attacked Argos in 495 and killed 6,000 Argives in battle; for Argos was known to favour the side of Persia. Now Sparta sent her representatives to Aegina, arrested ten Aeginetan leaders and deposited them at Athens as hostages for the neutrality of Aegina in regard to Persia. This affair brought to a head the enmity between Cleomenes and Demaratus, the two kings of Sparta who had different policies. By intriguing with the priests at Delphi Cleomenes managed to persuade the Spartans to depose Demaratus and to put Leotychidas in his place, but the intrigue leaked out and in the end Cleomenes committed suicide. Leonidas, his brother, became king. In 490 Demaratus, the deposed king, fled to the court of Darius. Sparta was now clear of trouble with her kings, and the Council of Elders was able to implement its policy of leading any Greek states which were prepared to resist the advance of Persia.

CHAPTER 9

OFFENSIVE AND COUNTER-OFFENSIVE
490–466

In 490 Darius decided to send his fleet across the Aegean Sea and to attack Eretria and Athens with élite forces. This decision was as bold as it was unexpected. It was the army which had won the empire and extended its frontiers into India and Europe, and the fleet had always been an ancillary arm, providing supplies and transport. Even in the Ionian Revolt the army too had had the lion's share of the fighting and had come up in support of the fleet at the Battle of Lade. It might have been expected now that Darius would advance from Macedonia with a large army and a supporting fleet and overwhelm the resistance of the Greek states, if any, by vastly superior numbers. Instead, Darius decided – and it was probably a personal decision – to forego the advantage of large numbers and deliver a sea-borne attack for which there was no precedent.

The Battle of Lade must have opened his eyes to new possibilities. It was clear that such states of the Greek mainland as were likely to resist him would not be able to raise a fleet as strong as that of the Ionians had been, and that beyond Greece the Persian fleet might be able to co-operate with the fleet of the Carthaginians, colonists as they were of the Phoenicians. In fact Darius is likely to have realized the truth (clear to Britain and now to Russia) that any state which wishes to control the Mediterranean area must have supremacy at sea. If a seaborne attack were to succeed against the states of the Greek peninsula, he could use the same technique to acquire Sicily and then land élite forces in Italy with a view to conquering the Greek colonies and Etruria, which alone were capable of organized resistance in the western Mediterranean. The alternative method of conquering the West, namely an advance overland, was an immense task because, as Darius had found to his cost in Scythia, there were no foundations in uncivilized areas of great extent on which to build an imperial system. Thus the fate of the West was involved in the outcome of the campaign of 490 which was directed against Eretria and Athens.

The Persian expedition crossed the Aegean without meeting any opposition at sea or on the islands. Sacrifice was made to Apollo at Delos in order to appease religious sentiment among the islanders, and Naxos alone was punished for its earlier resistance by looting, burning and deportation. The islands were incorporated immediately into the Empire, and young men were conscripted to serve as troops against Eretria and Athens. The fleet had the advantage over any army in the matter of speed: it could attack either Athens or Eretria or Sparta and be sure of catching any one of them on its own. The best course might have been to land in Laconia and attack Sparta first; but the orders which had been issued by Darius to the commanders of the expedition, Datis and Artaphernes (a son of the satrap of the same name), were to proceed against Athens and Eretria. The Persians chose, probably unwisely, to move against the weaker first, Eretria, a state of Euboea. They were delayed for a few days en route at Carystus, a small state on the southern tip of Euboea, which refused at first to submit but yielded under siege. The delay enabled Eretria, now clearly the next target, to send to Athens for help. The Athenians ordered their 4,000 men at Chalcis (see p. 64, above) to go to the aid of Eretria. When the 4,000 arrived, they found that the counsels of the Eretrians were divided. Fearing that they might become involved in the collapse of Eretria, they crossed over to Attica. The Persians made unopposed landings at three places in Eretrian territory and attacked the town. On the seventh day it fell through treachery from within. The buildings were burnt and the population was deported.

A few days later the Persians crossed to the east coast of Attica, made an unopposed landing at dawn in the bay of Marathon, and camped in an easily defended position which provided excellent watering facilities and pasture for the cavalry horses. They were now some twenty-five miles away from Athens. Their cavalry and skirmishers began to ravage the plain of Marathon, which was completely undefended.

The Persian command has been criticized by modern writers for not landing at the bay of Phalerum, where the open shelving beach is close to Athens, but the critics fail to realize that to put cavalry and infantry from galleys into the water in the face of a determined enemy when covering fire was limited to the bow and arrow was to invite their destruction. Granted that they had to land at some distance from the city of Athens, in which the Athenian army was certain to be stationed,

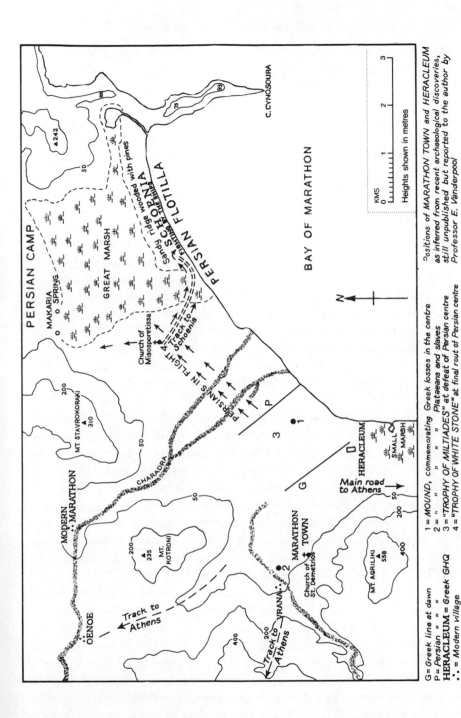

Map 8 The battle of Marathon, 490

G = Greek line at dawn
P = Persian " " "
HERACLEUM = Greek GHQ
∴ = Modern village

1 = MOUND, commemorating Greek losses in the centre
2 = " " " " Plataeans and slaves
3 = "TROPHY OF MILTIADES" at defeat of Persian centre
4 = "TROPHY OF WHITE STONE" at final rout of Persian centre

Positions of MARATHON TOWN and HERACLEUM as inferred from recent archaeological discoveries, still unpublished but reported to the author by Professor E. Vanderpool

Heights shown in metres

Map labels:

PERSIAN CAMP

▲242

50

MAKARIA SPRING

GREAT MARSH

sandy ridge wooded with pines

SCHOENIA

PERSIAN FLOTILLA

landing beach

Track to Schoenia

Church of Misosporetissa

PERSIANS IN FLIGHT

75

93

C. CYNOSOURA

BAY OF MARATHON

N

200

MT. STAVROKORAKI 310

50

CHARADRA

MODERN MARATHON

200

MT. KOTRONI 235

50

OENOE

Track to Athens

400

200

Track to Athens

VRANA

MARATHON TOWN

Church of St. Demetrios

MT. AGRILIKI 558

400

200

50

G

HERACLEUM

SMALL MARSH

Main road to Athens

P

1

3

4

KMS
0   1   2   3

77

why choose Marathon? The first consideration was ease and safety of supply; for ships could cross from their base at Eretria to the east coast of Attica in any wind, whereas they could not round Cape Sunium to reach Phalerum in some winds. Moreover, on the east coast of Attica, the most sheltered shelving beach was in the northeast corner of the bay of Marathon. The choice seems in fact to have been a wise one.

The élite fighting troops who landed at Marathon numbered at least 25,000. As it took some three men to transport and supply one fighting man, the total force on shore and offshore at Marathon was not far short of 100,000 men. A vital need for them was an abundant supply of fresh drinkable water. This was available just inland of the bay of Marathon. The arm in which Persia had undoubted superiority over the Greeks was cavalry. Darius had had transports specially designed to carry horses; they were made probably with let-down flaps for landing the horses. The plain at Marathon was admirably suited for the deployment of a large cavalry force. This point was appreciated by the Athenian émigré Hippias who acted as guide to the Persians, for he had landed there from Eretria with his father in 546, and on that occasion Peisistratus had advanced into the central plain of Attica to engage and defeat an army which had been slow to leave the city of Athens.

The Athenian army consisted of some 10,000 heavy infantry, a negligible number of cavalry and swarms of ill-trained skirmishing infantry. It was in camp at Athens when the news came by beacon-signal that the Persian expeditionary force was beginning to land at Marathon. The Athenian board of ten generals met at once. They sent off a runner, Philippides, to inform Sparta and ask for aid, and they had an emergency meeting of the Assembly convened at short notice. The debate was swayed by one of the generals, Miltiades, who had had much experience of the Persian army. His proposal was adopted, 'to provide themselves with supplies, to set out [from Athens] and to meet the enemy without delay'.[1] A runner was then sent off to Plataea to ask the Plataean army of some 1,000 infantry to join the Athenians at a rendezvous beside the plain of Marathon. The cavalry and the skirmishers stayed at Athens. The heavy infantry and some trained slaves marched that day and during part of the night along a direct but hilly route to a precinct of Heracles which lay in the southwestern part of the plain. When dawn broke, twenty-four hours after the first Persians had landed, the Athenian army was in position, covering its own supply-line and threatening or blocking the three routes which led from the western part of the plain towards the central plain and Athens.

If Hippias had had hopes of emulating his father and reaching the central plain first, he had been forestalled.

During that day the two armies reconnoitred one another's position. The Athenians saw the dreaded Persian cavalry manoeuvring in front of them on the level ground of the plain. By dawn next day the Plataean army came up to join the Athenians at the Heracleum. Soon afterwards the Persian forces moved into the southwestern part of the plain and took up position for battle, the infantry having its back to the dry watercourse (Charadra) and the cavalry manoeuvring in the plain. Should the Greeks advance into the plain and engage, or withdraw to a stronger defensive position on the foothills?

The decision lay with the ten generals sitting in committee. Five of them wished to engage, and five wished not to engage. The latter may well have argued that it was better to wait and see if the Spartans would come up, and then to reconsider the matter. But Miltiades invoked the casting vote of the ceremonial head of the armed forces, Callimachus. He voted to engage. Now the operational command rotated. It was vested not in the ten generals but in one general each day in turn. The four supporters of Miltiades gave their days of command to him; there was thus an even chance that if an engagement developed, Miltiades would be in command on the day. It was probably on his recommendation that the Greeks now felled trees in the foothills and made an abatis with them in the plain each night. When the abatis was constructed, the infantry could defend themselves behind it from the attacks of the Persian cavalry.

On the day after the decision to engage was taken, the Greeks learnt that for religious reasons the Spartans would not leave Laconia until full moon had passed and that they would come then to Athens. There was thus a week to go before the Spartans could reach Marathon. The abatis was advanced farther into the plain each night, and the Greeks were actually within a mile of the enemy infantry line when a message was brought by some Ionians in the Persian force shortly before dawn, saying 'The cavalry are away.'[2]

It happened to be a day on which Miltiades was to have the operational command. He seized the chance. As his men stood to in line, he thinned his centre so that there were less than eight men in a file and strengthened his wings above that number. Then in the grey light of dawn he sent the line forward at the double, shouting the words of command: 'Charge upon them.'[3] The line of bronze-clad infantrymen swept forward. Passing through the barrage of Persian arrows and keeping parade-ground order, they engaged the enemy all along the line, like a breaking wave, and fought with spear and sword at close quarters.

Miltiades knew the merits and defects of the Persian army from personal experience. The squadrons of aristocratic heavy-armed cavalry were deadly in action against any infantry which they might catch unprotected in an open plain; that was why it had been impossible up to that moment for the Greek infantry to engage the enemy. On the other hand, once two infantry lines were interlocked in a welter of individual combats, the cavalry could not intervene in formation, and any individual cavalryman rarely entered the melée of an infantry battle because a single horse was so vulnerable. The Persian infantry-men were much superior in archery. But in close combat they were at a disadvantage in their equipment and weapons. They wore a turban or cap, a leather jerkin, or fish-scale singlet of metal discs, or tunic, and trousers of quilted cloth, and they carried a wicker shield, short spear and scimitar, whereas the Greek 'bronze men' wore a metal helmet, a cuirass and greaves and carried a metal shield, a longer spear and a sword. The mere weight of the Greek line, some eight men deep on average charging fast into a stationary line, must have knocked the front row or two of the Persians onto their knees; and on this occasion Miltiades had deliberately increased the weight of his wings.

The battle went according to Miltiades' plan. The Persian wings broke and fled. The Greek wings wheeled inwards as pre-arranged. They then attacked the Persian centre, which had meanwhile broken the Greek centre and was now pursuing it. The whole Greek force was thus concentrated against the Persian centre. There was severe fighting, but the Persians broke and fled for the ships with the Greeks in close pursuit. Individual Persian cavalrymen were involved in the latter part of the battle but to little effect. The rout was now complete. The narrow exit from the plain which led to the strand and to the ships became blocked with fugitives. As the Greeks set upon them, the delay enabled the others ahead of them to get on board.

When the Persian army put out to sea, they left 6,400 dead behind them. They had not rowed far from land when a signal flashed from inland towards them. Thereupon the Persian fleet changed course and set sail with a following wind for Phalerum. They hoped to land the army there and take Athens, which was virtually undefended. By a forced march the Athenian army returned that evening just in time to save their city. The Persian fleet saw it was too late. It set sail for the Aegean Sea and Asia.

Next day the vanguard of the Spartans marched into Athens. They heard the news and went on to Marathon to inspect the dispositions and the equipment of the Persian dead. The Athenians had lost only 192 men. The dead were given heroic burial and a high mound of soil was raised over them. One may stand on this mound today and view the battleground. The Plataeans and the slaves who fell were buried beside the edge of the plain, near the road leading through the hills to Athens and Plataea and not far from the position they had held on the left of the original line. Their burial mound has recently been opened.

The victory electrified the Greeks. It showed the marked superiority of the Greek infantryman in close combat under good leadership, and it demonstrated that the tide of Persian aggression *could* be turned back. The Greek gods had proved to be on the side of the small battalions. But everyone knew that this was only the first round. In 489 Miltiades put to sea with the Athenian navy of seventy ships, hoping to win back some of the islands; but he failed and was wounded at Paros. He was put on trial for his conduct of the operation and sentenced to a large fine; he died shortly afterwards from the effects of his wound. The Athenian people gave credit where credit was due, but they were never sentimental about their famous commanders.

Defeat caused Darius to think again. This time he prepared to launch a massive invasion of the orthodox kind. But a revolt by Egypt, his own death and the need for his successor, Xerxes, to reduce Egypt delayed the final stage of the preparations until 483. Then gangs of forced labour began to dig a canal through the neck of the Athos peninsula, a huge and spectacular undertaking of which the purpose was clear. A Persian army and navy were about to invade Greece from the north and this canal was destined to provide a safe passage for the navy.

Athens drew two lessons from the campaign of Marathon: the danger of treachery from within and the importance of good leadership. In 488 she used for the first time the procedure of 'ostracism' ascribed to Cleisthenes. Each citizen wrote on a potsherd (*ostrakon*) the name of the man he wished to get rid of, and the man whose name occurred most often, provided that a certain quorum of potsherds was reached or exceeded, was then exiled on pain of death, but without loss of property, for ten years. The first men so ostracized were evidently suspected of pro-Persian leanings or dictatorial ambitions. The next went because the strategies they advised were not accepted; for example, in 483-2 Aristides, a colleague of Miltiades at Marathon and an advocate of resistance by the army, was ostracized. Finally the people accepted a proposal by Themistocles that she should raise her fleet from 70 to 200 ships. This was financially possible because of a lucky strike of silver in the state-owned mines at Laurium (the profit would usually have been distributed among the citizens as a bonus).

The decision to concentrate on the navy was intelligent and courageous. The great victory of the infantry at Marathon had not created any illusions. The army, however excellent, was too small to withstand a full-scale Persian invasion. On the other hand, a complete commitment to a navy of 200 ships and the training of their crews and marines, totalling nearly 40,000 men, would give to Athens and her associates a chance of reversing the verdict of the Battle of Lade. There was no question here of shilly-shallying between appeasement and war, no blimpish expectation of muddling through, no blurring of the issues. Rather, the Athenian people chose a course almost certain to lead to the evacuation of their country. Moreover, they did a rare thing. Before the enemy made his first move in the field, they committed themselves to the leadership of one man, Themistocles. Every month new warships were launched, and the naval training of all Athenians was intensified.

The Greek states which contemplated resistance at all looked not to Athens but to Sparta for leadership against Persia; for Athens was an individualistic state, hated by her immediate neighbours, whereas Sparta was the leader of a great coalition. The Greeks realized that Greece could be saved in the last resort only by a victory on land. Accordingly, their hopes of victory centred finally on Sparta and her allies. If Sparta had been narrow-minded and self-seeking, she might have insisted on all loyalist states joining the Spartan Alliance. Instead she looked for a wider form of coalition, capable of extension overseas and not tied by treaty to the special features of the Spartan Alliance (see p. 70). In autumn 481 representatives of all loyalist states met at Sparta. They took the oath to fight together against Persia, gave command by land and by sea to Sparta, and sent envoys to Argos, Crete, Corcyra and Syracuse 'in the hope that the Greek world might become one and that they should all get together and adopt the same policy, because danger threatened all Greeks alike'.[4] This was the voice of reason, speaking as it might have spoken to the democratic states before and after the Second World War.

The states which favoured non-resistance or appeasement or even collaboration were strong. The front-line states, Thessaly for instance and the islands, had little choice perhaps as they were likely to be flattened in any case by the Persian juggernaut. Others had more possibility of choice. Of these, Thebes was so hostile to Athens and Argos so hostile to Sparta that both were inclined to side with the

Medes and Persians, or, to use the contemporary Greek expression, to 'medize'. Their attitude was shared by the priests who controlled the utterances of the 'Pythia', the priestess-announcer of the will of Apollo at Delphi. Although the priests claimed that these utterances or 'oracles' were inspired by the god, there is good reason to suspect that the priests were influenced by the fears of the Delphian community and of the Amphictyonic Council which acted as secular sponsor and protector of the shrine. The members of the Council were mainly representatives of tribes which lay between Delphi and the borders of Macedonia, and they had little or no hope of resisting Persia success-fully. Consequently, although the 'oracles' were often ambivalent in meaning, their general tenor was in favour of neutrality and came very close to open 'medism'. This is apparent from the oracles uttered by the priestess in response to official enquiries from the leading states of Greece.

For instance, Sparta was told she would lose her city or a king, Argos was advised to sit still with her spear at the ready and Athens was told that her city would be burnt. When the Athenian envoys asked the oracle for a second utterance, they received an ambiguous but seemingly prophetic answer in hexameter verse, of which this is a crude translation in the same metre:

> Safe shall the wooden wall continue for thee and thy children.
> Wait not the tramp of the horse, nor the footmen mightily moving
> Over the land, but turn your back to the foe and retire ye.
> Yet shall a day arrive when ye shall meet him in battle.
> Holy Salamis, thou shalt destroy the offspring of women,
> When men scatter the seed, or when they gather the harvest.[5]

Syracuse said she would remain neutral. She sent an agent to Delphi, as the haven of neutrality, and she instructed him to offer tokens of submission and money as tribute if Persia triumphed in Greece. It was clear that there would be a landslide in favour of submission if Sparta backed down or mishandled the situation. It was assumed that Persia's next objective would be the conquest of Sicily and no doubt Italy.

In spring 480 the representatives of twenty or more states met at Corinth to organize resistance. We know from the experience of the Second World War how difficult it is to co-ordinate a coalition of states in the activities of war. The Greeks certainly created a more efficient system than the Western Allies did, both at the political level and at the operational level. Each member-state accepted the majority vote of a small deliberative body, the Congress of 'The Greeks', to which it sent a delegate or delegates, each state, large and small alike, having only one vote. The Congress took final decisions on military, diplomatic, financial, judicial and religious matters. The door was open for new members to enter upon the same terms. In operational matters the placing of the command on both elements in the hands of Sparta was confirmed, thus making a consistent and co-ordinated strategy possible. In practice the Spartan commander, whether he was one of the kings or a deputy, had full authority and full responsibility in making any decision in the field. Before coming to a decision it was wise for him to consult the commanders of the national contingents in his army or navy. With this in mind Sparta tried to rationalize the various systems of command which were in force in the allied states. For instance, Athens had ten generals in command of her national contingents. Sparta asked for one commander only in dealings with the Spartan command. Athens agreed. Themistocles was chosen by direct election from the whole population and acted for one year as commander in effect of Athenian forces against Persia. Similar arrangements were made in other allied states.

Xerxes was already advancing from Sardis to the pontoon-bridge over the Dardanelles, while the Greeks were hammering out their system of organization. His vast forces, numbering several hundred thousand men, moved with elephantine slowness constructing roads, dumping supplies, and conscripting local labour and troops. Midsummer passed before they made contact with the Greeks. It is a maxim of general application that a commander of greatly superior numbers should engage his enemy as frequently as possible and open more than one front by using flying columns or separate army groups. Xerxes adopted none of these tactics, familiar though they had been in the Ionian Revolt. When the Greeks offered battle in a fifty-foot-wide pass at Thermopylae, he made frontal attacks for three days and lost the flower of his infantry. When a detachment of his troops turned the pass by using a mountain-track which debouched behind the Greek position, the oracle of Delphi was fulfilled: the king, Leonidas, with the Spartans, their Helot attendants and the Thespians, stayed and fought to the death. The defence of Thermopylae was not in vain. It enabled the Greek fleet, which was stationed to the northeast of Thermopylae at Artemisium, to get the measure of the Persian fleet in the course of some indecisive actions. At sea the Persians suffered heavy losses through storms, particularly during an unsuccessful attempt to turn the Greek position by circumnavigating the island of Euboea.

They needed time to refit their ships and make good their losses by reinforcements.

When the Greek forces failed to hold the linked positions at Thermopylae and Artemisium, the Congress decided to leave central Greece undefended. Their plan now was to post the fleet in the Bay of Salamis in order to stop the advance of the Persian fleet and to fortify the narrows of the Isthmus as the army's next line of defence. This meant the evacuation of all territories between Thermopylae and the Isthmus. Most of the states which were now exposed to attack joined the side of Persia. But Megara and Athens stood firm in the allied cause. Indeed, Athens had decided long before on the proposal of Themistocles[6] in this event to entrust Athens and Attica to the gods and to take to the ships, 'the wooden wall' which the oracle of Delphi had mentioned. Now they put the decision into effect. When Xerxes' army came to Athens and the fleet moored at Phalerum, the Athenians at Salamis saw the smoke rising from their city.

The strategy which the Greeks had adopted required the fleet to remain in advance of the army's line and so prevent the enemy fleet from landing troops behind that line. Eurybiades, the Spartan in command, kept the fleet firmly in position at Salamis, despite the fact that most of the contingent commanders were advocating withdrawal. Themistocles clinched the matter on his private initiative. He sent a message to Xerxes saying that the Greeks were disunited; indeed they intended to escape and they were more likely to fight one another than to resist him. Duped by the message which corresponded so exactly with his own hopes, Xerxes sent his fleet out that very evening. His orders to the main body were that they should block the exits of the Salamis waters that night and advance into the channel at dawn. A separate flotilla was sent to block the distant narrows between Salamis and Megara. A commando force of picked Persian troops was ferried over to occupy a small island in mid-channel near the Greek position. It landed without being observed. Xerxes himself arranged to watch the battle next morning from a position by the bend of the Channel.

The Greek fleet of 380 ships lay on the beaches on the Salaminian side of the bend of the Channel. Just before dawn the Greeks launched their ships. They sent a squadron of seventy ships north to see if there was any enemy flotilla in the Bay of Eleusis; the remainder mustered in the northern arm of the Channel, visible to Xerxes himself, but not to the advancing Persian fleet. It was broad daylight when the 310 Greek ships rowed south in several columns, rounded the bend of the

Channel and turned facing left, their sterns towards the shore of Salamis. The eastern arm of the Channel was now filled with the oncoming Persian armada, row after row of some 1,200 ships, all pressing on under the eye of the Great King. To their surprise the Greeks evidently meant to make a fight of it. Moreover, the Persian fleet was now unable to go into reverse and back out of the Channel. They had to fight in the narrow waters, where most of their ships would be unable to engage at all.

Both sides fought under oar, and the crews were of comparable size, some 200 men to a ship. The ships, however, were designed for different tactics. The Persians had lofty decks and a high stern. Their aim was to shoot arrows and hurl spears at the enemy and then board an enemy ship. The Greeks had a heavier hull, a flatter build and a bronze-sheathed extension of the keel beam. Their aim was to ram and disable an enemy ship and leave her to sink. The Persian ships carried more marines on deck with a view to boarding than the Greek ships. This fact, together with the difference in build, made the Greek ships more manoeuvrable under oar and much steadier in a swell.

When the Greeks were in position and the Persians continued to advance, the Greeks backed water, drawing the enemy forward into the bend of the Channel, and themselves adopting a crescent-shaped formation which gave them more sea room. This delaying tactic had a further purpose. As a south wind had been blowing at dawn, Themistocles was expecting a swell. It came up the Channel when the front rows were already facing each other and set the higher Persian ships rolling so that they exposed part of their broadsides. The Greek ships made a racing start and charged and rammed their opponents, holing them below the water-line and splintering their oars down one side. They then disengaged and passed on to attack the next row. As the Persian front rows stopped, locked in combat or disabled, the Persian ships behind kept pressing on and added to the confusion. Ramming ship after ship, the Greeks extended their front line down the Channel and the Aeginetans on the right wing worked their way out and forward into mid-channel, thus narrowing the avenue of escape for the Persians who were now in flight, hoisting sail in a westerly wind which had come up. Thousands of survivors were in the water. They were speared like tunny-fish by the Greeks. Meanwhile, the commando force of Persian nobles which Xerxes had placed on the island in mid-channel during the night was butchered before his eyes.

Next day the Greeks prepared for battle. They were still much outnumbered but the Persian fleet had had enough. Thus the verdict of Lade was decisively reversed, the faith of Themistocles and Athens in trusting to their wooden wall was justified, and the strategy of the Congress of the Greeks and the firmness of the Spartan commanders were crowned with success at sea. As the campaigning season was now at an end, Xerxes withdrew to Thessaly, where he left his best troops to pass the winter under the command of Mardonius. He himself took the majority of the army and the entire fleet back to Asia.

Important though the victory at Salamis was in terms of sea power, the fate of Greece could be decided only on land. When the Congress of the Greeks met again in spring 479, they decided to station the fleet at Aegina and the army at the Isthmus line. This left the Megarid and Attica undefended. The initiative lay now with Mardonius. He made no attempt to breach the Isthmus defences. His aim was to draw the Greeks out of their defensive position on land and to engage them on ground of his choice. To this end he tried to drive a wedge between his chief opponents, Athens and Sparta, by offering an equal alliance and full reparations to Athens if she would make a separate peace with Persia. The Athenians replied that they would never come to terms with Xerxes 'so long as the sun stays on his present course'.[7] Mardonius then marched into Attica, and the Athenians fled again to Salamis. His plan now met with success. Athens told Sparta that she would consider accepting the offer of a separate peace if the Peloponnesians did not come out of the Peloponnese. Sparta decided to lead the Peloponnesians out, but she did not tell the Athenians.

Mardonius had not been reinforced by Xerxes, and the Persian fleet was still in the east Aegean when the Spartan Ephors issued marching orders to their army at nightfall. With a clumsy humour which exasperated the Athenian envoys the Ephors let the envoys make a final angry ultimatum next day and then remarked casually that the army was already on the way. Argos sent word of Sparta's move to Mardonius. He ravaged Attica thoroughly and then withdrew to his chosen ground on the north side of the Asopus River in southern Boeotia. He cleared the plain for cavalry action, built a stockaded camp and organized the bringing in of supplies from the rich Boeotian plain. His army, reckoned at 300,000 men and probably not far short of that figure, consisted of excellent cavalry, drawn from many parts of the empire including Thessaly and Thebes, and the finest Persian infantry including the 10,000 'Immortals' and the heavy infantry of central Greece.

Pausanias, who was a nephew of Leonidas and was acting as regent for his son, commanded both the Spartan army, which consisted of

87

10,000 heavy infantry and 35,000 Helots equipped as skirmishers, and the contingents sent by twenty-four states. The entire force exceeded 100,000 men. His dual command placed a severe strain on Pausanias, one which would be quite unthinkable in a modern system of command. He deployed his army on the foothills of Mt Cithaeron on the south side of the Asopus River, where they overlooked the lines of Mardonius. He relied for his supplies mainly upon a single carriageable road which ran from the Peloponnese through the Megarid and then crossed a pass on Mt Cithaeron to the southeast of Plataea. If the road were cut or blocked, he would be in a serious plight. Water too was a difficulty, for the only springs were situated on the lower slopes of the hills and were within range of a Persian attack.

The problem for both generals was much as it had been at Marathon. Mardonius was not prepared to attack the Greeks in their defensive position on the foothills, and Pausanias would not face the Persian cavalry in the plain. The initiative was taken by Mardonius. He used his cavalry to harass the Greek infantry on the lower slopes to cut off their access to the springs in the daytime and to intercept the supply-convoys as they were crossing the pass over Mt Cithaeron. Within three weeks the Greek position became untenable. The morale of the troops was affected by the attacks of the cavalry all day long and by the shortage of food and water in the broiling September heat. Pausanias called a conference of his contingent commanders. He decided to withdraw southwestwards to higher ground, where better supplies of water were available. Such a withdrawal in the face of the enemy being possible only at night and the position being already desperate, Pausanias issued orders for a withdrawal that very night.

Some three hours after nightfall the twenty-four contingents moved off, all except a Spartan regiment under a Colonel 'Flawless' (Amompharetus), who had not attended the conference and who now refused to retreat. He was stationed at the right (eastern) end of the Greek line, facing the best Persian infantry under the command of Mardonius. Pausanias in person hectored the colonel without success. He then sent a horseman to tell the contingents of Sparta, Tegea and Athens to halt and stay where they were. During the night Pausanias and his second-in-command argued with the obstinate officer. Dawn was upon them when Pausanias ordered the contingents of Sparta, Tegea and Athens to move, abandoning the one Spartan regiment to its fate. The colonel then changed his mind, but he was now out of touch with the main force. Pausanias halted the Spartan and Tegeate contingents again in order to let him catch up.

With daylight the Persian cavalry appeared on the scene. They immediately pinned down the troops under Pausanias. He got a horseman through to the Athenians, ordering them to join him, but it was too late; for the Greek cavalry in Persian service had already pinned the Athenians down too. The rest of the Greek army, having completed the withdrawal, was a mile or more away to the west, and Pausanias was not even in communication with them.

What Mardonius saw after dawn delighted his eyes, for it was apparently the break-up of the Greek army for which he had hoped. He could see one large body of troops, already halted by the Persian cavalry, on the hills opposite him, and he led the Persian infantry at the double towards this isolated body. He was followed by the rest of the Persian line which advanced in haste across the Asopus River. When the infantry of Mardonius came up, the Persian cavalry disengaged. It was now the turn of the infantrymen. Making a rampart of their wicker shields, they shot a hail of arrows into the Spartan and Tegean infantrymen who stood firm in close formation. When the chaplains declared the omens favourable, the Greeks charged with the slope in their favour, crashed through the rampart of shields, and bore down upon the Persian infantry. As at Marathon, Greek armament and Greek skill at arms prevailed. Even the best Persian troops were overwhelmed. Mardonius himself was killed in action, and the rest fled into the stockaded camp, hotly pursued by the Spartans and Tegeates. There they were eventually massacred. An army group of 40,000 men under Artabazus took evasive action and escaped to the north. Otherwise the expeditionary force left by Xerxes was almost completely annihilated for only 3,000 men were taken prisoner. In the decisive action the Spartans lost ninety-two men and the Tegeates sixteen men.

The deliverance of the Greeks at Plataea, against such enormous odds and at the cost of so few men, seemed almost miraculous. The Greeks gave thanks to the gods for the victory. They held that free men fight better than the subjects of a monarch, but otherwise they had high praise for the courage of the Persians themselves. The failure of the Persians in the whole campaign was due primarily to the stupidity of Xerxes in keeping all his forces in one lumbering mass and in not using the flying columns for which his first-class cavalry was so well fitted, and in being tricked by Themistocles into sending his fleet into the trap of the narrowing waters. Mardonius was a much better general than Xerxes. Yet he failed through a fundamental weakness in Persian warfare, an inability to integrate cavalry and infantry in assault. It was this weakness which Alexander the Great, was able to exploit a century and a half later, because in his army the Agrianians and javelin-men and even the Hypaspists were trained to attack together with the Companion Cavalry. On the Greek side courage and intelligence won the day at Salamis, and courage favoured by chance brought victory at Plataea. The steady judgement of Sparta and the readiness of Athens to sacrifice everything for the sake of freedom were qualities which brought success.

When Pausanias had marched out of the Peloponnese, the Greek fleet had advanced eastwards via Delos and chased the Persian fleet which beached itself at Mycale on the Asiatic coast in order to avoid an action at sea. The Greeks, totalling some 50,000 men, landed farther along the shore, destroyed the ships and killed 40,000 of the enemy. This remarkable exploit revealed how vulnerable Persia was to seaborne raids if conducted in strength. The commander of the fleet, Leotychidas, a Spartan king, accepted the Aegean islanders as members of the coalition of 'The Greeks'. But he would not accept any of the mainlanders, although Athens pleaded the cause of the latter, for the Spartans and the Peloponnesians were unwilling to commit themselves to continuous action on Asiatic soil. In any case, Leotychidas was no doubt acting in accordance with the policy of the Congress.

During the winter, while the Peloponnesians were at home, the Athenian squadron fought on in the Dardanelles. They captured Sestus, an important station in the Dardanelles, with the help of the Ionian members of the coalition. In 478 Pausanias, the victor of Plataea, commanded the fleet, and Aristides commanded the Athenian squadron. The strategy, which stemmed from the Congress of the Greeks, was excellent: Pausanias reduced most of Cyprus, thus keeping the Phoenician navy out of the Aegean Sea, and then captured Byzantium, cutting a line of communication between Persia and her European satrapy. But Pausanias was incompetent in the field of personal relations. He was dictatorial in dealing with non-Spartans and his methods provoked a mutiny, which was led by some Ionian captains. Complaints were made at Sparta, and Pausanias was recalled. During his absence the Ionians and the Aeolians asked the Athenians in the fleet to take command. Aristides did so, knowing that he could count on the full support of the east Greeks, the islanders and the mainlanders alike. When Sparta sent out a commander to take the place of Pausanias, the fleet refused to accept him. The transference of command was a *fait accompli*. However, it had not been ratified by the Congress of the Greeks.

As so often in a war which is won by a coalition of allies, there had been friction and hard feelings between the two leading states, Sparta and Athens, especially when Attica was overrun and the Spartans sat safe in the Peloponnese. In such cases when victory comes, there is likely to be rivalry in the division of any territorial spoils or the acquisition of political influence in liberated areas. In Europe Russia got the lion's share because the United States of America was not only trustful of Russia's aims but was also unwilling to become deeply committed on the east side of the Atlantic. So too in the winter of 478–7 when Athens was taking the lion's share in the east Aegean, Thucydides tells us that 'Sparta wanted to be rid of the war with Persia and reckoned Athens capable of exercising command and well disposed to herself at the time'.[8] Within fifteen years she was to regret her acquiescence, which was proving by then costly not only to her but also to many other states.

Athens was not slow to consolidate her gain. Two courses of action were open to her. She could wait for the spring meeting of the Congress of the Greeks, and in the climate of the day she could be confident that the Congress would vote the command by sea to her; but such a command was only for a year, and she might one year be voted out of command in a Congress of which she herself as a member had only one vote. The alternative was to create an Athenian Alliance, analogous to the Spartan Alliance, in which the command was conferred in perpetuity on one state and this state had a power in decision-making equal to that of all other members put together. Moreover such an alliance, whether centred on Sparta or on Athens, could be assimilated within the coalition of the Greeks against Persia.

During the winter Athens brought an Athenian Alliance into existence, first by making individual treaties with 'The Ionians', Mitylene and other states, and then by making a contract of alliance with her allies as a whole under the title 'The Greeks', a title chosen to mark the continuing war of liberation.[9] The terms of entry were an offensive and defensive alliance in perpetuity, the vesting of the command in Athens, and an undertaking to wreak revenge on Persia. The constitution was bicameral as in the Spartan Alliance (see p. 70, above), Athens deliberating in her own Assembly and the allies deliberating in a Congress which met at Delos. The strong position of Athens corresponded to the facts: her fleet of 200 ships was about equal to that of the allies at the time, equal not only in strength but in the requirements of manning and maintenance, and her presence was indispensable if the east Greeks were to win and preserve their freedom. The Athenian

Alliance, or as some call it 'the Delian Confederacy', was already in existence when the Congress of the Greeks met in spring 477. It was accepted by the Congress as being consistent with the famous oath to fight against Persia.

The Athenian Alliance was efficient from the start. Aristides fixed the liability of each ally in financial terms with such impartiality that he was nicknamed 'Aristides the Just'. The total contribution of the allies in the first year of the Alliance was one of ships and money, the two being worth 460 talents, a very large sum. Although the accountants or 'Treasurers of the Greeks' were by mutual agreement Athenians, the Treasury at Delos was under the control of the allies. Athens had nothing to do with its income and expenditure. During the first ten years of its existence, 477 to 467, the Athenian Alliance liberated many Greek states on the Thracian and Asiatic coasts, drove out or captured Persian garrisons, put down piracy and captured much booty in the coastal sectors of the Persian satrapies in Europe and in Asia. The reaction to the Greek offensive came in 467. A Persian fleet of 350 ships and a large army were assembled on the south coast of Asia Minor at the mouth of the river Eurymedon. The Athenian commander, Cimon, a son of Miltiades, based his fleet of 200 Athenian ships and 100 allied ships at Cnidus on the Asiatic coast opposite Cos. He then entered enemy waters and caught the Persian fleet in the river-basin where there was little sea room. The Greeks drove the Persian ships aground. They then landed and defeated the Persian infantry in bitter fighting. Later they caught a further Phoenician squadron at sea off Cyprus. In all, 200 ships were sunk or captured intact. In 466 Cimon drove the last Persians out of the Gallipoli peninsula. The Persian satrapy in Europe was now a thing of the past. Athens and her allies had carried the war of liberation and of retaliation to a triumphant conclusion.

In the west too there had been stirring events. The colonial expansion was brought to a halt by mounting opposition from other peoples and by dissension among the Greeks. For instance, attempts to found colonies in Corsica, western Sicily and Tripolitania were frustrated by Etruria and Carthage, which sometimes made common cause against the Greeks. In Sicily and Italy Greek states destroyed their neighbours, for instance Camarina, Siris and Sybaris, the last being fabulously wealthy with a total population of some 500,000 persons. Accumulation of capital and unsettled conditions favoured the rise of tyrants. They often employed barbarians as mercenary troops, liberated the slaves and massacred their opponents. To that extent they were social revolutionaries, but it was for personal and not ideological reasons that they upset the class structure.

Two of the ablest tyrants, Theron of Acragas, and Gelon of Gela, made a double marriage alliance and established something of an empire; Theron acquired Himera on the north coast and Gelon, supporting some exiled aristocrats, captured Syracuse on the east coast and made it his capital, leaving Gela to his brother Hieron. When he conquered other states, Gelon sold their poorer classes into slavery and removed the remainder to Syracuse. By such methods he made Syracuse the first great cosmopolitan centre in the Greek world and the richest Greek state in the West. His armed forces, stiffened with well-paid mercenaries, swelled rapidly. He soon had 20,000 heavy infantry, brigades of heavy cavalry and of light cavalry and companies of archers and slingers, each 2,000 strong, and 200 warships. He fortified Syracuse with such skill that it was to withstand assault for almost 300 years. As his war potential on paper exceeded that of any state in the old country, the Greeks who were preparing to resist Persia sought his aid in 481 (see p. 82). But in vain, for Gelon was aware that the Carthaginians were planning to conquer the Greek part of Sicily, while Greece itself was distracted by the Persian invasion.

Carthage and her colonies were well placed for an attack on the Greeks in Sicily. Their control of the western seas enabled them to transport troops and supplies from Tunisia and Sardinia to the bridge-head which her colonies in western Sicily provided. In 480 a fleet of 200 ships and a large army, which consisted partly of Phoenicians and mainly of mercenaries recruited from Africa and the western Mediterranean, were assembled in western Sicily. The commander, Hamilcar, decided to advance with his whole force along the north coast of the island. He hoped to join forces with the tyrant of Rhegium who controlled the straits of Messina, for Rhegium was at war with Syracuse and had asked for aid from Carthage. But on the way he made an attack on Himera, which was defended by Theron. Gelon now saw his chance of attacking Hamilcar before he joined forces with Rhegium. Making a rapid march from Syracuse overland with 5,000 cavalry and some 50,000 infantry of all kinds, Gelon raised the siege of Himera and joined forces with Theron. Gelon and Theron now had superior strength in cavalry. This enabled them to blockade the Carthaginians who had built a fortified camp. Then by a successful ruse some Greek cavalry got into the camp and admitted the infantry. The result was the slaughter or capture of the entire expeditionary force. Carthage was so badly crippled by this disaster that she bought peace with an indemnity of 2,000 talents and in gratitude for the peace made a gift of a golden crown to Demarete, wife of the victorious Gelon. Syracuse issued coins, great silver decadrachms, to commemorate the victory: they were named 'Demareteia' after her.

The victory at Himera established the supremacy of Gelon and his successor, Hieron, in Sicily. They made common policy with Theron of Acragas and Anaxilas of Rhegium, the latter forming a marriage alliance with Hieron after the defeat of Hamilcar. Peace and prosperity reigned among the Greek states, and Hieron won a great victory over the Etruscans in the bay of Naples in 474. Thus the power of a coalition of Greek states was demonstrated in the west as well as in the east. But each tyrant faced a mounting opposition which stemmed ultimately from the Greek concept of self-government, and any coalition of Greek states had to be contend with the centrifugal force of city-state particularism. Soon after the deaths of Theron and Hieron the whole system collapsed, and in 466 Syracuse emerged as the first democracy in Sicily. The methods which the tyrants had used to gain and retain power in Sicily had cut the strands of the old colonial tradition. The period of aristocratic rule was at an end. The era of the western democracies was dawning.

CHAPTER 10

THE MATURITY OF GREEK CULTURE IN THE AGE OF CONFIDENCE

In relation to the outside world the Greek states reached the peak of their achievement in the period 546 to 466. They resisted the aggression of the strongest imperial powers of their time and they won victories so decisive that the Greek world was to be free from fear of outside enemies for almost a century. The wars against Persia and Carthage were wars of conviction: men fought for survival, liberty and honour. Simonides expressed their purpose with simplicity. 'The Athenians fought for Greece at Marathon and routed ninety-thousand Medes.' The epitaph of the tragedian Aeschylus referred not to his victories in the dramatic festivals but to his part in the Battle of Marathon. 'The sacred wood of Marathon and the long-haired Mede will speak with knowledge of his glorious courage.' State and individuals alike were confident of the rightness of their cause, and men gladly took the oath before the Battle of Plataea and kept it. 'I shall fight to the death, I shall put freedom before life, I shall not desert colonel or captain alive or dead, I shall carry out the generals' commands, and I shall bury my comrades-in-arms where they fall and leave none unburied.'[1] The cause for which they fought was in their belief the cause of their special god, the cause of Zeus Hellenios; indeed several Greek gods and heroes were said to have appeared on the scene of battle at Marathon and at Salamis. Belief in the claims of god and country was general; there was no room either for conscientious objection or for cynicism. If we look for similar beliefs in our own society we have to go back to Kipling's call for the 'iron sacrifice of body, will and soul; there is one task for all, for each one life to give' and to the angels of Mons. But the true parallel is perhaps to be seen in the Victorian era; for it was then that society was confident of its values and secure in its religious convictions.

In their relations with one another the Greek states achieved a measure of co-operation which was never equalled in later centuries.

This was due initially to intelligent experiments in a new type of coalition. Military alliances with equal rights between members, involving arrangements for rotating or sharing a system of command, were as much a commonplace of the ancient world as they are of the modern world, and they form patterns which are constantly shifting and altering as new foci of danger are defined. But the type of coalition which Sparta created in the Spartan Alliance had a distinctive feature, namely one state acting as a permanent commander and receiving half the responsibility in policy-making; this feature endowed the coalition with an unusual strength in war and a stability in policy which often attracted new members. It was the Spartan Alliance which formed the nucleus in the coalition of the Greeks, and it was the conferring of the command by the Greeks on Sparta which made for a coherent strategy and an acceptance of discipline. On the other hand the much looser political and military union of the Ionians had proved incapable of becoming the basis for a wider coalition and had even lacked the ability within itself to provide a centralized form of command and to enforce discipline. When Athens succeeded Sparta as commander of the Greeks at sea, she modelled the Athenian Alliance on the Spartan Alliance. It proved equally strong and stable in policy at first, but only for as long as it remained a free association of states which had confidence in their leader.

To a great extent the stability of society and the confidence which men had in the rightness of their institutions were based upon the traditional beliefs of what we may call the aristocratic order in the individual states. One uses the term 'aristocratic' not in the Debrett sense of an accredited peerage but in the Greek sense of descent from citizen families of long standing, of clansmen as opposed to guildsmen in Athenian society and of original colonial stock as opposed to new citizens at Syracuse. The aristocratic element on the mainland was still attached primarily to the land and had the strong conservative qualities which are associated with any agricultural community. It is significant of this conservative outlook that a statesman as politically progressive as Cleisthenes did nothing to change the social and religious system of brotherhoods and clans in Attica. There was thus in the Greek world a community of belief and also of interest which formed a bridge between the separate city-states and made them aware of a common cause in facing external enemies. Cleomenes, Gelon, and Cimon were more internationally minded, more Panhellenic than their successors.

The aristocratic ideas of the period were most vividly expressed by Pindar, a Theban aristocrat, whose extant poems date from 498 to 446.

All the means that lead to human excellence come from the gods, and it is they who endow men with wisdom and eloquence and courage in action.

Inborn excellence confers great power upon a man, whereas one who has but learnt a craft is a shadowy, changeful figure who never enters the arena with confident step.

From the lovely games at Nemea the boy Alcidamas has come home victorious following his heaven-sent destiny; for he has shown himself a happy hunter in the wrestling ring, following in the footsteps of his ancestor Praxidamas.[2]

The aristocrat has god-given qualities within him, and the call to attain excellence (*arete*) is imperious; for his ancestors have set the example in winning their way to fame, and he must do likewise. When he obtains success, it is not for himself but for the glory of his family and his country.

The gods had always been and were very close to men. When Pelops prayed to the god Poseidon, 'he went close to the foaming sea, alone in the dark, and called upon the loud-roaring god of the trident; and the god appeared to him, close, at his very feet'.[3] When a man prays to god and sets out to win fame, he must 'know himself' recognizing his limitations and avoiding presumption; for all success is given only by the gods. And if he does win fame, he will be worshipped as a hero by posterity, like Pelops at Olympia who 'lies outstretched by the waters of the Alpheus, and many pilgrims come to honour the altar by his mounded tomb'.[4] So now men paid heroic honours to those who had died at Marathon and Plataea, and to Miltiades and Gelon and Hieron.

What we should call mythology was reality to Pindar and the audience for which he wrote, because for them the heroes were real persons and their acts were models for posterity. 'For a poet who would praise this famous island of Aegina broad avenues lie open on all sides; for the Aeacidae showed them examples of great excellence and gave them a distinguished destiny.'[5] When the Aeginetan fleet sailed to fight at Salamis, the statues of the Aeacidae were on board, and the descendants of the Aeacidae won the prize for valour in the fighting. So too the Spartans fought in the presence of the Tyndarid twins, Castor and Pollux, at Plataea. When the battle of Marathon was commemorated in the Stoa Poecile (the Athenian counterpart to a National Gallery), the painting showed Athena, Theseus, Heracles, Callimachus and Miltiades; for the victory was one of gods, heroes and men. So too gods and men were represented together in the magnificent sculptures on the pediments of the Aphaea temple in Aegina, built

c. 490, and gods and heroes figured in the metopes of Temple 'E' at Selinus c. 475–450. Even in the lesser art of vase-painting mythology provided most of the narrative sequences and the individual studies in the latter half of the sixth century, when the strong competition between Corinth and Athens led painters to a new mastery of technique.

In the Dorian states and at Athens the sense of belonging to a group, whether a clan or a state, was very much stronger than the sense of individualism. The poems which Pindar wrote to celebrate victories in the games were lyrics composed for song and dance by a chorus as an act of community thanksgiving and worship. They were not detailed descriptions of the contest or the contestant. Rather they celebrated the glory and the religious significance of a victory which was associated by the poet with the gods and the heroes of the state or the family. So too the statues of victorious athletes were not individualized portraits but represented the glory of achievement: a good example is the bronze statue of the victorious charioteer at Delphi which has survived from a Syracusan chariot-group. He stands serene and dignified, his long chiton falling in graceful folds.

In addition to these poems Pindar wrote processional-songs, dance-songs, songs of praise, funeral dirges, maiden-songs, and hymns of different kinds, appropriate to each god or goddess, which were designed for all aspects of communal and family worship. We gain from the poems an insight into the emotional power and the beautiful ritual of the aristocratic form of corporate religion. At the head of the innumerable states which we call the Greeks was Zeus Hellenios, the god of the Greeks, perfect in intelligence, courage and judgement, and perfect in physical beauty; for beauty too was part of the aristocratic ideal. These qualities are best portrayed in a remarkable bronze statue of Zeus which was retrieved from the seabed off Artemisium. He stands erect with his spear poised in defence of his people, the embodiment of physical perfection, serene in his divine strength.

In this period drama was born and grew to maturity. Earlier civilizations had produced epic poems and psalms or hymns and lyric verse, but Athens alone created drama. Its influence was to be profound in all areas of Greece: then throughout the Mediterranean world and the Near East during the Hellenistic period: and as transmitted by Seneca throughout Western Europe from the fifteenth century to modern times. The masterpieces of Attic drama – the *Oresteia* of Aeschylus, the *Oedipus Tyrannus* of Sophocles and the *Bacchae* of Euripides – have never been surpassed as close-knit organic representations of life. In their effect upon succeeding generations of spectators and readers they have no rival unless it be the masterpieces of Shakespeare.

Drama grew from religious ceremonies, conducted by village communities in honour of Dionysus, the god of growth and decay in the natural world. The dictator Peisistratus gave these ceremonies a national centre c. 534 when he introduced a competition in dramatic performances into an annual festival of state, the 'Dionysia'. For several days each year the people watched and judged a series of performances, at first sitting on temporary stands in the Agora (market square) and then, after a disastrous collapse of the stands, on the hillside of the Acropolis in the precinct of the god Dionysus. The early *mise en scène* was simply a large circular dancing-floor (*orchestra*), suitable for ring dances, and to one side of it a slightly elevated space, provided by the front of a building or stall. The dancing floor in its open setting was the centre of attention and the singing and dancing were the heart of the performance. It was the 'tragic chorus' celebrating the death of Dionysus which gave 'Tragedy' its name. The greatest period of tragedy coincided with the life of the chorus as an integral part of the performance.

Tragedy developed in response to the changes in Attic society. The choral element which expressed the communal spirit of Athens was predominant until the age of social confidence began to draw to a close. Thus the chorus was still the protagonist in the action of the *Supplices* of Aeschylus, produced c. 463, and the lyrics sung by the chorus in the *Oresteia* of Aeschylus (458) are unequalled in poetic quality in any literature. But the growing importance of the individual in society was reflected by the increase in the number of speaking actors from one to two shortly after 500 and to three c. 460. Thereafter this number proved sufficient, for one actor could play several parts if necessary. Detailed action by individuals and the interaction of personalities were portrayed for the first time in the *Oresteia*. The physical aspect of the theatre changed too. The acting space was moved from the side of the orchestra to the back of the orchestra where it became the centre of the spectators' vision. A temporary wooden building was erected there for the *Oresteia*. This consisted of a façade representing a temple or a palace, with a central door and probably two side doors. In front of the central door there was a portico and in front of the whole façade there was a shallow wooden platform probably with two or three continuous steps running along the length of the façade and leading down into the orchestra. Behind the façade there was a backstage area for the performers. But the great orchestra was not changed. It lay between the audience on the hillside and the stage platform. This fact serves to remind us that the judges of individual actions on the stage and the interpreters of their significance in a Greek play were the Chorus or community of citizens and not, as in a modern theatre, other individuals on the stage.

The performers wore contemporary dress but the subjects were drawn from religious legends. In this there was no paradox. The gods and the heroes and the men of legend were part of the present, as we see also from the poems of Pindar and the work of the sculptors and vase-painters of this period. Religion was an indispensible part of existence and any representation of life which omitted the gods would have seemed unreal. The bearer of the tragedy might be an individual such as the Persian King, Xerxes, or the Theban King, Eteocles, but the suffering of the community whether of the Persian people or of the royal house and the citizens of Thebes was the centre of attention. The ultimate message of the tragedy was an interpretation of a piece of life in which both gods and men were involved, and this interpretation was intended not for any individual but for a community.

The creator of tragedy in the form which was to be recognized as such by posterity was Aeschylus. The central message of his plays is clear. In the earliest surviving play, the *Persae* of 472, he dramatized the greatest event of contemporary history. As he interpreted it, the disaster of Persia in Greece was due on the divine plane to the operation of two forces (see above, pp. 10 and 36): the orderliness of the material universe which sets a limit to one nation's expansion, and the power of Zeus who punishes presumption. On the human side Xerxes and his advisers failed to understand the cosmic principle of orderliness and they offended against Zeus by acts of arrogance and impiety. In the *Seven against Thebes*, the last play of a trilogy (or set of three plays with a common theme) which dealt with the house of Labdacus, there was a similar duality of divine powers at work: the orderliness of the universe which establishes a proper relationship between father and son, husband and wife, and son and mother, and on the other hand, the Olympian gods, represented by Apollo and Zeus, who punish arrogance and impiety. Laïus and Oedipus and his sons, wittingly or unwittingly, all violated the proper relationship within the family, and on the other hand they disregarded with scorn the warnings of Apollo and acted in defiance of the gods. In the trilogy dealing with Prometheus the supreme power is the orderliness of the universe. Both Prometheus and Zeus are shown to have offended against the proper relationship between god and man and between god and god. They are both arrogant and stubborn and have not learnt the moderation and self-restraint which are appropriate. In the first play Prometheus and Zeus are equally uncompromising, and Zeus is tyrannical as well. But orderliness was re-established in the course of time when Zeus became merciful towards man and then towards Prometheus and when Prometheus became reconciled to Zeus.

In these plays the orderliness of the universe and the wishes of the Olympian gods either act in unison or become reconciled; or to use more modern terms, the principle of order and the principle of justice are shown to be or to become harmonious. But in the latest trilogy, the *Oresteia*, the two powers are thrown into discord by the action of Orestes; on the one hand his act of matricide has offended the orderliness of the universe, and on the other hand his motives in killing his mother have been approved by the Olympian gods. The representatives of the former are the Apportioners (Moirae) and the Furies (Erinyes); they drive Orestes mad and will torment him for ever. The representatives of the Olympian gods are Apollo, Athena and Zeus; they wish to free Orestes from the anguish of madness. In the sequel Athena persuades the Furies to become 'well-wishers' (*Eumenides*) towards mankind and to accept the verdict of Athena and her Court of Justice at Athens that Orestes is to be free. Thus Apportionment (Moira) and Zeus become reconciled. Moreover, they will act henceforth in unison for man's betterment. This confidence in the ultimate benevolence of the divine powers was peculiar to Aeschylus' generation. It disappeared thereafter.

In as much as religion and tragedy both endeavour to interpret life, Aeschylus' religious views are relevant to his form of tragedy. But what of tragedy in a more restricted or specific sense? Aeschylus saw that man brings suffering upon himself by lack of intelligence and by lack of restraint, and that his suffering is often not only disproportionate to the offence but also brings disaster upon innocent persons. Thus Xerxes' arrogance and Agamemnon's callousness in killing his daughter Iphigeneia bring suffering on Persians and Greeks alike and on Greeks and Trojans alike. We see innocent suffering in Cassandra and Orestes. The princess of Troy is involved in the fate of her city, being enslaved as a concubine to Agamemnon, but worse befalls her because she had aroused Apollo's love and broken her word to give herself to him; so she is brought to the palace of Agamemnon to be butchered by Clytemnestra. Prescient as she is of her own imminent death, she laments for the general lot of mankind whose happiness is so transient. Orestes is the victim of heredity. As a man he is innocent, pious and courageous, but as one of a family he is predestined like Oswald in Ibsen's *Ghosts* to suffer for the sins of his forebears. His form of suffering is *dementia praecox*. Eteocles in *Seven against Thebes* is also a victim of heredity. As a king he is a model of good sense and courage, but as one of the house of Labdacus, he goes to his death open-eyed, declaring: 'The gods have ceased to care for me. The only service they desire is that I die; so why fawn on death?'[6]

In Aeschylus' plays man is heroic in purpose and wilful in action, but he is also overconfident and in this respect unintelligent. The potentiality for greatness is inherent in us. We are free to choose, but we so often choose wrongly. Then we involve ourselves and many others in disaster.

Part III

IMPERIAL DOMINATION VERSUS NATIONAL INDEPENDENCE, 466–404

CHAPTER 11

ATHENS AND THE YEARS OF DECISIVE CHOICE, 466–460

In the years after 466 the Greek states were to an unusual extent free to decide their own future. Persia and Carthage were unaggressive and the other non-Greek communities, for instance Rome, were still innocuous. A century or so ago the states of western Europe were in an analogous position. At such times the initiative tends to lie with the leading state or states. On the mainland of Greece the initiative lay with Athens. She was under no external pressures. She was a leader of willing allies in the Aegean basin and she held the fulcrum of power in her own hands.

The crucial choice was made first in the field of internal politics. As we have seen (p. 63) the constitution of Cleisthenes was not democratic in the Greek sense of the word *demokratia*, 'the masses being in power'. Rather it was mixed or balanced, for two undemocratic features persisted: the power of the Council of the Areopagus, of which the membership was recruited from ex-magistrates, and the direct election of the chief officers of state by the whole people. The constitution of Cleisthenes had served Athens well at Marathon when the elected officers, namely the polemarch and the ten generals, had won the day, and in the year of Salamis when the Areopagus Council had acted as the emergency government and when the elected commander of the Athenian navy had lured the enemy into the narrows. Only one modification had been made during the wars. In 487 and subsequent years the chief officers of state (*archontes*) were selected by lot from candidates elected by the demes. The new procedure diminished the prestige of the officers, opened candidature to a wider number of persons and gave added importance to the generals who were still elected by the vote of the whole Assembly. In the immediate post-war period the Areopagus Council continued to be of paramount importance in the conduct of affairs. Its chief executive officer, Cimon, a son of the wealthy Miltiades, was elected by the Assembly year after year as the general in command of the Athenian and allied navies, and the choice was justified by a series of outstanding successes. Those who sought a change began their operations in the people's courts (the Heliaea), where charges of corruption were made sometimes successfully against members of the Council of the Areopagus. In these trials which were primarily political in purpose, the prosecutors were Ephialtes and Pericles. They also attacked the officers of state who supported the Areopagus, and finally they laid charges against Cimon himself. He was acquitted in 462. Later in the same year when Cimon and part of the Athenian army were on service abroad, Ephialtes and Pericles proposed and carried in the Assembly a reform of the constitution under which the Council of the Areopagus was stripped of all political powers; henceforth it was to serve only as a court of law in certain cases. When Cimon returned to Athens, he tried to have the reform revoked. During the winter Ephialtes was assassinated by a foreigner whose motives were a matter of speculation. In spring 461 the people had recourse to the decisive ostracism. The largest vote was against Cimon; he was sent into exile for at least five years. Pericles alone held the field. Thus the Periclean period of Athens opened. It was to last until his death in 429 BC.

The internal reason for this revolutionary change is not obvious. Corruption there may have been among members of the Areopagus, but corruption alone was not sufficient reason in a Greek state for a change of government. Athenians had emerged from the Persian wars with hopes of a new deal under which the poorer classes would benefit and the advantages of the traditionally wealthy class would be reduced. There is no doubt that Athens as a whole passed from the impoverishment which had been caused by two evacuations and by Persian looting to a financial recovery as victorious leader of the Athenian Alliance; but there are indications that the new wealth made the wealthy class, to which Cimon belonged, wealthier, and left the poor relatively poor and even dependent on the charity of the rich. Anyhow the hopes of a new deal were sterile until Ephialtes and Pericles emerged as the champions of 'the people'. In Greek politics personalities mattered enormously. As there was no party system, any policy was put forward not as a party line but as a personal line. What the electorate knew was similarly not a party programme but a person – a Cimon or a Pericles. If a policy was to be not ephemeral but lasting in its effect, the people had to back the judgement of the person who proposed it for a considerable time ahead. As we have seen in the cases of Solon and Cleisthenes, or Miltiades and Themistocles, the Athenians were prepared to do this. They did it now with Pericles. He was in a position to shape the future development of the state.

The struggle for power in Athens had repercussions in the sphere of foreign policy. During the ascendancy of the Council of the Areopagus Athens was bound by specific treaty obligations; under the terms of the Greek Alliance she was obliged to co-operate with 'The Greeks', that is, with the loyalist states headed by Sparta; under the terms of the Athenian Alliance she undertook to respect the autonomy of the allies both individually and as a body represented by its two organs, the Congress of Allies and the independent Treasury at Delos; and under the terms of both alliances she maintained a total war against Persia. The Athenians honoured these obligations in the years down to the Battle of the Eurymedon River, and on the face of it their attitude brought them very considerable success. Relations with the Spartans and the other freedom-fighters of the Persian wars remained friendly, and Cimon in particular was able to allay suspicion and cement goodwill. The allies gave full support to Athens at the Battle of the Eurymedon River, and, as the envoys of Mytilene were to say later, they willingly followed Athens as long as she led them in war against Persia. Her policy certainly brought honour and glory to Athens as a leader of others.

But there was a price to pay. Leadership on liberal principles, especially of a coalition of states smaller than oneself, may be a very costly business, as Great Britain has found during this century. The Athenians themselves seemed to carry a disproportionate burden, both individually in that service overseas seemed to be unending after 480, and collectively in that they provided no less than two-thirds of the victorious fleet at the Battle of the Eurymedon River. The material benefits may not have been so obvious to individual Athenians. For it was the freedom-fighters of the Greek mainland who now enjoyed the pleasures of peace, and even in the Aegean area it was the allies who were tending to cut down their participation by supplying money rather than ships.

During the years 465 to 462 Ephialtes and Pericles appeared for the first time among the elected generals. This marked the beginning of a possible swing in the electorate. Radical changes in foreign policy began to appear. The victory over Persia at the Eurymedon river was not followed up, as the Persians might have expected, by attacks on Cyprus or Phoenicia. Instead, Athens turned upon one of the most powerful of her allies, Thasos, and demanded a share in her commercial profits. Thasos refused, justifiably. On renewed pressure from Athens Thasos withdrew from the alliance. Athens then attacked Thasos. In these exchanges there is no doubt that Athens was the aggressor; and even if Thasos was under contract to stay in the alliance for war against Persia, the behaviour of Athens relieved her of that obligation. During the campaign against Thasos, Athens landed 10,000 settlers from Athens and the allied states at the mouth of the Strymon river, hoping to acquire permanently the rich Thasian possessions on the mainland.

These acts of frank imperialism were cleverly timed because Persia was weak after her defeat, Sparta was embarrassed by a rising in Messenia and Athens herself was particularly strong with 200 ships in commission. Even so all did not go well. In answer to an appeal from Thasos, Sparta gave a secret promise that she would invade Attica. The secret was well kept, but the invasion did not take place, as we shall see. Meanwhile, the 10,000 settlers were driven out by the native Thacians. Thasos fought hard, but she was compelled to capitulate in the summer of 462.

During the war against Thasos, Athens was distracted by events in Laconia. There the Spartans were able only to contain the Messenians who were in revolt. In 464 Sparta town was struck by a terrible earthquake, which caused much loss of life, particularly among the citizens themselves. The Helots rose in revolt and were joined by some of the Perioeci. Sparta was now in mortal danger. She sent appeals for help to her allies. Plataea, Aegina, Mantinea and other states responded by sending troops. At Athens the matter was debated in the Assembly. Ephialtes advised refusal: let Sparta's pride be trampled underfoot, he said. Cimon advised acceptance: let Greece not be maimed, he said, and Athens lose her yoke-fellow.[1] On this occasion the Assembly decided to send troops and appointed Cimon to the command. Allied help enabled Sparta to survive and even to assume the offensive. In autumn 462, as she was unable to capture the strongholds of the rebels in Messenia, she asked again for help. Again Athens sent troops under Cimon. But during their absence Ephialtes and Pericles carried the reform of the constitution. When the Spartiates learnt of the reform they sent the Athenian force home.

At this time the decision of Athens about the fate of Thasos was being put into effect. Athens herself dictated the terms; there is no suggestion that the Congress of Allies was consulted. The fleet of Thasos was confiscated, her walls were destroyed, her mint was closed, her gold mine and other possessions on the mainland were ceded to Athens, and she was required to make payments in money to the Athenian Alliance in perpetuity.[2] No doubt she lost her right of representation in the Congress of the Allies. She was in effect now a subject of Athens, 'enslaved' in Greek terminology or a 'satellite' in modern terminology. As Thasos had been one of the most powerful of all Athens' allies, her fate was a warning to the others that the demands of Athens must be met.

When Thasos fell, it is probable that Athens learnt of the secret promise which Sparta had made in 464. In any case she knew that her treatment of Thasos would be condemned by Sparta, for the policy of Sparta was to set herself up as the opponent of tyranny in any form, whether imposed by Persia or by Athens. It was now logical for Athens, if she intended to continue on these lines, to change her alliances in Greece. So in the winter of 462–1 Athens allied herself to two powers which had 'medized' during the Persian wars and had opposed Sparta, namely Argos and Thessaly. This was a shock to the ideas of the old freedom-fighters. In 461 Sparta crushed the Messenian revolt. Athens took in all the Messenian refugees, and later placed them at Naupactus, which she had seized as a naval base. She too could claim to be upholding the liberty of the oppressed. In 460 she took advantage of a frontier dispute between Megara and Corinth and obtained the alliance of Megara. She proceeded to occupy strategic positions in Megarian territory on each side of the Isthmus, thus penning up the Peloponnesians inside the Peloponnese and cutting them off from their friends in central Greece. In this year too her navy and her allies' squadrons sailed to Cyprus. If only they could secure the island they would be able to confine the naval forces of Persia to the waters of the southeastern Mediterranean.

These radical changes of policy towards a member of the Athenian Alliance and then towards Sparta and a member of the Spartan Alliance were made in defiance of treaty obligations. For Athens had sworn to fight in alliance with other states (e.g. Sparta and Corinth) against Persia and against the medizing states (e.g. Argos and Thessaly), to be an ally of Sparta and help her in the event of any revolt, and to respect the independence of the allies which had joined the Athenian Alliance. These obligations were treated merely as 'scraps of paper' which could be torn up unilaterally. *Realpolitik* was now Athens' principle in foreign policy. She had created a means to power in her navy and her Alliance, and she recognized no limitation to the pursuit of her self-interest. A new age in the relations between the Greek states was dawning.

At Athens there was a complete break with the past, marked not only by the demolition of the Council of the Areopagus in the working of the constitution, but also by the cutting of the bonds which had tied Athens to the other champions of freedom in the Persian wars. Even the heritage of constitutional precedents was irrelevant to the new thinking, of which Pericles was the chief exponent. There were of course still reactionaries at Athens. Aeschylus may have been one of them. In the *Oresteia*, produced in 458, he warned Athens against the dangers of anarchy and strife, and he emphasized the need for restraint and respect for the altar of justice. Others may have recalled the hope which had been expressed in 481 that 'the Greek world might become one, and all in concert might adopt the same policy'.[3] But their voices were rendered ineffective by the ostracism of Cimon and all he stood for in 461.

There is, of course, a strong case to be put for the Periclean point of view. It may be argued that national states are not capable of co-operation or co-existence unless external pressures hold them together, and therefore that Athens was merely anticipating the break up of the anti-Persian entente. Russia might justify her post-war policy on similar grounds. If this line of argument is accepted, Athens was justified logically in allying herself with Argos, Thessaly and Megara and in taking stern measures against Thasos. But one has still to bear in mind the ultimate objective. In the society of Greek states as it was in 460, Athens' actions were bound to lead to war. From such a war Athens expected to emerge as the victor, that is to trample Sparta underfoot and to keep the Athenian allies on a tight rein. If in fact co-operation was impracticable, then Athens above all other Greek states felt herself fitted to impose control.

Whatever view is taken on this issue – and it is only too familiar an issue in the modern world – the initiative of Athens turned the course of Greek history into a channel which led at first towards disintegration in inter-state relations inside the Greek world and towards the attrition of Greek strength in relation to the non-Greek world. In the long run Athens might win. What would she then be able to create? This is a question to which there can be no answer. What would Napoleon's France or Hitler's Germany or Stalin's Russia have created out of a subjugated Europe?

CHAPTER 12

THE GENERAL CHARACTERISTICS OF THE TWO PELOPONNESIAN WARS
460–446 AND 431–404

The attempts of Athens to impose her rule on the Greek states lasted from 460 to 404 except for two periods of uneasy peace. Her attempts were resented by the other Greek states whether or not they saw themselves individually to be in danger of subjugation. Because Athens' navy was unrivalled, open resistance by any maritime state in the Aegean was desperately dangerous. It therefore occurred only rarely. It was the landpowers which could resist with a fair chance of success, and they were traditionally organized round Sparta. The two Peloponnesian Wars were so named because landpowers in the Peloponnese formed the centre of resistance to Athens. The two wars had this in common, that the balance of power which existed between Athens and her alliance on the one hand, and Sparta and her alliance on the other hand, was upset in the course of them. In 446 the balance of power was re-affirmed by treaty. In 404 it disappeared for ever with the disruption of the Athenian Alliance and the defeat of Athens.

It was a feature of both wars that the existing pattern of free city-states was in danger of being destroyed by a new kind of power. For, as Thucydides explained in his history of the second war, Athens had created a naval, financial and imperial power which was radically different from anything that had gone before it. The ultimate question in the two wars was therefore whether Athens was capable of defeating her primary opponents and imposing her power-system on the remainder of the Greek world. The answer is unknown to us, because Athens committed her forces to major campaigns against secondary opponents – in the first war against the Persians in Egypt and in the second war against the Syracusans and their allies in Sicily – and it was her losses in these campaigns which reduced her to impotence in the final conflict. In any case the failure of Athens against her primary opponents was due to her own errors of judgement and not to an inferiority of power.

Athens began the First Peloponnesian War with two new weapons in her armoury: the navy and the democracy. The first enabled her to destroy the naval forces of her primary opponents within a few years, but her naval supremacy proved far from decisive thereafter. Seaborne raiders could inflict only relatively small damage on an enemy territory, and blockade by sea was very far from total because merchant ships were more seaworthy in rough weather than men-of-war and interception at night was rarely possible. At the start of the war democracy proved to be an exportable ideology. Democratic institutions were inaugurated at Argos and Megara when these cities became allies of Athens, but it soon became apparent that they were maintained only by the Athenian presence or by Athenian intervention. In the later phase of the war Athens imposed 'democratic' governments upon some of her so-called allies, but they were overthrown as soon as the fortunes of war went against Athens. The only lasting effects of this experiment in political warfare were a hatred of Athens, for instance at Megara, and the promotion of a bitter party-strife (*stasis*) which weakened each state from within.

On the other hand the Peloponnesians had a counterbalancing superiority in land warfare. This deterred Athens from invading the Peloponnese with her full army. Even in a period of uneasy peace when some Peloponnesian states came over to Athens, she was unwilling to commit her forces in strength to a campaign in the Peloponnese. In consequence the Peloponnesians were never afraid of a knock-out blow. But they found it difficult to apply their military supremacy at all effectively. During more than forty years of warfare only one major battle was fought between the full armies of both sides. That was at Tanagra in 457 when the Spartans had been weakened by the Messenian Revolt and by the Great Earthquake. The Athenian army was supported by troops from Argos and Thessaly and from some states in the Athenian Alliance, but even so it proved inferior to the forces of Sparta, the Peloponnese and Boeotia.

The battle at Tanagra was epoch-making in two ways. It was the first occasion on which almost all the states of the mainland were engaged in an internecine war between Greek and Greek. It was also the last occasion on which an outright victory by the Peloponnesians over Athens on land might have been decisive, for after the battle Athens completed an ambitious system of defences which rendered her almost impregnable. The city itself was surrounded by massive walls, and in addition the city was linked to the coast by two long walls which enclosed an avenue of access for seaborne supplies. Thus for purposes of defence and supply in wartime Athens made herself as far as possible into an island.

In both wars there were periods of stalemate when neither side was able to strike a serious blow at the other and when it looked as if there was no end in sight. During these periods Athens enjoyed a freedom of movement which was quite impossible for Sparta, for the Athenian fleet could sail away into the waters of the Mediterranean, but the Spartan army was unwilling to absent itself for long from its home front, let alone from the Peloponnese. The freedom which Athens enjoyed had its dangers. Indeed it was Athens' use of her freedom of movement which cost her any chance of success she may have had in each war. On the other hand Sparta learnt the lessons of patience and endurance which in a war of attrition were to prove of incalculable value. Indeed, the need to play safe preserved her from making costly mistakes.

Athens entered the First Peloponnesian War as the leader of generally willing allies. She emerged from it as their ruler. The road to empire was chosen deliberately by the Athenian people. In 457 they imposed on Aegina the sort of conditions which they had imposed in 462 on Thasos: surrender of her fleet, dismantling of her fortifications and an undertaking to pay tribute in money in the future. In this same year troops which were provided by states in the Athenian Alliance were fighting at Tanagra not against Persia but against their fellow Greeks in a war which aimed not at preserving their freedom but at the aggrandizement of Athens.

The allies were involved also in an adventure in Egypt where Athens had accepted an invitation to intervene in support of a local rising against Persian rule. During this adventure a fleet of two hundred ships sailed up the Nile. They won a resounding victory. But this stung Persia into action. First she offered to subsidize Sparta in her war against Athens, but Sparta refused. Then she invaded Egypt, whereupon the Egyptians made a separate peace. At this stage Athens would have been wise to withdraw, but she held on, confident in her sea-power, for another eighteen months. The base of her troops was an island in the Nile, and all supplies were brought up across the sea and then up the river by ship, at great financial expense. Finally the Persians diverted part of the waters of the Nile, opened the base to attack overland and captured the entire force. They went on to surprise a separate squadron of fifty ships which was coming up to relieve their predecessors. The loss of a large army drawn mainly from the allies and of between 100 and 200 ships, partly Athenian and partly allied, was a major catastrophe. It was due primarily to the overconfidence and the bad judgement of the Athenian Assembly.

When the magnitude of the disaster became known, a number of allied states in the southeastern Aegean which were close to Persia seceded from the Athenian Alliance. Athens moved rapidly. As her allies had sustained most of the casualties in Egypt, she was stronger *vis-à-vis* them than she had ever been. She now transferred the allied Treasury from Delos to Athens where it passed under the control of the Athenian Assembly. The balance alone enriched Athens beyond all expectation, and the annual income of the fund in the future would be of handsome proportions. In the years 454 to 448 Athens forced the seceding states to return to the Alliance but with the status not of Allies but of subjects. Her methods[1] have a modern ring. Vigorous military action was followed by the setting up of a puppet government under the eyes of Athenian 'overseers' and with the support of an Athenian garrison. The puppet government was small in numbers and was therefore called 'The Council'; but the whole set-up was optimistically labelled 'a democracy'. The councillors were a self-perpetuating body; their tactics were in fact those of an oligarchic clique, or in modern terms those of 'The Party'. All councillors had to take an oath of loyalty to Athens and the allies; the chief significance of this oath was that, if a councillor broke the oath, he and his sons were executed without more ado. Other members of the subject community had lesser rights than the councillors, that is than the party-members, but even they were sometimes compelled to take the oath of loyalty to Athens and the allies. While the oath was a device for putting the lives of some citizens at the mercy of Athens, certain cases had to be sent to Athens for trial. By 448 the number of states which had fallen into the status of subjects was between forty and fifty. They were widely scattered, from Aegina in the Saronic Gulf and Thasos in the northern Aegean to Miletus and Colophon on the Asiatic coast.

States which had not seceded from the Alliance were not disciplined in this manner. However, the money which they paid as members of the Alliance went now into the coffers of Athens. The policy of the Alliance was dictated by Athens; for it is probable that the Congress of Allies was never convened after 448. Three states only – Chios, Samos and Lesbos – were contributing ships to the Alliance by 448. The fact that they had navies of their own gave them a semblance of independence; but when they were invited by Athens to help her in disciplining states which had seceded they accepted dutifully, not because they were independent but because they were afraid of losing their independence.

The clearest sign of Athenian imperialism was the planting of a permanent garrison on the territory of some 'ally', for instance Andros and Naxos. The members of these garrisons were Athenians. In reward for their services overseas they were given plots of good land, and they were called 'plot-holders' ('cleruchs'). They were not themselves cultivators of the land (they used hired or slave labour for that purpose) but pickets of empire. Their citizenship was Athenian, and they voted in the Assembly when they were in Athens. The unfortunate 'ally' from which Athens confiscated the good land without any compensation was left to pay a reduced tribute out of its diminished resources. At the same time Athens reinforced the colonies she had planted earlier at places where the original population had been either subjected or expelled, for instance at Lemnos, Imbros and Scyros, and in Gallipoli.

Other measures contributed to the financial benefit or greater glory of Athens. She required all the allies to stop minting their own silver currency and use only the silver coinage of Athens, and to abandon their own systems of weights and measures and adopt those of Athens.[2] Thus Athens forced her allies to join the common market which she controlled. Some allies had been obliged to send presents to Athens at the time of the Panathenaic Festival; now the minimum value of these 'presents' was specified for the donor by the recipient. Religion was also pressed into service. Cults of the goddess Athena had to be set up in some allied states, and it was hoped that they would encourage an affection for the city of her name, Athens.

The word which Thucydides used to describe what the Athenian Alliance became by 448 was *arche* which literally means 'rule' (it lacks the overtone of 'authorised rule' which was inherent in *imperium*, the origin of our word 'empire'). It indicated that an area was under the rule of Athens without necessarily implying either direct rule by Athenians or any Athenian presence. In the same way we might say that Greece was under the rule of Rome in the second century BC or that some area today is under the rule of Britain or Russia or the USA. In 448 it was a form of imperialism which showed its true colour when a subject state tried to break away from Athenian 'rule', or, as we might say, from the Athenian sphere of influence. Then troops moved in; and the punishment imposed on the 'rebel' was normally enough to deter others from trying to break away.

Athens made two attempts to make her position as a ruler more acceptable to her allies and to the Greeks generally. In the first place she recalled Cimon, whose Panhellenic attitude had been popular with the allies, and she placed him in command of the operations against Persia. In 450 he won a great victory over the Phoenician fleet in Cyprus and restored the glamour which was traditionally associated with Greeks defeating barbarians. But he died while besieging the Phoenician base in Cyprus at Citium, and with him died the original concept of a free alliance formed between Greek and Greek to win liberation from Persia. In 448 a peace was concluded between the Great King of Persia and 'Athens and her Allies'. All prisoners of war were repatriated, the seas were declared open to traders of both sides, and the freedom of the Greek states in Asia was recognized by Persia. In terms of the hostilities between the Greeks and the Persians this treaty of peace was a triumph for the Athenian Alliance. But contemporaries in 448 did not see it in that light. This became apparent when, on the proposal of Pericles, Athens invited all Greek states of the mainland and of the Aegean basin to attend a Panhellenic Conference at Athens. Its purpose was to celebrate the end of the Persian War, establish the freedom of the seas for all Greeks, and discuss arrangements for peace among the Greek states.[3] What a wonderful idea! Thanksgiving and peace might have followed the Battle of the River Eurymedon c. 467 if Athens had taken such an initiative then (see p. 92, above). But in 448 the invitation came from the state which had provoked the first large-scale internecine war on the Greek mainland and had abused the trust of her allies by confiscating their Treasury and reducing many of them to subject status. No reply was made by the Peloponnesian states, and there was no conference.

Where diplomacy had failed, force might succeed. Athens renewed hostilities against the Peloponnesians, but with little effect. In 447 she suddenly found herself in a desperate situation. The states in the Megarid, Boeotia and Euboea which she had made subject to her rule rose in revolt simultaneously, and a Peloponnesian army marched through the Isthmus and occupied the plain of Eleusis. It seemed as if Athens would either risk her existence in a pitched battle against superior numbers, or surrender her territory to the enemy and retire behind her system of defences. Then an extraordinary thing happened. The Peloponnesian army was disbanded by its commander, Pleistoanax, a young Spartan king. On his return he was fined and his adviser was sentenced to death by the Spartan government. No explanation was published. However, the opportunity had passed. When the Peloponnesians withdrew, Pericles turned the tables on the unfortunate states in Euboea and stamped out the revolt.

Early in 445 the First Peloponnesian War was ended by a treaty of peace between 'Sparta and her Allies' on the one hand and 'Athens' on the other. The distinction was significant. The Spartan Alliance emerged from the war unchanged: it was still an association of Sparta and her free allies, and its membership now included Megara and the states of Boeotia. But Athens signed alone as she spoke in the name of those who had entered the war as her allies but were now subject to her rule. In terms of international diplomacy the Athenian Alliance had disappeared. Its place was taken by the Athenian Empire. One article in the treaty of peace recognized this fact: although Athens was required to give to Aegina a guarantee of 'autonomy', the obligation of Aegina to pay tribute to Athens was accepted by Sparta and her allies.

The treaty was the result of war-weariness on both sides. It was known as 'The Thirty Years Treaty' because its declared aim was to establish peace for thirty years. An honest attempt was made to avert a renewal of war. It was agreed that all disputes should be settled by arbitration and that any state which was not a signatory was free to join either side with the exception of Argos, whose accession for instance to Athens might constitute a danger to peace. In essence the Greek states returned to the balance of power which had existed before the outbreak of the war. In theory and to a great extent in practice a balance of power has been a promoter of peace in this century in the history of Europe and indeed in the history of the world. But by its very nature a balance of power is precarious. Its future depends on maintaining the status quo, and the growth and ambition of any one state may disrupt the status quo.

In 445 it seemed that Persia was quiescent and that Sparta was un-ambitious. The future of the peace seemed therefore to depend upon the behaviour of Athens. What was her policy to be? A relative of Cimon called Thucydides (not the historian) took the people to task in the Assembly. He said that they had abused the confidence and trust of their allies, and in particular they had stolen the funds of the allies. On the proceeds Athens was decorating herself with temples as a harlot decorates herself with jewels. She should now return to the liberal policy of the 470s, treat her allies as equals and resume the war against Persia as a cause common to all Greeks. Pericles replied with equal bluntness. The allies, he claimed, had contributed money and ships in order to obtain security from Persia. Athens had given them that security. Consequently the money belonged to Athens.[4] This clash between political principle and dialectical argument could not be solved in the debates of the Assembly. Ostracism was employed to decide the issue in 443. Thucydides lost. Pericles received the full support of the people in implementing his policy of which the keystone was the maintenance of the Empire.

The issue which the Athenians debated in these years is an interesting one. It is possible for an imperial state to abdicate from empire, but the process is costly in money and sometimes in men, as we have seen in this century. Moreover, it does not follow that those who are released from imperial rule co-operate freely with their ex-masters or even bear them any goodwill. The case of Athens was exceptional in that she was of the same race as her subjects and geographically close to them. Complete disengagement was impossible. If Thucydides' proposals had been implemented, it is at least arguable that Athens would have suffered an eclipse and the balance of power would have disappeared. Even in the modern world where other factors have preserved a balance of power it is not clear that abdication from empire has promoted the cause of peace in the liberated areas. On the other hand, the arguments of Pericles are an example of chauvinistic casuistry which is not unfamiliar in domineering states of our time. Yet we must admit the uneasy truth that a moderate use of imperial power may contribute towards the preservation of peace.

How far was Athens prepared to use her imperial power in a moderate manner? In 446, when the withdrawal of the Peloponnesian army left the rebels in the lurch, Pericles and Athens 'stretched Euboea on the rack'. Reprisals were taken at the expense of the leading citizens: some were deported and others were held in prison as hostages for the good conduct of their states. An example was made of Histiaea where some Athenians had been put to death during the revolt. The inhabitants were driven out at the point of the sword, and Athenian settlers took over the town and its territory. The treatment meted out to Chalcis, a powerful state in Euboea, is known to us from an inscription.[5] All members of the wealthy class were expelled, and the best land was confiscated and became the property of the Athenian state. The rest of the population was made to take an oath of loyalty to the Athenian 'demos', the word meaning 'people' being used with a democratic connotation. No doubt a 'democracy' was established at Chalcis, for special steps were taken to protect Chalcidian partisans of Athens from reprisals in Chalcis. Thus any Chalcidian who was condemned to death or exile or disfranchisement in a court at Chalcis had to be sent to Athens for re-trial in an Athenian court, if he so wished.

Did Athens intend to change her methods after the ostracism of Thucydides in 443? Samos provided a test case. Legally she was a free ally of Athens; for she had her own fleet, and she was entitled to freedom of action, except in relation to Athens as her ally and in relation to Persia as the common enemy. In 441 she went to war with Miletus. When Samos was winning, Athens ordered her to disengage and make peace. Samos refused, relying on her treaty rights. Athens declared war at once. Her fleet, which had anticipated the declaration of war, took the island by surprise and administered the usual medicine: the seizure of civilian hostages, the posting of an Athenian garrison, the setting up of a 'democracy' under the eyes of Athenian 'overseers', and the exaction of a substantial indemnity to pay for Athens' expenses. But the leaders had escaped. They raised 700 mercenaries, took the island by surprise and deposited all the Athenians whom they captured with a Persian satrap in Asia Minor. Athens acted quickly. She ordered Lesbos and Chios, the only allies which had a fleet, to send ships to reinforce her own fleet. They obeyed. Only one state, Byzantium, rebelled in sympathy with Samos. Both were forced to capitulate nine months later. Samos was made to surrender her fleet, dismantle her fortifications, pay the expenses incurred by Athens in the war, pay tribute in the future, surrender her leading citizens as hostages and take an oath of loyalty to Athens.

When Athens first attacked Samos, the free world of Greek states regarded her action as a flagrant breach of liberty. Sparta and her allies considered whether they should intervene. They decided not to do so. The decision gave Athens *carte blanche* in the treatment of those who were in her sphere of rule. She exploited it by branding Samian prisoners-of-war like cattle.[6] A wave of horror passed through the Greek world, yet no one raised a hand against Athens. Her policy succeeded to this extent that the Thirty Years Treaty and the Peace with Persia both held firm at a time when she was crushing a serious revolt within her empire. But her very success intensified the fears of others both within her sphere of rule and outside it.

The policy of Athens in these years was inspired by Pericles. He proposed the original declaration of war and he conducted the operations against Samos. At the conclusion of such a war the Athenians chose a leading statesman to deliver a funeral speech over the Athenian casualties. It was probably after this war that Pericles made a speech which contained his famous saying that the youth of Athens had passed away as the spring passes from the year. It was true at more than one level of meaning.

The central issue of the Second Peloponnesian War, 431 to 404, was the Athenian Empire, the Athenians seeking to conserve and extend its dominions and the Peloponnesians attempting to free the Greeks from the rule of Athens. This issue raised deeper fears on both sides. If Athens extended her dominions, the Spartan Alliance would feel itself encircled and in danger. Thucydides was correct in ascribing the cause of the war to 'the growing greatness of Athens and the fears of Sparta'.[7]

The friction which led to the outbreak of war began in a sensitive area, the northwest of Greece. There Corinth and her numerous colonies, headed by Corcyra, Ambracia and Leucas, had a monopoly of seapower. When Athens became mistress of the Aegean, the members of the Spartan Alliance preferred to import what they needed from the western seas. In consequence Corinth held a key position in the Spartan Alliance. However, her colonies chose to remain uncommitted; their allegiance was rather to their foundress, and as it was usually very strong they left her to represent them in international politics. A year or two after the reduction of Samos an Athenian fleet appeared in the northwest and helped the Acarnanians to defeat the army of Ambracia, a colony of Corinth. As far as the letter of the Thirty Years Treaty was concerned, Athens was within her rights, because Ambracia was not a member of the Spartan Alliance. Yet her unprovoked intervention in this Corinthian sphere of influence was a threat to the balance of power on which the Thirty Years Treaty was founded.

A year or two later, in 435, a quarrel arose between Corinth and Corcyra over their joint colony Epidamnus. Sparta advised them to go to arbitration, but in the summer a naval action was fought in which Corcyra defeated Corinth and her allies decisively. Among those allies there were some members of the Spartan Alliance who were eager to keep open the sea routes which Corcyra was now in a position to close. The success of Corcyra was likely to be short-lived because Corinth and her allies disposed of much greater resources and they were determined to equip a very large fleet and eliminate Corcyra. In 433 Corcyra invited Athens to intervene. The Assembly debated the matter for two days. The opinion of the majority was for rejection on the first day, and for acceptance on the second day. Athens granted a defensive alliance and sent ten ships to help Corcyra defend herself against the impending attack.

The action of Athens was regarded as aggressive and provocative; no one supposed that she was altruistic in helping Corcyra and enabling her to block the sea route to the west. On the other hand, if Corinth and her allies backed down in order to avert any chance of a general war, Corcyra and Athens would exert a stranglehold on trade with the west. The Corinthians decided to go ahead. A great naval battle was fought at Sybota in which the Athenian ten ships and a second squadron of twenty ships which was sent to reinforce the ten ships played a decisive part. The Corinthians and their allies were worsted. Athens and Corcyra were now the leading seapower in the northwest area.

At this point Athens might have refrained from taking any further action which could exacerbate the situation. But no, she chose otherwise. She ordered Potidaea, a colony of Corinth on the Aegean coast, which was a member of the Athenian Alliance, to break off her regular relations with Corinth, demolish her seaward defences and send hostages to Athens. Soon afterwards she laid an embargo on Megara. All Megarian ships and merchants were to be excluded from the market of Attica and from the harbours of the Athenian Alliance; and among the harbours were those of Megara's colonies, such as Byzantium and Chalcedon. The tactics of Athens may have been novel then. They have become only too familiar. The response to them varies: some states submit to an erosion of their liberties, others resist even if the odds are against their success.

Corinth and Megara were determined to resist, but being members of the Spartan Alliance they appealed to their allies. Separate debates were held in the Spartan Assembly and in the Congress of Allies; in each case the decision was that Athens was committing aggression and that Sparta and her allies must go to war with her unless they could obtain concessions by other means. In his account of the war Thucydides concentrates our attention upon Sparta which alone could lead the Spartan Alliance into action. In the past Sparta had advised belligerents to go to arbitration, but now her people decided by a large majority in favour of war. The fundamental reason for their decision, said Thucydides, was 'the growing greatness of Athens and the fears of Sparta'.

Diplomatic negotiations followed for many months, while each side keyed up its state of preparedness. They were of no avail as neither side was willing to give way. At Athens the opening words of Pericles in a crucial debate of the Assembly were reported by Thucydides. 'There is one principle which I hold to through everything, and that is the principle of making no concession to the Peloponnesians.' These words have the plausible ring which any astute politician can impart to a direct and simple statement; but it was Pericles himself who, having proposed the defensive alliance with Corcyra and the embargo on the ships and merchants of Megara, had created the situation in which 'concessions' were sought by the Peloponnesians. In effect Pericles preferred war to any form of compromise. The majority of the Athenian people went with him, although a minority favoured negotiation in the hope of prolonging the peace under the terms of the Thirty Years Treaty, which Sparta and her allies had done nothing to upset. So 'the Athenians, considering his advice to be the best, voted to do as Pericles bade them'.[8] The die was now cast on both sides. Early in 431 Thebes, a member of the Spartan Alliance, made an unwarranted attack on Plataea, an ally of Athens. The war was on at last.

The strategy for the Athenians to follow in the Second Peloponnesian War was laid down firmly by Pericles: they were to undertake the offensive by sea and avoid any pitched battle on land. When the strategy was implemented, the actions of the navy lowered the morale of the Peloponnesians but were very far from becoming decisive. The inaction of the army inevitably lowered Athenian morale; for the troops and the civilians watched the enemy lay waste the countryside of Attica year after year. The Peloponnesians and the Boeotians became even more confident of their superiority in land warfare, but they found it difficult to bring their opponents to any kind of battle. They planned to take to the seas and raise Athens' subjects in revolt, but they had neither the ships nor the money to challenge the supremacy of Athens at sea. For ten years a series of damaging but inconclusive actions were carried out by both sides. In 421 a peace was concluded. It was the product of exhaustion. The war had made no real change in the status quo, but it had weakened the reputation and the strength of the leaders, Sparta and Athens.

A cold war followed. Here Athens appeared to be achieving some success, for a reshuffling of the traditional alliances and an agreement made by Athens with Argos weakened the whole fabric of the Spartan Alliance. But Sparta did not let matters stop at diplomacy. Her superbly trained army took the field in 418 and won a decisive battle against the malcontents, who received only small assistance from Athens. Thereafter the military supremacy of Sparta was unquestioned. The Spartan Alliance was reconstituted in a stronger form than ever, and Argos had to make terms with Sparta.

The policy which Pericles had advocated at the outbreak of war had a further component: the Athenians were to keep their subjects in hand and they were not to try to extend their dominions during the war. Pericles had learnt the need for concentration in the Aegean area from the bitter experience of the First Peloponnesian War, when the expedition to Egypt had proved disastrous. But Pericles died in 429, and a new generation which had had no experience of the First Peloponnesian War was looking for some new avenue to success in 416. At the psychological moment an invitation came from the people of

Segesta asking Athens to intervene in Sicily. Envoys were sent, and on their return in 415 the Assembly decided to send a large expeditionary force to the island. The mood of the Assembly on this occasion has been brilliantly described by Thucydides (see p. 145, below).

The expedition to Sicily, like the expedition to Egypt in the First Peloponnesian War, proved to be more and more expensive and more and more hazardous. Meanwhile Sparta and her allies sent help to Syracuse and invaded Attica. But the Athenians at home refused to disengage and cut their losses in Sicily. In 413 the net closed. The Athenian forces were annihilated. The total losses of the expedition were 200 warships and their complements of some 40,000 men, a large number of infantry which included 4,000 Athenians, and a huge amount of shipping, equipment, supplies and money – all incurred in pursuit of a secondary objective. The home front split under the shock of the disaster. A revolutionary party seized power, and for two years oligarchs were in control of the city of Athens. Meanwhile the empire began to break up. The future lay with the Athenian fleet which stayed in the eastern Aegean, fighting under the flag of democracy and holding down some parts of the empire. In 410 their successes were such that democracy was restored at Athens in a bloodless revolution.

The revival of Athens after the disaster in Sicily was due in part to the slowness of Sparta and her allies. They lacked the money and the bases which were required for the mounting of a naval offensive in the eastern Aegean. They turned with reluctance to the Great King who offered them money and bases but at an embarrassing price, namely the recognition that the Greeks in Asia were the subjects of Persia. Sparta accepted the offer and the price, hoping against hope that she might never have to pay the price. Persian gold and one capable Spartan commander brought the war to a conclusion. In 405 the Athenian fleet was completely and utterly broken at Aegospotami in the Dardanelles, the last of her subjects were liberated, and the Peloponnesian fleet blockaded Athens into starvation and surrender. In 404 a Peloponnesian fleet under a Spartan commander sailed into the Peiraeus, and the Peloponnesian and Boeotian soldiers began to demolish the long walls of Athens to the music of flutes, 'believing that day to inaugurate the freedom of Greece'.[9]

The central issue of inter-state politics in the Greek world seemed to have been solved at last after almost sixty years of war and uneasy peace. Athens had failed to impose her system of power upon the Greek states; she had been stripped of all her empire; and she was now reduced to impotence. On the other hand the right of every Greek state to independence, self-government and liberty had been vindicated by force of arms. So in 1945 we saw the end of German imperialism and a declaration of human liberties. But wars between peoples of the same culture are destructive not only of lives but also of ideals. Animosities become more bitter, class divisions deepen, and the collective strength of the whole complex may be so impaired that it proves unable to check the advance of outside powers, more primitive indeed in culture but more robust in health.

CHAPTER 13

THE CULTURAL LEADERSHIP OF ATHENS
IN THE INTER-WAR PERIOD, 445-431

The victories of the Greeks over Persia, Carthage and Etruria led to an enormous expansion of Greek seaborne commerce. The fleets of the Sicilian tyrants, of Corinth and her colonies and of Athens and her allies controlled the seas and protected the passage of goods throughout the Black Sea, the Aegean basin and the western Mediterranean. Then goods came not only from the coastal areas but also from the hinterlands of Asia, Europe and Africa. There was a great demand for Greek products, and the markets for them were constantly expanding throughout the fifth century. It was an age of plenty, such as had never been known before in the relatively unproductive peninsula and islands of Greece. The only check on economic growth came from the wars of Greek against Greek. In periods of peace, for instance from 445 to 431, prosperity grew apace in all Greek states, whether free or subject in political terms.

The centre of Greek commerce was Athens. As the leading naval power and as the head of the Athenian Alliance in the Aegean, she attracted trade and traders from all parts of the Black Sea and the Aegean basin to her magnificent harbour at the Peiraeus. Her earlier rival, Aegina, fell far behind her; she was soon made subject to Athenian rule, and then in 431 she was eliminated by Athens. Trade from the West still came to Corinth; but all exchange between East and West went through the waters east of the Isthmus, and these were controlled by Athens. With trade came very large numbers of non-Athenians. Prominent among them were those engaged in the carrying trade: Greeks of the islands and of the Asiatic coast who were mainly of Ionian stock and came from member-states of the Athenian Alliance, and non-Greeks from Cyprus, Syria, Phoenicia, Egypt and so on. Others who were attracted to Athens as the cosmopolitan, international centre of the Greek world were capitalists, craftsmen, doctors, writers and, in general, persons of ability.

These non-Athenians were not offered the citizenship of Athens. Indeed under the democracy which was instituted by Ephialtes and Pericles Athens became more exclusive and inbred than she had ever been; for in 451, on the proposal of Pericles himself, the citizenship was made the prerogative of those alone who were of citizen birth on both sides. Exceptions were very rare. If non-Athenians wished to stay on in Athens, they had to apply for registration as resident aliens and, if approved, they were classed as 'metics' (*metoikoi*). They were then free to engage in business and in social life on the same terms as the citizens, except that they could not buy land in Attica, and their lives and property within Attica were safeguarded by the granting of certain legal rights. But they had no voice in politics; they paid a considerable amount annually in tax to the Athenian state; and they were conscripted into the Athenian armed forces. Though these terms may seem illiberal to us, they proved most attractive to the aliens; for instance in 431 one in five of the Athenian hoplite infantrymen were metics. The wealth, the skill and the services of the metics were invaluable to Athens, and in consequence they enjoyed much greater security than resident aliens did in Sparta or indeed do in many modern states. In addition there were many aliens at Athens who did not seek to become metics but were mere birds of passage.

Inevitably the Athenians became more and more exposed to the ideas of the outside world. Whereas the generation of Aeschylus had drawn its inspiration from the glorious past of Athens and the religious ideas of Homer and Hesiod, the next generation became familiar with the philosophies and religions of other peoples and especially of the Ionians, who were closely akin to the Athenians. As we have seen (p. 45, above), the Ionians were the pioneers in a new way of thinking, which shed the traditional beliefs and trusted in the ability of the individual intellect. Thus Xenophanes, who flourished c. 530, dismissed all myths and legends as man-made fictions, and among them the myths about the Olympian gods whom he regarded as simply man-made in man's image. If cows could draw, he said, they would make their gods in the likeness of cows. He discarded many standard values: Olympic victors and Olympic victories were in his opinion worthless. What his own enquiries led him to believe was that an incorporeal, unmoving constant was in control of all matter; it can be called God, but men being corporeal cannot have any certain knowledge of God's nature. At best men may have a personal opinion. How different Xenophanes is from Pindar and Aeschylus! Yet at times how close to Euripides and Thucydides!

The influence of Heraclitus, a citizen of Ephesus, who flourished c. 500, was no less disturbing to the traditionalist. In his philosophy the only constant was inconstancy: 'Everything is in a state of flux'. He saw the world as a continuum of changing opposites – day and night, birth and death, hunger and satiety. Thus the soul was destructible, absolute good and evil were imaginary, and restraint (*sophrosyne*) was not a principle of nature at all. Yet within the cycle of change a unity persists. This unity stems, he thought, from a plan or *logos*, 'the word', made famous centuries later by the evangelist St John.

The distinction between inconstancy and unity was carried further by Parmenides of Elea (a colony founded in south Italy by Phocaeans from the coast of Asia). He boldly dismissed all the evidence which has been and is provided by sensual perception. So the world which we apprehend through our senses – the world of seeming – became for him unreal. The real world – the world of truth – was apparent to the reason alone; it was, he said, a sphere, single and stationary and unchanging. Parmenides believed himself to have been transported beyond the world of seeming and to have experienced the world of truth through pure reasoning (*noema*). Thus the ultimate instrument of revelation was the individual mind.

Anaxagoras (c. 500–428), a child of this Ionian milieu, settled at Athens where he became a close friend of Pericles. He concerned himself with the problem of mind and matter. Assuming that particles of matter were infinitely diverse, divisible and numerous, he ascribed the individuality of an object to the predominance of certain sorts of particle in its make-up; and he held that changes in the object, such as are observable e.g. at birth and in death, were due to a rearrangement of its particles. But mind (*nous*), being a purer substance, was self-existent and separate; where it existed, e.g. in man, it was in control. Starting from these assumptions, Anaxagoras maintained that at first all matter was inert; then mind set up a movement at a point within matter; this movement spread outwards and threw the particles into collision, so that objects kept forming and changing. This movement of Mind is continuous, affecting the infinite expanses of the universe or indeed of infinitely numerous universes. Mind is thus the initiating and controlling force of existence, being itself conscious of what it creates. Thus everything is corporeal. Qualities which we ascribe to objects, such as heat, brightness, smoothness etc. are not abstractions but properties of particular particles, perceptible to a limited extent by the senses inherent in particles. Celestial phenomena – sun, moon and stars – consist of matter; they move on the circular course which Mind initiates, so that the sun, for instance, gives its light to the moon; in the same way eclipses and rainbows are due to physical causes (which he explained correctly).

The assumption of the infinitely divisible particle was challenged by Zeno. He posed the paradox that Achilles never overtakes the tortoise, because, if the distance between them is infinitely divisible, whenever he reaches the point where the tortoise has just been the tortoise is in front of him. Zeno's attack may have led Leucippus of Miletus to postulate indivisible units, called 'atoms' (*atoma*, or uncuttable things), infinite in number within infinite 'space' (*kenon*, or void). He and Democritus of Abdera (c. 460–370) formed an atomic theory of the universe in which an eddy initiated movement and brought the atoms into collision. Atoms alone are real in nature; all other aspects of matter, e.g. colour, texture, temperature, are relative to man's fancy, which derives from fallible senses and is founded on convention (*nomos*). But 'intelligence' (*dianoia*) is still there; it alone in man is able to form the concept of invisible and intangible atoms.

To these Ionian thinkers the Olympian gods and the ideas of justice which Aeschylus expressed were simply irrelevant. In terms of material realism the great initiator – Zeus, God or whatever – might be an eddy in the void, and the regulator which maintains order and continuity in the universe might be mere chance or mechanistic necessity. Leucippus preferred the latter explanation. 'Nothing happens at random,' he wrote, 'but all things happen of purpose and necessity' (*logos* and *ananke*). But others preferred chance (*tyche*). And it was chance which appealed most to those who lived in times of frustration and chaos.

Such thinking was unprecedented. It was to have no successor until the dawn of what we call science. Yet these Ionians were not scientists testing hypotheses by experiment but thinkers who were concerned with life as well as matter. They meant to live up to their beliefs, regulating their own conduct by the principles of material realism as they understood it. Moreover they were missionaries. Some of them taught at Athens and hoped to convert men to their way of thinking and behaving. They were the initiators in fact of what became the 'sophistic movement', a movement which attempted to sell and popularize the new thinking on a great range of topics.

No less remarkable was the development in medical thinking. Alcmaeon, who flourished c. 509 and came from Croton in southern Italy, dissected animals. He deduced that the centre of the intellect was the brain, to which sensations were conveyed through ducts. When the brain was at rest, these sensations were organized by memory and inference into knowledge. Thus knowledge (*episteme*) had a physical genesis. In the same way, disease was treated pragmatically. Hippocrates of Cos (c. 460–400) wrote as follows of epilepsy, which was generally regarded as due to possession by a god (or later by a devil, as we see in the New Testament): 'This disease is, in my opinion, no whit more sacred than other diseases. It is of the same nature and causation as they; it is also curable, no less than they . . . provided it is not at too virulent a stage for the remedies which are applied to be effective. Its origin is in heredity . . . and its cause lies in the brain; this is so with all the most serious diseases.'[1]

Exploration by sea revolutionized man's knowledge of the world. Phoenicians circumnavigated Africa and sailed out into the Atlantic in the early fifth century, landing in Cornwall to the north and in Sierra Leone to the south. Greeks too reached the Atlantic coasts of Spain and northern Africa, and they sailed via the Red Sea and the Persian Gulf to the mouth of the Indus. This knowledge was collected and systematized by Hecataeus of Miletus who compiled c. 500 his *Periodos Ges* or *Tour of the Earth*, the first geographical description of the world. Peoples and places were the main themes; but he gave information also on fauna and flora, local legends, and various products.

Hecataeus and other Ionian thinkers broke away from the tradition that verse was the only form of literary expression – they made prose the voice of reason. In his attitude to the tales which had been related by chroniclers, known as *logographoi*, Hecataeus was rationalistic. 'Thus speaks Hecataeus of Miletus; what I write is as I believe it to be true; for the tales which the Greeks tell are many and ridiculous in my opinion.'[2] These words formed the introduction to his *Genealogies*, a work which provided a chronological framework for what we should call ancient history or pre-history. His approach and his matter had a profound influence not only on his successors Herodotus and Thucydides but also throughout antiquity.

The greatest of all *logographoi* was Herodotus who lived c. 485 to c. 428. He came from Halicarnassus on the Asiatic coast and he travelled widely. He wrote his tales of all parts of the known world in a flowing prose of exceptional clarity and charm, drawing sometimes upon the work of his predecessors but often reporting what he himself had seen and heard in the course of his travels. Everything was of interest to him: the fat tails of the sheep in Arabia, the colour of the salt in Libya, the circumnavigation of Africa, the origin of the Phoenicians, the burial-rites of the Scythians and so on. His interest and his enthusiasm infect the reader today, as they infected his hearers at the time; for he composed his tales for recitation to an audience, and it is this fact perhaps which accounts for the unparalleled ease and directness of his style.

The last of the *logographoi*, Herodotus was also the first historian in the sense that the Greek word *historia* means 'inquiry'. He was the great questioner: why are Egyptians healthy, why does the Nile flood, why are the Scythians nomadic? He realized the continuity between past events and contemporary events, and he believed that all the tales, however remote in time or space, were relevant to the understanding of human experience. He took as the main theme of his history the conflict between East and West which culminated in the Greco-Persian Wars. The beginning of his history ran as follows: 'This is the result of the inquiry made by Herodotus of Halicarnassus, in order that time should not blot out the past from the minds of men, nor fame be denied to great and wonderful deeds accomplished by Greeks and by non-Greeks, and in particular why they went to war with one another.'

He was astonishingly impartial as between Greeks and non-Greeks. For instance in describing the Battle of Plataea he said that in boldness and in warlike courage the Persians were not a whit inferior to the Greeks. Yet he was discriminating; he saw the conflict as one between the freedom of the Greek spirit and the oriental form of despotism which imposed servitude on others both politically and intellectually. To him freedom was not a political catchword but an essential condition of human dignity and of human progress. He therefore realized how important the outcome was for the future of the world.

Reaching beyond human affairs he inquired into the ultimate causation of historical events. He saw God as the final arbiter in the lives of nations and of great men, punishing them for any arrogance or impiety which they commit but destroying many innocent and lesser persons in the process. In any individual's life the element of chance is so predominant that no man can be called happy before the day of his death. When we compare the outlook of Herodotus with that of Aeschylus, who was a generation older, we realize that the age of confidence in the gods who were led by Zeus on the path of benevolence to man has receded, and in its place there is a less specific divine power which is generally destructive and seems to be actuated more by jealousy, that is by the desire to keep man in his place, than by any sense of the justice which man aspires to in human relations.

The History of Herodotus was written within living memory of the Persian Wars but by a man who had himself grown up with the greatness of Athens. His home at Halicarnassus, on the fringe of the Greek settlements in Asia Minor, owed its freedom from Persia to the initiative of Athens. His own travels were made possible by the freedom of the seas which Athens and her allies had established. He stayed frequently and probably for long periods at Athens, and he gave recitations there, perhaps first in 445. He made his home after 443 at Thurii, an international colony in south Italy which Athens founded on the proposal of Pericles. It is evident that his sympathies were formed during the period of the First Peloponnesian War when he was a partisan of Athens and probably a friend of Pericles, but hostile to Corinth and critical of Sparta. His 'History' repaid a debt of gratitude to Athens, for nothing has done more to magnify the image of the City of Athena.

A visitor to Athens who had an extensive influence from c. 450 onwards was Protagoras of Abdera, who taught the art of rhetoric for a fee and was regarded as one of the earliest Sophists. The power of persuasion was all important in politics, at law and in the daily life of the Athenian democracy, and the Sophists claimed to be able to understand this power and to transmit it to others. They were of course exponents of techniques in oratory, but they were much more than that. Protagoras, for instance, was a polymath; he expounded the latest theories in ethics, politics, metaphysics and mathematics, drafted the laws of the newly-founded colony at Thurii, discussed the problems of epistemology with Democritus, and advised Pericles on matters of state. His influence on young Athenians was all the greater because Athens, unlike Sparta, had no system of state education. In regard to the gods he was frankly agnostic, declaring himself unable to know whether they did or did not exist, and on that account he took the senses of men to be the true discerners of reality. Thus man became 'the measure of all things', and each individual man was the judge of what is true and right for him. Protagoras differed in one other respect from the Ionian thinkers we have mentioned: he brought the state into his analysis of life and he maintained that the state teaches men through its laws to practise virtue. At Athens he held that the laws had been established by good lawgivers – no doubt with a side-glance at Pericles.

The brilliance of these Ionian thinkers is dazzling even today. They are analogous to the rationalists of the twentieth century, but the influence they exerted was more intense and more immediate for it was concentrated within a relatively small community at Athens and then only on those who had the leisure to listen to them. They inaugurated the first period of intellectual enlightenment in human history, at least in the opinion of those who identify rationalism with enlightenment. They provided a higher education in a very exciting way as they were a closely-related and yet cosmopolitan intelligentsia which owed nothing to any patron or any institution. Nor were they departmentalized specialists. Democritus, for instance, was renowned for the atomic theory and for fundamental work in mathematics and astronomy, but he also wrote and lectured on psychology, logic, music and poetry. They taught their pupils not with any particular vocation in view but to think for themselves in all fields of knowledge and above all to obtain a complete intellectual emancipation. The concept of free thinking was in line with the theory of democracy which prevailed at Athens; for, as a comic poet had expressed it, Ephialtes had 'poured out a full and unadulterated draught of freedom for the citizens'.[3] Yet in a state which was suppressing the liberties of others and was engaged in a great war there were some dangers in a form of free-thinking which challenged all conventional values.

The reaction of the Athenians to the influx of Ionian free-thinkers seems to have been guided at first by Pericles, who was himself a man of brilliant intellect and a powerful speaker. He became the centre of the intellectual circle in Athens because he was a close friend of Anaxagoras, Zeno and Protagoras and he had as his mistress a Milesian woman, Aspasia, who was famous for her free-thinking and free-living. The fact that the first citizen was in the vanguard of the movement gave some reassurance to the traditionalists, and Pericles was able to some extent to channel the new influences to suit his own purposes. It seems likely that he was behind Protagoras' advocacy of the state laws at Athens, and he used arguments himself which had the sophistic ring of the day, for instance in the debate against Thucydides, son of Melesias (see p. 117, above).

The chief indication that Pericles kept his concept of the state in harmony with the intellectual life of his time is found in the so-called Funeral Speech, which Thucydides the historian attributed to him. There Pericles emphasized two freedoms: the freedom of opportunity for every citizen which stemmed from a disregard of such traditional criteria as social class or financial circumstances, and the freedom of behaviour which stemmed from a general permissiveness and an absence of raised eyebrows or injurious looks. Yet the Athenians, he claims, combined these freedoms with obedience to the written and unwritten laws alike, that is to the laws of the statute-book and those of common decency. In war too they did not rely on traditional forms of training and discipline (as at Sparta), but upon native courage and intelligence, which were linked together at Athens. Decisions were taken by the community after free discussion and full deliberation; they were not delegated to any executive board as the Athenians had confidence in their own ability and versatility. Such a society, he claimed, was an example to all others, and aroused in its own citizens a deep patriotism, a love which filled the heart.[4]

In this speech the gods have no place. It is a noble expression of humanism, in which man is the sole measure of society. Yet orthodox religion, in respect of the state's gods, was strong in the period of Pericles. The Propylaea and the Parthenon, which were built between 447 and 432 when he was at the height of his power, were the greatest tribute men could pay to Athena Polias, the goddess of the city. Within the same period temples were built in the vicinity of the Agora to Athena, Hephaestus and Ares, and at Sunium to Poseidon and at Rhamnus to Nemesis; and such festivals as the Panathenaea and the Dionysia were celebrated with unrivalled splendour and devotion. The web of religious beliefs in Attica may have been loosened by the free-thinking of the Sophists but it was very far from broken by 432 when the Second Peloponnesian War was about to start.

The great poet of the Periclean period was Sophocles (c. 496-406). The people accorded more victories to him than to any other dramatist. He was a well-born Athenian who served in the highest offices of state and fought for the democracy and the empire. His love of Athens shines through his work, especially in his last play, *Oedipus at Colonus*, written when Athens was facing utter defeat. His plays have the technical brilliance and the mastery of composition which are the marks of Periclean thinking and of Periclean art and architecture. But they are set within a deep religious faith, which accepts unquestioningly the divine power and the divine will as the final arbiters of human life. There is no attempt, such as we have seen in Aeschylus (p. 100, above), to justify the ways of Zeus and to find a divine benevolence, albeit exercised within the limiting conditions of physical existence; nor is there any attempt to mitigate the ruthlessness of Athena in driving Ajax mad or the cruelty of Apollo in destroying Oedipus the King. The gods are not to be denied or ignored in any of their manifestations. In the *Oedipus Tyrannus* they dashed Oedipus to the ground, but in the *Oedipus at Colonus* when Oedipus hears the thunder overhead he calls out:

> The gods themselves make clarion call to me.
> In all that went before no word of theirs was false.[5]

Thus Sophocles belongs to the great age of Athens when men testified to their faith in Athena by building the Parthenon in her honour.

The centre of Sophoclean tragedy is man: self-willed, independent, acting upon consciously held and explicitly stated principles. Ajax is determined to live nobly or else die nobly. That is what his own sense of honour demands. He will not compromise and therefore he chooses to die nobly, that is open-eyed to take his own life. Tecmessa, his wife, understands him. 'He took the death he wanted', she exclaims.[6] Antigone is determined to uphold the unwritten laws. She does so at the price of her own life, and as she goes to the dungeon the Chorus of Theban Elders see that she is *autonomos*, a sovereign personality. Oedipus the King will know the truth, whatever the cost; and when he learns the dreadful truth, that he has killed his father and married his mother, he tears out his own eyes of his own free will. The characters all state the principles upon which they base their decisive choices, whether they are the central figures or lesser persons such as Tecmessa and Teiresias. Indeed the speeches of Sophoclean characters, as Aristotle has remarked,[7] resemble those of statesmen in that they reveal the issues which are involved and give reasons for a preferred course of action. Even the less admirable characters, such as Creon and Lichas, who are misguided rather than mean, have reasonable grounds for their actions and express them in a convincing manner.

Each play is an entity in itself; for Sophocles soon abandoned the trilogy form, which Aeschylus had preferred. It was his achievement to bring to its most perfect form and highest dramatic intensity the play of classical dimensions, which passed through the Latin versions of Seneca to the Elizabethan dramatists. But in his plays we are not watching individuals acting and interacting merely with one another, as in most of our modern dramas. Rather the action is set firmly within the community, and the decisions of the chief actors affect the fortunes of the community, which is represented by the Chorus. For example, Ajax is a fascinating study both in himself and in his impact on others; but the play is concerned with the position of a great man in a community and with the obligations which the community has towards him. So too Antigone; but the play is concerned with the clash between a personal conviction and a ruler's policy in a matter which raises a religious issue for a community. The study of character in its own right is deeper in the latest plays; but even in the *Philoctetes* the future of the Greeks at Troy is at stake throughout the play, and in the *Oedipus at Colonus* the destinies of Athens and Thebes are dependent upon the outcome of the action.

Thus the tragedy of Sophocles presents the tragedy of man in the full setting of his life in society and in the presence of the gods. It is, much more than in Aeschylus' plays, a tragedy of situation – Oedipus the King caught in the nexus of an inherited situation, like Hamlet the

Dane. Yet we are still in the period of religious tragedy. Everyone is aware of the presence of the gods; in the last resort it is they who over-rule *not* the choices but the outcome of the choices made by an Oedipus or an Antigone in a Sophoclean play. But the tragedy of man is initiated not by the gods but by man himself. It is he who chooses and so often chooses wrongly in self-will or arrogance or folly, setting his own superb qualities on the road to disaster; indeed by an irony of circumstance he is sometimes led by his own best qualities – Oedipus the King by his intelligence and integrity – into a disaster which will affect his descendants and his associates.

There are many wonders, but nothing is more wonderful than man. He crosses the white-capped sea in the teeth of the wintry gale, and he rides the thundering surf. Year after year he furrows the breast of Earth, the oldest of gods, who knows neither toil nor decay, as he drives his plough to and fro and turns his horses around. . . . Man is exceedingly intelligent . . . He has an invention for everything. The future contains nothing he cannot master except that he will not devise a means of escaping Death. . . . Intelligent, inventive, resourceful beyond imagining, he goes his own way – to what is good? Only sometimes, raising his city on high if he honours the laws of the land and keeps his oath to the Justice of the Gods. At other times he goes his own way to disaster, bringing loss to his city because he is reckless and does not abide by what is right.[8]

These words come from the *Antigone*, a play which has had and still has a remarkable influence on European drama. They sound the key-note of the tragic outlook. Shakespeare expressed the same thought on the lips of Hamlet[9]: 'What a piece of work is man! How noble in reason! How infinite in faculty! . . . the paragon of animals! And yet, to me, what is this quintessence of dust?' For Hamlet knew that Claudius had murdered his father and was bringing disaster to the state of Denmark. Moreover, in Hamlet himself those very qualities of intelligence, wit and sensitivity were playing their part in leading him and others to destruction.

It is interesting to compare the last play of Aeschylus with the last play of Sophocles, separated as they are by a gap of some fifty years. In the finale of the *Oresteia* Aeschylus reached the summit of man's hope that justice is enlightened and that the gods are benevolent towards man. From this summit there was a vista of progress towards a higher level of understanding, tolerance and co-operation. But the future was to bring something very different. Sophocles wrote the *Oedipus at Colonus* in his old age, when he was nearing ninety, and he acknowledged the benevolence of the gods only in one thing – that they granted to the old

Oedipus the release from suffering which is death. One thing still delights Sophocles; the beauty and fame of Attica and Athens, not as they were in contemporary time, but as he imagined them to have been in the lifetime of Theseus. Looking back over his long life, as the Chorus of old men did in the play, he wrote these words for them to sing:

Not to be born is best. But if one is born, the next best by far is to return thither whence one came with least delay. For when the light-hearted thoughtlessness of youth is gone, then we meet the blows of life: woe on woe, weariness on weariness, envy, sedition, strife, war, carnage. Last of all is abhorred old age, ineffectual, companionless, unloved: in it there are all miseries of miseries.[10]

It is a cry almost of despair. In this play Oedipus, like Lear, has met the blows and plumbed the depths of suffering, as the Chorus go on to say in these words, which were to be echoed in Shakespeare's *King Lear*:

> E'en as some headland on an ironbound shore,
> Lashed by the wintry blasts and surge's roar,
> So is he buffeted on every side
> By drear misfortune's whelming tide,
> By every wind of heaven o'erborne,
> Some from the sunset, some from orient morn,
> Some from the noonday glow,
> Some from Rhipean gloom of everlasting snow.[11]

Yet he is not overwhelmed. As he is about to go to his release, he utters to his faithful daughters, Antigone and Ismene, the words which save us from despair. 'Your life with me was hard, I know; yet there is one word alone which wipes out the sum of all our sufferings. That word is love.'[12] Not divine love but human love, the power of mutual love which is as strong between man and man as the power of mutual destruction.

Some of the qualities which mark Sophocles as a Periclean are found also in Thucydides the historian (c. 460–c. 400): the wholeness of vision, the clarity of thought, a certain detachment and anonymity which enables characters and situations to stand out in their own right. Of the surviving plays of Sophocles the majority were written perhaps after the death of Pericles, but the mind and the heart of Sophocles grew to maturity in the Periclean period. So too, Thucydides wrote his history mainly after the death of Pericles, but his cast of mind was shaped in the mould of the Periclean period. He began as soon as war broke out in the expectation that it would be a war of unprecedented significance, and he prefaced his actual history of the war with a review of the past which seems to be the fruit of earlier research. In it we see the focus of his interest.

Man's accumulation and use of power is the centre of attention. In mythical times Minos first acquired a navy. He first used sea power to rule others and to obtain revenues, while Agamemnon was superior to his contemporaries in terms of power and he used his power to raise a coalition against Troy. In archaic times Corinth obtained financial power by exploiting her geographical position and by her own enterprise in building a fleet, safeguarding trade and exacting tolls. Sparta owed her political power to her stable institutions and she used her political power to arrange matters in other states. In recent times Sparta had been the leading power, particularly at the start of the Persian Wars; then Sparta and Athens came to be on the same level, one in land power, the other in sea power – turning their weapons at first in the same direction (against Persia) and then against one another, including their own allies in each case and developing their own system of control over those allies. Sparta exacted no money but saw to it that her allies had an oligarchic form of government because oligarchs fostered Sparta's interests; Athens exacted money and confiscated the fleets of all her allies except Chios and Lesbos. The effect of their rivalry was that, when the Second Peloponnesian War began, Sparta and Athens had each accumulated a degree of power which surpassed the sum of their joint power at the time when they had been at war with Persia.

This is incisive, realistic thinking. There are no bulls of Minos. The power of Agamemnon is more important than the oaths of Tyndareus under which the suitors of Helen were said to have followed Agamemnon to Troy. There are no Olympian gods who were offended by the rape of Helen or by the arrogance of Xerxes. Rather there is a deliberate attempt to probe beyond poetic exaggeration and reveal the real factors of the situation. Thucydides tackles the past as Hippocrates tackled the so-called 'sacred disease', epilepsy. There is nothing mystical about the past, and the same diagnosis may be made of it as of any other period.

The object of his search is narrowed down to the study of power in its various forms – political, financial, military and naval – and in the end he concentrates on the importance of financial power, which accrues from revenues and accumulates in the form of capital. Thus the length of the Trojan War was due to lack of money rather than to shortage of men, and it was financial power which enabled Minos to control other territories and reduce lesser states to subjection. Money, sea power and rule over others are closely linked in his mind. Even the small navies of past times 'brought to their owners great power in the form of revenues and rule over others'.[13] Much more so the great navy of contemporary Athens which, under the guidance of Pericles, had amassed vast reserves of capital, exacted substantial revenues and ruled over some three hundred city-states.

This new power which had been created by Athens differed radically from land power – at least in Greece, since Thucydides does not draw any comparison with Persia – in that its capacity for expansion and imperial control was so much greater. Indeed its potential was almost unlimited in the mind of Pericles, as Thucydides portrays it. 'Your naval resources are such that your vessels may go where they please without the Persian King or any other nation in the world being able to stop them.'[14] Moreover, the Athenians excelled in the spirit of enterprise. Just before the outbreak of war the Corinthians described them as follows: 'Their inventiveness is revolutionary; they are quick to conceive a plan and quick to execute it; adventurous beyond their power, daring beyond their judgement and confident in danger; . . . swift to exploit success to the utmost degree and slow to give ground under a reverse. . . . It might be said in short that their nature is to have no peace themselves and give no peace to the rest of the world.'[15]

The psychology of power, in a state such as Athens was in 432 BC, was analysed by Thucydides with the objectivity which the Sophists applied to the study of individual psychology. Its mainspring is acquisitiveness, 'grasping after more', and its appetite is insatiable. It cannot stand still, because the hatred of its subjects and the alarm of its neighbours are constantly increasing. Therefore it must forestall opposition by action, and 'constant necessities of action must be accompanied by constant improvement of methods'. Morality is almost outside its considerations. 'To withdraw from empire is no longer possible: your empire is already a negation of liberty, a tyranny, wrong to impose (it may be said) but dangerous to let go.'[16] The reality (*aletheia*) and the nature (*physis*) of power are what need to be understood; not its relation to conventional thinking (*nomos*).

When war broke out in 431, Thucydides asked why the situation came to war (as the situation in a play comes to a climax). Fashions change in the explanation of what was to Pericles (as he was reported by Thucydides) 'the greatest of follies – for those of course who have a free choice in the matter and whose fortunes are not at stake'. We may think of religious ideologies, political ideologies, economic pressures, racial antipathies, commercial rivalries and so on as causes of war. Thucydides penetrated deeper. He and his contemporaries at Athens believed in the free will of the individual and in the sovereignty of a people to make decisions of policy, and in this case he saw that the war originated in the free will of the Athenian people on the one hand and the free will of the Peloponnesians on the other hand. They both chose to go to war. Their acts of deliberate choice were prompted on each side by various considerations, but in the considered judgement of Thucydides the most fundamental reason for their choices was that 'the growing power of Athens and the alarm of Sparta drove them to war'.

Thus to Thucydides the outbreak of the Second Peloponnesian War was a milestone, as it were, in the development of a new type of power which Athens had created and which could neither recede nor stand still. A collision was made inevitable by the reaction of Sparta; for Sparta was determined not to submit to fear but to go to war. The question which made this war significant was not whether the traditional land power of conservative Sparta would survive but whether the new power, based on sea power, capital and empire, would continue to innovate and expand almost without foreseeable limits.

The Periclean Age opened up to the Athenians new vistas in almost every sphere of human activity: in the refinement of art, architecture and literature, in mathematics, astronomy, and understanding of the universe, in psychology and the understanding of man, in the development of capitalism and the acquisition of power, and in the promotion of empire. The capacity of one city-state to create so much which is still deeply woven into the fabric of our modern world is indeed amazing.

CHAPTER 14

THE EVOLUTION OF THE ATHENIAN STATE BETWEEN 431 AND 414

The political development of a state during a long war may have an important influence on the outcome of the war. It was so at Athens. She entered the war as a progressive democracy in which there had been for a generation, and still was, an overwhelming support for the leading citizen, Pericles, elected year after year as general and able to influence every department of policy. Above all he gave consistency and stability to the foreign policy of Athens in respect both of the empire and of further adventures in peace and in war. Thucydides put forward the following reason for the influence of the great statesman in the democracy

As he owed his power to his personal prestige and his intellectual pre-eminence, and as he was transparently incorruptible in the matter of money, he controlled the mass of the people freely and gave them the lead rather than being led by them. His own acquisition of power being from reputable sources, he did not have to please them in giving them advice; but being there by merit he opposed them even to the point of enraging them. Indeed, whenever he saw that their confidence was at all untimely and arrogant, his words reduced them to alarm; and on occasions of unreasonable panic he restored them again to confidence. In fact what was in name a democracy became in practice rule by the first citizen.[1]

To those who lived under the leadership of Winston Churchill in the last war these words need no amplification. Yet one point has to be made. Thucydides says not 'one-man-rule' but 'rule by the first man'. The expression is to be understood in the context of the Athenian democracy, in which every year the whole electorate declared by a free vote who was to be the leading citizen or *strategos ex hapanton*.

When Pericles took Athens into the war, he outlined a strategy which put his leadership to a crucial test. He claimed that his strategy would bring victory, namely to maintain the fleet, deliver naval offensives against the Peloponnese, and keep Athens' subjects in hand; and, on the negative side, not to engage in pitched battle on land, not to try to expand her dominions and not to do anything which might endanger the safety of the state. He pointed out that Athens had greater reserves of capital than her opponents and that her naval power was unlimited; and that in a protracted war of attrition these facts would help her to win. Pericles' strategy was logical. Indeed Thucydides, who placed much emphasis on logic, expressed approval of it when he reported it and again in retrospect when he was reflecting on the subsequent course of the war. But more than logic is involved in a people's reaction. The Athenians who watched their property being destroyed in Attica were filled with detestation of his strategy. Upholders of Athens' military tradition disliked the tacit admission that her army was no match for the invaders. Young men resented the resumption of the tedious and expensive strategy which had been the mark of the First Peloponnesian War; it seemed as frustrating as the return to static warfare in France did in 1939. It was this reaction to his strategy which first split the people radically; it was to keep them divided until the Peace of Nicias.

In 430 a terrible plague started at Athens. It was all the more disastrous because the city was crammed with refugees from the countryside who were living in shacks and were short of water. One third of Athens' first-line troops died and many were maimed; but the damage to Athenian morale was more deleterious still. Pericles was called to trial and fined for his policy both in going to war and in conducting the war. However, he lifted the people out of their despair by his superb oratory. It was not long before he was restored to his position as war-leader. He died in 429, being himself a victim of the plague. However his strategy lived on. It was no longer a strategy of deliberate choice. It had become almost a strategy of necessity; for the countryside had been completely ravaged and the Athenian army had lost a third of its effective strength. This fact did not make the strategy less unpopular or reconcile the minds of the Athenians to its continuation indefinitely.

The death of Pericles was the end of an era. For as long as most men could remember only two men had led the democracy, Cimon and Pericles. As members of the most distinguished and experienced families in the state, and as men of exceptional talents, they had imposed their will upon the electorate to a remarkable degree. Now the people did not find a successor to them, perhaps because it wanted something quite different. The consequences were noted by Thucydides. 'The politicians who came after Pericles were on a level with one another. As they endeavoured each to gain first place, they had recourse to the practice of surrendering the conduct of affairs to the whims of the people.'²

One effect of the change was that direct government was now exercised by the people or rather by the group of individuals who formed a majority of those present at any single meeting of the Assembly. This kind of direct government tended to be inconsistent. A striking example occurred in 427. The people of a small state, Mytilene, which had risen in revolt, capitulated on condition that no citizen should be summarily executed by the Athenians without trial. The Assembly met and voted the execution of all adult males and the enslavement of all women and children forthwith, and the appropriate order was sent to the general who was in command at Mytilene. Next day the Assembly met, changed its mind and cancelled the order. The cancellation reached Mytilene when the general had just published the order.

Another effect was that politicians now fulfilled a different role at Athens. They were concerned not to advocate a reasoned strategy but to propose from day to day any *ad hoc* move which might win a majority of the votes of those present. In consequence each meeting of the Assembly saw a closely-contested struggle by rival politicians for the people's favour. Thucydides has given us a graphic description of such a meeting, held in 425. Cleon, having no military position himself, criticized Nicias' conduct of a military operation and hinted that he himself could have done better. Nicias then resigned his command in favour of Cleon, his object being simply to make a fool of Cleon. Thereupon Cleon tried to back out of the situation. However, the people, enjoying the fun, shouted at Cleon 'Go'. So in the end they sent him off as commander. To everyone's amazement he won a spectacular success. In this affair the people acted as the master. Nicias and Cleon were not its elected leaders but its pawns.

Strategy was now determined by the Assembly. Its course was erratic but not disastrous in the years down to the Peace of Nicias. Naval and amphibious operations which were generally in accordance with Periclean principles brought many successes, and only one group of allies (in Chalcidice) got out of hand. Two deviations from the policy of Pericles were unsuccessful: attempts to obtain a footing in Sicily for imperial expansion failed, and a military adventure in Boeotia ended in heavy infantry losses. Commanders were chosen by the Assembly with less attention to military experience and expertise than in the past. The final blow which led a war-weary people to make the Peace of Nicias came in 422, when Cleon whom they had chosen as commander committed an elementary error of tactics at Amphipolis and was killed together with some six hundred Athenian infantrymen.

Ten years of war had decided absolutely nothing. The major states, Athens and Sparta, had only weakened themselves both materially and spiritually. The power structures which they led had been so undermined by the tensions and actions of war that the leaders made an alliance with one another in order to protect themselves from their former associates. The 'peace and alliance' which Athens and Sparta made with one another in 421 was only the opening gambit in a long diplomatic game, in the course of which Athens tried to obtain by diplomacy what she had failed to achieve by war – the break-up of the Spartan Alliance. During the diplomatic negotiations a new politician became prominent at Athens as one of the extreme democrats. He was Alcibiades, young, aristocratic, handsome and wealthy, comparable in his background to the Pericles of the democratic revolution in 462. His exceptional cleverness and his ostentatious extravagance both fascinated and alarmed the Athenians, so that they found it difficult to decide finally for or against him.

The split within the people, apparent at the beginning of the war, was now much wider. Holders of property in the countryside, who had seen Attica ravaged, burnt and looted, were eager for peace with Boeotia and the Peloponnese, and they supported Nicias as the architect of the peace. Those who obtained their living from the empire in one form or another were more interested in preserving and extending the empire than in cultivating Attica, and they viewed a renewal of war with less concern. The division was not by financial classes, for some peasants were middle-class small-holders and some exploiters of empire were well-to-do. The division was more by outlook and occupation. But there was one significant factor. In time of war the poorest citizens served in the fleet and earned pay as oarsmen, and their hopes of financial advancement lay in an extension of imperial possessions. This group regarded itself as 'the Demos', the Athenian equivalent of John Bull.

The diversity of interests within the people was played upon by the politicians who identified themselves readily with this or that sectional interest, and in the period of uneasy peace the Assembly made a series of unwise and sometimes inconsistent decisions. When Thucydides viewed this period of Athenian politics in retrospect he wrote as follows:

The people did everything contrary to the strategy of Pericles and even adopted policies which seemed extraneous to the war. They did so to further personal ambitions and personal financial interests at the expense of Athens and her Alliance as a whole. In the event of success their policies served the prestige and the advancement of individual persons, and in the event of failure they impaired the state's ability to conduct the war.[3]

At the instigation of Alcibiades in 420 the Athenians entered into alliance with Argos while they were still in alliance with Sparta. As Argos and Sparta were deadly enemies, it may have seemed clever to run with the hare and hunt with the hounds. Its effect was to precipitate a trial of military strength between Argos and her allies and Sparta and her allies. If Athens really intended to commit herself to Argos, this was the chance for her to put her entire army in the field and aim a knock-out blow at Sparta. But Alcibiades was no longer in favour. He was not even one of the ten generals in 420. The people compromised. They sent only a token force to help Argos in 418. It arrived late. By that time a truce had been made between Argos and Sparta. Alcibiades who was present at Argos as Athenian representative persuaded Argos to break the truce unilaterally and to resume operations against Sparta. A pitched battle resulted. Sparta won a decisive victory, made peace and alliance with Argos and re-established her supremacy in the Peloponnese.

Thus the half-measures which the Assembly adopted lost Athens the only chance she had in this century of making a successful intervention in the Peloponnese. At the same time they rekindled Sparta's animosity towards Athens. It became obvious to the Athenians that a choice must now be made once and for all between the policies advocated by Nicias and by Alcibiades, and the Assembly decided to hold an ostracism in the spring of 417 BC. This time the politicians outwitted the Assembly. Nicias and Alcibiades joined forces and arranged that their supporters should vote against a third party, Hyperbolus. In the event Hyperbolus was ostracized. Thus the constitutional mechanism was deflected, and the all-important choice of a political leader was left unsolved.

Nicias and Alcibiades were both elected to serve as generals for 417–6. Nicias conducted operations against some states in Chalcidice which were still at war with Athens. Alcibiades began to intrigue again with a democratic group in Argos. Two other generals led an unprovoked attack on Melos, a neutral state, whose inhabitants were of Spartan origin. During the war the Melians had sent gifts of money but not troops to their foundress, Sparta. Even when Athens had ravaged their territory and demanded the payment of tribute, they had maintained a strict neutrality. Now Athens issued an ultimatum: submit to superior force or be destroyed. Because Thucydides regarded this as an act of naked imperialism, significant not only for Athens but also for posterity, he has left a record in the form of a dialogue,[4] which includes arguments expressed and unexpressed at the time. He did not name the speakers; for they represented the people of Athens and the people of Melos.

To the Athenian speakers in the dialogue might is right. 'As the affairs of men are, any question of right exists only between equals. The strong do what they have the power to do. The weak submit.' When the Melian speakers declared their faith in their foundress and in international law, the Athenians pointed out that Sparta was guided solely by her own interest and that in international affairs the strong rule the weak in accordance with a natural law of the world; indeed, as far as one can guess, the gods do likewise. The Melians said that this attack on them as a neutral state would turn other neutral states against Athens, but the Athenians were unmoved, for neutral states were few and feeble in fact. Appeals to justice and honour were equally ineffective. When Melos again offered a treaty of neutrality, Athens went to war. Later in the year the Melians capitulated, entrusting themselves to the mercy of the Athenian people. 'The Athenians executed all the adult men they had taken and enslaved the women and children. They occupied the place themselves, sending out five hundred settlers later.'

During the winter when this massacre was perpetrated the Assembly debated whether or not to send an expeditionary force to Sicily. The leading politicians gave conflicting advice. Nicias thought it unwise to disperse Athens' forces in view of her present commitments, and he regarded the conquest of Sicily as too large an undertaking in itself. Alcibiades had no doubt of Athens' ability to conquer Sicily, and he argues that a spectacular success of this magnitude might cause all Greek states to submit to the rule of Athens. He appealed to the adventurous spirit of the people. 'We have reached a stage of empire at which we must not be content to keep what we have, but we must plan to extend our dominion; for if we fail to rule others we are in danger of being ruled ourselves.'[5] Meanwhile most of those in the Assembly knew nothing of the size of Sicily. They thought of it as an Eldorado, and their excitement became infectious. Thucydides described the motives of those who were present at the last assembly which took the decision:

A passionate desire to make the expedition fell on everyone alike. The general mob and the soldiers had expectations of pay for the present and of an extension of empire in the future which would provide an unending source of pay. The younger generation welcomed the prospect of adventure and excitement; they were confident that they would come through all right. The older men thought that the very size of the expedition ensured its safety, if not its success. In such an atmosphere of excessive enthusiasm anyone who had misgivings kept quiet, lest he be regarded as a traitor.[6]

Thucydides described the Melian dialogue and the debate about the expedition to Sicily at considerable length because they indicated so clearly the changing nature of the Athenian state. There was no Pericles to expound the issues involved, but those who spoke were individually prompted by personal considerations. It was the Assembly which set its own mood and the Assembly decided to destroy Melos and subjugate Sicily without reference to any concept of international justice or even of elementary logistics in a distant campaign overseas. The people were moved by passionate ambition and wishful thinking and not by rational exposition or intelligent debate.

The decision to send so large an expedition to Sicily did not heal the division in the state, because the great number who voted in favour of it voted with differing motives. Nor did it end the rivalry between Alcibiades and Nicias, because although the people were dazzled and flattered by the brilliance of Alcibiades they still felt safe with the conventional, respectable and experienced Nicias. Unable to choose between them, the Assembly foolishly appointed both of them, together with an unpolitical military figure, Lamachus, to take command of the expedition. When they reached Sicily, each member of this ill-balanced trio advocated a different strategy. The cleverest of them, Alcibiades, got his way. But he was recalled soon afterwards.

The recall of Alcibiades arose from an episode which illustrated the nervousness of the Athenian people. Just before the expedition was due to sail, some stone busts in the streets which represented the god Hermes were mutilated. This act of sacrilege was thought by the superstitious to be a bad omen for the expedition, and the perpetrators were supposed by some to be anti-democratic revolutionaries. The name of Alcibiades was mentioned as one of the suspects because he was known to be a reckless and irreligious character, and some saw in him a would-be dictator. Aware of such rumours Alcibiades asked for an immediate trial. This was refused. When he had sailed, his enemies in Athens aroused much feeling against him and the Assembly recalled him and some others. On the way home he escaped. Later he reached the centre of the enemy camp, Sparta; for the Peloponnesians had renewed the war in order to help their friends in Sicily.

The Athenians did not replace Alcibiades when he was recalled or Lamachus when he was killed in battle. They left Nicias in sole command of an expedition which he thought to be unwise. When he fell ill and asked to be replaced, the Assembly made him stay and even sent out reinforcements. It was his mishandling of the campaign which led finally to complete and utter disaster in 413.

Later, when Thucydides passed his judgement on Athens, he wrote as follows:

As a great power in possession of an empire Athens made many errors. Chief among them was the expedition to Sicily. The error of judgement which the Athenians made in the assessment of their enemies was not as serious as the errors committed by those who sent the expedition out; for they did not take the decisions they should have taken in support of those in the field. Instead the politicians engaged in intrigues, struggling to win the leadership of the people. The consequence was that the keen edge of military operations was blunted, and open dissension appeared for the first time at home.[7]

The change in the Athenian state between 431 and 413 was astonishingly rapid and profound. The internal cohesion which derived from the statesman-like leadership of Pericles and the readiness of the people to follow the dictates of reason had brought Athens to a high level of power by 431. As Thucydides saw it, her successes were due to intelligence rather than to circumstance, and he himself began writing his history in the constant belief that politically intelligent man can shape his own future in a decisive manner. As an example it seemed to Thucydides in 431 and right on until the end of the war that, if the intelligent policy of Pericles was implemented, Athens would win the war without any doubt; for her margin of power over her adversaries was so very great. What then went wrong? As Thucydides analysed the course of events, he saw that the cohesion of the state was falling apart and the rifts widened and widened until open dissension appeared in the events of 415 to 413 at Athens. The deep patriotism, the sense of common decency and the intelligence which had been typical of Periclean Athens were now replaced by a self-seeking at all levels of society which put profit before patriotism, expediency before decency and emotion before intelligence. In Thucydides' phrase, 'the people were grasping after more', whether at home in Athens or abroad at Melos and in Sicily. In a democracy the people elect the leaders who reflect their ideals: in 431 one statesman Pericles, and in the years after 421 two or more politicians who appealed to sectional interests and were themselves influenced by personal ambitions.

CHAPTER 15

THE EVOLUTION OF THE ATHENIAN STATE DURING THE YEARS OF DIVISION AND WEAKNESS, 413–404

When the full extent of the disaster in Sicily was known, even the democrats themselves lost faith in a form of democracy which had shown itself so incompetent. The Assembly set up a commission of ten advisers to guide the state through the immediate crisis. One of them was Sophocles the poet, a good Periclean, now in his eighties. The commissioners were no doubt moderate democrats. More radical critics of democracy who had lain low since the ostracism of Thucydides in 443 realized that there might be some chance of coming into power at last. They were of two kinds: moderates who belonged to the upper income groups, and extremists who held doctrinaire 'oligarchic' views. The former wanted to administer the state economically and prosecute the war efficiently. The latter were more interested in seizing power; they were prepared to come to some understanding with Sparta if it enabled them to gain their primary objective. Of the two parties the extremists were already organized for a *coup d'état*; for they had been working underground in clandestine clubs or 'cells of comrades' (*hetaireia*). The opportunity for them to act came from that extraordinary man, Alcibiades.

When Alcibiades joined Sparta, he was condemned to death as a traitor by the Athenians, deservedly, because it was he who persuaded Sparta to send an officer into Syracuse and to place an army of occupation in the countryside of Attica. When disaster struck the Athenians at Syracuse, Alcibiades moved to the eastern part of the Aegean in order to instigate revolt among the 'allies' of Athens and win the aid of Persia for the Peloponnesians. After his departure from Sparta it was discovered that the wife of King Agis had been seduced, and the general opinion was that Alcibiades was the seducer. Whatever the truth may have been, Alcibiades quickly transferred his services from Sparta to Persia. He realized that the outcome of the war depended

1 A jug in Protocorinthian, Early Orientalizing style with a griffin's head, c. 700–650. Found on Aegina. *British Museum.*

2 A jug in Early Corinthian, Orientalizing style from Rhodes, c. 600. *National Museum, Athens.*

3 *Above:* The inside of a Laconian cup, *c.* 565. A masterpiece of the school of vase painting at Sparta, which was widely exported. King Arcesilas of Cyrene oversees the weighing and loading of silphium (used for seasoning) onto a ship, indicated by the yard-arm overhead. Found at Cyrene. *Bibliothèque National, Paris.*

4 *Left:* The inside of an Attic black-figure cup, mid-sixth century. Found at Tarquinia, Italy. Still influenced by Corinthian style, the painter shows a 'ring-dance' and, in the centre, Heracles, wearing a lion-skin headpiece, wrestling in the sea with Triton, a sea-god. *National Archeological Museum, Tarquinia.*

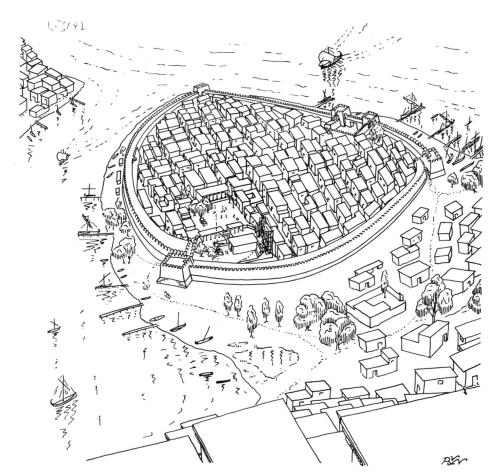

5 *Above*: Plan of Smyrna in the late seventh century, as reconstructed by the excavators. Streets running north by south and east by west are on the grid system. Temple and public buildings are alongside the open square inside the walled town, which is set on a peninsula.

6 *Right*: The Temple of Apollo at Corinth, mid-sixth century. The columns, numbering fifteen on each flank, are monolithic and the capitals are in the Doric style. Size *c.* 70 by 178 feet on the stylobate.

7 *Opposite*: Archaic marble statue, 'The Peplos Kore', with the archaic smile. Almost four feet high, with traces of the original paint, *c.* 540–30. *Acropolis Museum, Athens.*

8 *Below*: Archaic bronze statuette of mounted warrior, *c.* 550. *British Museum.*

9 *Above:* The Temple of Hera (in the background) at Posidonia (Paestum), mid-sixth century. The columns, eighteen on each flank, nine on each facade, three in the porch and eight in the cella or interior, are 'cigar-shaped' and made of drums. Size *c.* 80 by 175 feet on the stylobate.

10 *Below:* Conjectural restoration of the temple of Artemis at Ephesus by A.S. Murray. Designed *c.* 550, completed *c.* 450 in the archaic Ionic style. The columns, perhaps 127 in all, are solid marble. Size *c.* 180 by 360 feet.

11 A silver tetradrachm of Athens under Peisistratus and Hippias. *Left:* Head of Athena with helmet and earring. *Right:* Owl with olive spray. *British Museum.*

12 A silver didrachm of the Boeotian League, latter part of sixth century. *Left:* Shield of Athena Itonia. *Right:* Incuse mark with initial letter of a member state, here *theta* for Thebes. *British Museum.*

13 A silver didrachm of Syracuse, a so-called Demareteion, commemorating the victory over the Carthaginians in 480. *Left:* Four-horse chariot with victory crowning the driver and lion below. *Right:* Arethusa wearing a laurel crown, earring and necklace, and around her four dolphins. *British Museum.*

14 A silver tetradrachm of Eretria in Euboea, late sixth century. *Left:* Cow scratching her nose with a hindhoof, and a bird on her back. *Right:* Incuse square with a cuttlefish. *British Museum.*

15 *Above:* Painting on a Protocorinthian vase found at Veii, Italy, *c.* 650–40. It shows the Hoplites going into battle, the front ranks about to engage and a piper between the ranks on the right. *Villa Ginlia, Rome.*

16 *Left:* Bas-relief found on the Acropolis of Athens, showing the side of a trireme in the late fifth century. The rowers of the top level only are visible, but oars of the two lower levels are shown. *Acropolis Museum, Athens.*

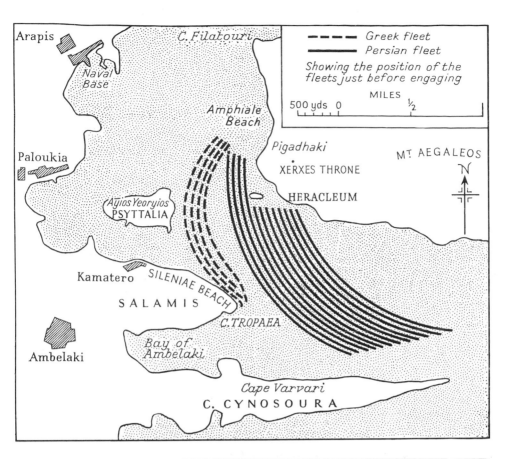

Arapis

C. Filatouri

Naval Base

Amphiale Beach

Paloukia

Pigadhaki

XERXES THRONE

HERACLEUM

MT AEGALEOS

N

Ayios Yeoryios PSYTTALIA

---- Greek fleet
—— Persian fleet

Showing the position of the fleets just before engaging

500 yds 0   MILES   ½

Kamatero

SILENIAE BEACH

SALAMIS

C. TROPAEA

Ambelaki

Bay of Ambelaki

Cape Varvari

C. CYNOSOURA

17 *Above:* The battle of Salamis. The fleets about to engage inside the Salamis Channel.

18 *Right:* Aerial view of the Piraeus (bottom right) and the Salamis Channel.

19 *Above left:* Scene from the theatre at Athens on a red-figure crater, *c.* 500–490. The six youths, probably a half-chorus from the *Neanisci* by Aeschylus, dance bare-footed on a clay *orchestra* towards an actor, seated as a suppliant on the *thymele. Museum of Art, Basle.

20 *Below left:* Scene from the theatre at Athens on a black-figure lecythus. The six men, holding branches and seated on altars as suppliants, are a half-chorus probably from the *Heracleidai* or *Eleusinii* by Aeschylus, *c.* 470–60. No doubt the other half-chorus were similarly placed on the other side of the open *orchestra. National Museum, Athens.*

21 *Above:* The theatre at Epidaurus. Late fourth century.

22 *Above:* The Propylaea of the Acropolis of
Athens, begun by Mnesicles in 437. In
Doric style with some Ionic features.
View from east Portico looking west.

23 *Above right:* Horsemen of the Panathenaic
procession from the west side of the frieze
of the Parthenon, designed by Phidias
and executed *c.* 440.

24 A silver tetradrachm with (*left*) Zeus of Olympus and (*right*) a bearded rider raising hand in salutation, probably Philip II of Macedon. *British Museum.*

25 A gold coin of Philip II, called *Philippeios*, with (*left*) head of Apollo, and (*right*) two-horse car, commemorating a victory in the Olympian Games. *British Museum.*

26 *Left:* Hermes and the infant
Dionysus by Praxiteles, *c.* 340.
Museum at Olympia.

27 *Above:* Perseus freeing Andromeda. A painting
at Pompeii, after an original of the fourth
century probably by the painter Nicias. *Pompeii.*

28 Bronze statue of Zeus, *c*. 460. Found from a wreck off Artemisium.
The god, slightly more than human life-size, was aiming a spear
probably in defence of the Greeks. *National Museum, Athens.*

now on Persia; for whoever had his finger in the purse of the Great King could build ships and hire rowers. He therefore set himself up as the purveyor of the Great King's favours. Both the Peloponnesians and the Athenians were duped by him. Upon reflection he decided to make use of the Athenians. He told the commanders of the Athenian fleet which was operating off Samos that he would switch the aid of Persia from Sparta to Athens but on two conditions: that he was recalled with a full pardon and that an oligarchic government was set up at Athens.

The offer of Alcibiades came at a time when the power of Athens was at a very low ebb and defeat seemed to be almost unavoidable. But if Alcibiades could switch Persian aid to Athens, then there would really be a chance of winning victory over Sparta. The prospect was so pleasing that the whole fleet at Samos and the people at Athens accepted the offer of Alcibiades and the attendant conditions. This turn of events inspired the extremists to put their plans into action. Some members of the cells were detailed to assassinate the leading democratic politicians; they succeeded without being detected. Others briefed certain individuals whom they had chosen to speak in the Council and in the Assembly. These speakers presented as their programme a very moderate form of oligarchy. Anyone who opposed these speakers was tracked down and assassinated. The names of the organizers and the killers were known only by some members of the cells. The speakers themselves were usually persons whom no democrat would have suspected of holding oligarchic views. Thus mutual distrust and confusion spread, and the assassinations created an atmosphere of terror in the crowded city.

Meanwhile the oligarchs in the fleet at Samos had moved more rapidly. As the crews expected that oligarchy would bring Persian gold into their hands through the services of Alcibiades, the oligarchic leaders took command without any opposition. They proceeded to set up oligarchic governments in some of the subject-states, and they then raised troops among their sympathizers there. But they did not recall Alcibiades; for they distrusted him profoundly and suspected he was bluffing. Now that they were in control of the fleet, they sent some of their number together with some of the troops they had raised to carry out a *coup d'état* at Athens. The leader of this group, Peisander, made a moderate speech in the Assembly on his arrival, and it was agreed to set up a commission of thirty men who should draft a new constitution by a specified date, the idea being generally held that a change of constitution would switch Persian aid from Sparta to Athens.

When the day came for the commission to report, the Assembly was

149

convened not in Athens but outside the walls at Colonus, where it was conceivable that the enemy might deliver an attack. Under these conditions attendance by those who were not supporters of a change was naturally sparse. The commission then reported that the constitutional safeguards of the democracy were suspended and that any proposals were legitimate. Peisander himself made the proposal which was adopted, that all the democratic magistrates be deposed and that a provisional government be appointed forthwith in the Assembly.

The manner in which the provisional government was appointed revealed the nature of the dominant party. Those present in the Assembly elected five 'presidents'. The presidents at once named one hundred persons as their collaborators, and each one of the hundred then named three men as his personal collaborators. Thus, mainly by selection from the top échelon of the party, a body known as 'The Four Hundred' was created. It was then empowered to administer the affairs of the state on its own authority and to convene at its own discretion 'The Five Thousand', a body of persons whose names and qualifications for appointment were not made known. The implication was that 'the few' were not the four hundred but some five thousand persons who held and would soon exercise the political franchise. In the Assembly which witnessed these transactions not a single dissentient voice was raised.

It remained for 'The Four Hundred' to take power. At this time when the enemy were encamped in Attica the citizens manned the walls of Athens during the day and then dispersed to their homes. The conspirators chose an evening for their coup. Peisander and the troops he had brought with him from the islands occupied the approaches to the town centre (*agora*), where the Council House was situated. The four hundred oligarchic 'councillors', armed with daggers and supported by a hundred and twenty young extremists, then went into the Council House. The democratic councillors offered no resistance. They were paid off and sent home. The new Council installed itself with the usual ritual. Thus a complete revolution was carried out in time of war with no loss of life after the initial assassinations. Thucydides the historian made a point of praising the organizers and in particular Antiphon, Peisander, Phrynichus and Theramenes for their exceptional ability.[1]

The change from democracy to oligarchy was not just a change of the men in office, such as occurs when a government changes within a modern parliamentary system, but a change of the politically franchised community. Whereas under the democracy all male citizens over eighteen years of age, exceeding 30,000 in number, had exercised the vote, now only the chosen five thousand citizens possessed the vote. The rest had legal rights only. Thus 'the many' (*hoi polloi*) were replaced by 'the few' (*hoi oligoi*). Moreover, within 'the few' in this sense, only The Four Hundred actually governed, so that here too the principle of 'the few ruling' (*oligarchia*) was in operation. Such a system may be employed equally effectively by right-wing extremists and by left-wing extremists. In the modern world it is more commonly employed in left-wing 'one-party' states. Within such states the party élite governs, the party-members have political rights, and the rest of the citizens have equal legal rights if they are lucky.

The chief claim of any right-wing government is that it corrects the faults of its left-wing predecessor. The Four Hundred was no exception. Expenditure was cut back, administration was centralized and foreign policy was decided *in camera* and not in public, as it had been. These were sensible measures, especially in time of war. There was much to be said in favour of The Five Thousand as constituting a political electorate of those who paid taxes and served in person as infantrymen; for they would be voting on policies for which they would have to pay in money and in service. But the theory of all this, important though it was for purposes of propaganda, was far from the actual practice. The party-organizers controlled The Four Hundred, and they had no intention of convening The Five Thousand. Their agents executed or imprisoned all known opponents without trial. In effect the word of The Four Hundred was law within the city. Outside the walls their troops inflicted losses on the Peloponnesians, but the party-leaders opened negotiations with Sparta in the hope of obtaining a settlement. There was some sense in this double game; for they knew that, if peace could be made, Sparta would support an oligarchic régime at Athens.

What the revolutionaries needed, if they were to stay in power, was a monopoly of control over the armed forces of the state. This eluded them at Samos. There the sailors, who had heard exaggerated reports of atrocities at Athens, refused to obey the representatives of The Four Hundred. Instead they elected their own commanders and called themselves 'The Democracy'. At this point Alcibiades came into play. 'The Democrats' at Samos still supposed that Alcibiades had influence with Persia; they therefore recalled him and elected him as one of their generals. As far as the favour of Persia was concerned, Alcibiades was a broken reed. But he saved Athens from being plunged into civil war when he dissuaded The Democracy from sailing to the Peiraeus and attacking The Four Hundred; for he saw that a civil war within a general war was certain to end in disaster both for him and for Athens. But, having a good understanding of the politics of oligarchy, he sent a message to Athens, asking that The Four Hundred should be replaced by The Five Thousand.

The message of Alcibiades split the oligarchic front. Theramenes left the party élite and joined the moderates, who then pressed The Four Hundred to publish the names of The Five Thousand. Alarmed by this development, the extremists occupied a strongpoint which controlled the entry from the Saronic Gulf into the Peiraeus. They then sent some of their leaders to Sparta. The moderates naturally suspected that a plan was afoot to surrender the city to a Spartan fleet. When such a fleet appeared and proceeded to attack an Athenian base on Aegina, Theramenes and his supporters stormed the strongpoint and seized the Peiraeus. The extremists were now confined to the upper city; the moderates set up The Five Thousand as a separate government at the Peiraeus; and the fleet at Samos continued to call itself The Democracy.

Alcibiades' initiative might seem to have been disastrous in fragmenting the Athenian state still further, but it soon paid off handsomely. The extremists were now hamstrung; for they were unable to obtain supplies. In September 411 they abandoned the upper city and took refuge with the Spartans who were encamped in Attica. Their failure was now total; for they had been unable either to win general support or to control the armed forces, or even to put the city in the hands of the enemy and survive as a puppet government. On the other hand the moderates at the Peiraeus and The Democracy at Samos had two things in common, namely patriotism and some naval power; moreover, the moderates depended on the seaborne supplies which the Democratic fleet allowed to pass through their area of control and reach the Peiraeus. Co-operation grew steadily, and Athenian squadrons defeated the enemy at Cynossema and Cyzicus. Theramenes persuaded The Five Thousand to cancel the banishment of Alcibiades, and Theramenes himself served under the general command of Alcibiades at Cyzicus. These two men, Alcibiades and Theramenes, more than any others, saved Athens from collapse and defeat. In June 410 the two states coalesced. They formed a 'Democracy', elected leaders from both camps, and passed an amnesty which was intended to cover all past acts of whatever political colour.

The Five Thousand had had a good record in regard to the war. The soldiers had defended the city against the enemy in Attica, and the fleet had operated successfully at Corcyra, off the coast of Macedonia and in the western Aegean. They had had the good sense to collaborate with the Democratic fleet at Samos both in the bringing of supplies to Athens and in the prosecution of the war in the eastern Aegean. The basic principle of the constitution was that political rights were exercised only by men over thirty years of age who came from the well-to-do classes and were in a position both to pay taxes and to serve in the forces. At the time of the revolution the number of such men was estimated at five thousand, but later it was said that those who were eligible had numbered nine thousand. The electorate of The Five Thousand was divided into four councils, each being 1,250 strong, and each council in turn was the executive administrative body for one year. The members of the other three councils were convened, at the discretion of the council in office, to form a consultative body. The chief magistrates were chosen by election from a short list of elected candidates to serve for one year. The whole electorate voted at each stage, but the candidates for magistracies were drawn only from the members of the council which was in office for that year. No one was paid for political services, and there were fines for non-attendance at meetings of the council in office. The administration was thus tight-knit, economical and stable. It relied upon its members to show an altruistic patriotism.

Thucydides the historian stated his opinion of The Five Thousand with surprising directness. 'Athens proved to have a good constitution for the first time, at least within my lifetime; for as regards "the few" and "the many" the mixture was a moderate one, and it was this constitution which enabled the state to recover from its poor condition for the first time.'[2] Modern intellectuals tend to praise democracy whether in the Periclean form or in a more developed form. Not so Thucydides who lived under both forms. On the other hand he clearly condemned the narrow oligarchy of The Four Hundred, although he acknowledged the ability of the leading organizers. His desire seems to have been for a responsible, moderate and patriotic government, and he found it in The Five Thousand. His judgement is that of a historical realist, who observed all these constitutions in action during a critical war. We came nearer to The Five Thousand in the Second World War by forming a Coalition Government. It is an open question now whether such a coalition is desirable not only in war but also in peace.

When democracy was restored at Athens in June 410, every adult male citizen over the age of eighteen was made to take the following oath.[3] 'I shall kill with my own hand any person who overthrows the democracy at Athens, holds office under a non-democratic régime, seeks to set up a tyranny, or collaborates with a tyrant. The killer of any such person will be regarded by me as clean in the sight of the gods and the spirits.' This formula was characteristic of extreme democracy. It was no idle oath. The killer of an oligarchic leader,

Phrynichus, was publicly honoured by a grant of Athenian citizenship. Despite the amnesty legal proceedings were taken in the People's Court against those who were thought to have supported the extreme oligarchs. At the same time the hallmarks of democracy returned: state pay for political and other services and state subsidy for the poor. The financial balance which had enabled The Five Thousand to maintain their armed forces soon became a deficit.

As Pericles had said, financial resources were the sinews of naval war. Now neither Athens nor Sparta had sufficient money to outbuild one another or to buy up all available mercenary oarsmen by offering higher pay. Athenian squadrons raided the coast of Asia Minor and taxed all shipping in order to stay at sea. Sparta received only small amounts of money from Persia; for the Great King preferred to prolong the war and let the Greeks wear one another down. During a period of restricted warfare from 410 to 407 the most striking feats were performed by Alcibiades as a commander of the fleet in the eastern Aegean. In spring 407 he put all his booty on board, sailed at the head of his fleet to make a daring reconnaissance of the Spartan naval base at Gytheum, and then proceeded to the Peiraeus which he reached on a day of festival. Crowds awaited the most controversial figure of their time. When he saw his friends among them, he landed and was escorted to the city. His fine rhetoric and his scintillating ability soon charmed the people into the belief that he could regain control of the empire and win the war. The curse which the state had laid on him as a traitor was now revoked, and he sailed off as supreme commander at the head of the Athenian forces.

Victory, however, did not depend on Alcibiades' abilities. The decisive factor now was Persian aid, and Darius had decided to back Sparta strongly. He sent his younger son, Cyrus, to the coast where he formed a close friendship with a new Spartan commander, Lysander, and enabled him to offer better wages for oarsmen than Athens could afford to pay. In spring 406 the Athenian fleet suffered a minor defeat when Alcibiades was absent. The Athenian seamen lodged complaints against him, and he was not elected for a further year. When he was told to lay down his command forthwith, he made off to a fortress which he owned in the Chersonese; for he knew better than to put himself at the mercy of a People's Court at Athens. There was some truth in Aristophanes' words in *Ranae* (l. 1432), that, if you have a lion, it is better to humour him, i.e. to have him fighting on your own side than to let him loose.

Conon who replaced Alcibiades was even less successful, because hired oarsmen left his service in order to obtain better pay in the Peloponnesian fleet. Athens enfranchised anyone, free or slave, who would row, issued an emergency coinage in gold and tried to obtain aid from Carthage. In 406 a major battle was fought off the Arginusae islands. In all some 20,000 Greek lives were lost. The Athenians won but they suffered heavy losses, which occurred mainly after the engagement when a detachment of ships under the command of Theramenes and Thrasybulus failed to pick up the survivors in stormy weather. Their casualties came to 5,000 Athenians or at least 5,000 men in Athenian employment. The loss was the more serious because Athens could not replace them, whereas the Peloponnesians could obtain fresh crews with Persian gold. Sparta, however, still wanted peace. She offered to take her army of occupation out of Attica and to negotiate a peace on the basis of the *status quo*. Cleophon, the democratic leader, persuaded the people to reply that Athens would not negotiate unless Sparta withdrew her troops from the cities of the Athenian Empire. It was to be war to the death. Lysander was sent out again and Cyrus provided the necessary subsidies.

Meanwhile the aftermath of the Battle of Arginusae produced a *cause célèbre* at Athens. Archedemus, a colleague of Cleophon, opened the attack by indicting one of the generals responsible for the battle on a charge of misconduct. This general was imprisoned pending trial in a People's Court. Then the Council decided as a precautionary measure to arrest the other generals. Two of them escaped. Theramenes and Thrasybulus could also see trouble ahead, and they made their plans accordingly. When the newly-arrested generals were brought before the Assembly for a preliminary hearing, Theramenes and others turned on the generals and blamed them for the loss of so many Athenians who had been left to drown. The generals stated their case and many witnesses supported them. The discussion became protracted. When it became too dark to count hands the meeting was adjourned, the Council being instructed to confer meanwhile and to recommend procedure for a full trial.

In the interval before the next meeting the Athenians celebrated a festival at which all bereaved families mourned their dead and in particular those who had died at sea off Arginusae. There was lamentation and keening throughout the city. When the Assembly met, many men were wearing black clothes, their heads being shaven in mourning, and emotion ran high against the generals. This was exploited by a member of the Council called Callixenus, who was a supporter of Theramenes. He proposed the resolution which the Council had formulated, namely that, as the generals had already had a hearing, there should be an immediate vote for or against the execution of the generals collectively. A speech in support of Callixenus was made by a survivor of the battle who said that he was floating on an empty barrel when his mates in the water told him to report their words to the people; 'The generals have failed to rescue those who served their country best'. A few speakers attacked the proposal of Callixenus as illegal in terms of procedure and equity; for at least one of the generals whom it was proposed to try collectively had been in the water at the time. An uproar then broke out, and many voices were heard shouting that it was monstrous to stop 'the People' from doing what it wanted. All opposition was silenced except that of Socrates, who as a member of the Council insisted on conforming with the law. 'The People' then proceeded to the trial. An advocate spoke in defence of the generals (for they were not allowed to speak themselves), and he ended by asking for a trial of each general individually. On the first vote he won. However, a second vote was demanded and granted. This time the proposal for collective trial was carried, the vote was taken at once, and the eight generals were condemned to death. The six generals under arrest were executed forthwith.[4]

The trial showed the sovereign people at its worst. Indifferent alike to the written laws and the unwritten laws, which Pericles believed the democracy of his day to have upheld, the Assembly abused its own legal system and executed some at least who were innocent of any misdemeanour. In this ugly affair 'The People' acted as a dictator, doing what it wished. Soon afterwards it repented; however, repentance took the form not of self-criticism but of putting on trial those 'who had deceived the people'. Five men were arrested, but they escaped during a riot. One of them came back after the war, Callixenus; he was left to die of starvation. The son of Pericles was one of the generals who were executed. It was ironical that a lack of competent generals precipitated the collapse of Athens in 405.

Lysander mustered a large fleet in that year. He sailed into the Hellespont, cut the supply-route from the Black Sea to Athens and based his fleet in the fine harbour of Lampsacus on the Asiatic coast. As he expected, the Athenians followed him. They encamped on the open beach of Aegospotami, which was on the European coast opposite Lampsacus. The fleets were two miles apart. Next day at dawn both fleets were manned and under oar, ready for battle. The Athenians rowed out into mid-channel, offering battle, but the Peloponnesians remained in harbour. Later in the day the Athenian fleet returned to

Aegospotami. There the ships were anchored off shore or even beached and some of the crews made off to Sestus, two miles away, in search of food. The same thing happened on four consecutive days, except that more and more of the crews made off each evening. On one of these days Alcibiades, who was living in a castle nearby, called on the Athenian generals and told them urgently to move the fleet into the harbour of Sestus. They paid no heed. Late on the fourth day Lysander sent his ships into action. They captured 171 ships which were either half-manned or abandoned; only nine Athenian ships got away. The naval power of Athens was irretrievably shattered, thanks to the incompetence of the generals and the nonchalance of the crews.

The fate of the prisoners was discussed at the conference of the commanders of the Peloponnesian fleet. It was agreed to let all go free except for the Athenians who numbered some 3,000. They were then accused of various atrocities. For a general, Philocles, had recently captured a Corinthian and an Andrian ship and had had the crews thrown from a cliff into the sea; it was also known that the Athenian Assembly had voted to amputate the right hand of all seamen who might be captured that year. It was decided to execute the Athenians; the only exception was a general who had opposed the vote of the Assembly.

When the news of the defeat reached Athens, 'it was night,' wrote Xenophon, 'and cries of grief passed from the Peiraeus up the Long Walls and into the city as each man told his neighbour of the disaster. That night nobody slept; for they were mourning not only for the dead but rather for themselves, because they expected that they would now be treated as they had treated the people of Melos, Histiaea, Scione, Torone, Aegina and many other places.'[5] Next day the Assembly was convened. It was decided to prepare the Peiraeus and the city for a siege. Yet no one doubted that the end of the war was in sight. All that remained was to obtain the best terms possible under the circumstances.

Cleophon and the other democratic leaders of the moment, who had initiated the policy of 'Schrecklichkeit' (ruthless reprisals against the allies and the enemy seamen), intended to fight to the last ditch, because they knew that they personally had no hope of escaping execution. Many shared their view for similar reasons. The size of the population was increasing rapidly as streams of refugees came in from the islands, where Lysander was proclaiming the day of liberation and letting any Athenians and Athenian sympathizers depart to Athens. When the circle of blockade was drawn tight by the Peloponnesian army outside the walls and by the fleet of Lysander off the Peiraeus, it became obvious that the Assembly had to choose between a negotiated peace and the onset of famine. It decided to open negotiations with an offer of peace on condition that an alliance was made between Athens and Sparta and the fortifications of Athens were left intact. Peace on these terms would save Athens from the humiliation of acknowledging her defeat and give her security against her bitterest enemies. Sparta refused to negotiate at all on these terms. She required Athens to demolish part of her Long Walls as a preliminary to negotiations.

When a member of the Council at Athens proposed that the Long Walls should be demolished in this way, he was arrested. When the Assembly met, Cleophon proposed that anyone advocating the demolition of the Long Walls should be executed. His proposal was carried. At this point Theramenes, the leader of the moderate oligarchs, took the initiative. He offered in the Assembly to go as an envoy to Sparta with a view to ascertaining whether Sparta was demanding the demolition of the Long Walls in order to send her army into the city and 'andrapodize' the population, i.e. kill all adult males and enslave the rest, or simply as a guarantee of good faith during subsequent negotiations. He knew that it was the fear of andrapodization which made the majority support Cleophon, and his offer opened up a plausible alternative. The people accepted the offer. Theramenes departed as their negotiator. It was the first sign of a switch of power in Athenian politics.

Theramenes stayed away for three months. Meanwhile starvation took its toll in the beleaguered city, and the people condemned and executed Cleophon. Xenophon believed that Theramenes waited deliberately until he thought that Athens would accept any terms at all. But it is equally probable that Lysander detained him for the same purpose. When Theramenes came back to Athens he may have allayed the people's fear of andrapodization; for they appointed him and nine others to go to Sparta as plenipotentiaries and negotiate terms of peace. There they were brought before a Congress of Sparta and her allies. The representatives of Corinth, Thebes and many other states proposed not to treat with Athens at all but to destroy her. The representatives of Sparta refused to andrapodize the city which had served Greece so brilliantly in the Persian Wars. Finally Sparta, apparently alone and on her own authority, offered peace to Athens if the fortifications of the Peiraeus and the Long Walls were demolished. The Athenian plenipotentiaries accepted.

For the first time in history a Peloponnesian fleet sailed into the Peiraeus, and the Boeotian and Peloponnesian soldiers began to demolish the Long Walls. The tyrant city had been overthrown and the day of liberty was celebrated.

CHAPTER 16

CHANGES IN ATHENIAN SOCIETY DURING THE SECOND PELOPONNESIAN WAR

The Second Peloponnesian War had a much deeper effect upon Athenian society than the First Peloponnesian War had done. The chief reason was that the two-thirds of the citizen body which had lived in the countryside for countless generations was compelled to move into the city and live there as evacuees for stretches of some years at a time. Land became alienable, land values fluctuated rapidly and age-old traditions of all kinds were abandoned. Inside the walls of the over-crowded city there was a ferment of new ideas to which the younger generation was particularly susceptible, and the crises of the long war lent a feverish fervour to political life and excited many passions.

In 431 Athenian society was at the height of prosperity. The Athenians themselves numbered some 168,000 men, women and children, and they lived either in the countryside of Attica or in the city or in Athenian dependencies overseas. They were divided into four classes by property: the two upper classes numbered perhaps 4,000 persons, the middle class about 100,000, and the lower class about 64,000. The citizens of the upper classes usually owned estates of good land in Attica which they had inherited, and they possessed capital which they invested at a high rate of interest. Those of the middle class were mainly smallholders of land, whether in Attica or overseas, or owners of shops, lodging-houses and small businesses in the city or the Peiraeus, or master-craftsmen who owned their own equipment and a few slaves as operatives. Those of the lower class, being called *thetes*, depended mainly on wages earned from the state or from casual labour as harvesters, fishermen, salesmen, seamen and so forth. Thus the citizen society of Athens was based on an advanced form of capitalism, but it was unlike most capitalist societies in having a swollen middle class, larger than the lowest class. As an adjunct to this society the metics increased the size of the wealthier element, for no metic came to Athens as a thete. As they were not

permitted to acquire land in Attica, their capital was invested in commerce and handicrafts, and some of them were high-grade craftsmen
themselves. They numbered about 30,000 persons.

The number of slaves in Athenian society in 431 is not known.
Estimates vary considerably. The present writer puts the total at some
200,000, that is at one slave more or less to each free person, if we allow
some 2,000 foreigners in transit in that year. As slaves were a form of
capital, their number fluctuated with the tide of prosperity in the state.
A few very rich men owned gangs of slaves; for example, Nicias owned
a gang of 1,000 slaves, which he let out on contract. A rich household,
like that of Alcibiades in his hey-day, had twenty or thirty domestic
servants and retainers. But in general they were owned in small numbers
by individuals who put them to work in domestic employment, agriculture and handicrafts. The state too owned slaves who were used as
public servants, clerks, police, messengers and labourers. In short, what
would today be the labouring class in a western European state was
made up almost entirely by slaves at Athens.

In general slaves were humanely treated. They worked alongside free
men and manumission was not infrequent; there was no form of segrega-
tion and no distinction in dress. It is true that almost all slaves were
non-Greek, because Greeks enslaved in war were usually ransomed, but
there seems to have been little racial prejudice. Slaves were accorded
some legal rights and could possess property. But there were some black
spots. Girls were let out as prostitutes; if a slave were involved in a
lawsuit, he was tortured before giving evidence; and in the mining area
of Laurium slaves were kept in pens and lived in manacles, and not
surprisingly the life-span of mining slaves was short. The Athenian democrats prided themselves upon the freedom of life which they allowed
to most slaves, but it was slavery that men feared most and runaway
slaves were common. During the latter part of the Second Peloponnesian
War 20,000 slaves escaped from their masters, and most of them were
skilled workers who could make a living elsewhere in freedom. The
institution of slavery was not questioned in any extant writings of this
period; for those who wrote, being in the free sector of society, gained
prosperity and security by exploiting a form of labour which was safe
and cheap and incapable of becoming organized.

The prosperity of Athens was derived partly from commerce.
Productivity was enhanced at home by the growing number of metics
and slaves who swelled the ranks of the craftsmen and operatives;
moreover, the metics played a considerable part in the carrying trade.
As a writer of oligarchic views – 'The Old Oligarch' – pointed out at

this time, 'The state has need of metics because handicrafts are numerous and we have shipping' (specifically in time of war).[1] While individual Athenians profited from the expansion of commerce as investors and participants, the state took 400 talents a year in revenue from the taxes which it levied on non-citizens and in the form of purchase-tax and tolls. But the chief source of Athenian prosperity was the empire. In 454 the state capitalized itself to an unprecedented extent by seizing the accumulated funds of 'The Allies', a sum of 8,000 talents or so. With this large capital reserve the state was able to expend 2,000 talents on the building of the Propylaea and the Parthenon – money which went into the pockets of the citizens as contractors rather than as labourers. Lavish as her expenditure may have seemed, Athens still had a capital reserve of 7,000 talents when war broke out. In addition Athens exacted some 600 talents a year from her quondam 'allies' in the form of tribute, indemnities and profits from confiscated land. Nor had Athens reached the limit, for within a few years Cleon raised the tribute alone to an estimated total of 1,500 talents a year. Individual Athenians enriched themselves at the expense of their subjects when they became 'cleruchs', that is owners of land acquired overseas, and they were then able to employ native labourers to work their holdings.

The theory of the democracy was that the prosperity of the state should be used to benefit the citizens. Thus state pay became the hallmark of democracy. In peacetime half of the adult male Athenian citizens drew money from the state for services in government and in national security at home, and as inspectors, garrison-troops and naval personnel overseas. In wartime the proportion increased considerably, and Cleophon introduced a further benefit for the needy in the form of a dole of two obols a day. The individual payments were relatively small, but the great spread of benefits in one form or another gave an added dimension to the well-being of the Athenian citizens as compared with their less fortunate neighbours, not least their quondam allies.

When the Athenian Alliance was converted into the Athenian Empire, the basis of Athenian power in the field of foreign policy began to move from the army to the navy. It was the navy which patrolled the seas and imposed imperial control upon the three hundred or so small states which were subject to her rule. The army served mainly in Attica as a home guard; it did not bring the revenue into the treasury of Athens. Since the navy was manned principally by the lower class of citizens and the cavalry and hoplite infantry were recruited from the upper and middle classes, the economic structure of society began to change to the advantage of the lower class and the lower middle class. When the Second Peloponnesian war broke out, Pericles advised Athens above all to maintain her fleet in readiness, 'for our strength lies in the fleet'. The sociological deduction was made by 'The Old Oligarch': 'Because the common people row the ships and bring power to the state . . . rather than the hoplites, the high-born and the gentlemen, it is right that the poorer element among the citizens should have more say than the well-to-do.'[2] When the inner logic of the situation was realized, it was natural that the democracy introduced by Ephialtes and Pericles became an extreme democracy in the course of the Second Peloponnesian War, and that the politicians who came to the top were sometimes members of the common people, such as Cleon and Cleophon.

The economic and social structure of the Athenian state was not affected radically by the first part of the Second Peloponnesian War down to 413, although there was a very considerable decline in overall prosperity as a result of the plague, the expenses of war and the ravaging of Attica. The basis remained secure: the Athenian Empire and the domination of the Aegean Sea by the Athenian fleet. In 413, when the Athenian expeditionary force was totally destroyed in Sicily, men expected that the empire would rise in revolt and naval control would be lost by Athens. The oligarchic movement took power prematurely. If men's expectations had been realized, the survival of Athens would indeed have depended on the army's ability to defend the city and upon a much less extravagant form of public expenditure than that in which the democracy had been indulging. With these aims in view the oligarchs limited the franchise to the members of the upper and middle classes, which had in fact shrunk to 9,000 adult males as compared with some 26,000 in 431, and they set up a form of government which practised financial austerity. But their expectations were belied. The fleet revived; the sailors set up a democracy; and most of the empire was kept in subjection. The future of Athens still lay at sea, and democracy in the unified state of 410 became an extreme democracy.

In the last phase of the war from 410 to 404 Athens was impoverished because Attica was permanently occupied by the enemy. Maritime commerce was open to attack and her sea power was under challenge. She had used up all her capital reserves, and the sources of imperial revenue were drying up. Life for the citizens was very different. The general affluence of the Periclean Age was replaced by increasing pauperization. The index of private wealth is apparent in the decline of the upper and middle classes from 26,000 men in 431 to 9,000 in 410 and 3,000 in 404. But the pinch was greatest in the common people, where despite the overall decline in population the numbers rose from 16,000 in 431 to perhaps 27,000 in 404.

The beliefs of Athenian society underwent a revolutionary change in the course of the war. At the start the ties of traditional religion were strong. The majority of Athenian families had their ancestral homes in the countryside, where they worshipped their gods in family shrines and buried their dead in family cemeteries. To have roots in the countryside and in the past is a stabilizing factor in any society, ancient or modern, and Thucydides remarked that the Athenians in particular regarded their country home as the centre of their life. In 431 the countryside was evacuated, and the houses and shrines were destroyed. Children were brought up in the overcrowded city alongside metics, slaves and foreigners, and the young men enjoyed the freedom of speech, thought and morals which went with city life and city politics. In terms of religious beliefs and traditional morality a gap developed between the generations of those who had grown up in the countryside and those who had grown up in the city. By the end of the war no one under forty years of age remembered much of pre-war Athens and Attica.

If the effects of evacuation from the countryside were gradual, the plague of the years 430 to 428 had an immediate impact upon men's beliefs. This is apparent from Thucydides' brilliant description.

The terrible suffering was aggravated by the evacuation of the countryside and it hit the evacuees hardest. For as they had no houses but were living in stifling hovels at the height of summer, mortality among them knew no restraint. Dying men lay on top of one another, and half-dead creatures reeled about the streets and crowded round the fountains in their longing for water. Some had camped in the sacred places; these became full of corpses, as people died upon the spot. Caught in the relentless grip of the plague no one knew what was to become of him, and men lost any respect for religious and social sanctions alike. . . . To persist in what was regarded traditionally as honourable conduct appealed to nobody, when survival to see the consequences was so uncertain. Instead, whatever proved pleasurable or brought advantage, whatever its source, was accepted as honourable and useful. No limitation was imposed by fear of the gods or man-made law.[3]

In a city which lacked hospitals, medical resources and such amenities as water in the houses it is difficult for us to imagine the horrors endured by the sick and the dying. Yet what was of more significance for the future was the effect of this unparalleled and incurable plague on the survivors. Faith in divine justice seemed to be incompatible with the incidence of death; indeed those who went to the help of others through love or loyalty or goodness of heart only died the sooner themselves. Normal habits were abandoned. As demoralization spread, a wave of lawlessness swept over the community. Life seemed to be characterized only by self-interest, chance and instability. The family system was greatly weakened as property changed hands with bewildering rapidity and long-established traditions of conduct were cast aside. The plague and the evacuation of Attica upset the economic structure of society. Land-values and rents in the city shot up, while real estate in the countryside slumped. Family land became alienable, and country people who had lost their holdings had to look for occupations in the city. For all these problems the democracy had no policy. *Laisser-faire* was the order of the day in social and economic matters alike.

A society in such a state of flux was open to the new thinking which had come from Ionia. Hitherto its influence had been canalized by Pericles (see p. 132, above). With his death the link between the Sophists and the state was broken, and the new thinking became an uncontrolled solvent of traditional beliefs, including belief in patriotic duty, particularly in the younger generation. Here too the policy of the democracy was one of *laisser-faire*; for Athens had no state education, no censorship and no concept of 'non-Athenian activities'.

In 427 two Greeks from Leontini in Sicily, Tisias and Gorgias, came to Athens. They amazed the Athenians with their eloquence. They claimed that the art of persuasion could be learnt by the study and the practice of rhetorical techniques, and their own speeches seemed to justify the claim. Pupils flocked to them. The training involved semantics, logic, composition, rhythm and so on. Their ideas had a revolutionary effect upon the composition of speeches and on narrative prose, as we see from the works of Thucydides and Isocrates, but they had a more immediate effect on the practical side of life in the fields of politics and law. If one wished to influence others on the democratic Council of Five Hundred or in the Assembly one had to speak so persuasively that people would be convinced even against their wills. In the past a statesman like Pericles, 'most capable in speech and in action', as Thucydides called him, had acquired this art first as a young man because he had grown up in a family conversant with statesmanship, and then he had developed it himself during his long experience of public life. But now it did not matter what one's family origins were; all one had to do was pay a fee and attend the lectures of the itinerant Sophists. Almost overnight political leadership was democratized. Men of non-aristocratic families, such as Cleon and Cleophon, came to the top and challenged successfully those who had been born in the houses of great statesmen.

The Athenian legal system also gave great importance to the art of persuasion. Although the juries were by our standards enormous, consisting of several hundreds in major cases, the jurors had had no legal training and were keen judges of rhetoric. As the prosecutor and the defendant had to speak in person, much depended upon the individual's power of delivery and force of argument. The provision of briefs was already a trade, undertaken by speech-writers when Tisias and Gorgias imported their new techniques into the law-courts. The influence of their style is apparent in some specimen speeches, written for the training of clients by Antiphon. He himself was a politician, who led the oligarchs in 411 and was subsequently put on trial. His speech in his own defence was brilliant; but feeling ran high against the oligarchs and he was executed.

In the conditions which developed with the evacuation of Attica, the incidence of the plague and the impetus to the new thinking which was given by Tisias and Gorgias, it was inevitable that a gap developed between the old and the young. Thus the Sophists in general seemed to the old to be threatening their conventional standards, but they were to the young an elixir which opened their eyes to new vistas of thought and action. For when the Sophists gave their lectures they had no responsibility towards an institution (such as a university in modern times) or towards society (most of them being non-Athenian anyhow). They simply expounded their advanced views, like Hyde Park orators, in order to obtain a following, and their young Athenian hearers, quick-witted as they were but without educational training, were easily converted to the latest novelty.

The chief outcome of the Sophists' teaching was a growing individualism, as each pupil was invited to think for himself and set up his own standards. Thus Thrasymachus, for instance, taught that true Justice was the interest of the stronger and that city-state laws were designed to protect their promoters who were in a democracy the masses and in an oligarchy the minority. For him there was no absolute Justice and there were no inviolable laws, whether written or unwritten. Callicles went one step further, for he claimed that might was right. The political relevance of such concepts becomes apparent in the treatment of Melos by Athens. Since the days of Xenophanes the anthropomorphic nature of orthodox Greek religion had been an easy target for the individualistic rational thinker. Now men made gods of ideas, especially social ideas, such as wealth and power. Critias, one of the Four Hundred oligarchs in 411, maintained that religion had been invented by some astute person who saw that he could line his own pocket if others duly practised moderation in all things. Self-seeking began to predominate over the claims of one's country or one's political associates. Alcibiades and Critias were examples of the new intellectual Athenian, willing to serve any master and espouse any political party, if it meant personal advancement and power.

The weakening of traditional obligations and the revolution in the economy which arose from the war were among the factors which led to the outbreak of *stasis*, civil war, in 411 and 410 at Athens. This in itself was a sign of the growing disintegration of society. We have already described the onset of stasis in the archaic period when the aristocratic form of state was collapsing. Thereafter it had been rare, because the Greek states were expanding and the defeat of Persia and Carthage brought prosperity. But the Second Peloponnesian War brought the age of stability to an end and caused a recrudescence of stasis on a large scale, indicating the collapse of the orderly city-state. Thucydides took the stasis which broke out at Corcyra in 427 as his model, and he wrote a brilliant analysis and account of the civil war there which is just as relevant today.

The cause of all these evils was the lust for personal power, arising from greed and ambition, and this lust made the contestants passionately desirous of victory. The leaders used the most plausible slogans – 'equal terms for the masses' and 'fair play under the meritocracy' – but what they wanted for themselves were the prizes of office as leaders of the cause they were championing. In the struggle to overcome one another men went to any lengths in reckless daring and in cruel reprisals, being restrained by no consideration of moral right or public interest but simply glutting their appetite as partisans. . . . Meanwhile, the moderate elements in society were annihilated either because they failed to take sides in the fight or because the envy they aroused was their undoing.[4]

In the intensity of the struggle words lost their meaning and took on the colours of the revolutionary life. It became more important to wreak revenge on one's enemy than to save oneself. One gained the trust of one's comrades by sharing in their atrocities, and one won their regard by devising a more outrageous form of vengeance. As Thucydides remarked, 'Such suffering and atrocities will always occur in civil war, as long as human nature remains the same; they will vary in degree and in the forms they take in accordance with the attendant circumstances at the time.'[5]

The upheavals which took place in Athenian society in the course of the Second Peloponnesian War reached a climax at the time of the civil war. The state disintegrated into three sections, each practising its own political ideology. The lines of division corresponded generally with the economic pattern which had evolved during the war: a group of well-to-do extremists, a relatively small upper middle class (the Nine Thousand in practice), and a very large lower class. There were other cross-currents. One was due to the generation gap between old and young, which affected the foreign policy of the state as well as many aspects of social life. Another was a conflict between the sexes which arose in part from the new thinking and the weakening of family ties. In the past citizen life had been man-centred. The father arranged the marriage of a daughter to suit the convenience of the family. Chastity was demanded of a girl, and fidelity of a married woman; the position of a woman in a citizen family before and after marriage was more or less that of a family chattel. The virtues which were admired in them was loyalty to the family and skill in household management.

On the other hand, the men had a social life outside the family in their daily occupations and in politics at various levels. They allowed themselves a sexual licence which they refused to their womenfolk. Pericles, for instance, had as his mistress a famous woman of non-Athenian origin; he lived openly with her, and she was renowned for her advanced views. The city brothels were full of foreign women who came to Athens in pursuit of higher pay, and they were in great demand at men's drinking parties. Many vase-painters made portraits of famous harlots in the nude, and scenes of love between men and women and between men and boys were painted on fine vases which had wide circulation. It was a permissive society for everyone except the women in citizen families.

Free thinkers, whether men or women, called into question the position of women in citizen families in the latter part of the war. No doubt the women themselves saw the absurdities of the men's policies which led only to war and commotion and loss of life. As they had no vote and no right to speak in an assembly, their discontent must have been voiced in gatherings of married women and to their menfolk. Even in the courts of law they were not allowed to speak for themselves. The male next-of-kin acted for them. It is only from the writings of Athenian poets that we have some insight into the antipathy between the sexes.

Many of the strains and stresses in Athenian society provided material for the most versatile and in many ways the most provocative of the tragedians, Euripides, an Athenian with property in Attica (c. 484–c. 406). Although he was only some ten years younger than Sophocles and died before Sophocles, his outlook was totally different. Indeed these two great poets may be taken as representatives of the split personality of wartime Athens: the one conventional, pious, representing persons 'as they should be' in their grasp of principle and sense of responsibility, and the other unconventional, agnostic if not atheistic, representing persons 'as they are' in self-centred despair, unrestrained passion and individualistic self-seeking. Contemporary audiences rated Sophocles far above Euripides, the former winning twenty-four victories and the latter only five. But posterity reversed this judgement; for Euripides was the favourite poet of the fourth century, and his influence on playwrights of tragedy and comedy was paramount in the Hellenistic period. It is for this reason that so many of his plays – eighteen or nineteen – have survived. Here it seems best to take one play as an example of the way in which he portrayed the social conditions of his day.

In the *Hecuba*, produced c. 424, when the full impact of the war was being felt at Athens, Euripides took a traditional story about the Queen of Troy and translated it into a drama of realistic, contemporary life and beliefs. A 'Ghost' opens the play. It announces itself as the ghost of Hecuba's youngest son, Polydorus, whose death is unknown to Hecuba; for he has been murdered in Thrace by his wartime guardian, the king Polymestor, who threw the corpse into the sea. Polymestor's motive was that he coveted the gold which had been deposited in trust together with Polydorus, and he also hoped to ingratiate himself with the victorious Greeks by killing the Trojan prince. The Ghost tells us that the gods of the underworld have granted it a favour: the corpse is to be washed up and come into the arms of Hecuba on this very day, when one of Polydorus' sisters, Polyxena, will be a sacrificial victim because the ghost of the Greek warrior, Achilles, is holding up the departure of the Greek fleet with adverse winds and demands the blood of Polyxena. The coincidence of these two events on one day is due to Fate. Some god is engaged in coverting past prosperity into present misery for Hecuba.

In this prologue the divine setting has shifted from the intelligible, if harsh, Olympian deities of Sophocles' plays to the vague purposes of Fate and the sinister power of the dead. It is a shift from religious faith to superstitious fear. The ghosts are concerned only with their own needs, to obtain burial in one case and recognition in the other; it is no matter to them that they inflict misery and suffering on Hecuba and Polyxena. The backcloth to the ghosts is Fate and a faceless deity which operates like the swing of a pendulum between prosperity and misery.

The Ghost of Polydorus has been troubling Hecuba for three nights and now, at dawn, announces her approach from the tent of Agamemnon; for as a prisoner-of-war she is his slave. As the Ghost disappears, Hecuba shuffles in, leaning on a twisted stick and supported by her companions, some of the enslaved Trojan women, who are to form the Chorus in the play. White-haired, dirty, doddery and in rags, she is a pitiable figure; moreover, she is distraught by her fears for Polydorus and Polyxena, fears which have been implanted by the nightmares of the Ghost's contriving. The Chorus then tell her that the fears for Polyxena are justified: the Assembly of the Greeks has decided to sacrifice Polyxena to the ghost of Achilles which, rising in golden array from his tomb, has demanded her blood. It is true that the decision was for long in doubt, but it was the Athenian orators and that honey-tongued demagogue, Odysseus, who persuaded the masses to opt for human sacrifice.

In her despair, Hecuba sends for Polyxena and tells her that she will be slaughtered at the grave of Achilles. Odysseus and some soldiers now enter, intending to take Polyxena away. When Hecuba appeals against such barbarous treatment of a defenceless woman, Odysseus answers with the cold, calculating logic of political necessity. When she asks to die in place of Polyxena or together with her, Odysseus quotes the words of Achilles' ghost. Polyxena herself refuses to plead for mercy. Life offers nothing to her as a slave except rape and drudgery. When her mother breaks down, Polyxena asks to be taken away, her head covered with her cloak, lest she too should weep in sympathy. Hecuba is left swooning and prostrate on the ground.

After a choral song a herald announces the death of Polyxena. The whole army of the Greeks was present when she bared her throat to the sword of the executioner, and all men admired her courage. He summons Hecuba now to prepare the corpse for burial. While Hecuba is getting ready to go, a slave girl enters, carrying in her arms a wrapped-up corpse. Hecuba supposes it to be the body of Polyxena. The slave girl tears off the wrappings and exclaims grimly: 'Look and see if this will be for you an unexpected surprise.' The corpse is Polydorus, mutilated by sword-cuts and rotted by the seawater. Hecuba realizes that the nightmare is fulfilled. Polydorus has been murdered by Polymestor.

Up to this point events have corresponded with the prophetic utterances of the Ghost in the prologue. What follows is presented without the overdrive of Fate. Humans now take the initiative. Hecuba plans revenge on Polymestor, and tries to obtain the help of Agamemnon both as her master and as the owner of another of her daughters, Cassandra, his concubine. When Agamemnon turns a deaf ear to her appeals for justice, Hecuba realizes that what one needs in life is not a just cause but the art of persuasion. Accordingly she deploys every argument which may help, invoking Cassandra's caresses of Agamemnon in bed. But in vain. Agamemnon is afraid that, if he helps her, he will be criticized by the army. But he will turn a blind eye to what Hecuba is planning (for he regards all women as unpractical anyhow), and he will let her send the slave girl to bring Polymestor and his sons to the camp.

When they arrive, Polymestor does not know that Hecuba knows that he has murdered Polydorus and stolen the gold. We watch him telling lies in a brazen manner and then being drawn into the tent by the lure of more gold. Shrieks ring out, as his eyes are pierced by the women's brooch-pins and his sons are murdered by Hecuba and her helpers. Then she comes out, exultant, taunting Polymestor, as Regan taunts Gloucester in *King Lear*, and the corpses of the young boys are brought into full view. Last comes Polymestor on hands and knees, eyeless and bleeding, and he tries to catch his tormentors in a ghastly game of blind man's buff. The Chorus pity him. Hecuba crows over him, triumphant in the totality of her revenge. Agamemnon is brought in by the noise and adjudicates between Hecuba and Polymestor. He treats them as racially inferior, lectures Polymestor on the duty of a guest friend, and pronounces in favour of Hecuba's action. Now Polymestor wants revenge, so he tells Hecuba she will be turned into a bitch and Agamemnon he will be murdered by his wife. Then he is dragged away by the guards. Agamemnon issues his last orders. Polymestor is to be put on a desert island to die a lingering death. Hecuba is to bury her dead. The winds having changed, the Greeks are to set sail for home. The day's doings are done. The complacency of the Greeks is unruffled.

In this play the harsh necessity of circumstances dominates the persons. For 'war, a violent teacher,' as Thucydides said, 'brings the passions of most men to the level of contemporary conditions.'[6] So Hecuba is reduced to a blood-thirsty monster who rates revenge on others above her own survival. The leaders of the Greeks have degenerated also; indeed they are leaders only in name, as Hecuba points out: 'No mortal man is free; rather he is a slave to wealth or circumstance, or he is prevented from following his inclinations by the opinion of the masses in society or by the word of the law.'[7]

Those who hold positions of authority in time of war – Odysseus, Agamemnon and Polymestor – are cynical and callous in their treatment of those who are at their mercy. Desire for power and money has driven out all finer feelings, and self-justification is a matter not of principle but of oratorical skill. The theme of suffering is expounded by the Chorus which consists of enslaved prisoners-of-war. In their odes they sing of the miseries which the warring Greeks have let loose upon the world, miseries past, present and future. This play and several others by Euripides expressed the tragedy of war in terms of suffering and degradation. There is no doubt that they were plays of protest which formed a satirical comment on the policies of Athens and other states.

In other plays which had a less immediate application to contemporary politics, Euripides excelled in the portrayal of human passions, especially of women in love and women in hate such as Medea, Phaedra and Electra. Intelligence and principle played a much smaller part than emotion in the motivation of the characters, and the disastrous results of uninhibited passion were rarely relieved by any nobility in the sufferer. The tragic *dénouement* is sometimes all the more pitiful because it is so pointless, being the product of illogical passions. His contemporaries regarded Euripides as a realist, introducing into his plays the affairs of everyday life with which men and women were living at the time. Thus he imported new elements into the form of Tragedy as it had been developed by Aeschylus and Sophocles: humour, cynicism, satire, sensationalism, soliloquy, philosophizing, parody, mistaken identity, thrilling intrigue, romantic interest, and vivid description without dramatic purpose. Similarly, his characters were much more varied and came from a wider range in the social spectrum. Innocence and faith were found only in the inexperienced young, and wisdom born of experience was shown in ineffective old men and women such as Iocasta and Oedipus in the *Phoenissae*. Plays of this kind are closer to Anouilh's *Antigone* than to Sophocles' *Antigone*. Yet he could also write fanciful and romantic plays, such as *Iphigeneia in Tauris*, and a remarkable play in the classical mould, *Bacchae*, at the end of his life. Thus, he portrayed many facets of a society which was artistic, sensitive, intelligent and questioning.

The most famous questioner in wartime Athens was an Athenian of middle-class standing, Socrates (469–399). He was a man of action as well as a philosophical thinker. Thus he served his country loyally and bravely in war and in politics, and he stood firm in support of the proper legal procedure at the trial of the generals (see p. 156, above). When Pericles was at the height of his power in the 440's, Socrates was fascinated by the new thinking of the physicists and by their speculations on the nature of the material universe. From there he moved into the spheres of epistemology and moral philosophy, and for the rest of his life he sought the criteria and the purpose of existence. His chosen method was to question others and to move through discussion or 'dialogue' to a conclusion. He himself began with a claim which he made in all humility, that he himself knew nothing and was eager to learn from others. Whenever someone tried to teach him what was what, Socrates questioned him with such sustained and penetrating logic that the beliefs he advocated were shown to be devoid of logical foundation. Subsequent discussion led to the conclusion that it was necessary to abandon one's preconceived ideas and build a philosophy of life upon first principles.

What were these first principles to be? In the modern world the answer may seem to be only of academic importance because we associate philosophical principles with abstract speculation or university departments. This was not so in fifth-century Athens. Socrates and his pupils put their ideas into practice. Philosophy for them was a way of life, not just a way of thinking. If there is an analogy today, it is to be found in a religious creed. Thus the significance of Socrates' philosophy, like the significance of Christ's beliefs, was expressed by the way in which he lived. Because he believed material phenomena to be transient, he scorned all material things and lived like a pauper; indeed he scorned life itself and accepted death as an unimportant physical transition. Because he believed that truth and goodness are essential to the health of the mind or soul, which is the core of man's being, he devoted his time to the pursuit of truth and goodness in the workings of his mind and in the acts of his body. There were occasions when logical analysis could not solve his problems and answer his questions. Then he listened to the voice of 'the god', *to daimonion*, and obeyed it; for he acknowledged the existence within himself of something which we might call a religious or spiritual intuition.

As far as we know, Socrates did not leave any writings, nor did he influence men of his own age. On the other hand he talked interminably and he fascinated many younger men. As they portrayed him after his death, he was a uniquely charming and magnetic personality. He was physically robust but ugly; he was married, perhaps twice, but his closest ties of affection seem to have been with young men. He was brilliantly logical, penetrating and witty, and at the same time spiritually confident, serious and idealistic. His complete integrity and his indomitable courage were shown repeatedly in his actions and most splendidly in the manner of his death (see p. 234, below). It was in the nature of the Socratic method and outlook that he did not dictate to others the principles which he followed himself. Some of his pupils did adopt them; most did not, and their principles varied very widely as we see in the case of Alcibiades, Critias, Xenophon and Plato, to name a few of those who had sat at his feet. This was to be expected; for when a young man is cut off from all traditional and preconceived beliefs, he finds his own level. Socrates' influence was a solvent and not a panacea.

When modern democracies are at war, they impose certain restrictions upon freedom of expression. This was not so at Athens. Even in public at the state festival in honour of Dionysus complete freedom of expression was the prerogative of the poet. The writer of comedy could ridicule anyone he pleased, politician, general, priest, private citizen or prostitute. Even if he was taken to court by an individual, the degree of licence he enjoyed was such that he was usually acquitted.

The greatest writer of comedy was the Athenian, Aristophanes (c. 450–c. 385). Coming to maturity with the outbreak of the war, he was more typical of the wartime period than any other writer. He saw and dreaded the growing gap between the older and the younger generation. But above all he feared the degeneration of Athenian policy. In his earliest plays he attacked the imperialistic policy of Athens and those who were in his opinion its advocates. *Babylonians*, produced in 426, showed Athens behaving to her 'allies' as Darius, the Oriental Despot, behaved to his Babylonian subjects; and the Chorus, representing the 'allies', were shown as slaves on a treadmill, one being 'branded with letters', because Athens had branded Samian prisoners c. 440. This performance led to a prosecution, which was unsuccessful.

He attacked Pericles as an instigator of the war, Aspasia as a keeper of prostitutes, and Cleon for every trick of demagogy; and there is no doubt that he longed for peace, as we see from his play, *Eirene*, produced in 421. The Athenian people, represented by the character, Demos (which has a politically democratic connotation), was the butt of much humour. But if Demos was denounced as gullible, cruel, vindictive and changeable, he was always very close to the heart of Aristophanes. What was needed was a grasp of just principles and their application in foreign policy towards the allies and the other Greek states, and inside the city towards the old, the weak, and between citizen and citizen.

The serious purpose of Aristophanes was in accordance with the tradition of Attic Comedy which had developed since its inclusion in the state festival c. 486. At one point in a comedy the Chorus stepped forward out of its dramatic context and delivered some home truths to the assembled people. The ridicule which he poured on Socrates as the representative of the Sophists and on Euripides as a free-thinking dramatist sprang not from any personal dislike of Socrates and Euripides, but from Aristophanes' conviction that what they taught led to a form of individualism which was causing the dissolution of loyalty and unity in Athens. When he preferred Aeschylus to Euripides in *The Frogs*, it was because he believed it to be the function of tragedians 'to teach adults not shameful things but good things', and he made the god of the underworld send Aeschylus back to Athens with the words: 'Go on your way rejoicing, Aeschylus, and save our city with your good principles and educate the fools – and there are many of them. And give this to Cleophon. . . .'[8]

The gaiety and vivacity and variety of Athenian society in wartime are revealed to us most vividly in the plays of Aristophanes. If freedom had its blemishes, its virtues far outshone them. The incomparable greatness of Athens is always in Aristophanes' mind, an idealized Athens perhaps but in the image of the actual democracy. It comes across to us most in the beautiful and imaginative lyrics which the Chorus sang and in the affection of the poet for old Demos. The same love for Athens was a characteristic of Sophocles, even in his last play, *Oedipus Coloneus*, and of Euripides in *Medea*, *Heracleidae* and *Supplices* which were produced in the first part of the war. Although Thucydides was critical of Athens on many occasions he wrote the greatest encomium of her as an example to others and put it on the lips of her greatest statesman, Pericles. His emphasis is on freedom in all its forms and on its products – enterprise, versatility, courage, tolerance, energy and resilience. When disaster followed disaster, the Athenians rallied with superb spirit. When the state split into three parts, it was the good sense of the sailors in the fleet at Samos and of the soldiers at Athens which saved the situation – a good sense which was shown in open debate in free assemblies in both cases. Throughout the war Athens was the centre of Greek culture, creative in poetry and prose, tragedy and comedy, oratory and essay. The democracy voted the funds which led to the building on the Acropolis of the small Ionic temple of Athena Nike, 427 to 424, and the much larger Erechtheum, 421 to 407, famous for the porch of the Caryatid Maidens. These beautiful and graceful buildings were an expression of patriotic devotion to Athena and the cults of Athens' past. No other state in history has responded to the strains of a long war by making so magnificent a contribution to the culture of the world in poetry, prose, philosophy and architecture.

CHAPTER 17

THE EVOLUTION OF THE PELOPONNESIAN STATES AND THEIR ALLIES DURING THE SECOND PELOPONNESIAN WAR

The states which ranged themselves against Athens in 431 were at the height of their prosperity and power. Sparta and the Peloponnesian states had suffered hardly any losses in war since the Battle of Tanagra in 457, and they had kept the peace of 446. Although the operations which preceded the outbreak of war impaired the strength of Corinth as the leading naval state in the Peloponnese, the military power of the Spartan Alliance in 431 was so much superior to that of Athens that the possibility of defeat seemed remote. Sparta and her allies were confident also of their moral superiority. The war was for them a crusade in the cause of liberty, and it became a holy crusade when Apollo, the god of Delphi, declared himself to be on their side.

The opening years of war seemed to confirm their expectations of victory. Their army ravaged the Athenian countryside with impunity and their military predominance was not even challenged. The god himself showed his partisanship as the god of plague; for while he struck the Athenians down he left the Peloponnesians unscathed. The leadership of Sparta was readily accepted by her allies; for it was they who had pushed her into war, at least as far as appearances went, and her conduct of their joint military operations was beyond reproach. Indeed, after the second invasion of Attica the Athenians sued for peace, in 430. Sparta rejected the overture; for her sights were confidently set on total victory. Plans were made to bring the Thracian king Sitalces and the Great King of Persia into alliance, and a seaborne attack was launched against Zacynthus in order to improve communications with the allies in Sicily.

In 429, when the plague was raging at Athens, the Peloponnesian army turned its attention to Plataea, a small state in close alliance with Athens. It had an important strategic position. It was able to enfilade from the west the only main road leading from the Peloponnese to Boeotia which did not pass through Attica. However, Sparta had to solve a religious problem before she could attack Plataea. During the Persian Wars Plataea had fought gallantly in the cause of liberty, and as leader of the Greeks Sparta had declared Plataea inviolate for all time and bound herself by solemn oaths to preserve this inviolacy. Now Sparta and her allies demanded that Plataea should renounce her alliance with Athens and be neutral for the duration of the war. The Plataeans refused. Thereupon as commander-in-chief, the Spartan king Archidamus went through a solemn ritual. He appealed to the gods and heroes of the Plataean land and called them to witness that the Plataeans were at fault in rejecting the request for their neutrality. He then brought his army into action and laid the city under blockade.

Whatever the rights and wrongs of Archidamus' appeal were, worse was to follow. The small garrison held out for two years – a remarkable example of the superiority of Greek defences to Greek siegecraft. When they surrendered they did so on receiving a promise that they would be given a fair trial by the Spartans. When the five judges arrived from Sparta, they thought it fair to put only one question to each of the surviving Plataeans, some two hundred in numbers: 'Have you rendered any service to Sparta and her allies in this War?' When the Plataeans claimed that this was unfair and put their own case, the Thebans were allowed to speak in the role of prosecutors. The judges then summed up by declaring their question to be a fair one, and as each Plataean replied to the question in the negative he was taken away and executed. Twenty-five Athenians who had been with the garrison were also executed. The Plataean women who had cooked for the garrison were enslaved. The inviolable city was handed over to the Thebans, who later razed its buildings to the ground.

In her dealings with Plataea Sparta showed herself cynical and hypocritical. It was an accepted convention at this time that men who surrendered on terms and men captured in war, as the Athenians were in this instance, were not put to death unless they were proved to be war criminals. Sparta disregarded this convention. The appeal to the gods and heroes and the so-called trial were empty gestures which did not conceal the fact that Sparta was governed by considerations of expediency and swayed by the vindictiveness of her ally Thebes. Yet these actions were determined mainly by the Spartan executive officials. It is probable that the Spartan people were left with an uneasy conscience in 427.

Two years later the military confidence of Sparta was shaken to its foundations. In 425 a small Athenian force landed on Spartan territory in Messenia and fortified the rocky promontory of Pylos. The Spartan government thought little of it at first and delayed to act. When they did act, they committed several errors which enabled the Athenians to isolate 420 Lacedaemonian infantry soldiers on the island of Sphacteria. Of these perhaps 200 were Spartiates, a picked force drawn from important families. The possibility of losing these Spartiates threw the government into a panic, and an armistice was concluded while envoys set off to Athens to open negotiations for their recovery. Meanwhile the Peloponnesian fleet of some sixty ships was handed over as a security, returnable at the conclusion of the armistice. At Athens Sparta proposed a separate peace and suggested an alliance, which would enable Athens and Sparta to dictate their joint wishes to the rest of Greece. Such proposals alarmed Sparta's allies indeed, and to no point, because Athens rejected Sparta's overtures and kept the Peloponnesian fleet on the grounds that there had been some technical infringement of the armistice. A few

Map 9 Pylos in 425

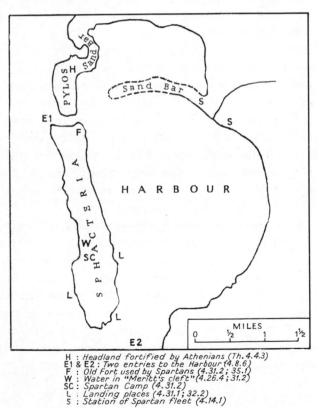

H : Headland fortified by Athenians (Th.4.4.3)
E1 & E2 : Two entries to the Harbour (4.8.6)
F : Old Fort used by Spartans (4.31.2; 35.1)
W : Water in "Meritt's cleft" (4.26.4; 31.2)
SC : Spartan Camp (4.31.2)
L : Landing places (4.31.1; 32.2)
S : Station of Spartan fleet (4.14.1)

weeks later Athenian forces landed on Sphacteria, fought the Lacedaemonians to a standstill and persuaded the survivors to surrender. Among them were 120 Spartiates. In this operation Sparta lost her fleet, her reputation for invincibility in battle and to some extent her nerve; for when Athens threatened to execute her prisoners, if Sparta should invade Attica again, the Spartans abstained from entering Attica. Moreover, Athens used Pylos as a base from which she sent some of the independent Messenians into the countryside as agents to raise the Messenian Perioeci in revolt and encourage the local Helots to run away.

These reverses undermined the confidence of Sparta to a remarkable extent. As Thucydides observed, her strength was derived from her social order (see p. 17, above). As long as this order was secure, the Spartiates formed a highly-trained military élite which was supported economically and in the field by a relatively vast number of Helots. At the beginning of the war this élite may have numbered 4,000 men of military age, while the Helots of the same age numbered some 75,000. The chief task of the 4,000 Spartiates was to maintain the social order, their very presence under arms sufficing to deter the Helots from rising in revolt. The Perioeci provided some 5,000 well-trained infantry who fought alongside the Spartiates in the hoplite line, and a number of Helots were used as light-armed infantry and batmen. These troops, however, were not used to maintain order within Laconia and Messenia. Thus the social order of Sparta may be likened to a steep-sided pyramid with an élite of 4,000 in the top part and 80,000 or more underprivileged adult males in the lower parts of the pyramid. In 425 the pyramid was suddenly shaken: the military élite lost the magic of invincibility, the enemy was established within Spartan territory, and the Perioeci and the Helots might be brought into revolt by enemy agents or enemy action.

Another factor which alarmed Sparta was that her prestige as leader of the Spartan Alliance was now impaired not only by her failure in six years of war to gain any significant advantage over Athens but also by her inability to defend even her own territory. The loss of the Peloponnesian fleet at Pylos exposed her allies in the Peloponnese and also her allies outside the Peloponnese to the full and now unchallenged naval power of Athens. For the first time Sparta and her allies realized that they might conceivably lose the war. Sparta tried to negotiate a peace with Athens at this time, but the Athenian Assembly rejected her approaches.

In 424 Athens captured the island of Cythera off the coast of southeastern Laconia and raided the outlying districts of Spartan territory. Her ships having greater rapidity of movement than any concentration of Spartiate troops, Athens could strike at any one point in greater strength. The Spartan government played into her hands by decentralizing its troops and placing small garrisons at many points, where they could operate only on the defensive. Thus the Spartan war effort became paralysed and from the point of view of their allies totally ineffective. Moreover, the Spartiates had to deal with their internal problems, which were of alarming proportions. On one occasion they wiped out 2,000 leading Helots whom they managed to identify by a treacherous offer of freedom.

The initiative and enterprise which the Spartan government so signally lacked were supplied by a most untypical Spartiate, called Brasidas, who had already distinguished himself as a daring commander. He was chosen, together with a force of 700 Helots, trained as hoplites and liberated for the purpose, to open a new front in Macedonia and Chalcidice, where the Macedonian king, Perdiccas, was anxious to co-operate against Athens and there were some 'allied' cities still in revolt from Athens. For the expedition Brasidas engaged 1,000 Peloponnesian hoplites who were to be paid for their services. While the force was mustering at Corinth, he was informed that a large Athenian army, which was unaware of his presence there, was threatening Megara. Brasidas seized his opportunity at once. With remarkable speed and brilliant organization he managed to save Megara for the Spartan cause, without incurring a single casualty in his own army. With equal skill he passed through Thessaly, although most of the states there were friendly to Athens. Then he opposed the wishes of Perdiccas and persuaded several more states in Chalcidice to revolt from Athens and join Sparta which pledged herself through Brasidas to respect and defend their independence.

In the winter months of 424–3 Brasidas was so successful that Amphipolis, the chief city to the east of Chalcidice, fell into his hands and Athens was faced by a landslide of her 'allies' in Chalcidice. Brasidas asked for reinforcements but in vain. The Spartan government, having at last gained a point of leverage, opened negotiations with Athens and concluded an armistice for one year with the intention on both sides of making a general peace. But in the interval between the ratification of the armistice and the news of it reaching Macedonia another state, Scione, revolted from Athens and was accepted into alliance by Brasidas, who pledged himself and Sparta to its defence. Athens protested. She refused to include Scione under the terms of the armistice, and Cleon persuaded the Assembly to pass a sentence of execution upon the citizens of Scione. Then Mende revolted. It was accepted by Brasidas, who accused the Athenians of some infringement of the armistice. In this matter Brasidas acted rashly and probably improperly. In any event Athens excluded the area of Chalcidice from the armistice and sent a naval force to reduce Mende and Scione.

Brasidas now had to pay the price which Perdiccas demanded for the provisioning of his forces. Brasidas went off inland on a campaign with Perdiccas which resulted in a military fiasco and a rift between himself and Perdiccas. He had put garrisons into Mende and Scione, but during his absence Mende was lost to the Athenians. The Spartan government had meanwhile sent off an army to join Brasidas; but through the machinations of Perdiccas it did not get even as far as Thessaly and only a few Spartans reached Brasidas. Their orders were to review the situation and take control of the states which had come over to Sparta. They found Scione under blockade and could do nothing to help it. When the armistice ended in spring 422, an Athenian force under Cleon's command captured a number of the cities in Chalcidice which had joined Sparta but was decisively defeated at Amphipolis. In this operation both Cleon and Brasidas were killed.

To the peoples of Chalcidice and Amphipolis Brasidas had appeared as a liberator, and he was worshipped after his death as a hero. The Spartan government, however, had viewed him with some suspicion and indeed jealousy; for they were less concerned with the liberation of others than with the recovery of the Spartans who had been captured at Sphacteria. In 421 a treaty of peace was ratified, but Scione and two other towns were left out of the treaty. Moreover, the other states in Chalcidice which had joined Sparta were protected from reprisals only by the letter of the treaty, and they had to pay tribute to Athens. Sparta thus showed little scruple in trading her friends in Chalcidice in order to gain peace for herself.

The allies of Sparta suffered severely during the years 431 to 421. Corinth lost her navy and was defeated on land; of the colonies which were loyal to her Potidaea was destroyed and Ambracia was ruined. Megara was reduced to penury by Athenian raids by land and sea; the state split into factions, and when Brasidas managed to keep it within the Spartan Alliance the oligarchs massacred the leading democrats to the number of a hundred or so. Other allies in the Peloponnese were raided repeatedly by Athenian forces, which landed from their ships at undefended places. They were impoverished by the disruption of trade, especially at sea to varying degrees. Outside the Peloponnese the Boeotians gained possession of Plataea, but they too suffered from Athenian raids. As discontent grew in the Boeotian cities, some democratic leaders began to intrigue with Athens. The result was a pitched battle at Delium on the Boeotian side of the border in which the Boeotian cavalry and infantry defeated the Athenian army decisively.

From the point of view of the allies Sparta failed miserably in these years. The war of liberation on which the Spartan Alliance had engaged in 431 liberated no one except a few Chalcidian states which were left virtually unprotected by the peace of 421. The attempts to save Potidaea and protect Megara from economic blockade had been totally ineffective, and the rule of Athens over her subjects was as strong as ever. More objectionable even than Sparta's inability in the conduct of operations was her attempt to make a separate peace with Athens on several occasions, and her obvious readiness to sacrifice any ally if it suited her interest. When the peace treaty of 421 was brought before the Congress of Allies, a majority of votes was cast in its favour but the minority included the important member-states of Corinth, Megara, Elis and Boeotia. Sparta unwisely went ahead and ratified the treaty. The dissatisfied states rejected the treaty; they thus refused to abide by the decision of the majority which was binding on all members, and they in effect indicated their withdrawal from the Spartan Alliance.

The split in the Spartan Alliance left Sparta in a dangerous situation. For the dissident states formed a strong block which might seek a separate arrangement with Athens or enter into alliance with Argos. In view of this danger Sparta made an alliance with Athens, under which each undertook to defend the other's territory and Athens undertook to help Sparta in the event of a revolt by the Helots. Thus Sparta sold her soul to the devil and abandoned all the principles which she had claimed to be maintaining at the outbreak of the war in 431.

Between 421 and 418 international diplomacy sank to the lowest level of chauvinism. Treaties were made and discarded as if they were temporary expedients, and the most solemn oaths were broken by all contracting parties. The situation was made more complicated by the emergence of Argos as a leader of the democratic states in the Peloponnese, and as an aspirant to supremacy. Meanwhile Sparta tried to set her own affairs in order by enfranchising the Helots who, having fought under Brasidas, had returned home, and by disfranchising the Spartiates who had been captured at Sphacteria and were now released by Athens. The latter were later re-enfranchised. But the moral had been made clear: Spartiates do not surrender with impunity.

In summer 418 Sparta abandoned diplomacy and took up arms. She paraded her own army with the full complement of Spartiates, Perioeci and Helots, and she was supported by the picked troops of her allies, among whom were Corinth, Megara and Boeotia. Never had so fine an army been seen on Greek soil in the experience of Thucydides. The king-in-command, Agis II, out-manoeuvred the army of Argos and her allies (all were present with the exception of Athens). He seemed to have the enemy at his mercy when he suddenly made an armistice on his own initiative without even informing his allies. He may have acted thus in the expectation of a treaty being made between Argos and Sparta, but his hopes were belied. The full Argive army, supported by Mantinea and some other Arcadian cities and by an Athenian force of 1,000 hoplites and 300 cavalry, broke the armistice; captured Orchomenus, an Arcadian city which was in the Spartan group; and prepared to move against Tegea.

Thus Argive bad faith turned the tables on Sparta, which was cut off from her allies in the northern Peloponnese and in central Greece. The Spartans saddled Agis for the future with a group of ten 'advisers' but sent him off now in command of their army in accordance with their law. The oldest and youngest age-groups were recalled to keep internal order; the remainder picked up the Tegean army and some other Arcadians and sought an engagement with the Argive coalition. The incompetence either of Agis or of two of his brigadiers caused the line to split in two, but as at Plataea a tactical blunder by the command was retrieved by the superb discipline and fighting spirit of the Spartan soldiers. They outfought one group of opponents after another, inflicted 1,000 casualties in all and remained masters of the field. The military pre-eminence of the Spartans was now beyond question. No one was prepared to face their serried spears.

The military victory opened the way for a new policy. Could Sparta devise one? In the past Sparta had tried on several occasions to establish an alliance with another leading power, namely Athens. This time she offered alliance to Argos. Moreover the alliance was to be open to all states in the Peloponnese and to the allies of Sparta and Argos outside the Peloponnese. Argos accepted the offer, thus casting off her alliance with Athens and some Arcadian cities. The treaty of alliance was concluded for fifty years and was publicized. The terms included guarantees of territorial integrity and political autonomy for its members, recourse to the law for all disputes within a member state, and international arbitration as a means of settling all disputes between members. The two big states, Sparta and Argos, reserved the right of decision to themselves, if a need for combined action should arise, but they claimed that such a decision would be in the interest of their allies.[1]

In theory the Sparta-Argos alliance was an important innovation in international politics because it provided the basis for a 'general peace' (*koine eirene*) in which an attempt was made to call a halt to revolutionary violence inside member-states and inter-state war between member states. Indeed it was the first of many such attempts to establish a 'general peace'. In practice, however, Sparta and Argos aimed to exclude Athens and her allies from the general peace, and they soon showed that states within the general peace were not secure at all from political intervention. Late in 418 a force of Spartan and Argive troops took the field together and visited Sicyon, where the Spartan element took steps to strengthen the grip of the oligarchs in power. The army then marched into Argos, overthrew the existing democracy and installed an oligarchy. Similar steps were taken by Sparta in the cities of Achaea. It was obvious that 'political autonomy' in this treaty meant the subjection of a state to an oligarchic group of pro-Spartan sympathy.

As the trend in politics at this time was towards democracy rather than oligarchy, Sparta's policy was reactionary and short-sighted. Moreover her unscrupulous manipulation of political terms was condemned by all shades of opinion. In summer 417, when Sparta was celebrating a religious festival, the democrats in Argos seized power and killed or banished the oligarchs. An extraordinary inertia now overcame Sparta. She did nothing to check the democrats in Argos, who were intriguing with Athens, and in 416 the Athenians gained admittance to Argos and took away some 300 oligarchic sympathizers, whom they interned on islands in their empire. This combination of political ineptitude and sheer lethargy in the government caused Sparta's new policy to collapse in ruins. During the ensuing winter she sat inactive while the Athenians attacked her loyal colony Melos and later put the adult Melians to death.

Two things roused Sparta from her inactivity, the departure of the Athenian Expedition to Sicily and the arrival of Alcibiades at Sparta. Although the Ephors and the Gerousia had no intention of sending military aid to Syracuse, Alcibiades addressed the Assembly and persuaded the Spartans to send to Syracuse a Spartan officer, Gylippus, in charge of some Corinthian ships, and to prepare to invade Attica and garrison a fortress at Decelea in Attica. In 414 Gylippus reached Sicily where he played a major part in the ultimate victory of Syracuse, and the Spartans decided to renew the war against Athens because in their opinion Athens had blatantly broken the terms of the peace and alliance of 421. In 413 Sparta and her allies invaded Attica once again, fortified

Decelea as a permanent base for an army of occupation and sent off troops to the help of Syracuse, these being Helots and enfranchised ex-Helots (neodamodeis) to the number of 600. The victory at Syracuse filled Sparta with optimism, and she planned to send ships across the Aegean Sea to instigate revolts in Ionia. But her plans developed slowly and were executed so timorously that it was in fact Alcibiades who prompted and accompanied the first group of ships, only five in number, which reached the Asiatic coast. He and the Spartan commander organized the revolts of Chios and Miletus and made the first alliance between Sparta and Persia in 412.

The keys to ultimate victory – naval bases in the East and Persian aid – were now in the hands of Sparta, but it took her another eight years of frustrating and expensive warfare to defeat Athens. There were several reasons for her slowness. She was reluctant to commit herself fully to 'medism'; yet she could not win without Persian subsidies of money. Her lack of experience in naval warfare cost her many losses, and the building of naval vessels took time. Meanwhile Athens was given many reprieves, and she was quick to recover. The chief reason was the timorousness of the Spartan government and its reluctance to elevate any officer to a position of supreme command overseas for any length of time.

The Spartan government, in the sense of the office-holders who took decisions in executive matters and initiated or even formed policy, consisted normally of two kings elected for life, twenty-eight *Gerontes* or Elders elected for life as councillors, and five Ephors elected annually to represent the citizens. The authority within this government lay with the *Gerousia* or Council, which consisted of the Elders over sixty years old, and the two kings. During most of the Peloponnesian War one king, Pleistoanax, was in disgrace for his withdrawal from Attica in 446, and the other king, Agis II, who reigned c. 427–c. 399, was headstrong and erratic so that he tended to unite the Gerontes against himself. By tradition a king commanded a Spartan army whenever it marched beyond the frontiers of Laconia, and from 445 to 409 this had to be Agis II, who was not judged fully dependable. From 413 to 409 when he was permanently away at Decelea and had the army at his disposal, he tried to make policy on his own authority. However he was outsmarted by Alcibiades who, having seduced his wife, joined the Ephors in advising the opening of a naval front in Ionia and himself accompanied the first naval force. As the government of Sparta found it so difficult to control a king in command abroad, they did not intend to give much licence to any officer they put in charge of a naval force. So the first expedition went off to serve in different zones under three separate unco-ordinated commanders.

The naval command was rationalized in 412 when a *navarch* or supreme commander was sent out, namely Astyochus. He found it difficult to co-ordinate, or even keep in touch with the various flotillas, and he refused to help Chios, which had revolted from Athens. When complaints reached Sparta, the government sent out a Spartan eleven as 'advisers' to Astyochus, whom they had been authorized to replace. The first action of the advisers was to offend the Persian satrap Tissaphernes, who had been supplying money to the fleet of Astyochus. On the other hand Astyochus was an incompetent officer; he was suspected of accepting bribes from Tissaphernes, he drove his troops to the verge of open mutiny, and he raised his baton against some allied seamen. In 411 he was replaced by Mindarus who concentrated all his ships in the Hellespont and was defeated there by a smaller Athenian fleet. Nevertheless the government kept him in command, and in 410 he was defeated and killed off Cyzicus in the sea of Marmara. His adjutant sent the following despatch to Sparta: 'Ships lost, Mindarus dead, men starving. At a loss what to do.'[2] What indeed? Sparta offered to treat for peace with Athens on the basis of the status quo. The offer was rejected on the proposal of Cleophon.

. The next navarch, Lysander, was cautious. He won a minor victory at sea, but his main success was to establish a good understanding with the allied flotillas and a close friendship with Cyrus, the younger son of the Persian king, who had been sent to co-ordinate aid to the Peloponnesians. His good work was all undone by the next navarch who offended Cyrus, sailed off to challenge the Athenian fleet and went down with seventy-five Peloponnesian ships in the defeat at Arginusae. Once more Sparta offered peace on the status quo, except that she would evacuate Decelea. Again she was refused. The allies in Ionia now demanded the return of Lysander, and Cyrus supported their request. But the law was that a man could be navarch only once. With their usual duplicity the Spartan government sent Aracus as navarch and Lysander as his flag officer or 'epistoleus', but with the proviso that the flag-officer should take charge of the fleet.

At last the right man was in the right place at the right time, when Cyrus was supplying plenty of money and the fleet could be raised to a total of 200 ships. In August 405 Lysander annihilated the enemy fleet at Aegospotami (see p. 157, above). Master of the seas, he sent all Athenians and Athenian sympathizers to Athens and blockaded the Peiraeus in November. Meanwhile Pleistoanax had died, and his son,

Pausanias, brought up a second army to join forces with the army of Agis in Attica. They encamped outside the walls of the upper city. Total victory came in April 404.

It often happens that the victors in a long war emerge from the war in a weakened condition. Sparta's leadership of her allies was far less assured than it had been in 431. Indeed Sparta had felt so estranged from her allies and therefore so isolated at various times in the war that she had made alliances with Athens and even with Argos. These were desperate and short-sighted expedients. She had come back to her allies in the last part of the war, when she needed their help at Decelea and in the naval campaigns, but her incompetence in naval matters and the tremendous losses suffered by her allies at sea made her unpopular. Moreover, her commanders often acted without consulting any allied leaders, and Sparta conducted diplomatic negotiations sometimes as if her allies did not exist. Thus the original power system of Sparta was severely shaken by 404.

Sparta herself had suffered considerable losses during the course of the war. In so far as these losses were borne by the Perioeci or freed Helots, they were of no great significance to Sparta. What hit her hard was any loss of Spartiates, because they were needed to keep the Perioeci and the Helots in their place and to act as officers and magistrates abroad. In fact the number of Spartiates of military age was a closely guarded secret, and the casualties of the Spartiates in a battle were not published, as they were for instance in democratic Athens. We can see from the panic at Sparta how vitally important the recovery of the 120 Spartiates captured at Sphacteria was to the Spartan Government. There seems indeed to have been a steady wastage in the ranks of the Spartiates during the years of war, and it is probable that the number of men of military age, that was between eighteen and sixty, sank as low as 3,000 by 404.

Because there was a shortage of Spartiates for foreign service, Sparta recruited freed Helots, later called 'new citizens' (Neodamodeis), in increasing numbers. It is interesting that in the critical Battle of Mantinea in 418 the Neodamodeis served in the line but one-sixth of the Spartiate forces returned home to keep internal order. A group of 600 Neodamodeis was sent out to Sicily to help Syracuse. In service abroad they remained remarkably loyal to Sparta, and they were usually kept abroad because they might have dangerous sympathies with the Helots f they were based at home. In general, however, Sparta excelled in maintaining her military expertise. As Thucydides said, the men at Mantinea were as they had always been – superb soldiers in every way.

The command in the Spartan army stemmed from the king who was named for the campaign, and the chain of command ran down from him through five grades of subordinate officers, exactly as in a modern European army. There was also an order of seniority in each grade so that, if a colonel was killed, the next officer in seniority succeeded him. The whole system seemed to the Athenians undemocratic, but it was efficient in a strictly military sense, as Thucydides remarked in describing the Battle of Mantinea. There were and are corresponding defects which result from such a system in a regular army that normally has little active service. Too many officers remain subordinate and fail to show initiative or gain experience of leadership. The exceptions were as rare as they were notable: for only Brasidas, Gylippus and Lysander could be described as original and inventive commanders.

Behind the army stood the government, of which the twenty-eight Elders formed the core. Themselves the élite of a military system with an average age of perhaps seventy years, they suffered sometimes from an old age of the mind, as Aristotle said, and we may blame them, as well as the whole Spartan form of training, for the dilatory, cautious and conservative methods which marked Spartan policy and strategy during the war. This slowness made Sparta unlike Athens, and in many ways she was a convenient enemy for Athens. But in the end it was Sparta and the Spartan government which proved superior. For the Spartiates were a united group, and the major decisions of the war were taken in the Assembly of the Spartiates, on the whole with good sense. Indeed Sparta made fewer mistakes than Athens. She kept her word alike in success and in adversity, and she had the self-control and self-discipline which enabled her to concentrate first on military supremacy in the Peloponnese and then on the naval war in Ionia.

Among the Allies of Sparta Corinth showed most initiative and independence during the Peace of Nicias, but her attempt to form a rival group of states failed and she returned to the fold of the Spartan Alliance before the Battle of Mantinea. When the Athenian expedition threatened her colony Syracuse, the envoys of Corinth pressed the Spartans to go to war again and Corinth played the major part in supplying ships and men for the defence of Syracuse. She was supported, too by her loyal colonies, Ambracia and Leucas. It was her skill at sea which enabled the Peloponnesian convoys to reach Sicily and dispel the illusion of Athenian invincibility at sea. When the centre of operations shifted to Ionia, the Corinthians and the Syracusans provided the largest flotillas in the Peloponnesian fleet and suffered correspondingly heavier losses in the defeats at sea, for which they must have blamed the Spartan command and the Spartan government. During the last years of the war slaves were used as rowers in the Corinthian fleet and general financial exhaustion must have impaired the resources of the state. By 404 Corinth was much less strong than she had been in 431, and her oligarchic government which had stayed in control throughout the war was now critical of Sparta.

Megara suffered more than any other ally of Sparta; for she was exposed continually to raids from her neighbour Athens, and in the closing years of the war her army had to be reinforced with Spartan troops. Split by faction into two warring factions in 424, the state had been saved by Brasidas from falling into the hands of Athens. The oligarchs then gained power with his support, tried the democratic leaders in an open court and had a hundred or so executed on a charge of treason. Megara fought on to the end and sent help to her colony Byzantium when it rose in revolt from Athens. But by 404 she was impoverished and resentful of Spartan leadership.

The ally of Sparta which grew in power during the war was the Boeotian League and in particular its leading state, Thebes. Early in the war Thebes acquired possession of Plataea and leased its fields to Theban settlers. Then the Thebans distinguished themselves at Delium, when the Boeotian army defeated the Athenian army in a pitched battle. The League at this time consisted of eleven cantons, each of which contributed troops to the federal army and provided one federal general or *Boeotarch*. Of the eleven cantons and Boeotarchs two were Theban, and it happened to be the day of command for one of the Theban Boeotarchs, Pagondas, when the Boeotian army mustered near Delium (for the operational command was held by each commander for one day in turn, as in the case of the Athenian generals at Marathon). Pagondas was unable to convince his ten colleagues in committee to adopt his proposal to attack the enemy, but he then addressed the troops as their operational commander and persuaded them to follow him into action. He placed his Theban troops, which were holding the right wing of the line on that day, in the unusual depth of twenty-five men to a file and the other Boeotians in the normal depth of eight men to a file. As the Athenians had their men in the normal depth all along the line and as the numbers of hoplites in the two armies were about equal, the inevitable result ensued when the lines clashed. The Thebans steamrollered the opposition and the other Boeotians were driven back; but Pagondas, having foreseen this development, brought two squadrons of cavalry into action unexpectedly and they defeated the Athenian infantry who were pursuing the Boeotians. Thus the victory was due entirely to Pagondas and his use of the Theban element in the federal army.

The Boeotian victory at Delium raised their army to the level of prestige which was enjoyed by the armies of Sparta and of Argos. When the Peace of Nicias was made, the Boeotian League refused to accept the majority vote in the Congress of Sparta's allies and in effect ceased to be a member of the Spartan Alliance. It continued to be at war with Athens and arranged a truce with her which lasted for ten days at a time. It was an indication of the League's military strength that it could stand on its own in international politics and face Athens unaided. But in the cold war which followed the Boeotian League aligned itself again with Sparta, partly because the governments of its member-states were on an oligarchic basis, and partly because the combination of the Boeotian and the Spartan armies seemed superior to any other combination.

We know from Thucydides the size of the armed forces of some leading states in the course of the war. Thus the Boeotians at Delium mustered 7,000 hoplites, 1,000 cavalry, 500 specialized light infantry and more than 10,000 skirmishers, and they sent a high proportion of these forces into the Peloponnese to help Sparta in 418. The Spartans drew some 5,000 hoplites from the Spartiates and the Perioeci in that year; they made use also of 1,000 or more hoplites who had served under Brasidas, these being Neodamodeis and paid Peloponnesians. They had about 400 cavalry, and a large number of Helots served as skirmishers. The Argives had 6,000 hoplites, of whom 1,000 had been specially trained at public expense in order to emulate the Spartiates, and Athens had a field army of some 6,000 hoplites and 1,000 cavalry at this time. Other states belonged as it were to the second division. For instance Elis supplied 3,000 hoplites and Corinth 2,000 hoplites in 418. It is thus clear that the Boeotian League stood high in the first division of land powers.

On the economic side Boeotia was a rich agricultural area and during the latter part of the war it made use also of northern Attica and its installations. As it possessed harbours on the Corinthian Gulf and on the Euboean Channel it was little affected by the Athenian naval blockade, and it was no doubt able to export surplus cereals to the Peloponnese at favourable prices. It seems likely that the Boeotian states and especially Thebes were considerably stronger in 404 than they had been in 431, and they were certainly more powerful in relation to Athens and Sparta then they had ever been before.

The most serious effect of the Second Peloponnesian War was that internal disintegration of city-state society known as, as previously mentioned, *stasis* or civil war. Sparta seemed to be exempt from the trouble, but there are indications that coined money came into the city in contravention of the law and upset the simple agricultural economy on which the Spartiate system of a basic equality among its citizens had been based for some centuries. One consequence was that the number of Spartiate 'Equals' declined and the number of 'Inferiors' increased. The social system came under criticism from Spartiates who had held responsible posts abroad and from freed Helots who returned with a good war record. Sparta herself was a promotor of stasis in other states; for she was determined to keep one-party oligarchic governments in power in the allied states, and she abetted the oligarchs in executing the democratic leaders. As Athens and on most occasions Argos were supporting the democratic leaders, it became customary for them to support reprisals against the oligarchic leaders. Thus the leading states in Greece fanned the flames of stasis and caused frequent and usually bloody revolutions in the lesser states, where appeal to the authority of the laws was useless and a political alignment to one extreme party or the other was essential. The gap which had developed between oligarch and democrat by 404 was as wide as the gap between fascist and communist in 1945. 'The ideological split vitiated the whole concept of world order.'[3]

Part IV

IMPERIALISM, FEDERATION OR AUTOCRACY:
THE SEARCH FOR A POLITICAL SOLUTION
404–336

CHAPTER 18

SPARTA'S DOMINATION OF THE GREEK STATES, 404-379

A state which wins a great war does not necessarily win the peace. Sparta stood supreme in 404. She was hailed by a contemporary publicist as 'justifiably the leader of Greece because of her innate excellence and military skill; unrivalled in her freedom from invasion, revolution, and defeat, and always conservative in her ways'. But the facts were different. The struggle for victory had upset the system of internal balances upon which Spartan society was based. The Spartiate 'Equals' sank to some 3,000 in 404, and if the male line ended in a family, the estates passed into the hands of the women. The 'Inferiors' rose correspondingly in number, the Perioeci formed a higher proportion of the army than ever, and an alarming number of freed Helots (Neodamodeis) were under arms. The iron curtain which served to insulate Spartan conservatism against outside influences had been lifted when her citizens had served overseas and returned with new ideas and foreign luxuries. Corruption spread through individuals into society as a whole. The Sparta of 404 lacked the inner cohesion and the unity of purpose which had made her strong in 431.

Sparta had gone to war as the champion of liberty, but the war itself was a corroder of liberty. Even within the state Sparta treated Spartiates who had surrendered in battle and Helots who had shown initiative with unusual harshness. The solemn undertaking to respect the liberty of Plataea was violated, and some cities were freed from Athens only to be looted by the army. Finally, the liberty of the Greek states in Asia Minor was traded for Persian aid, and the liberated states in the Aegean found they still had to pay tribute, to Sparta instead of to Athens. As the leader of a free coalition in 431, Sparta had enjoyed the good will of almost all men, but it proved no easy matter to preserve freedom of relations between allies in time of war. Indeed Sparta acted unilaterally on many occasions. For example, in making the Peace of

Nicias and allying herself with Athens, she sacrificed the interests of her oldest allies, Corinth and Megara, in order to secure herself. Consequently in 404 she stood alone. The sympathies of her allies were alienated, and this was the more serious because she owed her victory less to her own fighting power than to the efforts of her allies on land and at sea.

In ideological terms oligarchy overcame democracy in 404. But its victory was rendered insecure by the ebb and flow of revolution, and the current of political change seemed to be setting in favour of extreme democracy not only in Sicily but also in the Peloponnese except at Sparta and Corinth. Where oligarchy was securely entrenched, it was becoming less extreme in its system of government. For instance in the states of Boeotia and in the Boeotian League itself, where four small councils had conducted all the deliberative and executive functions of government, there was now in each case a single council with strong executive powers and the electorate was given some part in the formation of policy. Yet as the war came to a close Sparta made the mistake of introducing into the 'liberated' states an extreme form of oligarchy which was becoming obsolete elsewhere. In the same way at the end of the Second World War forms of 'socialism' and 'communism' which were not acceptable to the recipients were imposed on some states at the time of the liberation.

The transition from war to peace may be seen by a historian as a sudden and decisive event, which marks the close of one period and the beginning of another. But in the actual march of events there is no such pause. The final policies of war continue with a powerful momentum into the opening years of peace. In the Aegean theatre of war Lysander was the director of policy because he drew money from his personal friend Cyrus, the Persian viceroy, and he had full control of the victorious fleet. His policy stemmed from his year of command in 407 when he had made contact with the leaders of oligarchic resistance movements in the subject-states of Athens, and had cultivated the friendship of oligarchic émigrés who joined his fleet. During the two years 405 to 403 he delivered the liberated states into the hands of these friends, and he supported their rule with men and money. Their first task was to carry out the de-democratization of their societies with or without judicial procedures; for instance at Miletus they massacred eight hundred of their fellow-citizens who were denounced as democrats, while Lysander and his fleet were in the harbour. When the purge was complete, Lysander's partisans assumed the government, and were usually supported by a Spartan governor (*harmostes*) and a Peloponnesian garrison. Because many of these governments consisted of only ten executive leaders, they were called 'decarchies', 'ten-men-rules'. Thus a most narrow and ruthless form of oligarchy was imposed upon the liberated states.

The system of oligarchies was inevitably associated with the wishes and the name of Sparta, but it depended in practice on Lysander as the focal point of political intrigue and executive action. His personal influence and power were unprecedented. He was worshipped as a hero or a god by his admirers, and the oligarchs of Samos gave his name to a religious festival. Nor was Lysander averse to cultivating this cult of the individual. After the victory at Aegospotami he placed a statue of himself alongside those of the gods at Delphi and wrote the dedication for 'Lysander, who set the wreath of victory on unsacked Sparta, the citadel of Greece, the country of beautiful dances, his fatherland.'[1] But his pre-eminence was less acceptable at Sparta where the citizens were 'Equals', and the State alone was supreme. In 403 the opposition to Lysander came to a head, and he fell from power. The occasion of his defeat arose from a situation at Athens which we must now describe.

When Athens capitulated and the oligarchic émigrés returned, in early summer 404, Lysander supervised the installation of a provisional government of thirty men, known to their victims as the 'Thirty Tyrants'. Their outlook is represented by two sayings of their leader Critias: 'the finest constitution is that of Sparta', and 'all changes of constitution involve bloodshed'.[2] While the Thirty were carrying out a purge of the democrats, they obtained from Lysander the services of a Spartan governor and a Spartan garrison in order to intimidate the mounting opposition. One member of the Thirty stood out against this policy, namely Theramenes, the moderate oligarch, who had negotiated the terms of the capitulation with the Spartan government. He persuaded his colleagues at least to publish a list of 'Three Thousand' who were to hold the franchise and to be committed to the support of the 'Thirty'. All other citizens were deprived of their weapons and had no right of appeal against the decisions of the Thirty.

In October 404 Critias prosecuted Theramenes in the court of the Council. He prepared the scene by bringing the police commissioners and a gang of armed youths into the Council House, and by posting the Spartan garrison in the forecourt. Theramenes defended himself so forcefully that the councillors showed their approval. Thereupon Critias called his armed youths forward, struck Theramenes' name off the list of the Three Thousand, and condemned him to death in the name of the Thirty. The police commissioners set upon him and dragged him protesting from the altar in the Council House and across the Agora. There he drank the cup of hemlock. As he tossed the dregs to the ground, he made the mocking toast, 'To the fair Critias.'

By the end of 404 the Thirty had killed 1,500 and banished some 5,000 of their fellow-citizens, and they relied confidently upon the continuing support of the Spartan governor, the Spartan garrison, and Lysander. For Sparta evidently intended to use Athens as a satellite which would be ready to provide troops in support of their policy. But the future of Athens was a matter of interest to other states also. For instance, the discontented allies of Sparta saw that they might use Athens for their own purposes, if they could oust the Thirty and introduce a democratic government instead. These states accordingly gave protection to the democratic émigrés, and in January 403 Thebes enabled a group of them, headed by Thrasybulus, to establish a base at Phyle, just inside Attica, from which they defeated a patrol of Athenian and Spartan troops. Success followed success until in May 403 the democrats defeated the joint forces of the Three Thousand and the Spartan garrison. They then occupied the Peiraeus and cut the main supply-lines of the city.

Attica now split into three parts. The Thirty held Eleusis and Salamis; a new group, 'the Ten', who represented the moderate oligarchs, held the city and collaborated with the Spartan garrison; and the democrats held the Peiraeus. The Thirty and the Ten obtained money from Sparta, and the democrats got help from Thebes and other sympathetic states. It was a civil war of rival ideologies which also reflected the divisions within the Spartan Alliance. At first the Spartan Government procrastinated, because some of the governors appointed by Lysander to control other states had been found guilty of treason, and his whole policy was under criticism; but when the democrats laid siege to the city and endangered the Spartan garrison, it was no longer possible to delay. Lysander and his brother were sent in command of an army and a fleet respectively and their instruction was to settle the rebellion at Athens once and for all in favour of the Thirty.

At this critical moment the two kings at Sparta, Agis and Pausanias, made common cause with the newly-elected board of Ephors and decided to oust Lysander. Pausanias entered Attica at the head of a levy of the Spartan Alliance, superseded Lysander as commander-in-chief of the army, inflicted a defeat on the democrats, and then by secret negotiations persuaded the leaders at Athens and those at the Peiraeus to come to terms with Sparta if occasion should offer. He then summoned a special commission of Spartiates to draw up the terms of a final settlement. In 403 Attica was partitioned. The western sector was governed by an extreme oligarchy with the seat of government at Eleusis. The eastern sector was governed by a coalition of moderate oligarchs and moderate democrats; they held Athens and the Peiraeus. Both states were bound by treaty to follow the dictates of Sparta in all matters of foreign policy. The Spartan garrison was withdrawn, and the independent states were left to manage their internal affairs.

When the influence of Lysander was broken by the action of Pausanias, the Spartans had a chance to review their policies abroad and at home in the post-war situation which was now emerging. The decision of first importance was whether or not to withdraw from the Aegean area. In 475 Sparta had withdrawn, but in 403 she stayed as ruler of the 'liberated' states, which were now paying her an annual tribute of 1,000 talents. She modified Lysander's system of control only slightly, by pronouncing herself in favour not of decarchies but of 'ancestral constitutions' by which she meant less extreme forms of oligarchy. It was a difference only of degree; for the Spartan governors (called 'harmosts') and the garrisons stayed in the subject-states to keep her puppet governments in power, which were still one-party minority governments. Her aim was to be the leading sea-power in the Aegean basin, replacing Athens as the head of a maritime empire.

Her relations with Persia posed a fundamental problem in foreign policy. If she honoured her promise and let Persia occupy the coast of Asia Minor, her own empire in the Aegean would become vulnerable to attack; moreover, she would be sacrificing the liberties of the Greek states in Asia not just in treaty but in fact. It was true that as long as Cyrus remained active it was likely that no decision would be required. But it seems that the Spartan government did decide to resist if Persia should at any time advance against the Greek states in Asia Minor. Such a decision was a logical corollary to her continued involvement in the Aegean area.

A major anxiety to Sparta was the discontent of the leading members of the Spartan Alliance. In particular, Thebes, Corinth and Megara gave asylum to the democrats who fled from Athens, and when Pausanias took the levy of the Spartan Alliance into Attica in 403, Thebes and Corinth refused to send contingents. Sparta did not attempt to force these states into line despite the fact that any decision taken by the Congress of Allies in the Spartan Alliance was in theory binding on all members.

Most serious of all was the internal situation within the Spartan state. If Sparta aimed to dominate Greece despite the discontent of so many states, and also to oppose any advance by Persia, she needed able leadership and more manpower than she possessed. Lysander indeed was said to have advocated the abolition of the monarchy so that the ablest men could be elected to the high command, but he was now in disfavour and any such proposal lapsed. Laconia and Messenia had great numbers of able-bodied men, and the qualifications for citizenship could have been altered so as to yield a much larger number of Spartiate troops. But in this vital field Sparta did nothing at all. Conservative to the point of stupidity, the Spartans retained their social system and went forward on the path of imperialism with an effective force of only 3,000 Spartiate soldiers. If the Spartans did review their situation in the autumn of 403, there is no sign in their later actions that they established any order of priorities. Rather they let events dictate the sequence of their moves and the inter-relationships of their policies, and it is remarkable that they managed to surmount their difficulties through sharp executive action rather than by any strategic planning.

In spring 401 Cyrus informed the Spartan authorities that he was about to attack Artaxerxes Mnemon and oust him from the Persian throne, and he asked for Sparta's co-operation. This was given un-officially; the Spartan fleet in the Aegean helped Cyrus to turn the coastal defences of Cilicia and enter Syria. When Cyrus failed, Arta-xerxes ordered his satrap in Asia Minor to take over the Greek cities in accordance with the terms of the treaty between Sparta and Persia. The Greek cities appealed to Sparta as the liberator of Greece to come to their aid, and Sparta and the Spartan Alliance took up the challenge. In 400 the first Peloponnesian army landed in Ionia. It consisted of 1,000 enfranchised Helots, 4,000 infantry from the Spartan Alliance, and 300 Athenian cavalry. During this year and the following years when Sparta was committed in Asia, her enemies in Greece seized their opportunity. In Laconia an Inferior called Cinadon organized a rising in which the Inferiors, the Perioeci, the Helots and the Neodamodeis were to set upon the Equals whom they outnumbered by about twenty to one. However, the plot was betrayed at an early stage, and the Ephors forestalled them, by arresting the conspirators.

A member of the Spartan Alliance in the Peloponnese, Elis, had refused to pay an overdue contribution to the costs of the Peloponnesian War, and was now pursuing a policy towards her neighbours of which Sparta disapproved. In 399 Sparta persuaded the Congress of Allies to declare war on Elis and she did so herself. Corinth and Boeotia refused to send their contingents to the levy, but Sparta went ahead without them. In 398 Elis was forced to accept an alliance with Sparta, under which she surrendered her fleet, demolished two fortresses and gave up some of her recent acquisitions. Meanwhile the partition of Attica came to an end. The moderate group in Athens eliminated the leaders of the oligarchic group at Eleusis by an act of treachery, and then made a merger of the two states into a single democracy. Thus Athens became again a united state in 401 without asking the leave of its conqueror Sparta. In central Greece, where Sparta was alarmed by the independent and truculent attitude of Boeotia, she took steps to confirm her hold on Heraclea in Trachis, where a task force executed 500 citizens as a warning to the others in 399.

The war in Asia was a gamble as far as Sparta was concerned. Its outcome depended not on Sparta's ability to damage the Persian Empire (which was immensely stronger) but upon the extent of Persia's reaction to trouble on this particular frontier. For three years the Greeks ravaged and looted the territories of the Persian satraps, but they were unable to capture or hold any significant cities and the Greeks in Asia became disenchanted with Spartan leadership. Late in 397 it seemed that Persia might accept a settlement which would be regarded as honourable in Greece, whereby the freedom of the Greeks in Asia was to be recognized by Persia and Sparta was to withdraw her armed forces. But during the winter the reaction of Persia proved to be quite different. Artaxerxes put a stop to negotiations and laid down the keels of a large fleet which would be ready for action in 395 or 394. Sparta decided to step up her offensive during the intervening period and entrusted the command of the army to one of the kings, Agesilaus.

The chief adviser of Agesilaus was Lysander, who had helped him to become king in a disputed election, but Agesilaus was a strong character and soon sent Lysander home. Being an excellent marauder, he enriched his troops and himself with loot, but he failed entirely to strike at the growing Persian fleets or to capture Rhodes, the key to entry into the Aegean. In 395, in preparation for the Persian navy's offensive, Artaxerxes sent an agent to Greece who gave subsidies to Sparta's likely enemies on the mainland. He arrived when trouble was brewing between Boeotia and the Spartan Alliance, and the Theban leaders, encouraged by a Persian subsidy, attacked an ally of Sparta in central Greece. Sparta declared war on Boeotia. She sent two armies which mistimed their invasions; one, commanded by Lysander, who fell in battle, was defeated, and the other, commanded by the king Pausanias, did not engage but came home with the corpses of the dead. Pausanias was condemned to death at Sparta but escaped into exile. But the damage was done; Boeotia was joined by Athens, Corinth, Argos and other states. In 394 with one army in Asia and her fleet threatened in the eastern Aegean, Sparta had to fight a decisive battle in the Peloponnese for her survival.

The confederate army of 24,000 hoplites, 1,500 cavalry and many light-armed infantry outnumbered the forces of Sparta and her faithful allies, Mantinea and Tegea, in all arms. But it had an inferior system of command, each ally taking supreme command for one day in turn, whereas the Spartan force was led by an able general, Aristodemus, who out-manoeuvred his opponents and got them on to ground unsuitable for cavalry beside the river called Nemea. When the confederates attacked, the Boeotians had the command and therefore held the right end of the line with their files sixteen men deep, and the Athenians held the left end with the normal depth of files of eight men. Whenever two lines of infantry advanced to attack one another, each soldier tended to incline to his right in order to cover his unshielded side. On this occasion the consequence was that, when the lines engaged, the Spartans who held the right end of their line overlapped the Athenians, enveloped them on the flank and rear, and destroyed many of them. Meanwhile the confederates overwhelmed and pursued the rest of their opponents, but as each confederate contingent came back it was attacked in the flank and defeated by the Spartans. It was a resounding triumph for Sparta. She lost eight men, her allies lost 1,000, and her enemies lost thrice as many. Later in the summer, when Agesilaus brought his army back from Asia, he defeated another confederate army at Coronea in Boeotia. More than twenty years were to ensue before anyone was willing to challenge Sparta in pitched battle again.

Nevertheless Sparta was in a very weak position. The confederate forces held the massive fortifications which blocked the best route through the Isthmus of Corinth and threatened any army which used alternative routes. In effect Sparta was almost confined to the Peloponnese and her commander, Agesilaus, succeeded only in ravaging enemy territory in the Argolid, Corinthia and Acarnania. The Persian fleet, commanded by a Persian satrap and by an Athenian *émigré*, Conon, destroyed the Spartan fleet in a naval battle in 394 and swept the Aegean Sea, driving out the Spartan governors and garrisons and puppet governments and proclaiming the freedom of the island states. On the advice of Conon the fleet ravaged the coasts of Laconia and Messenia, established a base on Cythera, and helped Athens to rearm and in particular to rebuild her Long Walls. Persian gold enabled the confederates to build fleets and to hire mercenary seamen and soldiers. Thus Conon was recreating an Athenian fleet under the Persian flag.

With her usual tenacity Sparta weathered the storm. She kept her western communications open by driving the Corinthian ships from the Gulf of Corinth; she concentrated her attacks by land on Corinth and Argos; and she did not recall the section of her army which Agesilaus had left at the Hellespont. As in the last phase of the Peloponnesian War, so now Persia was the trump card in the game of war and diplomacy. When the new Athenian fleet began to operate in the Aegean and later gave help to Evagoras of Cyprus who was in revolt from Persia, it became clear that Persia might transfer her aid from Athens to some less aggressive state. At the same time the interests of the confederates were diverging as Corinth and Argos grew weaker and Boeotia and Athens, always uneasy neighbours, grew stronger. Without reducing her naval and military efforts, Sparta opened negotiations with Persia late in 392. She proposed peace with Persia on the condition that the Greek states in Asia were ceded to Persia and all other Greek states were given a guarantee of autonomy. The confederates also sent delegates to Persia. They opposed the concept of autonomy, which, if it was applied strictly, would involve the dissolution of the Boeotian League, the surrender by Athens of some recent acquisitions, and the separation of Argos and Corinth which had formed a close union under the stress of war. The negotiations in Persia broke down. In the winter Sparta proposed to the confederates that the Greek states should exclude Persia from Greek affairs and form a general peace among themselves, and that the terms of such a peace should be autonomy for all states except that the Boeotian League should continue in existence and Athens should keep Lemnos, Imbros and Scyros which she had recently acquired. Her proposal was rejected, principally by Athens, which had imperialistic ambitions.

In 387 Sparta reopened negotiations with Persia and obtained a reversal of Persian policy. She was granted alliance and financial aid by Persia for the purpose of finishing the war and imposing terms of peace. The Spartan fleets, fully manned by mercenary seamen on Persian subsidies, took control of the Hellespont and blockaded the Peiraeus. In autumn 387 the Greek states accepted the invitation of Tiribazus, the Persian satrap in Asia Minor, that they should send envoys to his court and learn the terms of the settlement which the Great King of Persia had sent down from his Chancery. Tiribazus read it out: 'King Artaxerxes thinks it right that the states in Asia and Clazomenae and Cyprus among the islands should be his, and that the other Greek states, small and great alike, should be left autonomous, except Lemnos, Imbros and Scyros which should belong to Athens as in earlier times. I shall wage war, together with those who share my aims, by land and by sea, with ships and with money, against any who do not accept this peace settlement.'³ When the terms were reported to the Greek states on the mainland, Thebes proposed to sign on behalf of the Boeotian League and Corinth and Argos proposed to continue their union and sign as a single state. In spring 386 Agesilaus called up the levy of the Spartan Alliance. The threat of action was enough. The Boeotian League dissolved itself, the Argive garrison left Corinth, and all Greek states took the oath of acceptance of the edict of the Persian king, backed by the spears of the Spartan hoplites.

'We cheat boys with dice and men with oaths'⁴ was a saying attributed to Lysander which might have been applied to Sparta's relations with Persia and the Greek states in Asia from 412 to 386. Oath after oath was broken, and no consideration except expediency affected Sparta in her foreign policy whether towards Persia, the 'autonomous' allies of the Spartan Alliance, the 'liberated' states of the Aegean or the Greek states in Asia. Such despicable chauvinism was not peculiar to Sparta. Other states were equally culpable. The confederate states which had accepted Persian aid against Sparta when Sparta was defending the liberties of the Greeks in Asia could not now accuse Sparta of betraying those liberties with any moral justification. Greek interstate politics was entering a phase of complete cynicism.

The most influential statesman at Sparta was Agesilaus. He overshadowed the other king, Agesipolis, and later his successor Cleombrotus, and he dominated the annually-elected Ephors who were the chief executive magistrates. At this period policy seems to have been formed more by executive actions than by decisions of the Assembly, and the actions of Agesilaus were designed to suppress democracy, to weaken Thebes and to maintain the primacy of Sparta. He interpreted the term 'autonomy' in the King's Peace as meaning the restoration of exiled oligarchs and the placing of them in power; for example at Corinth the restored oligarchs banished the democratic leaders. Where the restored oligarchs were ineffective, as at Phlius in the Peloponnese, Agesilaus demanded the surrender of the acropolis and when he was refused he blockaded the city. When it fell as a result of famine, he placed a garrison in the city for six months and empowered the oligarchs to put on trial and execute any citizen of Phlius. After the purge an extreme oligarchic government took control.

Even when Agesilaus was not in command, Sparta acted in a dictatorial manner. Mantinea was ordered to demolish her fortifications. She refused and fell after a long siege; the state was split into four village communities, each becoming an ally of Sparta perforce, and an oligarchic government was set up in each village. In 382 when a Spartan army was passing Thebes, the oligarchic leader offered to betray the acropolis. The commander of the Spartan army, Phoebidas, accepted; he garrisoned the acropolis and arrested the head of the democratic party, whose supporters fled to Athens. Phoebidas was defended by Agesilaus on the grounds that his action had been expedient. The Spartan court fined Phoebidas and kept the garrison on the Acropolis at Thebes. The democratic leader was passed to a court of the Spartan Alliance, which condemned him to death on a charge of Medism – itself now the basis of Spartan policy! The most impolitic of Sparta's acts was to attack the strong Chalcidian League because it had helped Athens and Thebes in the past and might do so again. In the third year of a major campaign by the forces of the Spartan Alliance the strongest city of the League, Olynthus, was starved into surrender. In 379 the League was formally dissolved and each of the individual states was compelled to enter into an offensive and defensive alliance with Sparta and obey her orders in time of war.

During this period of autocratic imperialism Sparta relied not on freed Helots (Neodamodeis) who were dependable far from home, but on foreign mercenaries who had no political scruples, like their modern counterparts. The Congress of Allies in the Spartan Alliance was persuaded to provide money instead of men, and Sparta herself employed mercenaries to serve under Spartan officers, as France did in her Foreign Legion. By this means she conserved her own soldiers who were required at home to hold the Helots down. In 379 she had garrisons of occupation at Thebes, Thespiae, Plataea and Heraclea, and her puppet governments were in control of a large number of her so-called allies. She was supported in the west by Dionysius, tyrant of Syracuse, and in the east by the Great King of Persia. The unprincipled application of expediency as the sole measure of policy seemed to have gained success for Sparta, but in fact she had lost the sympathy of her former allies and she had weakened the sole basis of her authority, the Spartiate army, by continuous attrition in war and by the decline of her own institutions.

CHAPTER 19

THE GROWTH AND SUCCESS OF
FEDERAL MOVEMENTS, 377–371

When great states become imperialistic, small states tend to band together for security. Thus the expansion of Athens in the fifth century and the growth of Macedon led the small states of Chalcidice to found a federal union which developed by 382 into a 'sympolity' with some aspects of 'isopolity'. A *sympolity* is based on a common citizenship. 'Chalcidian' in this case, which is usually additional to the individual citizenship of a member state e.g. of Olynthus. While a sympolity is a necessary feature of a federal union or 'League', the extent of its common citizenship may vary. An *isopolity* is a reciprocal exchange of equal rights, for instance the rights of holding property and marital status. The United States of America is a federal union or sympolity in which isopolity has been carried almost to its fullest limits. On the other hand in ancient Greece a sympolity could exist without any form of isopolity between its member states.

The acknowledged leader of the federal movement in Greece was the Boeotian League in which each member state had Boeotian citizenship and retained its own citizenship also. Early in the fourth century its central organ of government was a Council of 600 delegates elected severally by eleven cantons and holding office for one year. In modern terms the Council embodied the principles of proportional representation by election, as the House of Commons in England does today. In ancient terminology such a system was oligarchical; for democracy meant direct government by the demos. Each member state had its own government, and in each case this was oligarchical in form; at the same time the full franchise was limited to adult males who possessed property above a fixed level. Thus the Boeotian League was a federal union with an oligarchic constitution, and its member-states were oligarchical in constitution and in citizenship. The eleven cantons elected officials to command the federal army (Boeotarchs), preside over the federal Courts of Justice, maintain the federal treasury and so on. There was however no development in the direction of isopolity. Indeed it was always a feature of the Boeotian League that Thebes far outweighed any other member state in importance. Early in the fourth century she held four of the eleven cantons because she included in her electoral area some subject states, such as Plataea, and therefore had four of the eleven Boeotarchs. Being a rich agricultural area which prospered during the Peloponnesian War (see p. 189, above) Boeotia was able to support an army of 11,000 hoplites and 1,100 cavalry which had shown itself superior to the Athenian army at Delium.

Sparta's policy of *divide et impera* had broken up the Boeotian League despite the protests of Thebes, and now in 379 Thebes herself was treacherously occupied by a Spartan garrison. But political cynicism and ruthless oppression in this case proved self-defeating, because it created the will to resist. On a December evening in 379 seven *émigrés* joined a gang of labourers and entered Thebes undetected. During the night they and their fellow-conspirators killed the pro-Spartan oligarchs. At dawn their supporters in the city were in arms, and a group of armed *émigrés* reached Thebes from Attica where they had received asylum. The Spartan commander of the garrison, which numbered 1,500 men, sent a message to Sparta and held his position. But when an Athenian army appeared he obtained a safe-conduct and marched his garrison into the Megarid, where he met a Spartan relief-force under the command of the young King Cleombrotus. The garrison commander was sent on to Sparta where he was executed. Cleombrotus made a parade of strength, reinforced the Spartan garrison at Thespiae, and marched through Theban territory without attacking any Theban force or the Athenian army. This was a well-calculated action, for the Athenian force withdrew and the Athenian Assembly condemned to death the two generals who had been in command of it. The Theban conspirators were now isolated.

At this moment the commander of the Spartan garrison at Thespiae, Sphodrias, marched his men by night into Attica, pillaged some houses between Eleusis and Athens at dawn and withdrew into Boeotia. This extraordinary action in time of peace caused the Athenians to protest to some Spartan envoys who were in Athens on other business, and they gave assurance that Sphodrias would be executed for his irresponsible behaviour. In fact Sphodrias was tried *in absentia* and defended by Agesilaus, who secured his acquittal. Athens thereupon entered into alliance with Thebes and sent an army of 5,000 infantry and 200 cavalry to her assistance. Instead of offering battle, as was customary, in the plain, the joint forces of the two states prepared field defences on a ridge above Thebes, something which had not been done in Greek warfare since the campaign of Marathon, and when Agesilaus invaded Theban territory at the head of an army of 18,000 infantry and 1,500 cavalry the Theban and Athenian forces remained behind their field defences. Agesilaus did not attack, because he was alarmed by the disaffection in his allied contingents and he was unwilling to commit his Spartiates, who on this occasion represented five-sixths of Sparta's entire citizen army, to the hazards of unconventional combat. The same thing happened in 377, and when Agesilaus was ill in 376 Cleombrotus failed to force an entry into Boeotia.

When Agesilaus failed to crush the revolt, Thebes and Athens acted rapidly. In accordance with the anti-Spartan feeling of the day the conspirators introduced democracy into Thebes and proceeded to reconstitute the Boeotian League on a democratic basis. Thus all Thebans, unless engaged in certain menial occupations, possessed the full franchise and voted in the democratic Assembly. When a state was liberated, as Thespiae was on the defeat of the Spartan garrison late in 378, it adopted a democratic constitution and became a member of the incipient Boeotian League in which all fully franchised citizens formed the 'General Assembly of the Boeotians', meeting at Thebes. This Assembly became now the sovereign body in the constitution of the League; for the Council served as its executive committee, and the officials such as the Boeotarchs were answerable to the former. In 374 when the League was almost fully reconstituted, some states which had helped Sparta were made subject to Thebes, the leader of the rising, and the cantonal system was modified so that Thebes henceforth held three of the seven electoral cantons and elected three of the seven Boeotarchs. Influential among them were two heroes of the resistance to Sparta, Pelopidas and Epaminondas.

Meanwhile Thebes' democratic ally, Athens, had taken a lesson from the principles of federalism. In March 377 she published a manifesto with the following invitation: 'Any state, Greek or non-Greek, provided it is not subject to Persia, may become an ally of Athens and her Allies on conditions of freedom and autonomy, preserving its chosen form of constitution, receiving neither garrison nor governor, and paying no tribute.' The contrast was with the practice of Sparta, which had denied the right to freedom and autonomy, had imposed garrisons and constitutions, and had exacted tribute. This was made explicit in the manifesto by the passage 'that Sparta may leave the Greek states in peace, in enjoyment of liberty and autonomy, and in secure possession of their territory.'[1]

What the manifesto offered was an alliance not with Athens but with 'Athens and the Allies', an already existing and hopefully expanding block of powers. As such a block needed a system of administration, its constitution was framed as follows. The Athenian State deliberated separately. The Allies deliberated in a Council, each state having one vote, and the decisions of the Council, being reached on a majority vote, were binding on all members. If the decisions of the Athenian State and of the Council of the Allies were different, the matter lapsed; if they were the same, then 'Athens and the Allies' adopted a particular policy. This policy was put into effect by Athens as the executive authority or *hegemon*; for the Allies entrusted to her the command in war and the conduct of preliminary negotiations in diplomacy. Each body handled its own financial affairs. Athens taxed her citizens, mainly by exacting levies on capital, and the Council of the Allies raised from its members 'contributions' in money or in ships to meet the needs of the moment. A joint court of Athens and the Allies judged anyone who proposed to alter or annul the terms of the constitution, and a court of the Allies alone judged any Athenian citizen who was accused of acquiring property in the territory of an ally. The admission of new members was carefully regulated. Both Athens and the Council had to approve an application which could be either to enter the Alliance and become a member of the Council or to make an alliance with 'Athens and the Allies' and not become a member of that body. The basis of the contract was a defensive alliance, so that any member which was the victim of aggression could invoke the protection of 'Athens and the Allies'. We do not know whether each member undertook to limit its freedom in foreign policy, e.g. in making an external alliance, but such a limitation was desirable in order to limit the possible commitments of 'Athens and the Allies'.

Because no joint citizenship was involved, 'Athens and the Allies', or 'the Athenian Alliance' as we may call it for convenience, was not a federal union, but it possessed some of the features of a federal union: the means of reaching a joint decision, implementing a joint decision, raising ships and money, and trying breaches of contract. Its aim (and its appeal) was to protect its members from oppression and victimization at the hands of Sparta or any other external force. At the same time it placed the Allies in the position of accepting the executive authority of Athens and ultimately perhaps of exposing themselves to exploitation by Athens. Assurances against such exploitation were written into the manifesto, but the only true safeguard lay in the liberal attitude of Athens in 377 towards present and potential members. The statesman who inspired the manifesto and guided Athenian policy for some years was Callistratus, one of the new generation which was not steeped in the tradition of fifth-century imperialist Athens.

The alliance of Thebes and Athens was at first of great mutual benefit. While Sparta was concentrating on Thebes in 378 and 377, Athens was free to build ships, launch her manifesto and enrol members of the Alliance from Euboea to the Propontis, thus controlling the importation of corn from the Black Sea ports to Boeotia and Attica. In 376 and 375 when Sparta was conducting an offensive against Athens, Thebes wiped out the Spartan garrisons in Boeotia except at Orchomenus, and reconstituted the Boeotian League on the new democratic basis. During these operations the Sacred Band of Thebes, a *corps d'élite* of 300 hoplites, commanded by Pelopidas, routed a superior force of two Spartan brigades at Tegyra. As Athens had helped Thebes in Boeotia, so Thebes helped Athens by becoming a member of the Athenian Alliance and making a 'contribution'. In September 376 the Spartan fleet, based on Aegina, was defeated by the Allied fleet, and most of the Cyclades joined the Alliance. In 375 operations were undertaken in the Ionian Sea, a Spartan fleet was defeated, and Corcyra, Cephallenia and Acarnania joined the Alliance. At the beginning of 374 the Athenian Alliance was the leading sea power in the Ionian and Aegean Seas.

The remarkable successes of Thebes and of Athens endangered the alliance between them, because they became less dependent on one another for protection from Sparta. Thebes resented the disproportionate growth of Athens' power through the Athenian Alliance and her own inferior position in that organization, and she knew that any expansion of Boeotian power in central Greece would be regarded with suspicion by Athens. In the spring of 374 Thebes attacked Phocis, traditionally a friend of Athens; she had previously subjugated Plataea, always a protégé of Athens, and she failed to pay her contribution to the Athenian Alliance. Sparta, quick to exploit the division of interest between Thebes and Athens, sent a large army across the Corinthian Gulf into Phocis where it would be able to operate against Thebes alone. At this moment Athens acted unilaterally in seeking and obtaining peace with Sparta on the status quo, under which the Athenian Alliance and the Spartan Alliance were recognized. Thebes was a beneficiary of the peace only in that she was a member of the Athenian Alliance. No provision was made, as far as we know, for recognizing the existence of the Boeotian League, and Sparta may have intended to use her army in Phocis to insist on the dissolution of the League.

It was Athens which prevented the peace from becoming effective.

Most of the states which entered the Athenian Alliance had previously been controlled by pro-Spartan oligarchies. Sometimes an oligarchy stayed in power when the state entered the Athenian Alliance, for instance at Corcyra; in other cases the oligarchy was overthrown from within and a democracy took power. Under the terms of the manifesto Athens had undertaken not to interfere but to leave the choice of constitution entirely to the member-state. When the peace was signed, the fleet of the Athenian Alliance was recalled from western waters, and its commander, Timotheus, sailed past Zacynthus, which was held by a pro-Spartan oligarchy and was a member of the pro-Spartan group if not of the Spartan Alliance. Timotheus had some Zacynthian *émigrés* on board and he landed them on Zacynthus with a view to their seizing power and bringing the island into the Athenian Alliance. When Sparta protested at this attempt to upset the status quo, the Assembly at Athens insisted on supporting the *émigrés*. The peace with Sparta was thereby terminated. At the same time the action of Timotheus augured ill for the members of the Athenian Alliance, because in supporting it Athens was departing in principle from her undertaking in the manifesto.

The breach with Sparta brought Athens and Thebes together again for a time, for Thebes made her 'contribution' to the Alliance and a Theban was elected President of the Council of Allies in 373. But relations deteriorated when Thebes destroyed Plataea and Athens gave citizen rights to the Plataean refugees. In her operations at sea Athens was crippled at first by lack of money. Then in 372 she sent a fleet to defend Corcyra; in the course of operations the commander, Timotheus, placed a garrison and some Athenian officials in Cephallenia to ensure its loyalty, in contravention of Athens' undertaking in the manifesto. As it became clear that Athens could not hope to defeat Sparta, she informed Thebes in 371 that she was about to negotiate peace with Sparta. The Great King, having arranged the terms of the previous treaty of 386, sent envoys to Sparta. Other states joined in. Consequently a general peace conference was held there at which Sparta proposed terms, Athens and Persia supported them, and the other states then accepted them. The terms were general disarmament, withdrawal of garrisons, independence of all Greek states except those in Asia, and Amphipolis and the Chersonese to be Athenian possessions. If any state broke these terms, the others could act against it but were not obliged to do so. The oaths were then taken by Sparta on behalf of the Spartan Alliance, by Athens and her allies separately and individually, Thebes included, and by all other states present. As in 386, Persia was present to guarantee the peace. No doubt the diplomats of Sparta and Athens congratulated one another, for they had set the seal upon their own power-blocks and excluded the power-block led by Thebes even from consideration.

That the exclusion was deliberate became clear on the next day when the leader of the Theban delegation, Epaminondas, asked to substitute 'Boeotians' for 'Thebans' and the leader of the Spartan delegation, Agesilaus, refused.[2] Epaminondas then withdrew Thebes from the treaty and *ipso facto* from the Athenian Alliance. She alone was now the only state at war with the Spartan Alliance, and she might find other powers in league against her.

The terms of the peace were implemented immediately by Sparta and Athens, with the exception of the disarmament clause, because Sparta retained her army in Phocis. When the commander, Cleombrotus, asked for orders, a speaker in the Assembly at Sparta proposed that the army should be disbanded in accordance with the treaty and that thereafter, if the autonomy of any state was infringed, Sparta should invite the co-operation of other states against the offender. This sensible proposal was defeated and Cleombrotus was ordered to attack Thebes. Taking an unusual route along the south coast he entered Boeotia un-opposed and deployed his army of 1,000 cavalry and 10,000 hoplites in the plain of Leuctra. He himself held the right end of the line, where some 2,000 Spartiates were stationed, and the cavalry formed a screen in front of the line, as the Boeotian League had not yet mustered its forces. Epaminondas and six other Beotarchs had only some 600 cavalry and 6,000 hoplites under arms, but Epaminondas persuaded his colleagues to attack. Concentrating his best troops on his left wing and ordering the rest of the line to advance slowly, he took the initiative. First his cavalry drove the screen of enemy cavalry back on to the Spartan end of the enemy line, then the massed spearhead of élite Theban infantry charging at the double struck the Spartans where Cleombrotus and his staff were stationed, and finally the main Theban force led by Epaminondas engaged the shaken line. At the first onset Cleombrotus fell mortally wounded, and the fierce fighting came to an end when half of the Spartans lay dead. The remainder, followed by their allies who had not engaged at all, fled to their camp. As Epaminondas said, if the head is scotched, the body of the snake is useless.

A Theban envoy took the news of victory to her ally Athens and asked for assistance. He received none. Another ally of Thebes, Jason of Pherae, arrived with an army after the battle and arranged for an armistice, during which the survivors of the Spartan army withdrew. At

Aegosthena in the Megarid they met a second army under Archidamus, son of Agesilaus, which had been sent out to retrieve the situation. But appalled at the heavy loss in Spartiates, Archidamus turned back and disbanded the army of the Spartan Alliance at Corinth. The triumph of the Boeotian League was complete. Thebes and federalism had defeated Sparta decisively.

CHAPTER 20

DECLINE AND DICTATORSHIP IN SICILY
413–343

The instability of democracy was shown very clearly at Syracuse in the years 413 to 405. Success against Athens gave Syracusan democracy a unique opportunity to unite Sicily against outside intervention. But, as Thucydides observed, the Syracusans were similar in national character to the Athenians: they were eager for innovation in politics and the acquisition of more power. Hermocrates, who had led them to victory and then had taken a fleet to help Sparta in the Aegean, was away from Syracuse when the extreme wing of the democrats, led by Diocles, came into power. It was characteristic of Hermocrates that he had advocated lenient treatment of the Athenian survivors, and of Diocles that he had proposed the torturing and killing of the Athenian generals and a lingering death for the rest in the quarries on starvation diet. Once in power the extreme democrats drafted a new legal code, raised the number of their annually-elected generals from three to ten, and adopted from Athenian practice the use of the lot in selecting magistrates. They passed a sentence of banishment on Hermocrates and his supporters, who were in command of the fleet but for patriotic reasons did not use their position to contest the issue. Whereas Hermocrates had advocated reconciliation among the Greek states in Sicily, the extreme democracy went to war with the Chalcidian states in Sicily and became involved in reprisals by Selinus on Segesta, which had invited the Athenians into Sicily in 415 and now in its distress called upon Carthage.

In spring 408 Hannibal, grandson of the Hamilcar who had been killed at Himera in 480, assembled in western Sicily an army of about 100,000 men, a siege-train of catapults, battering-rams and movable wooden towers, and a large fleet. When he invested Selinus, the Assembly and the ten generals of Syracuse were very dilatory in sending help. The city was taken and destroyed on the tenth day, and the bulk of the population was massacred. He then laid siege to Himera with an army of more than 60,000 men, now including some of the non-Greeks in Sicily, Sicels and Sicans. Eventually Diocles came up at the head of 4,000 troops drawn from Syracuse and other states, but he soon withdrew, taking some of the non-combatant inhabitants of Himera with him to Syracuse. The Carthaginians captured Himera and razed it to the ground; they killed most of the population and tortured 3,000 prisoners before they executed them. Hannibal returned to Carthage, leaving a mercenary force to hold his gains.

During the winter Hermocrates came to Sicily with a private army. He recruited survivors from Selinus and Himera, and pillaged the Carthaginian territory in Sicily with great daring. He sent to Syracuse the bones of some Syracusans who had been abandoned by Diocles outside Himera, but he himself stopped at the frontier because he was an exile. During this time Syracuse had been inactive. The Assembly now exiled Diocles but did not recall Hermocrates. Some months later Hermocrates tried to force his way into the city. He and most of his men were killed, but among the few who escaped was an officer aged twenty-three called Dionysius who evaded massacre by shamming dead. While the democracy was concerning itself with Diocles and Hermocrates, Carthage was entering into friendly relations with Athens[1] and preparing to conquer the Greek part of Sicily. In 406 a Carthaginian army of 120,000 men laid siege to Acragas. A combined force of Greeks from eastern Sicily and South Italy was mishandled by its Syracusan general and proved completely ineffective. The Carthaginians took Acragas and razed it to the ground. In spring 405 they advanced on Gela. The confusion and the panic of the refugees and the citizens at Syracuse was exploited by Dionysius who, having distinguished himself in action at Acragas, was now playing the part of a demagogue. He got the current generals deposed, then himself and others elected in their place, and finally his own colleagues deposed and himself elected as sole general. It was a classic example of demagogue becoming dictator in an unstable democracy.

Dionysius gave his mercenaries double pay, recruited a bodyguard from refugees who had nothing to lose and owed no particular loyalty to Syracuse, put his own friends into military commands and persuaded the Assembly to execute all the deposed generals. Thus, when the Carthaginian army came to Gela, Dionysius controlled Syracuse. The democracy would certainly have been incapable of saving Gela or itself. Could Dionysius succeed? His first campaign was disastrous. He lost Gela and Camarina, but thanks to his mercenaries he won a civil war in Syracuse and prepared to hold the city. At this juncture, late in 405, plague decimated the Carthaginian army, and Carthage offered terms of peace which Dionysius accepted. The west of Sicily was to be Carthaginian, central Sicily to be without fortifications and to pay tribute to Carthage, and the Sicel communities and the Greek cities which were enemies of Syracuse were to be autonomous. The Carthaginians then took the plague back to Africa. Dionysius made good use of the respite. He suppressed a revolt of the Syracusan people in 404. It was the last, for he thereafter kept the masses disarmed and under observation. His dictatorship was destined to last for thirty-eight years.

Relations with Carthage were a continuing problem. In a series of wars Dionysius almost succeeded in driving the Carthaginians out of Sicily, and the Carthaginians almost drove Dionysius out of Syracuse. When he died in 367, his son made peace and the frontier was fixed at the river Halycus. Both sides were exhausted and Carthage did not return to the attack again until 343. Dionysius certainly saved Sicily from occupation by Carthage. As no one doubted that his rule was more acceptable than massacre and torture under Carthage, the Greeks in Sicily might have been grateful to him, for it was unlikely that democracy would have succeeded. He staved off Carthage by making Syracuse the largest, strongest and best fortified city in the Greek world. During his dictatorship the population rose to half a million, the walls, which were fifteen miles long, proved impregnable for centuries, and his forces in his last campaign against Carthage were 300 warships, 30,000 infantry and 3,000 cavalry – a force far superior to that of Athens or Sparta or Thebes.

He made great advances in Greek warfare, using catapults, rams, moles and towers for sieges, building quinqueremes with five men to a sweep (they needed less expertise than the rowers of a trireme), training specialist mercenary units, combining fleet and army in amphibious operations and using specialist arms in combination. He and his staff of mercenary captains had professional skills which were beyond those of any annually-elected band of generals, and they could afford to be more ruthless than a citizen commander in the use of troops when the need arose. He was able not only to defeat the armies of Carthage which consisted of the best mercenary and native troops in the western Mediterranean, but also to overcome the forces of the Greek states in south Italy.

To pay for his army of mercenaries, his fleet, his armoury and his public works Dionysius needed vast sums of money. He obtained these initially by confiscating private capital, by selling prisoners or entire populations into slavery, by looting temples or exacting ransoms. But he was also concerned to promote the prosperity of Greek Sicily and particularly of Syracuse. When he ruled two-thirds of Sicily and the toe of Italy and had planted colonies and trading-stations in the Adriatic Sea, Syracuse became the centre of a trade with Carthage, Italy and Greece which flowed through the Straits of Messina and the Straits of Otranto. Her coinage was the strongest currency in the West, and she reached an unprecedented level of prosperity.

A man of brilliant ability, indomitable courage and remarkable resilience, ruthless, vindictive and cruel, he and his mercenary bodyguard lived inside Syracuse in a castle on Ortygia, itself a peninsular fortress, where he hoarded his armaments and kept a special fleet in a locked harbour. In times of peace he and the male members of his family were heads of state with whom foreign powers negotiated. The normal magistrates of a democracy were in existence and their names were included in formal treaties, but only as the executors of his wishes. In time of war he was commander-in-chief with unrestricted powers (*strategos autokrator*). He hired mercenary soldiers and sailors, paid them generously, and settled veteran mercenaries on lands confiscated from Greek cities. The mercenaries looked to him as their leader, as legionaries looked later to Augustus. On occasions he liberated slaves and armed them to serve in his army and his fleet. As far as we know, the mercenaries and the freed slaves were always faithful to him.

Dictators usually favour a particular class or some vested interest, or fan a racial prejudice in order to gain support within the existing state. But Dionysius was different. He destroyed oligarchs and democrats alike and confiscated property and persons to suit his purposes. At first he helped the poorest class and enfranchised the slaves he had liberated, but these 'new citizens', as his opponents called them, remained a powerless element in society. The truth is that Dionysius destroyed the state as men had known it. The social order of the Syracusans was now torn to shreds, and the citizen population was enormously enlarged and adulterated by the addition of refugee populations from cities destroyed by Carthage or by himself, both in Sicily and south Italy. Syracuse thus became a cosmopolitan conurbation, confined within its great walls of fortification. Nor did this happen at Syracuse alone; for Dionysius planted new cities of mixed populations, poured populations of one city into another city and added veteran mercenaries whom he had enfranchised – these last often being of Iberian or Campanian origin. In as far as a state existed, it consisted of Dionysius and his mercenaries alone.

The achievement of this one man in a position of supreme power amazed his contemporaries. The individual seemed more capable than the polis. This had been no doubt potentially true of Alcibiades and Lysander but it was demonstrably true with Dionysius. His alliance was sought on all sides. He and Sparta gave one another mutual help; Athens made him an Athenian citizen and awarded him the first prize for his tragedies at the Dionysiac festival of 367. Two political philosophers, Plato and Aristippus, came to his court in the vain hope of influencing him, and Isocrates, who appreciated his defence of Hellenism in the West, urged him to unite the Greek states against Persia.

When Dionysius died in 366, his son Dionysius, aged thirty or so, succeeded to the command of the mercenaries and the dictatorship. By making peace· with Carthage and with the Lucanians in Italy, and modifying the rigorous methods of his father, Dionysius II kept Syracuse under subjection and the empire under control for nine years. The dangers to his safety came from within his own family and from the Syracusan *émigrés*. Dionysius I, being a polygamist, had saddled his successor with two half-brothers, Hipparinus and Nysaeus, three sisters or half-sisters, Virtue, Equity and Prudence, and an uncle called Dion, who was also his brother-in-law, having married Virtue. As Dion was an experienced officer and administrator, he guided Dionysius II, and persuaded him to invite Plato to the court. When the entourage of Dionysius realized that the philosopher's idealistic precepts might impair the practical sense of the dictator and that Dion might be trying to rise to power on the shoulders of the philosopher, they alerted Dionysius and secured the exile of Dion; but the dictator let Dion take his vast fortune with him. Plato left soon afterwards, but returned in 361, when he tried in vain to persuade Dionysius to recall Dion. This caused a rupture between Plato and Dionysius, and Dionysius deprived Dion of his wife and of his property in Sicily.

Where philosophy had failed, force succeeded. In 357 Dion, an oligarch by conviction, and a democratic *émigré* called Heraclides made joint plans. Dion sailed with 1,500 mercenaries direct from Zacynthus to Heraclea Minoa in Carthaginian territory where the commander was a personal friend, and marched towards Syracuse, collecting supporters at Acragas, Gela and Camarina. Meanwhile Dionysius happened to be in Italy and his fleet was patrolling the approaches from Greece via Italy. The governor of Syracuse panicked, the mercenaries withdrew into Ortygia and Dion entered the outer city, where he was proclaimed 'liberator' and appointed general with full powers together with his brother. But Dionysius came back into Ortygia, and soon afterwards Heraclides arrived with a fleet. Fighting in and around Syracuse lasted for two years. Dion and Heraclides fought against one another as well as against Dionysius, and Pharax, a Spartan adventurer, made a separate attempt to seize power. In 355 Dion emerged as victor and had Heraclides assassinated; he was setting up an oligarchical constitution after the model of Sparta and Corinth, when he was murdered by the agents of a Platonic philosopher, Callippus, who had a short run as a dictator. The half-brothers Hipparinus and Nysaeus followed for five years; then Dionysius expelled Nysaeus and ruled once more for three years; he was driven out by a Syracusan called Hicetas, then ruler of Leontini, who intrigued with the Carthaginians. In 343 a Carthaginian fleet sailed into the Great Harbour of Syracuse.

In these years liberation was worse than dictatorship. As there was no effective organization or grouping among the citizens of Syracuse, liberation led at once to party-strife, anarchy and dictatorship. When the central control was broken, the empire of Dionysius in Sicily and Italy fell apart. Each city went its own way; some suffered the same experiences as Syracuse, and some were destroyed by a Greek or barbarian neighbour. The collapse of organized society in the Greek states of Sicily and of inter-state systems was the result, perhaps the inevitable result, of an authoritarian dictatorship which had held Syracuse and Sicily in its grip for fifty years. By suppressing liberty, corrupting morality, prohibiting political experience and debasing the coinage of citizenship Dionysius and his son left an anarchic society at the mercy of adventurers similar to themselves. To quote the words of a contemporary which have survived in a Platonic letter, 'There is never any end. What seems to be an end always links on to a new beginning, so that this circle of strife is likely to destroy utterly both factions, those of tyranny and democracy alike, and the Greek tongue will almost die out in Sicily as it becomes a province of Carthage or Italy.'[2]

Any harsh and prolonged authoritarian rule, whether in the form of a one-man dictatorship or a narrow oligarchic group, was and is likely to produce such disastrous consequences in its aftermath

CHAPTER 21

THE CORRUPTION OF FEDERALISM AND THE FRAGMENTATION OF POWER, 371–354

When Sparta was defeated at Leuctra, Athens was the first to exploit the new situation. She put the Athenian Alliance in the place of Sparta as guarantor of the King's Peace, and on her invitation all mainland states except Sparta and Elis made individual defensive alliances with the Athenian Alliance. She came close to uniting the Greek states in the cause of peace, but it proved only a diplomatic success. Peace was not for the asking.

In the Peloponnese the enemy of peace, party faction, was in full spate. The democrats rose against the oligarchs who were in power through the support of Sparta. The villages of Mantinea coalesced again into a single state, the Mantineans drove out their own oligarchs and then helped the democrats to seize power in Tegea and exile the oligarchs, who found refuge in Sparta. Inspired by the example of the Boeotian League, Mantinea and Arcadia formed an Arcadian League on a democratic basis and tried to force two recalcitrant Arcadian states to join. These states obtained help from Corinth and Phlius, and they expected Sparta to come to their aid. On the other hand, the Arcadian League entered into an alliance with Argos and Elis, and later on sent an offer of alliance to the Boeotian League. Aware of the gathering storm the Spartans entrusted themselves to Agesilaus, authorizing him to make any constitutional changes or other dispositions at his discretion. The fundamental weakness of Sparta was that after the losses at Leuctra she had only some 800 Spartiate soldiers as the professional core of her army, which consisted otherwise of Perioeci, mercenaries and freed Helots (Neodamodeis). Agesilaus made no constitutional changes. He spared the Spartiate survivors of Leuctra the ignominy of being reduced to the rank of Inferior in accordance with the standing law, and left the initiative in the hands of the enemy.

After their victory the Boeotians turned their attention to Orchomenus, the only state in Boeotia which still supported Sparta. On the advice of Epaminondas it was treated generously and it was given membership of the Boeotian League. The growing power of their doubtful ally, Jason of Pherae, caused anxiety, but he was assassinated in the course of 370. The Boeotian League then created its own power-block in central Greece. Defensive alliances were made with Acarnania, Aetolia, western and eastern Locris, Phocis, Malis and Euboea, and the resulting coalition created a central organization which met probably at Delphi. It was similar to the Athenian Alliance and the Spartan Alliance in that the hegemony was accorded to the Boeotarchs in the field. When the Arcadian League approached the Boeotians for help late in 370, it was granted an alliance by Boeotia and may also have entered the Boeotian Alliance of central Greek powers.

Contrary to all precedent Epaminondas campaigned in midwinter 370–369. Entering the Peloponnese unopposed and mustering 40,000 hoplites and as many light-armed troops, he invaded Laconia, crossed the swollen Eurotas at Amyclae and probed the field defences of Sparta which was without walls of fortification. Agesilaus stayed on the defensive. His smaller but highly-trained army was augmented by 6,000 Helots whom he had liberated and armed for this emergency. While the Boeotians and their allies were at hand, a number of Perioeci and Helots deserted from the Spartan force, and a conspiracy was suppressed by Agesilaus, who executed the ringleaders without a trial. Epaminondas then withdrew and ravaged Laconia for three months, during which time help from some Peloponnesian states reached Sparta, but Agesilaus maintained the defensive.

When Epaminondas marched home in 369 he was opposed at the Isthmus by Corinth and Athens, which had abandoned her alliance with Thebes and taken the side of Sparta. He eluded their forces without difficulty. In 368 Sparta and her allies fortified the Isthmus and manned the fortifications with an army of 20,000 men, but Epaminondas broke through them in a night attack with an army of only 600 cavalry and 7,000 infantry and joined his Peloponnesian allies. During this campaign he liberated Messenia and built massive fortifications at the new capital Messene, and he helped the Arcadians to make a strong federal capital at Megalopolis. Thus the economic basis of the Spartan state was broken, and she was pinned down by her neighbours, Messenia, Arcadia and Argos.

The imperial power of Sparta was broken for ever. As Isocrates had said some years earlier, Sparta's claim to rule others was utterly false.[1] She conferred no benefits of culture or trade or political progress on her subjects. In the end she did not even give them security from conquest. Her own methods were suppression, treachery and brutality, and she trained her puppet-governments to rule by the same methods. Her claim to be the champion of liberty and autonomy was sheer hypocrisy, for she denied to others the right of self-government and she fostered in them the evil spirit of party strife for her own ends. Like Dionysius in Sicily, she left a legacy of hatred and discord when her empire fell.

When repressive régimes collapse, it is always to be hoped that some liberal principles will take hold in the resultant chaos. At this time both Thebes and Athens had shown the power of the liberal principles which underlay the successful formation of the Boeotian League and the Athenian Alliance. The champions of those principles were Epaminondas and Callistratus respectively, and they still held leading positions in their states.

Epaminondas secured the forgiveness of Orchomenus and her admission into the Boeotian League on equal terms, and in his settlement of the Peloponnese he justified the claim which was later written into his epitaph that he had made the states 'free and independent'. The new Boeotian form of federalism was adopted by the Aetolian League and the Acarnanian League which hitherto had been a loose union of tribal groups. The Aetolian League in particular established a cantonal system, an administrative council and a sovereign democratic assembly, and it laid the basis at this time for its future importance. The Arcadian League formed itself on the same model; but the name of the federal assembly, 'The Ten Thousand', indicates that citizen rights were granted only to those who had a certain amount of property, perhaps enough to enable them to arm themselves as hoplites. In 368 Pelopidas organized the numerous states of Thessaly, apart from Pherae, into a Thessalian League with the same features except that an elected President of the League was given wide powers. In 367 Boeotia extended her influence in the north at the expense of Athens. Pelopidas and Ismenias were sent on a diplomatic mission to Ptolemy, the regent of Macedon, who had received support from Athens, and they brought him into an alliance with the Boeotian League. They also received as guarantees of Ptolemy's good faith a number of hostages whom they sent to Thebes. One of them was a young prince, Philip, son of Amyntas. The presence of Pelopidas and Ismenias in Macedonia is probably to be connected with the withdrawal of the powerful Chalcidian League from the Athenian Alliance at this time. In Thessaly Alexander of Pherae attacked some of the states in the Thessalian

League, which applied to Boeotia for help. When Pelopidas and Ismenias put diplomatic pressure on Alexander, he arrested them and entered into an alliance with Athens, which later sent him an expeditionary force of 30 ships and 1,000 men. But a Boeotian army of 600 cavalry and 8,000 infantry arrived first. However, it failed in its mission because Alexander had a superior force of cavalry and well-trained mercenary infantry, and a second army led by Epaminondas was needed before Pelopidas and Ismenias were released.

It was more difficult for Athens to maintain her liberal principles. Naval warfare was very expensive. The system of 'contributions' from the allies yielded less in money and ships than she had hoped, and her fleets were crippled by lack of funds from 374 onwards. Unfortunately too Thebes and Athens had a long tradition of enmity, and they looked askance at each other's success – first Thebes when the Athenian Alliance attracted some seventy member-states by 374, and then Athens when the Boeotian League defeated Sparta and drew into the Boeotian coalition two states which had been in the Athenian Alliance, Acarnania and Euboea. In the winter of 369–8 Athens made the decisive break with Boeotia. She allied herself with Sparta and tried to hold the Isthmus defences against Epaminondas.

As the Athenian Alliance had been formed expressly to free the Greek states from oppression by Sparta, it seemed unnatural that Athens should become now the ally of the oppressor; moreover, she went on to ally herself with Dionysius, tyrant of Syracuse, and Alexander, ruler of Pherae, both notorious for their oppression of other states, and with the Great King of Persia. Nevertheless, if Athens had continued to interpret her relations with the members of the Alliance liberally, such vagaries of policy might have been accepted. Her intervention on behalf of the democratic *émigrés* at Zacynthus in 374 and the placing of Athenian officers and a garrison at Cephallenia in 372 had been reminiscent of Athens' fifth-century imperialism, but they were still only straws in the wind.

In 367 Sparta sent an envoy to Persia; Athens followed suit as Sparta's ally; and Boeotia, Arcadia, Argos and Elis, being their enemies, did likewise. In the humiliating competition which ensued, the Great King pinned his favour on Pelopidas, the Boeotian envoy. Peace was to be made on the basis of autonomy and liberty (except for the Greeks in Asia), the independence of Messenia was to be recognized by Sparta, that of Amphipolis by Athens, and the fleet of Athens was to be withdrawn from the seas. The initiative of Sparta and Athens had indeed rebounded to their disadvantage, and the peace became known as The

Peace of Pelopidas. In the spring of 366 the Great King's representative came to Greece and announced his master's terms at a conference of Greek delegates. Athens felt herself threatened; for if she disobeyed the Great King, the Persian fleet and perhaps a Boeotian fleet as well would enter the Aegean against her. Even so, she and several other states refused to accept the Peace of Pelopidas.

A long list of failures annoyed the Athenian people. They turned against their officials; the envoy who had represented them in Persia was executed, and Callistratus, as the advocate of liberal policy, was prosecuted for treason; although acquitted, he was stripped of his authority. The Assembly then decided on a new policy, to make alliance with the Arcadian League which was acting independently of Boeotia, and to discard her alliance with Corinth, where she had already placed some troops. In order to get the best of both worlds before the new alliance was published, her general at Corinth was told to seize the Acropolis, eject the oligarchic government and install a democracy. The plot failed. Athens' double-dealing was exposed, Corinth and her allies joined Boeotia in disgust, and Athens added another failure to her list. The Assembly then decided to adopt a new policy in the Aegean and appointed Timotheus to carry it out. He supported a Persian satrap who was in revolt from the Great King, and with the money he received he undertook a series of operations. He captured Samos, Sestus, Crithote, Potidaea, Torone, Pydna and Methone and proceeded to plant Athenian citizens as cleruchs on the best land of Samos, Sestus, Crithote and Potidaea. His actions were a flagrant breach of the charter of the Athenian Alliance and of the avowed purpose for which Timotheus was collecting 'contributions' from the allies. The mask of principle had fallen, and Athens was revealed as a stark imperialist; her methods in diplomacy and in war were those of piracy.

The Boeotian League was also overstrained. This was due not so much to financial expenditure as to the continuous call-up of her men, for the Boeotians fought in person and not at second-hand using mercenaries. The Boeotian Assembly accordingly became critical of Epaminondas and Pelopidas. They were impeached in 369 but acquitted. Epaminondas was not elected a Boeotarch in 367.

When the Peace of Pelopidas was not accepted by some states, the Boeotian Assembly tried to enforce it. In 366 Epaminondas, once more in command, broke through the defences at the Isthmus, joined forces with Argos, Arcadia, Messenia, Elis and Sicyon, and brought the Achaean League into his coalition. This League was of long standing. It had previously been loyal to Sparta and its constitution was oligarchical. Some of Boeotia's allies wished to replace oligarchy in the League with democracy, but Epaminondas announced that no change of constitution by revolutionary methods would be permitted and that the oligarchs then in power were not to be exiled. Thus he showed respect for the principles of autonomy and liberty, and set his face against political intervention. In the same way he left the oligarchs in power when Sicyon became an ally of Boeotia.

The policy of Epaminondas annoyed the Peloponnesian allies. They sent complaints to Thebes and obtained a reversal of his settlement. The Achaean oligarchs were exiled, democracies were installed, and Boeotian governors and garrisons were imported to support the democratic governments; thus for the first time the Boeotian League stooped to the methods of Sparta and Athens. But not with success. The Achaean exiles returned to their cities, threw out democrats and garrisons alike, and took the Achaean League into alliance with Sparta. Epaminondas' arrangements at Sicyon were also overthrown. As the result of intrigue by Arcadia and Argos a democracy was proclaimed at Sicyon, and a demagogue made himself dictator. He was eventually assassinated. But during these vicissitudes the Boeotians placed a garrison in the acropolis of Sicyon, endeavouring to keep the city by force within their own sphere of influence.

The Boeotians were involved also in Thessaly. Two large armies of citizen troops fought there in 364, and Pelopidas lost his life in the moment of victory. The whole of Thessaly was brought into the Boeotian coalition, and the priests of Delphi granted to Thebes the precedence in consulting the oracle of Apollo.

Only the naval hegemony was lacking. In 363 Epaminondas put to sea with a fleet of a hundred new triremes and reached the Bosporus, where Byzantium, Chalcedon and probably some other states left the Athenian Alliance, joined Boeotia and intercepted the convoys of corn which were bound for Athens from the Black Sea. He was not challenged by the Athenians either then or on the voyage home. During his absence it was discovered that the leading men of Orchomenus and some Theban émigrés were plotting to install an oligarchy at Thebes by a coup d'état. The Boeotian Assembly destroyed Orchomenus, killing all adult males and enslaving the women and children. When Epaminondas returned he denounced this act of cruelty.

In the Peloponnese too the federal states failed to live up to their principles. The Arcadian League became aggressive and tried to annex Triphylia from Elis. The quarrel spread and two groups of states fought in 364 for the control of the Olympic Festival. The leaders of the

Arcadian force robbed the temple at Olympia to pay their men, but this act of sacrilege split the Arcadian League into two factions in 363. Because the Arcadians had acted in defiance of their treaty obligations with the Boeotian League, Epaminondas announced his intention of entering the Peloponnese.

In speed of movement and in strategic conception the campaign of Epaminondas in 362 opened a new chapter in the history of military warfare. As his enemies – Athens, Achaea, Elis, Mantinea and Sparta – were dispersed, he took the field first and tried to catch them individually before they could concentrate their forces. He laid an ambush for the Athenians at Nemea; but nothing came of it because the first Athenian force was sent by sea. He then pressed on to Tegea, where he dumped his transport and supplies and proceeded to use the fortified city as a base for free manoeuvre. He now lay between Sparta and Mantinea. An advance party of Spartans was already at Mantinea. When he ascertained that the main Spartan army commanded by Agesilaus was at Pellene on the way to Mantinea, Epaminondas took a different but roughly parallel route and marched some thirty-five miles overnight to descend on the open and undefended town of Sparta shortly after dawn. As Xenophon put it,[2] he would have taken Sparta like a nest of fledgelings, had not a Cretan deserter informed Agesilaus and enabled him to send a flying column back into the town. Even so Sparta was within an ace of being captured. It was saved only by desperate street fighting in the hour or so before the main army of Agesilaus arrived. At noon Epaminondas disengaged and rested his horses and men. Guessing that the Spartan force at Mantinea and the Mantineans would now be marching via Pellene to the relief of Sparta, Epaminondas left his camp-fires burning and marched through the night to Tegea. From there he sent ahead a force of Theban and Thessalian cavalry to surprise Mantinea which, as he had guessed, was unguarded. By a freak of chance a full brigade of cavalry had just arrived from Athens. They were still in the saddle when the Theban and Thessalian cavalry rode towards the city, and they beat off this unexpected attack.

The forces of the Spartan coalition, being now concentrated, took up a defensive position in a narrow part of the plain just south of Mantinea. Their straight and solid line of 20,000 hoplites, drawn up twelve men deep, extended across the flat ground for a mile between the steep hillsides which enclosed the plain. Because the army was in Mantinean territory, the Mantineans held the supreme command. They stationed themselves on the right wing; the Spartans came next, then the Eleans and the Achaeans, and finally the Athenians on the left wing. The cavalry, 2,000 in number, was placed on the wings in advance of the infantry. Epaminondas ordered his army of 30,000 hoplites and 3,000 cavalry to burnish their equipment and sharpen their weapons, and then during a hot morning in June at a distance of some two miles from the enemy position, he marched his men to and fro across the plain in parade-ground manner, their helmets and their shields glistening in the sun. As no attack developed by noon, the Mantineans and the Spartans ell out to take a meal in the shade of the wood behind their line. At that moment Epaminondas was executing his final manoeuvre behind a cloud of dust raised by the main body of his cavalry, namely, the massing of his infantry against the western foothills in an oblique line of

Map 10 The battle of Mantinea 362

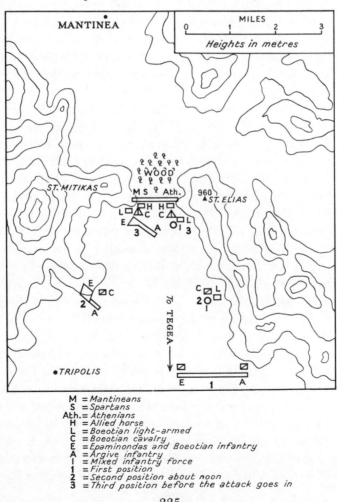

M = Mantineans
S = Spartans
Ath.= Athenians
H = Allied horse
L = Boeotian light-armed
C = Boeotian cavalry
E = Epaminondas and Boeotian infantry
A = Argive infantry
I = Mixed infantry force
1 = First position
2 = Second position about noon
3 = Third position before the attack goes in

which the head on the left was formed by the best Boeotian infantry in deep formation. Meanwhile a smaller force of cavalry, supported by light infantry, was manoeuvring on the eastern side of the plain.

Epaminondas then delivered the attack. The smaller force on the eastern side of the plain engaged and defeated the Athenian cavalry and then pinned down the Athenian infantry by attacking its flank. The main force caught the Mantineans and the Spartans unprepared. First the cavalry in a deep wedge, mingled with slingers and javelin-men, smashed its way through the extended formation of the enemy cavalry, six horses deep and unsupported by infantry, and then Epaminondas, at the head of the picked infantry, in mass formation broke through the thinner and hastily reformed line of Mantineans and Spartans, who collapsed under the impact and fled into the wood. The victorious Boeotian cavalry and infantry then turned right to roll up the enemy line from flank and rear. But at this moment they halted. Epaminondas lay dying. His trumpeter sounded the recall. No one issued a new command, and the Boeotian light-armed troops who had advanced furthest were cut to pieces by the Athenians who were also now in full retreat. The victory of the Boeotian coalition was still-born.

As far as the Boeotians were concerned, the vision of Epaminondas died with him: that is the vision of a grand coalition of self-governing leagues which would accord leadership to the Boeotian League and hold in check the imperialist ambitions of Athens and Sparta. But during the winter after the battle there came into being the boldest of all Greek federal experiments, a League of City-States. The participants in this League – all the mainland states except Sparta – called themselves 'The Greeks'. They swore to maintain 'a general peace and alliance'. They undertook to settle any disputes with one another by negotiation and to go to the help of any member who was attacked. The aim of the League was expressly to enable its members to develop their prosperity and strength on the basis of the status quo. The organization of the League probably included a council of delegates, a federal court and a federal treasury. We know of only one decision by the council (this decision having survived on an inscribed stone).[3] When a group of satraps invited 'The Greeks' to support them in their revolt against the Great King, the League rejected the invitation. Political prudence was in favour of isolationism, though by their decision 'The Greeks' showed themselves more interested in promoting their own security than in helping their fellow Greeks who were deprived of freedom by the Great King.

In the world of political ideas the League of City-States foreshadowed the United States of America or the Union of Soviet Socialist Republics

with its common citizenship and its single policy in matters of importance, and the League of Nations or the United Nations Organization
with its concepts of collective security and a growing economic prosperity within the framework of a federal council, court and treasury. But
in practice it could succeed only if the strongest of its member-states led
the way in implementing its policy. As this leadership was not forthcoming, the League of City-States left hardly a ripple on the surface of
Greek history.

In 361 a Boeotian army helped the federalist elements in Arcadia to
maintain Megalopolis as the federal capital, and Athens made alliances
with the anti-Boeotian group – Achaea, Elis, and Phlius. In the north
Athens managed to seduce the Thessalian League from its allegiance
to Boeotia but she was unable to unite Thessaly, for Alexander of
Pherae turned against her and damaged her allies and fleets in the
Cyclades. As Boeotia was now showing signs of complete exhaustion,
Athens redoubled her efforts to consolidate and extend her own power.
Callistratus, the advocate of moderation, was condemned to death *in
absentia*, and pressure was put upon the so-called 'allies'. For instance
at Iulis in Cos a pro-Athenian democracy was imposed, the oligarchs
were exiled, serious law-suits in which an Athenian citizen was involved
were to be tried in the Athenian courts, and Athenian commissioners
were given *carte blanche* in collecting arrears of 'contributions'. From
361 to 357 Athens made desperate efforts to keep or acquire control of
Euboea, Amphipolis, the Chersonese and the Bosporus, and to obtain
dependable allies among the satraps of Asia Minor, so that the Aegean
might become a *mare clausum*, and the conversion of her alliance into an
empire might proceed without intervention from other powers. But the
struggle against Boeotia, Macedon, the Chalcidian League, the
Thracian kings and the rebellious states in the Bosporus was proving
too much for her financial resources, and the commanders of her fleets
had to resort time and again to piracy and requisitioning in order to
pay their sailors and marines.

In summer 357 the satrap of Caria, called Mausolus, and Byzantium,
still in revolt from the Athenian Alliance, helped Chios, Rhodes and
Cos to eject their pro-Athenian democratic governments and quit the
Athenian Alliance. Their naval forces defeated one Athenian fleet in
357 and, as the revolt spread, another in 356. Her sea-power was
broken. In desperation she attempted to force the new Great King,
Artaxerxes Ochus, to call off his loyal satrap Mausolus by supporting
a disloyal satrap Artabazus against him. The Great King reacted
vigorously; he threatened to bring the Phoenician fleet into action

unless Athens withdrew her forces from Asia. Athens complied. In 355 she ended the so-called Social War by recognizing the independence of the rebels. She was left with the rump of the Athenian Alliance – Euboea, the Cyclades and a few places in the northern Aegean – and she drew the trivial sum of 45 talents a year in 'contributions'. Her second attempt to establish an empire in the Aegean and then to dominate Greece ended in bitter failure.

The Boeotians were inactive in the years 360 to 358. But they took advantage of Athens' involvement in the Social War to regain their influence in Thessaly and to discipline their ally Phocis, which had shown some signs of favouring Athens. The Thebans persuaded the Council of the Amphictyony of Delphi to require payment in April 356 of fines previously imposed by the Council for various offences upon Sparta and upon Philomelus and some other Phocians who were suspected of pro-Athenian sympathies.

The expectation was that the Phocian state would disown Philomelus and his associates and remain meekly in the Boeotian fold. But the use of a professedly religious body for secular purposes enraged Sparta and Phocis, and they entered into alliance. The Phocian people rallied round Philomelus and electing him 'general with full powers' put the conduct of the inevitable war in his capable hands. Philomelus seized Delphi, claiming that it was part of the Phocian state, hired some 5,000 mercenaries, and beat off the attacks of the Boeotian forces; for his position on the precipitous slopes of Mt Parnassus was almost impregnable. Success brought him the alliances of Athens and Achaea. When Athens lost the Social War, Thebes persuaded the Council of the Amphictyony at its meeting on October 355 to declare a 'Sacred War' upon Phocis. Thus the war against Philomelus became a war against Phocis, and a war of a special kind, in which no prisoners were to be taken and no mercy was to be shown to the excommunicated state, in the name of Apollo, the god of Delphi.

As Phocis was threatened with extermination, Philomelus felt justified in 'nationalizing' the temple funds, and with the proceeds he hired more and more mercenaries. In 354 he made skilful use of his central position among his enemies. Taking the offensive with an army of 10,000 men, he defeated the Locrians and the Boeotians separately and then forced the Thessalians out of the war. The great Boeotian coalition which had come into existence in 370 was no more. The Boeotian League was left with only one effective ally, Locris. Her once unrivalled citizen army was being worn down in battle after battle by highly paid and easily replaceable mercenaries.

Xenophon, the historian of the period 411–362, died in 354. Having described the battle of Mantinea, he added this sentence. 'After the battle there was even greater indecisiveness and confusion in Greece than there had been before.'[4] His words ring true. In the past three states had created power-blocks which seemed capable of imposing a settlement on the Greek world – Sparta, Athens and Boeotia. Now they had been reduced to the position of minor powers, and no other state had shown itself capable of leadership. As the great powers fell, wars multiplied between state and state all over the Greek peninsula, and confusion reigned in a constantly changing sea of alliances.

CHAPTER 22

THE POLITICAL AND SOCIAL SITUATION OF THE GREEK STATES BETWEEN 400 AND 350

The first half of the fourth century BC in Greece bears a striking similarity to the first half of our century in Europe because society was repeatedly disrupted by wars which were conducted in order to impose hegemony or to shake it off. As the years passed, the chance of any one state becoming ruler over all the others lessened. If an imperialist state is to be successful, it needs a wide margin of superiority over its victims, such as Athens had built up by 431, at least in the opinion of Thucydides. Sparta, Athens and Boeotia never had that wide margin of superiority in the fourth century. In the early years of the Second World War, Germany was very much stronger than her immediate victims, but she lost this advantage when she attacked Russia. We can say with hindsight that the policy of these states was ill-conceived. The alternative, a partial hegemony, was easier to achieve than to hold, as Athens found after the collapse of Sparta, because restricted empire, whether within Greece or within Europe, is open to neighbouring influences and to intervention by outside powers, especially at a time when rival ideologies are rife. Thus both periods are marked by instability in interstate politics.

On the other hand particularism, that is each state acting for itself, is hazardous in a world where imperialist states are active. Individual states were swallowed up one after the other by Athens in the 390s and by Dionysius whenever Carthage was off his back. 'Liberty and autonomy' is an excellent motto for the small state, but to believe that it can be realized by a policy of particularism may be wishful thinking. It soon became a general truth that lesser states could only retain their freedom if they were willing to diminish it by entering into a partnership. For example, when the imperial yoke of Sparta was temporarily shaken off in the years 394–385, Corinth and Argos formed a close union; and a number of states in the eastern Aegean area adopted a common coinage and entered into a coalition. Where loose federal unions existed as in Acarnania and Aetolia, they tended to become increasingly close-knit in the interests of solidarity and survival. But the tightening of the bonds within a federal union some-times aroused the centrifugal forces of particularism. This happened in the Boeotian League, the Chalcidian League and the Arcadian League at various times.

Federalism offered more hope of stability than either particularism or imperialism in the conditions of the fourth century. Federal states in general proved superior in power to single states in their vicinity; for example, the Boeotian League was stronger than Megara or Corinth, and the Chalcidian League than Amphipolis. Federal states were, broadly speaking, of two kinds. They were made up either of city-states or of tribal units. The Boeotian League was an example of the former class. In northern Greece the Molossian League consisted of tribal units, that is racial units, such as have gone to make up the modern federal state of Yugoslavia. Such federal states called them-selves often by a tribal name such as 'the Molossi', or 'the Orestae'. In a few cases a federal state was made up mainly of city-states and only to a small extent of tribal units; this was so in the Aetolian League at its inception. These federal states had all the organs of central govern-ment which were needed for permanency. Federal systems grew up in the fourth century which were different from federal states in that they did not become permanent and developed only some of the organs of central government. Thus the League of City-States in 362 proclaimed itself as a federal system under the name of 'The Hellenes', but only a few organs of central government were formed in its short life. In the same way Timoleon and Philip created federal systems for Sicily and Greece.

The ideal form of federalism is of course a federation of equals in which every state, great or small, has one vote, or one representative in the federal council. This was a characteristic of the Ionian League in the 490s and of the League of Nations between the two World Wars. The danger of such ideal or egalitarian federalism is that, like a team without a captain or a body without a head, it finds it difficult to reach a decision and is then slow to implement it; indeed, it may lose its sense of direction altogether. As Thucydides said, 'Where all repre-sentatives have an equal vote and are of different races they each endeavour to advance their own interest, and as a result it usually happens that nothing is accomplished.'[1] In practice the federal states which grew powerful were non-egalitarian in the sense that one member was stronger in fact or *de jure*; for example, Thebes was richer economically and, by virtue of having subjugated some other states, had an extensive territory, to which three-sevenths of the total votes in the Boeotian League were allocated *de jure*; and Olynthus, being itself a union or 'sympolity', of several settlements, played the predominant part in developing the military strength and the sophisticated constitution of the Chalcidian League. But in such federal states the actual command in war and the executive authority inherent in what the Greeks called *hegemonia* were not vested *de jure* in any one state.

In coalitions which were formed 'for all time' in the hope of permanence, it was customary to vest the hegemony in one state *de jure*. For instance, Athens and Sparta were given this position in the alliance which they formed in the fifth and fourth centuries; and Boeotia held the same position for a time in the coalition of Leagues in central Greece. In such coalitions the burden of hegemony proved extremely heavy, for instance for Sparta during the long Peloponnesian War, Athens in the early years of her second Athenian Alliance, and Boeotia in invasions of the Peloponnese; and the temptation to lighten it by obtaining larger contributions from the allies was almost irresistible. Yet larger contributions were not usually to be obtained for the asking. The hegemonic state had either to have a compliant ally, which was often achieved by imposing or arranging for a puppet government in the allied state, or to use force in exacting a higher contribution. Athens employed both methods in the latter days of her second Athenian Alliance. What was needed to avoid this form of deterioration in a large coalition was a hegemonic state so strong in itself that it did not need to make heavy demands on its allies. As long as peace reigned, Athens and Syracuse came closest to being in this ideal situation, but their home base in terms of territory and citizen population still remained relatively small. The other possibility was that an outside power might appear as a hegemonic state. Macedonia was to assume this role in relation to the Greek states, even as the United States of America was in a position to assume it in the post-war period.

The inventiveness which the Greek states showed in their political practice is extraordinary. We have written here mainly of interstate relations, but the constitution of individual states showed an infinite variety from constitutional monarchy at Sparta and dictatorship at Syracuse to extreme democracy at Athens and communism at Lipara. Political experiment was frequently carried out, sometimes with a political philosopher as consultant, and the political theory of the fourth century was unrivalled in its range and perceptiveness, as we see from Plato's *Republic* and *Laws* and Aristotle's *Politics*. While these two philosophers were faithful to the almost divine right of the polis as a form of social existence, Antisthenes and Diogenes reacted against the claims of the polis and advocated a return to primitivism and simplicity for individuals and for groups of individuals who found the harshness and hollowness of contemporary life intolerable.

When interstate relations become chaotic, it is natural to question the validity of the state, whether city-state or national state. There was certainly much to criticize in the fourth-century poleis. In their treatment of one another they were perfidious in the extreme; oaths meant nothing, and alliances were discarded at will. Worse were the atrocities they committed against one another. Thucydides related the butchering of the entire population of a Greek city by Thracian mercenaries as terrible beyond belief, but in the fourth century such massacres were organized by Greeks themselves, for instance by Alexander of Pherae who had the population of Scotussa massacred and the corpses thrown into a ditch. Again the annihilation of a city by andrapodismos (the adult males being slaughtered and the rest being sold into slavery) was a rare occurrence in the fifth century, and Thucydides drew attention to Athens as being more guilty of this crime than any other state. But in the fourth century andrapodismos became common enough in Greek warfare, especially in Sicily and south Italy under the rule of the dictators.

The use of mercenary soldiers, which was rare in the Peloponnesian War, became general in the fourth century. The expedition of Cyrus, so brilliantly described by Xenophon in his *Anabasis*, showed that Greek hoplites were the finest infantry of the time; for his force of 13,000 mercenaries, led by a Spartan officer, routed the Persian infantry without suffering a casualty, and then marched from the heart of Mesopotamia to Trebizond on the Black Sea, defeating all who attempted to stop them. Thereafter the market for mercenaries was almost unlimited; every satrap in revolt and every general or admiral of the Great King hired thousands of them and paid high wages to distinguished mercenary commanders. Within the Greek world the professional mercenary soldier became more efficient than the average citizen soldier, and many states used mercenaries to fight for them. They were inevitably more ruthless and unscrupulous than citizen soldiers.

Unemployed mercenary armies were also a menace to peace. For example at the end of the Sacred War, the army of 8,000 mercenaries commanded by Phalaecus set sail from Corinth for Italy and Sicily, 'hoping either to capture some city or find employment', but the mercenaries mutinied, put back to the Peloponnese, and found employment with Cnossus in Crete. First they captured a city, Lyctus, and expelled the population. But a Spartan army appeared and drove them out; they then laid siege to another city, Cydonia, but their siege-engines were struck by lightning and burnt. Next they were employed by *émigrés* from Elis. Returning to the Peloponnese, they attacked the Eleans, who got help from the Arcadians and defeated them. The 4,000 survivors were divided up between the victors; the Arcadians sold theirs as slaves, and the Eleans executed theirs as sacrilegious miscreants.

The collapse of the accepted standards of humanity was even more marked within states which were torn by revolutionary factions. Thucydides noted that every form of depravity occurred in the civil wars of his own lifetime; and in the fourth century, which was even more fiercely torn by civil wars, depravity was more widespread still. Frequent changes of government, often engineered by outside powers, were attended by massacres of the rival party. Thus in 392 the democrats at Corinth set upon their opponents during a religious festival and killed 120 of them at the altars and in the temples, and in 370 the democrats at Argos clubbed 1,200 persons to death. The oligarchs were little better; in some states they took the oath 'I shall be evil-minded to the people and devise any mischief I can against them'.[2] Indeed hatred of the opposite faction made men blind to the interest of the state as a whole, and they had more feeling for a similar faction in another state than for their rivals at home. The dictators were generally in a class by themselves. Afraid of all the citizen classes, they were ruthless and merciless, and let their mercenaries run riot. Faction and inter-state wars produced a constant flow of refugees or as the Greeks called them 'apoleis', 'stateless' persons. This floating population reached a dangerous size in Sicily and threatened the existence of the smaller states. One of Dionysius' tasks was to resettle the better elements among them; many of the able-bodied refugees became mercenaries. As Isocrates said and as Philomelus demonstrated in 356, 'It is easier to raise a bigger and better army from the floating population than from the citizen population.'[3]

The deterioration of political standards at Athens was shown in the trial of Socrates on a charge of impiety, for which the prosecutor proposed the death-sentence. The case was tried by a court of probably 501 jurors under the restored democracy in 399, and the fact that Critias and other oligarchic leaders had been his pupils helped to arouse prejudice against him. That he, a man of the highest integrity was found guilty by the court, was a miscarriage of justice. That he was put to death was partly his responsibility because he chose not to propose an acceptable alternative penalty, as he was invited to do. In the speech of defence, as it was subsequently related by his pupil Plato,[4] Socrates said that, if a man who really fights for what is right wishes to survive, he must engage in private life and not in public life. In fourth-century Athens this was so. Intellectuals of high principle such as Plato, Antisthenes and Isocrates did not enter the arena of Athenian democratic politics, and it is to be noted that one of the few liberal statesmen of Athens, Callistratus, was condemned to death on a charge of treason, escaped into exile, and on his return as a supplicant was removed from the altar of the Twelve Gods in the Agora and executed.

The bitterness of politics was partly due to the social situation. Slaves being plentiful and employed on manual work, there was no citizen working class or 'labour component' in a city-state. If a citizen fell to the level of manual work, he was despised and such work was labelled 'menial' (*banauson*). Aristotle listed the occupations of the poorest class of citizens as follows:[5] 'farming', i.e. owning and working a small hold-ing, 'retail trading', i.e. owning a small shop or business, 'salaried work', e.g. as a doctor, lecturer or artist, and 'menial work'. He added for a maritime city 'fishing' and 'passenger-carrying', i.e. owning and oper-ating one's own boat in these activities; and specifically for Athens 'rowing in the fleet', which was a respectable citizen occupation and earned a good wage. Thus the bulk of the lowest class owned property of one kind or another, and probably had a slave or two to work it; for Aristotle mentioned only one group in the lowest class as not possessing enough capital to have leisure, that is the 'menial workers'. It was this particular group which some states helped by paying a dole. Aristotle condemned the dole as wasteful and non-productive. He preferred to make outright grants of sufficient size to equip the recipient either with a small holding or with a small business in commerce or agriculture. His aim was to make *all* members of the citizen body owners of property, i.e. capitalists, in however small a way.

Those above the poorest class were divided into holders of larger pro-perties and holders of smaller properties. The rich man had fifty slaves or so in his household (as Plato remarked c. 375), owned fine horses, and adorned his women with gold jewellery; some of them could afford to hire a private army and Heraclides, Dion and Philomelus did so. At Athens the three hundred richest men were able to advance the entire sum which was due to be paid in a capital levy for one year. It was this topmost class which sometimes gained power by a *coup d'état*, or was put in power by the intervention of an imperialist state; it would then estab-lish an extreme oligarchy. The well-to-do capitalist had a less lavish establishment, but he too owned horses and he could equip himself for service as a cavalryman. Next came the prosperous man who owned some slaves, could live at leisure if he pleased, and was able to equip himself for service as a hoplite. In a moderate oligarchy those who enjoyed the full franchise usually came from these three classes. The class structure was reflected in the armed forces of the state. Thus in Boeotia at the height of her power there were 1,500 cavalry drawn from the two upper classes, 13,000 hoplites from the middle class, and an unknown number of light-armed infantry from the lower class, while Athens had 1,000 cavalry, perhaps 15,000 hoplites, and enough naval personnel to man a hundred triremes, that is perhaps 17,000 servicemen drawn mainly from the lowest class in about 370.

Class warfare in most Greek states was between the well-to-do classes and the lowest citizen-class which had usually a small amount of capital and sometimes none at all. As Plato put it, 'There must not be severe poverty in any section of the citizen body, nor yet opulence; for either breeds faction, which may more correctly be called disruption.'[6] The well-to-do fought to keep or improve their favourable position. The lowest class tried to improve its position either by becoming the sovereign element in a democracy which was able to tax the rich and help the poor, or by effecting a revolution in which property was re-distributed in its own favour. At Athens where the democracy was so firmly established, 'the people' were very jealous of their powers. As Aristotle noted, 'The people have made themselves master of every-thing; all administration is conducted by decrees of the Assembly and decisions of the Courts in which the people are sovereign.'[7]

In foreign policy the democracy tended to be aggressive. Thus Aristophanes described the feeling at Athens in 393, when hopes of obtaining sea-power were rising again, as follows: ' "Let's launch the fleet" [an orator cries]; the poor vote "Aye", the rich men and the farmers vote "No".'[8] Again in 355 when imperialism had failed, Xenophon attributed the aggressive policy of Athens to the poverty of the majority of the citizen-body – for they had nothing to lose but their poverty. One can indeed see that the lowest class had much to gain if an imperialistic policy should be successful; for there was the opportunity not only of earning good wages in the fleet and its ancillary services, but also of obtaining land as a cleruch and so becoming a prosperous member of the hoplite class. In the same way the Boeotian League and the Arcadian League became aggressive when their constitutions were democratic, and it was the Assembly of the Boeotians which overruled Epaminondas and adopted imperialistic methods.

The corruption of the city-state by party strife afforded ideal conditions for the emergence of dictatorship, especially when foreign powers intervened in support of the rival ideologies. The alarming feature of dictatorship was that it appeared to provide a form of stability by ending the ebb and flow of party strife and often by achieving some success in foreign policy. Dionysius and his agents or imitators in Sicily, Euphron at Sicyon and Jason and Alexander at Pherae were more powerful than the city-state whose liberty they had usurped had ever been. This was partly because the dictators made unscrupulous use of power, exploited capital resources, and employed unprincipled troops whether natives or refugees or mercenaries; but there is the more fundamental point that, where society was disrupted, the able individual had more opportunity to assume and exercise control, as is indeed the case in modern times.

Despite the instability of the political situation, the wealth of the Greek states increased rapidly as capitalism and commerce spread into the hinterlands of the Mediterranean and Black Seas. The flow of intercontinental traffic in goods and slaves passed mainly through the Greek cities of the coastal lands of Europe, Asia and Africa, and by sea through the maritime states of mainland Greece, southern Italy, and Sicily. Athens and Syracuse were still the richest states in time of peace, and had an astonishing power of economic recuperation, but hundreds of other states came not far behind them. The practices of a booming capitalism were adopted throughout the Greek world – monetary pacts, trading concessions, commercial agreements, interstate banking and marine insurance; and they were beginning to develop in some of the non-Greek areas which were adopting a Greek way of life. The fourth century was internationally an age of plenty and an age of affluence in the city-states.

Wealth and urbanization developed together. Every Greek city had massive walls of defence, civic centre, theatre, stadium, gymnasium, and well-planned housing areas, such as have been found by excavation at Olynthus. Entirely new cities were built in the Peloponnese at Messene and Megalopolis, and in Sicily, for instance at Leontini and Aetna, or rose again from the ashes of a Carthaginian invasion. The bulk of the citizens now lived in the city where life was more exciting and the walls gave some security. From there they could supervise the work of the young and the old and the slaves in the fields which were never very far away. City life became standardized from one city to another. The best plays were taken round by touring companies of actors and the fashionable sophists or architects or political consultants travelled from city to city. A standard form of literary Greek was beginning to evolve and its adoption was facilitated by the circulation of books.

As city life became so typical of the Greek world, a common culture grew up alongside the traditional particularism of individual city-states. Isocrates of Athens, who founded the first school of higher education, believed that Greek culture could best be preserved by restricting the rights of the city-state and creating a Panhellenic union of states, preferably on a basis of equality but, if necessary, under the aegis of one benevolent power. The greatest historian of the period, Ephorus of Cyme in Asia Minor, saw all Greek history in terms of themes and not of city-states, and he saw the desire for 'general peace' culminating in the unification of Greece under the protection of Philip of Macedon. The last comedy of Aristophanes, *Wealth*, produced in 388, was on the theme of wealth and poverty, and its characters were drawn from the gallery of city life. The strongly political tone of Old Comedy and the particular localization at Athens had almost disappeared.

The weakening of the city-state meant a loosening of the sense of community, and it was due to this perhaps that great poetry ceased with the end of the Peloponnesian War. The fourth century was marked by reason rather than enthusiasm, by prose rather than poetry. The four great philosophies of antiquity, Platonism, Aristotelianism, Stoicism and Epicureanism, developed at this time from the teaching of Socrates, and their interest was centred on man as an intelligent being rather than man as a political animal. The foundations of science were laid by systematic studies of zoology, botany, psychology and musicology, and much progress was made in mathematics and mechanics. The one form of literature which was tied to the conditions of city-state life was oratory, and no other period in history has been marked by such a galaxy of talent in oratory, headed by Demosthenes. Written prose reached a high level in the dialogues of Plato and Aristotle, the essays of Isocrates, and the journalistic history and memoirs of Xenophon. Admiration for the outstanding individual led to biographical writing, and a leading historian, Theopompus of Chios, named his history of the period after Philip, King of Macedon.

Specialization and individualism developed rapidly in city life. Competition was keen, and one had to specialize to succeed. The versatile amateur became rare. Even in the theatre script-writing, producing and acting became separate professions. In public life an orator was rarely a general. Specialization in war became such that citizen troops could rarely be trained to the same high level as the professional soldiers, and many states preferred to employ mercenaries. Successful city-state generals did not revert to civilian life at the end of a war but took service overseas as mercenary commanders; even at the age of eighty, Agesilaus, king of Sparta, with 1,000 of his troops, took service for pay in Egypt. Men wrote treatises on special subjects of practical life such as the defence of fortified positions and horsemanship for the cavalry officer. Scholars and antiquarians wrote elaborate local histories and studied mythology and ethnology.

Individual pursuits and interests were no longer bounded by the horizons of the city-state or restricted by the nexus of relationships which had once tied a man to his tribal and familial associations. The free-ranging individualism which Euripides had portrayed in his plays became more common in the fourth century, and it was then that the plays of Euripides became more popular than those of Aeschylus and Sophocles. The choral element in tragedy and comedy declined in the plays and the productions of the period, and fewer temples were built to the patron gods of communal life. Individuals turned to the oracular gods of Delphi and Dodona for an answer to their personal problems, and to the mystery religions for standards of personal life and hopes of personal survival after death. Secular buildings of this period rivalled the earlier temples in magnificence. At Megalopolis the Assembly Hall which was built to house the meetings of the Arcadian League measured 218 feet by 172 feet and its roof was carried throughout on stone columns. At Olympia a vast hostel for visitors, called the Leonidaeum, was constructed in stone with an outer colonnade of 138 Ionic columns. At Epidaurus a stone theatre was built c. 350 for the entertainment of visitors who came to the shrine of Asclepius, the god of Healing; it seated some 17,000 spectators and had amazingly good acoustic properties.

Sculpture and painting found their inspiration less in idealism than in realism and naturalism. A famous statue of Peace with her child Wealth, sculptured by Cephisodotus of Athens in 370, gave expression to the yearning of this age for release from war and its effects. The mother looks towards her child with a tenderness which is found also in the statue of Hermes with the child Dionysus on his arm, sculptured by Praxiteles of Athens and now preserved in the museum at Olympia. These two statues have a sentimental quality absent from sculpture of an earlier period. Praxiteles used Phryne, a courtesan who was his mistress, as a model for his statue of Aphrodite. The goddess stood in a relaxed but conscious pose, laying her clothes on a water jar to one side – a human rather than a divine representation; and a gilded statue of Phryne herself was dedicated by the sculptor to the god at

Delphi. Realistic portraits were made in marble, for instance of Mausolus and his wife Artemisia and of Philip of Macedon. Passionate feeling was also a subject for representation whether in battles of Amazons and Greeks or in scenes of love. The painter Apelles of Colophon in Asia Minor showed Aphrodite rising from the sea and wringing out her hair, as any woman might do. The gods have come down to earth, and man is the centre of a secular universe.

The civilization of the fourth century with its growing individualism and secularism, and its combination of affluence and divisiveness in a capitalistic, city-centred society was the beginning of a way of life in the eastern Mediterranean world which lasted under Macedonian and then Roman rule until the beginning of the Byzantine age. It is also closer than the civilization of the Periclean period to European civilization of the twentieth century. That it was vigorous and inventive there is no doubt, but by 354 it had failed to solve the overriding problem of an interstate order which would put an end to the circle of internecine revolutions and wars. Despairing of contemporary politicians and democratic assemblies, Plato and Aristotle pinned their hopes on the education of a new generation of citizens within the city-states. Such an education was to be state-controlled and compulsory, and make its pupils so just and wise that they would obey the laws willingly and produce an intellectual élite to guide the state. The setting for such an educational panacea was an ideal city-state surprisingly like Sparta in its economy and class-structure and in its rejection of developed capitalism and urbanization. Their eyes were turned back to the heyday of the city-state, and their faith in the power of education was perhaps illusory. Isocrates believed in a more practical form of voluntary education and looked for a practical solution to the problem of peace and war in the development of a federal union for all city-states.

CHAPTER 23

THE RISE OF MACEDONIA TO POWER
359–346

City-state life on the Athenian model became for the Greeks of the fourth century the hall-mark of Greek civilization, and the racialist distinctions of the past were now of comparatively little significance. Isocrates made the point succinctly in 380: 'The name "Greek" suggests no longer a race but an outlook, and the title "Greeks" is given rather to those who share our culture than to those who share our blood.' It thus came about that peoples who may have been racially of the same stock as the Greek-speaking peoples of central and southern Greece were regarded as non-Greek and so barbarian, because their outlook and their culture were from the Greek point of view retarded and un-Greek. This was particularly so if the political unit was the ethnos or tribal system and the constitution was monarchical.

The peoples of what we call northern Greece were at the tribal stage of development, and many of the tribes were still ruled by constitutional monarchies at the beginning of the fourth century. The tribal and personal names, for instance, of the Thesprotians and the Molossians in Epirus were Greek in terms of language, and there are strong grounds for believing that they were predominantly Greek in race in the sense that they were descended from the original nucleus of Greek-speaking peoples. But in their institutions and in their outlook they were different from the Greeks in the south, and an Athenian, say, of the fourth century regarded them as 'barbarians'. Nor did they think of themselves as anything but Molossians or Epirotes; in their own eyes they were neither Greeks (except in language) nor barbarians. There were, of course, some 'Greeks' living in Epirus; they were the descendants of the colonists from Corinth and Elis; they lived in city-states such as Ambracia and Pandosia, and their outlook and culture were Greek and not Molossian or Epirotic. In Macedonia the distinction was drawn with the same clarity. The tribal systems known as

Macedones, Orestae, Lyncestae, Paeones, Bottiaei, and so on, were one and all 'barbarian', whether or not they were Greek in language or race. Here too there were 'Greeks living in Macedonia', as Thucydides called them; for they were descendants of Eritrean and Corinthian colonists who had founded their city-states on the coast of the Thermaic Gulf, for instance at Methone, Dicaea and Potidaea. But they were exceptions. An Athenian like Demosthenes regarded the Macedones, for instance, as barbarians; and the Macedones regarded themselves as Macedones, certainly not as Greeks nor yet as barbarians.

The Macedones were originally a group of tribes, like the Molossi; the leading tribe in the sixth century was the Argeadae, but by the fourth century the internal tribal distinctions had disappeared. The language of these Macedones was probably Greek, but of such a strong and archaic dialect that it was not intelligible to a southern Greek. Some tribes in western Macedonia, for instance the Orestae, spoke a different dialect of Greek which was related rather to the Greek spoken by tribes in Epirus. Other tribal groups in what we now call Macedonia spoke non-Greek languages such as Illyrian, Paeonian and Thracian. When they came under the rule of the Macedones, they no doubt continued to use their own language and names, but in course of time they learned Macedonian and so became bilingual, just as the remnants of conquered peoples in the Chalcidic peninsula learned Greek and became bilingual.

In some of the tribes of Epirus and Macedonia the royal house claimed to be descended from Greeks of peninsular Greece, and such claims were entirely independent of the question whether their own subjects spoke a form of Greek or not. Thus the kings of the Argeadae Macedones held that their dynasty had been founded by members of the royal house of Argos in the Peloponnese, the Temenidae, who having been exiled went to Illyria and then crossed into Macedonia around 650. The kings of the Lyncestae traced the origin of their dynasty to some members of the Bacchiadae, a noble clan which was banished from Corinth c. 650; descendants of this clan came to Lyncus from Illyria and founded the royal house c. 450. As these claims were accepted by southern Greeks, it is certain that these kings and their families originally spoke Doric Greek as their mother-tongue, but may have adopted the standard cultural Greek in the fourth century. They were bilingual only in the sense that they learned whatever archaic dialect of Greek was spoken by their subjects.

As soon as the Temenid dynasty was established, the Macedones issued from their homeland in northern Pieria and gained possession of central Macedonia west of the Axius river and southern Pieria, from which they expelled the inhabitants. Later, in the first half of the fifth century, they acquired Eordaea and central Macedonia east of the Axius river and expelled only the royal tribe of the Thracians from this area. The Macedonian kingdom was now well defended by the high mountain ranges which circle the great plain of Central Macedonia, and it included one district, Eordaea, which extended into the higher inland country known as 'Upper Macedonia'. At some time the king of the Macedones claimed suzerainty over Upper Macedonia, perhaps originally by right of conquest, but in the early fourth century the claim was not substantiated.

The history of the kings is to a remarkable extent the history of the Macedonian state. For the king was the embodiment of the state. He owned all land, commanded all troops, controlled all finance, conducted religious ceremonies of state, and was judge in most cases. All Macedones owed him fealty. The heads of the noble families which had once led the original constituent tribes were treated by the king as his Companions. They hunted with him, attended his court, and served as his élite cavalry. Another élite group, which served as infantry, was known as The Foot-Companions; it existed in the time of Philip II. Economically the country was backward; for the raising of stock and the transhumance of sheep were more important than agriculture, and the export of animal products and timber was mainly in the hands of the Greek city-states on the coast. The first urban centre was Pella in the plain of Central Macedonia, just west of the Axius, and other urban centres developed in the plain during the first part of the fourth century. An able Macedonian king, Archelaus, made Pella his capital and treated the towns as administrative centres to which the Macedones were attached for military and other purposes. When such towns grew up, the corps of Foot-Companions was recruited from the more capable of the Macedones in the towns; but the towns had no independent existence, no sovereignty, such as a city-state on the coast possessed.

Thus the land of the Macedones was a national territorial state, capable of expansion by conquest and incorporation. The head of state and the director of its destiny was a constitutional hereditary monarch with almost unrestricted powers once the Macedones had elected him. He could create Macedones by granting land and citizenship. Not all freeborn males in his realm were citizens; for many such in eastern central Macedonia were the descendants of conquered peoples and remained subject to the king without being either in a racial sense or in a privileged sense Macedones. The king had many enemies adjacent to his realm: the Greek city-states on his coast, the Chalcidian League, the Thracians, the Paeonians, the tribes of Upper Macedonia, and beyond them the dreaded Illyrians. The great powers in the Greek world – Athens or Sparta or Boeotia – also intervened in his kingdom during the first half of the fourth century.

In 367 Philip, a young prince of the Temenid house, was taken as a hostage to Thebes where he lived until 364 in the house of a Theban commander, Pammenes, and saw the development of Boeotia under the leadership of Epaminondas. Early in 359 Macedonia suffered a shattering defeat at the hands of the Illyrians. The king, Perdiccas, and 4,000 Macedonian soldiers were killed. Philip, as brother of Perdiccas, was appointed at the age of twenty-two to act as regent for the infant son of Perdiccas, and was elected king, perhaps in 358, if not earlier. The kingdom was in danger of liquidation. In Upper Macedonia Lyncus was held by the Illyrians, and Pelagonia had been intriguing with Athens. The cities on the coast of Central Macedonia were independent, and Athens was a declared enemy, hoping to gain a footing in the Thermaic Gulf and also to capture Amphipolis, which Perdiccas had strengthened with a garrison. The Paeonians and the Thracians were always ready to invade when Macedonia was weak, and Philip's only ally, the Chalcidian League, had its own territorial ambitions in Macedonia. In addition there were rival claimants to the throne.

Philip acted with characteristic speed. He engineered the assassination of two rivals, paid the western Thracians and the Paeonians not to invade, and withdrew the Macedonian garrison from Amphipolis. He was thus free to deal with his most dangerous enemy, Athens, when she sent a strong fleet and an army of 4,000 mercenaries into the Thermaic Gulf to put the strongest rival, Argaeus, on the throne in the place of the infant king. The landing of Argaeus and the mercenaries and their march to the old capital, Aegae, was unopposed. As there was no rising in his favour, Argaeus set off back to the coast, but Philip now intercepted and defeated him and then surrounded the survivors. On condition that Argaeus and any Macedonians were surrendered to him Philip let the mercenaries go free, asked Athens for peace and recognized Athens' claim to Amphipolis. Peace was granted in winter 359.

His vulnerable coast now safe, Philip reduced Paeonia in 358 and then invaded Lyncus where the Illyrian king, Bardylis, offered peace on the status quo. But Philip had trained his army in the Theban manner, and chose to engage before Bardylis could obtain any reinforcements. Each army had some ten thousand infantry, and Philip had a larger force of cavalry. Bardylis drew up his infantry in a square so that they could not be taken in the flank or rear by the Macedonian cavalry. Philip massed his best infantry on the right of his line, advanced in oblique formation delaying his left wing, broke the corner of the enemy square and sent his cavalry into the gap. When the enemy broke, the cavalry chased them and killed 7,000 men. Bardylis asked for peace which Philip granted on his own terms: the cession of Illyrian territory up to the western side of Lake Lynchnitis (Ochrid) and the hand of an Illyrian princess in marriage. His victory over the Illyrians was a relief to the Molossians in Epirus, and he cemented an alliance with them by marrying Olympias, a princess in their royal house, who, as his favourite, became influential in the court of Macedon.

In 357 Philip attacked Amphipolis. By playing on the enmity between Athens and the Chalcidian League, who both wanted to control the town, and by taking advantage of Athens' involvement in the Social War, Philip was able to proceed without interruption and gained possession of Amphipolis. He pronounced it free and autonomous, to the delight of the Chalcidian League, and he then attacked the Athenian base on his coast, Pydna, where his sympathizers opened the gates. Athens now declared war on Philip, but her forces were fully engaged in the Social War. Both Athens and Philip now sought the alliance of the Chalcidian League, which had a formidable army of 1,000 cavalry and 10,000 hoplites and excellent harbours for a large fleet. It was a question of who could offer most, and Philip obtained the alliance by ceding a rich territory, Anthemus, to the Chalcidians and by promising to help them capture the city of Potidaea, where the Athenians had planted a clerurchy. No sooner was the alliance concluded than Philip laid siege to Potidaea. An Athenian force was sent to its relief; but Philip had already captured the town, and gave it to the Chalcidian League. He set all his Athenian captives free and sent them back to Athens at his own expense – a sequel to war which was very different from the andrapodismos sometimes employed by Athens – and he made an agreement with his ally, the Chalcidian League, that neither of them would negotiate unilaterally with Athens.

During the winter Philip helped Larisa in Thessaly against the tyrants of Pherae, and cemented his friendships there by marrying a Thessalian lady. In spring 356, in answer to a request from the citizens of Crenides for help against the Thracians, Philip sent settlers and built fortifications, and the citizens renamed the city Philippi in his honour. It lay beyond the Strymon, to the east of Amphipolis, and it had access to the rich gold and silver mines of Mt Pangaeum, which now passed into Philip's control and were soon to yield him a revenue of 1,000 talents a year. Because Athens was fighting desperately against her allies, she was not able to send a large expedition against Philip, but she organized a coalition of the neighbouring kings to attack him, namely Cetriporis of Thrace, Lyppeus of Paeonia, and Grabus of Illyria. As always, Philip moved first and defeated them individually in summer 356. During 355 he advanced along the Thracian coast and occupied the territories of two Greek cities, Abdera and Maronea, and in the winter of 355 he attacked the last Athenian base on his coast, Methone. He lost the sight of his right eye during the siege, but he captured it by assault before an Athenian fleet arrived. He did not kill or enslave the survivors but let them go free with one garment apiece. During this critical operation (for Athens was now at peace with her allies), the alliance with the Chalcidian League held firm.

The brilliant success of Philip was certainly facilitated by the decline of the Athenian Alliance and the Boeotian Alliance, but it was due primarily to the source of power which he organized within Macedonia. His first step was to restore the morale of an army which had suffered a disastrous defeat; to this end he concentrated his troops, trained them in the close formations and the tactical manoeuvres of Epaminondas, and inspired them with confidence by his own magnetic personality. Resounding victories over Illyrians, Paeonians and Thracians in 358 to 356 confirmed the allegiance of the Macedonians and gave a new security to his kingdom; for the frontiers were carried forward in the west to Lake Ochrid and the valley of the upper Drin, in the north to the valley of the upper Axius where the Paeonian king Lyppeus ruled as his vassal, and in the west to the valley of the middle Strymon where the Thracian king Cetriporis ruled as his vassal.

These achievements made it possible for him to create the greater Macedonia which was to be the basis of all future expansion. Behind the shield of client kings he incorporated into his kingdom the cantons of Upper Macedonia which had been independent from time to time under his predecessors; namely Pelagonia, Lyncus, Orestis, Tymphaea and Elimea. The natural defences of this greater Macedonia were extremely strong; for the high ranges of Olympus, Pindus, Grammus, Scardus, Babuna, Plaskovitsa and Dysoron formed a strong ring of defence, and the passes between them were narrow or high and sometimes both.

The chief task was to bring the peoples of these cantons within the fold of the Macedonian state. As each canton had been and in some cases still was ruled by a local dynasty, Philip gave the Macedonian citizenship to suitable members of the dynasties and elevated them to the position of Companions; but he also retained the cantonal divisions. Thus a scion of the Lyncestid royal house might become a '*Makedon Lynkestes*' and serve as a Companion in the King's own bodyguard. Intermarriage provided an additional bond; Philip married a princess of the royal house of Elimea, and the Macedonian nobility was doubtless encouraged to marry into noble families of Upper Macedonia. Philip also planted cities in Upper Macedonia, such as Heraclea Lyncestis (near Bitola-Monastir), and the administrative leaders in these cities held or were granted Macedonian citizenship. An able man could thus become for example '*Makedon ex Herakleias Lynkestes*', that is a citizen of Macedonia, a citizen of his own town of Heraclea and a citizen of his tribe Lyncestae, three separate categories of citizenship. It was a characteristic of Philip that he moved 'peoples and cities as shepherds moved their sheep from winter to summer pastures'.[1] Thus, when he founded Heraclea Lyncestis, he presumably moved some people from a city in Central Macedonia to the new city; similarly when he sent settlers to strengthen Crenides, they went from one of the Macedonian cities. So within Central Macedonia he created a new community on the site of Methone by granting land to his chosen settlers and giving or confirming Macedonian citizenship to some of them. During the period 359-4 Philip began the process of assimilation between Central Macedonia and Upper Macedonia in these ways.

The economic development of Macedonia was particularly important for Philip's plans. Hitherto the imports and exports had passed mainly through the Greek cities on his coast or those of the Chalcidian League, and the Macedonian currency being on the archaic Persian standard, was used for internal exchange and overland trade in the Balkan area. Philip, and perhaps Perdiccas before him, employed Greek experts, such as the exiled Athenian statesman Callistratus, to develop Macedonian ports and markets such as Pella and Therme, and he transferred his currency to the Thracian standard in silver and to the Attic standard in gold, so that he could foster trade relations with the rich hinterland of Thrace and compete in Aegean maritime commerce, where the strongest currency was that of Athens. By 354 he had taken over all the Greek cities on his coast and so dispensed with them as middlemen, and he was glad for reasons of policy to leave to the Chalcidian League the cultivation of Anthemus and the profits of acting as a centre of exchange. No less important was it to modernize Macedonian production, which was partly agricultural and partly pastoral in Central Macedonia and mainly pastoral in Upper Macedonia. Philip had seen the effects of intensive agriculture with controlled irrigation and rotation of crops in Boeotia, and he seems to have introduced similar methods into all suitable parts of his greater Macedonia by employing Greek experts and training Macedonians. For example, the plain of Philippi was deforested and drained, and crops of cereals were grown where small flocks of sheep had once pastured. As agriculture expanded, transhumant pastoralism was reduced, and more attention was given to the raising of horses and cattle. As more of the population abandoned nomadism and took to a settled life, towns grew up and the cities gained in administrative importance. As Alexander said in a speech to the Macedonian army, 'Philip found you nomadic and poor . . . gave you cloaks to wear instead of sheepskins, brought you down from the mountains to live in the plains . . . made you inhabit cities and civilized you with good laws and customs.'[2] A social and economic revolution of this kind was certainly inaugurated by Philip in 359–4, and we can see from modern analogies in Balkan countries that such a revolution can be carried through with surprising rapidity.

Although Macedonia was a foreign state, Philip himself was a Greek in the eyes of city-state Greeks, and as such, he competed, for instance, in the Olympic Games of 356, when his horse won the flat race. Moreover, he felt himself to be not only a Greek by blood, but a descendant of Heracles, son of Zeus. Some of the coins which he minted on his new standards were marked with representations of the victorious race-horse and the head of Heracles, and he commemorated his victory over Bardylis by naming his new foundations in Lyncus 'Heraclea'. Thus when he moved into the sphere of the Sacred War, he was not regarded as an intruder; for he had as much right as any to espouse the cause of Apollo, god of Delphi.

In summer 354 at the invitation of the Thessalian League, which had suffered severely at the hands of Philomelus, Philip captured Pagasae from the tyrants of Pherae, who were in alliance with Athens. Thus Philip aligned himself with the Thessalian League, Locris and Boeotia against Phocis, Athens, Sparta and Achaea, and in the spring of 353 he came into contact with Boeotia when a Boeotian army of 5,000 men marched through Thessaly and Macedonia on its way to help Artabazus, a satrap who was in revolt against the Great King and was prepared to pay handsomely for military aid. It appeared at that time that the Sacred War was virtually finished because Philomelus had been killed and his army had dispersed late in 354, and in a moment of over-confidence the Boeotian Assembly decided to recoup its finances in this way. The Boeotian commander, Pammenes, had housed Philip as a young hostage at Thebes, and the two men now met at Maronea. Philip secured safe passage through southern Thrace for Pammenes, and Pammenes negotiated a non-aggression pact for Philip with Cersebleptes, the king of eastern Thrace.

The Sacred War broke out again in spring 353. Because Phocis had been condemned to extermination and all captured Phocians had been executed, the Phocian people in their desperation rallied behind a new leader, Onomarchus, who hired more mercenaries and used bribery to obtain help from his allies; for he began to melt down the dedications of gold and silver from the offerings at Delphi. As the main Boeotian army was in Asia Minor, Onomarchus overran his enemies in Central Greece, destroying Thronium by andrapodismos and re-founding Orchomenus as a base against Thebes. Meanwhile Philip was invited by the Thessalian League to give help against the tyrants of Pherae and Crannon, who were in alliance with the Phocians. At this time the Macedonian army which Philip had created and trained had never fought against an army of Greek hoplites. If Philip refused the invitation, he could await the return of the Boeotian army from Asia Minor and together with it and his Thessalian allies challenge Onomarchus. If he accepted, he would probably find himself matching the Macedonian army against the most powerful force of professional Greek soldiers in the world. It is an indication of his confidence in his army and of his determination to pursue his policy that he accepted the invitation.

At first Onomarchus underestimated Philip. He sent his brother Phayllus and 7,000 mercenaries to join the army of the tyrants, and they were defeated by the Macedonians and the Thessalian League forces in summer 353. Onomarchus then came north with his full army, not far short of 20,000 well-trained men, joined the tyrants and defeated the Macedonians and the Thessalian League forces in two pitched battles. The Macedonians were driven out of Thessaly, and their losses were severe. Philip had to deal with discontent in his armed forces during the winter, but in spring 352 he returned to Thessaly with the full Macedonian army. For, as he said himself, he had withdrawn, 'like a ram, to butt the harder'. Meanwhile Onomarchus had laid his plans in concert with the tyrants and with Athens. While he was to march close to the coast of southern Thessaly, the Athenian fleet carrying an expeditionary force was to sail offshore, until they both reached a point where they could combine their forces on land and then join the tyrants at Pherae. Onomarchus brought 500 cavalry and 20,000 infantry; Chares, the Athenian commander, was transporting some thousands of hoplites; and the tyrants had excellent cavalry and a considerable force of mercenary infantry. Probably no unified command was envisaged.

Philip persuaded the Thessalian League to place its forces under his command. Then, being first in the field, he posted his army of 3,000 cavalry and somewhat more than 20,000 infantry before the walls of Pherae, so that the tyrants concentrated their forces in its defence. He was aware that news of his position would reach Onomarchus and the fleet of Athens as they came north, and his own intelligence service was on the alert to inform him of their approach. At the appropriate moment Philip's army left its position silently during the night and caught the army of Onomarchus next morning in a coastal plain known as the Crocus Field. The Athenian fleet was sailing offshore. Philip attacked at once. His infantry engaged the enemy infantry all along the line, so that Onomarchus had no freedom of manoeuvre, and Philip then sent his cavalry, superior in number and in quality, to attack one flank and the rear of the enemy infantry and drive them towards the coast. His victory was complete. Of the Phocian army 6,000 were killed in action; 3,000 were captured and killed by hanging or drowning, in accordance with the practice of the Greek belligerents on both sides in the Sacred War; and others drowned as they swam out to the Athenian fleet. The victorious Macedonians and Thessalians crowned themselves with leaves of laurel and gave thanks to Apollo, the god of Delphi, for their victory.

In the campaign of the Crocus Field Philip planned his moves and tactics as brilliantly as Epaminondas had done in the campaign of 362. The Greek states realized for the first time that the Macedonian army was the equal of the army of any leading state, such as Boeotia or Athens; but Philip did not yet know whether his infantry by itself was a match for the best Greek infantry because the cavalry had been the decisive arm in the battle. Victory brought great advantages to Philip in Thessaly. Pherae and other cities surrendered on condition that the tyrants and their mercenaries were allowed to go in safety; and the cities were then included in the Thessalian League. Thus the whole of Thessaly was united as a federal state. The Assembly of the League elected Philip commander of its armed forces and allocated to him all revenue from market taxes and harbour dues. With its approval he placed troops to safeguard the passes between Macedonia and Thessaly and to hold Pagasae; and the city of Gomphi, from which a pass led to Ambracia in southern Epirus, was renamed Philippi and received some Macedonian settlers. In midsummer 352 he marched at the head of his Macedonian and Thessalian troops towards Thermopylae.

Because Philip did not follow up his victory at once by invading Phocis, as he could have done, a new army of mercenaries was recruited by Phayllus and his allies sent reinforcements to him. Philip's delay in Thessaly had probably been intentional, so that he could gauge the reaction of the Greek states and in particular of Athens to his intervention in the Sacred War. When he approached Thermopylae, he found that the narrow pass was held by the army of Phaÿllus, 1,000 Spartans, 2,000 Achaeans, and an Athenian force of 400 cavalry and 5,000 hoplites which had come by sea. He now withdrew homewards, for he did not wish to provoke a head-on collision with these city-states at this time.

For three years Philip turned his back on the Greek states and extended his realm in the Balkans. By 349 he held in his own court the heir to the Molossian throne, Alexander, brother of Olympias, and he had annexed Parauaea, a frontier area marching with Epirus. He defeated the Illyrians of central Albania and left the native kings as his vassals, campaigned successfully against the Paeonians, and defeated the Thracian kings. His frontier now was at the river Hebrus, and his allies Byzantium and Perinthus controlled the Bosporus and the Propontis. Athens held the Chersonese on the European side of the Hellespont, for she had destroyed Sestus by andrapodismos and planted a cleruchy on the site. Philip managed to effect a reconciliation between the Great King and Artabazus, who came to his court; and relations of friendship and neutrality were established between Macedon and Persia. He built a fleet at this time which raided Athenian ships and bases in the Aegean. The whole area from the Ionic Gulf (the lower Adriatic) to the Black Sea and from Thessaly to central Thrace, except for Chalcidice, was now under his control.

Meanwhile a general war was fought out in the Peloponnese. Sparta attacked Megalopolis, which was then supported by the full citizen forces of Argos, Messenia and Sicyon. However, Phocis came to the rescue of Sparta with 3,000 mercenaries, and the exiled tyrants of Pherae helped her with their cavalry. In 351, Boeotia sent 4,000 citizen infantry and 500 cavalry to support Megalopolis, and the Theban contingent distinguished itself in battle. But Sparta rallied and won a major battle, whereupon a stalemate ensued and an armistice was made. The bitter rancour which marked the Sacred War had now seeped into the Peloponnesian states.

In central Greece Phaÿllus used the temple monies to hire a new army of mercenaries and gave bribes to leading men in allied states. He fought first in Boeotia and then in eastern Locris where he captured and looted the cities. But late in 352 Pammenes returned from Asia with his large army and much money; the Boeotians then overran and looted most of Phocis. When Phaÿllus died, his successor captured Chaeronea in 351, but was driven out again. As both sides grew weaker, the fighting degenerated into guerrilla warfare; Boeotia got a subsidy of 300 talents from the Great King in 350, and the temple funds of Delphi were running low.

Athens had the good sense to keep out of the Peloponnese and the Sacred War. An able statesman, Eubulus, husbanded her resources, built up her navy, and helped the poor by grants from the Theoric Fund, which received all surplus revenue. If Athens decided to undertake a major war, such surplus revenue would have to go into the Military Fund; thus the poorest class had an interest in preserving the Theoric Fund and would now hesitate to embark on a policy of war. Financial recuperation from the low level at the end of the Social War in 355 was very rapid, and interventionist policies, in the Peloponnese in 353, in Thrace in 352, and in Rhodes in 351 were advocated unsuccessfully by a young orator, Demosthenes. The influence of Eubulus and his supporters remained paramount until 349. Athens' position was improved by a number of alliances in the Aegean area, but an attempt to win over the Chalcidian League failed.

As an ally of the Chalcidian League since 357, Philip warned it in 351 not to flirt with Athens and then in summer 349 asked it to hand over two pretenders to the Macedonian throne, his half-brothers Arrhidaeus and Menelaus. Philip made his request when some of his sympathizers in Olynthus had secured the banishment of a democratic leader, and he may have expected them to persuade the League to comply. The choice for the League was a difficult one. All considerations of financial self-interest suggested compliance, because the Chalcidian cities profited from the boom in Macedonian production; but the danger of being absorbed by so large a neighbour alarmed those who put independence before prosperity. Class interests were also aroused, so that each city in the League was divided in its views. However, the majority in the Assembly of the League said no to Philip and asked Athens for alliance and immediate aid. The Assembly at Athens granted the alliance and sent a fleet of thirty-eight ships and 2,000 mercenaries forthwith.

Philip took no action for some months. He calculated perhaps that Athens would now become dilatory and the cities which made up the League might individually become alarmed. Meanwhile Demosthenes delivered the three Olynthiac speeches urging Athens to act promptly but not proposing openly to switch the surplus revenue from the Theoric Fund to the Military Fund. Towards the end of the year when sailing conditions were bad, Philip began to take the cities one by one, some opening their gates and others falling by assault, and in January 348 he promoted a rising against Athenian control in Euboea, sending mercenaries from Thessaly into the island. As Euboea lay on Athens' line of communications, she sent her citizen army there and concentrated on regaining control. In July she gave up the attempt. During the war in Euboea, she sent eighteen more ships and 4,000 mercenaries to Chalcidice. By July Olynthus was isolated and under siege. Its leaders begged Athens to send citizen troops and not mercenaries, who had proved unreliable, and a citizen force of 300 cavalry and 2,000 infantry sailed from the Peiraeus, but was delayed by the seasonal northerly winds. Meanwhile in an engagement outside Olynthus her cavalry deserted to Philip and in August 348 the city fell.

Philip demolished the defences of Olynthus and sold its population into slavery for betraying the alliance with him. Other cities seem to have been unpunished, but parts of their populations may have been moved by Philip to towns in Macedonia. Chalcidice was incorporated into Macedonia, and Anthemus became again a royal domain. There was now no base available for a seaborne expedition against Macedonia.

Athens had suffered a double defeat which was due as much to her dilatoriness and use of mercenary troops as to the superior planning of Philip. The Chalcidian League, having 1,000 cavalry and over 10,000 hoplites, and receiving 6,000 mercenaries from Athens, might well have resisted far longer, but as a League it collapsed in action and Olynthus fell partly through faction and treachery. What alarmed Athens most was that the loss of Euboea opened the door for Philip to enter the Sacred War, break the resistance of Phocis, and lead the coalition of anti-Phocian powers against Athens as the ally of Phocis. Eubulus sent envoys to the Greek states after the fall of Olynthus and invited them to combine against Philip. There was no response. Politicians at Athens, including Demosthenes, tried to persuade the people to negotiate peace with Philip and abandon Phocis to her fate.

Philip played a waiting game. He expressed a desire for peace and even alliance with Athens, but he sent no envoys. When the Boeotians kept asking him for help in the gruelling guerrilla war to which they were exposed, he sent only a small force early in 347, and gave merely verbal assurances in the winter of 347–6. By then the Phocian leaders, being in a desperate situation, made a secret plan with Sparta and Athens to combine their forces. Spartan and Athenian troops were to take over from the Phocians the fortified pass of Thermopylae and hold off any aid from Philip, and the main Phocian, Spartan and Athenian forces were to destroy what was left of Boeotian resistance. In February 346 the Spartan king Archidamus with 1,000 Spartan hoplites, and an Athenian force on board a fleet appeared at Thermopylae only to find a rival Phocian commander in control, who refused to hand over the fortifications. They withdrew discomfited. Still Philip made no move. In June 346 envoys from Athens, Thebes, Phocis, Sparta and Euboea waited on him at Pella, his capital in Macedonia. He concluded a treaty of peace and alliance with Athens and asked her on two occasions to send troops to help him end the Sacred War. The request was refused on the advice of Demosthenes and Hegesippus. Meanwhile Philip passed Thermopylae unopposed and received the capitulation of Phocis in July; he granted a safe-conduct to Phalaecus and his 8,000 mercenaries, and the Boeotians took possession of Orchomenus and Coronea from the Phocians.

The Amphictyonic Council had to decide whether or not to carry out its resolution of October 355 to exterminate Phocis by andrapodismos. As the Boeotians had destroyed Orchomenus and Coronea by andrapodismos where no one else had a say, it was certain that they would vote in favour of extermination. At the meeting of the Amphictyonic Council, the Oetaeans proposed the andrapodismos of Phocis, but the majority vote which Philip commanded through his control of Thessaly was for a different course: the towns were to be split into villages, and the Phocians were to pay to the temple of Delphi sixty talents a year as reparations. Because Phocis had acted impiously, the two votes she had had on the Council were transferred to Philip, the liberator of Delphi, and he was elected to preside over the Pythian Games of September 346. When he had done so, he returned to Macedonia. He left behind him not only an example of clemency towards a conquered enemy, but also an indication of his policy towards the Greek states, for the decree of the Amphictyonic Council which he had inspired contained recommendations for bringing about 'religious conduct, general peace and concord among the Greeks'.[3] Towards the end of 346 the members of the Amphictyony, Athens and Boeotia included, swore solemnly by the god of Delphi to observe the general peace on the status quo, submit disputes to arbitration, and combine against an aggressor. Philip also took the oath, and behind him was the power of Macedonia. Would the initiative of Philip lead to an era of peace and reconciliation, based upon respect for treaties and religion?

CHAPTER 24

PROPOSALS FOR PEACEFUL SETTLEMENTS IN SICILY AND GREECE

While the Greek states in Sicily were passing through the vicissitudes of dictatorship and liberation and fighting one against the other, Carthage was laying the foundations of her maritime and commercial empire in the western Mediterranean. To her domains in Africa she now added extensive territories in Spain and the island of Sardinia. Meanwhile in 358 Rome defeated the dreaded Gauls in central Italy, consolidated the Latin League and annexed southern Etruria. Because she was emerging as an important state on the coast of the Etruscan Sea, Carthage concluded with Rome a treaty of friendship which permitted Carthaginians and their allies to trade at Rome and Romans and their allies to trade in the Carthaginian part of Sicily and at Carthage. What Carthage wanted next was to conquer the eastern part of Sicily. She was already on friendly terms with Messana and she accepted the invitation to help Hicetas (see p. 217) in expelling Dionysius from Ortygia and occupying Syracuse.

It so happened that Hicetas had applied to Corinth for help before he turned to Carthage. The Corinthians and their friends equipped ten warships and engaged 700 mercenaries, and they placed in command of the expedition a middle-aged Corinthian, Timoleon, who had absented himself from public life for twenty years In 365 or so, his elder brother, having been put in command of 400 mercenaries at Corinth, had seized power and executed his personal enemies without trial. Timoleon had then arranged for the assassination of his brother and had been present at the execution. The Corinthians now believed that, if he became a liberator, he would not turn into a dictator. When Timoleon's force reached the coast at Rhegium in south Italy in 344, it was intercepted by a Carthaginian flotilla, but Timoleon slipped away and reached Tauromenium in Sicily, where he was welcomed by the ruling dynast. Hearing that a city between Tauromenium and

255

Syracuse was split by party-strife, Timoleon went off to it with a small force, but found that Hicetas had just arrived there with a larger force. Knowing now that Hicetas was collaborating with Carthage, Timoleon made an unannounced attack, dispersed Hicetas' troops and went on to Catana, where a Campanian adventurer, Mamercus, was dictator and lent him support. The next step was to make contact by messenger with Dionysius who, like Timoleon, was at war with Hicetas and Carthage. The two made common cause, Timoleon passing troops and a commander into Ortygia, and Dionysius coming out to Catana. Some months later Dionysius opted out of public life, and retired to Corinth.

In spring 343 the Carthaginian commander, Mago, sailed into the Great Harbour of Syracuse with 150 ships and a large army, blockaded Ortygia and sent a flotilla to south Italy to intercept any further aid from Greece. Mago and Hicetas led forces against Timoleon at Catana. But despite the odds Ortygia and Catana withstood the attack, and a second expedition from Corinth, ten ships carrying 2,000 hoplites, avoided the Carthaginian flotilla in south Italy and sailed into Catana. Mago and Hicetas quarrelled because Hicetas' mercenaries were seen fraternizing with the mercenaries in Ortygia, and Mago sailed away to western Sicily. Timoleon promptly moved into Syracuse, and Hicetas withdrew to Leontini. The liberation of Syracuse was celebrated on Timoleon's orders by the citizens demolishing all the works of the dictators – the palace, the citadel and the tombs. The first liberator not to turn dictator at the moment of success, Timoleon recalled all exiles, recruited new settlers and devised a constitution for the city after its sixty years of servitude. He came to terms with Hicetas and borrowed some of his mercenaries for the impending struggle with Carthage.

In 341 a Carthaginian fleet of 200 warships escorted a great convoy from Africa to Lilybaeum in westernmost Sicily. The army of 70,000 men was complete with siege equipment and supply-train, and it was unlike any previous army of invasion in that it included the citizen-troops of Carthage, headed by a 'Sacred Band' of 2,500 heavily-armoured infantry and a squadron of four-horse chariots. The rest of the army consisted of mercenaries from the western Mediterranean countries. Such an army was clearly designed for the occupation of Greek Sicily. Timoleon took the initiative by invading Carthaginian territory with an army of 12,000 men, which included 1,000 cavalry and 3,000 citizen troops from Syracuse; the rest were Greek mercenaries, a thousand of whom deserted during the march. Timoleon's bold strategy had the desired effect, for the Carthaginian army was drawn inland into hilly country where it camped by the River Crimisus.

When Timoleon's army reached the hills above the river, a thick mist lay over the plain and he halted his men. As it lifted the Carthaginian army was seen to be in the process of crossing the river, and Timoleon immediately attacked, his cavalry first engaging and halting the chariots and then his infantry in massed formation striking the Sacred Band and that part of the main line which had just crossed the river. The Carthaginians, wearing bronze helmets and iron cuirasses and wielding heavy spears, were not overborne by the charging infantry of Timoleon, but in the close fighting which followed the clash of the lines, they were less agile and skilful. At this critical moment there was a cloudburst with lightning and hail driven by the wind into the faces of the Carthaginians, and the ground became slippery underfoot. As the Greek cavalry concentrated on attacking the flanks and the Greek infantry broke through the front of the enemy formation, the head of the Carthaginian army fell back towards the river bed where the main body was pressing forward. The rising waters of the river added to the confusion; for the heavily-armoured infantrymen found it difficult to rise once they had fallen, and were easily drowned. Panic ensued. The Greek cavalry and light-armed infantry pressed the pursuit, killing 3,000 Carthaginians and 7,000 mercenaries, and captured the richly-equipped camp of the enemy.

The victory was decisive in that it halted the Carthaginian army of invasion, but the new Carthaginian commander sent mercenaries to help a league of dictators, headed by Hicetas and Mamercus, who were afraid that Timoleon would overthrow them. On this occasion Carthage hired Greek mercenaries for the first time, being convinced of their superior quality by the battle of the Crimisus River. In 339 Timoleon and Carthage made peace, adopting the Halycus river as the frontier, and Carthage undertook not to help the dictators, who were eventually captured and publicly executed. In 336 Timoleon the liberator brought his mission to completion, for every city in Greek Sicily was free to decide its own future. He retired from public life, went blind, and died soon afterwards; public games were instituted in his honour at Syracuse, to be celebrated 'for all time'.

Between 342 and 336 Timoleon carried out a great work of rehabilitation and reconstruction. When he first came to Sicily, grass grew in the streets of Syracuse and the sites of many cities had been totally abandoned. By offering land and citizenship, Timoleon attracted settler-families in hundreds of thousands from Sicily, Italy and Greece. Old cities such as Gela and Acragas came to life again; new cities were planted and prosperity returned to eastern Sicily. Coinage in gold and

257

silver commemorated the victory at the Crimisus River, and the head on the coins was that of Zeus the Liberator. When the dictators fell, Timoleon resisted the pressure to re-establish political life in the form of a democracy. Instead he set up first in Syracuse and then in almost all other cities a balanced or mixed constitution in which the chief magistrate or president was the priest of Olympian Zeus, chosen from three priestly families, the Council of 600 members was elected from members of well-to-do families, and the Assembly of all citizens discussed and decided only major issues. Thus the day-to-day administration of the state was firmly placed in the hands of the propertied class. Military matters were conducted by an elected board of generals, except that a commander-in-chief was to be obtained from Corinth in the event of war against a non-Greek power; and a new legal code for all states, replacing that of Diocles, was drawn up with the help of jurists from Corinth. Finally Timoleon created a union of Greek states in Sicily on the basis of a general peace and alliance, which was strengthened by the possession of a balanced constitution and a common legal code by almost all its members.

Timoleon showed what one man of principle, courage and faith could achieve in the troubled world of fourth-century Sicily. He was in a sense the mirror-image of Dionysius, working for good rather than evil and upholding the claims of religion, liberty and moderation. An admirer of Epaminondas, he tried to strengthen the Greek states for the future by forming a coalition of allies and introducing institutions which were calculated to achieve the very objectives which in a different context had been outlined in the decree of the Amphictyonic Council at Delphi in 346, 'religious conduct, general peace and concord among the Greeks'.

The decline which Timoleon arrested for a time in Sicily was gathering momentum in south Italy. When the empire of Dionysius collapsed, the coalition which he had imposed on the Greek cities broke apart and a period of anarchy and particularism followed. The Italian tribes were dangerous neighbours because they had been enlivened by contact with the Greek states and many of their men had become experienced in Greek warfare as mercenary soldiers. Now the Bruttians, Lucanians and Messapians took advantage of Greek disunity and captured city after city piecemeal – Terina, Hipponium, Sybaris, Thurii, and so on. Tarentum, traditionally the leading state in south Italy, which had had a citizen army of 30,000 men in the fifth century, was now so decadent and divided that it relied mainly upon mercenary soldiers and turned to its foundress for help in 343. Sparta sent one of her kings, Archidamus, with a fleet and an army, but he was killed in battle against the Lucanians in 338. Although Greek capitalism and Greek warfare, as exemplified by the professional mercenary Greek soldier and sailor, were unrivalled in the eastern and the western Mediterranean, the area of the free Greek states was contracting rather than expanding.

When a great power suddenly arises and its policy is directed by one man, it is exceedingly difficult for a foreigner to guess his intentions, and, if he expresses his intentions, to decide whether he is sincere or not. The critical question for the Greek states in 352, when Philip defeated Onomarchus, and in early summer 346, when he was likely to act in Phocis, was whether he would behave like the average city-state in carrying enmity to its logical conclusion and in imposing hegemony by traditional methods.

In early summer 346, when Athens and Philip had agreed to make peace and Philip was still in the north, Isocrates wrote and published an open letter to Philip which has survived under the title *Philippus*. He recognized that Philip's power was greater than that of any state in Europe, and that Philip had won the complete confidence of the Thessalians by his actions. Could he not go on to reconcile the Greek states and lead them in a campaign against Persia? This is what Isocrates exhorted him to do. His first objective, wrote Isocrates, should be to bring together Argos and Sparta, and Thebes and Athens, and the attempt would be more likely to succeed with Athens if he made clear his intention to attack Persia. Next, he should aim to conquer the whole Persian Empire, or at least to cut off Asia Minor, in order that he might extend his own rule over as many barbarians as possible, liberate the Greek cities in Asia, and relieve Greece from its troubles by founding cities in Asia and settling in them Greece's floating population of mercenaries, refugees and *émigrés*. Isocrates addressed Philip as a Greek, and as no ordinary Greek but a Greek descended from Heracles, son of Zeus, and a Greek in a position of kingship – on both these counts Philip being exactly like a Spartan king. The appeal to Philip to reconcile the Greeks and lead them on an anti-Persian crusade was made on the grounds that his ancestor Heracles had been a benefactor of the Greek race. The obligations of Philip were summarized at the end of the *Philippus*: 'To benefit the Greeks, be a king to the Macedonians [i.e. a true king and not a despot] and extend your rule over as many barbarians as possible.'[1]

Isocrates ascribed to Philip as motives for taking such a course not only a desire for power but also a desire for glory and a love of all

Greece as his 'fatherland'. He assumed that Philip believed in his descent from Heracles, son of Zeus, and he expressed the belief that the gods had promoted Philip's success in the past and were now prompting him to reconcile Greece and defeat Persia. Isocrates presumably chose his words with a knowledge of Philip's character and beliefs, for a personal appeal is of little worth unless it is directed towards the predilections of the recipient.

Some weeks after the publication of the *Philippus* the actions of Philip in Phocis and the decree of the Amphictyonic Council seemed to fulfil the hopes which Isocrates had expressed. For Philip did not attempt either to carry the Sacred War further or to impose his hegemony. Rather he sought to reconcile the Greeks by terminating the Sacred War with merciful treatment of the Phocians and by proposing, through the Council, measures designed to bring about in Greece 'religious conduct, general peace and concord among the Greeks'. Isocrates certainly regarded Philip as sincere, as we know from a later letter of Isocrates to Philip, but then Isocrates was a professor of education and not a politician in the arena of practical politics.

In the *Philippus* Isocrates made it clear that he was not speaking for the politicians. Rather he warned Philip against them. Their view of Philip's intentions (and here Isocrates was hitting the mark for some politicians, if we may judge from the speeches of Demosthenes, for instance) was that he would first deal with the Phocian situation, then gather the forces of his group in the Sacred War (Thessaly, Boeotia, Locris, Doris, etc.), link up with Argos, Messenia and Arcadia, destroy Sparta, impose his own hegemony on the Peloponnese and go on to reduce the rest of Greece. Such an expectation would not be unnatural, if one judged Philip by the standard of the city-state. Indeed, if Phocis and her allies had managed to exclude Philip from Greece early in 346, they would surely have destroyed Boeotia and her allies, tried to subjugate Argos, Messenia and Arcadia, and would have had no scruples in using temple monies and mercenary soldiers.

When Philip made arrangements for a general peace and returned to Macedonia in autumn 346, the politicians had to think again. Either Philip was sincere in his intentions as they were revealed in the Amphictyonic decree, or, if he was insincere, he hoped to lull suspicions for the moment, and intended later to subjugate the Greek states. Some politicians, Aeschines being one at Athens, expressed the former view; others, Demosthenes for example at Athens, expressed the latter view. That they believed their view in each case to be correct or at least probably correct (for it was a matter of weighing probabilities) cannot be assumed, for politicians deal with overall situations and not with one aspect of foreign policy alone. Thus an extreme democrat might have believed Philip to be sincere but still have represented him as a menacing imperialist rather than agree with an oligarchic sympathizer of Philip; and an extreme oligarch might have taken up the diametrically opposite position. In case this seems unduly cynical, it is worth noting that Isocrates blamed contemporary city-states for being guided solely by expediency and politicians for considering a general peace inimical to their personal interests.

For three or four years Philip left the Greek city-states to accommodate themselves to the new situation, and they for their part wavered in their attitude towards him. He expressed his goodwill towards Athens repeatedly, discussed matters arising from the treaty of peace, and rebuked her if she acted in breach of the treaty. He offered to cut a canal through the neck of the Chersonese, which would have strengthened her control of that strategic area; he inspired an award in Athens' favour by the Amphictyonic Council in 344/3; he offered to admit other Greek states to the 'general peace' of 346; he proposed in 342 to give to Athens a small island, Halonnesos, which he had cleared of pirates; and he was willing, in 341, to submit to arbitration some points of dispute affecting the Chersonese. It is probable that he dealt with other states in the same conciliatory way.

Athenian politicians had combined after the fall of Olynthus in 348 to extricate Athens from her exposed position in the Sacred War, and even Demosthenes who had previously led the way in denouncing Philip served on an embassy to Philip and supported a proposal to make peace with him. On the other hand, when Philocrates, the leader of the embassy, proposed peace and alliance in the Assembly, Demosthenes sat silent; and when the treaty of peace and alliance was finally concluded in July 346, Demosthenes opposed its implementation and persuaded the Assembly not to send troops at Philip's request in order to help him terminate the Sacred War. Thus before Philip's intentions were made clear in the decree of the Amphictyonic Council, Athens was split in its attitude towards him and some leading politicians had committed themselves up to the hilt, Philocrates and Aeschines advocating trust in Philip's intentions and Demosthenes advocating distrust.

The struggle between these politicians after the end of the Sacred War was conducted partly in the Assembly but mainly in the lawcourt. The first prosecution of Aeschines which Demosthenes arranged in 345 failed miserably, and Aeschines reaffirmed his confidence in

Philip's intention to benefit Athens. In 344 Demosthenes and his supporters were successful; the courts passed sentence of death on Philocrates, and imposed a heavy fine on Proxenus for failing to get control of Thermopylae early in 346. However, Demosthenes' chief target was Aeschines; he prosecuted again in 343, and this time Aeschines escaped the death sentence by only thirty votes before a mass jury of probably 1,501 jurors.

On the advice of Demosthenes and his supporters, the Assembly rejected the friendly overtures of Philip and tried to counteract his popularity with the anti-Spartan group of Peloponnesian states – Argos, Messenia and Megalopolis. When Philip offered in 343 to extend the scope of 'general peace', the Assembly sent the most violent of Demosthenes' supporters as head of a mission to Macedonia. While relations with Philip were so uncertain, Athens tightened up her security, put her fleet of 300 ships on to a war footing, reinforced her cleruchies in the Chersonese and obtained a base for her mercenary troops in Thasos.

In 344 Philip reorganized the Thessalian League, arranging administration by districts rather than by city-states; Macedonian coinage was adopted but alongside city-state coinages; and Philip was elected President of the League for life, a position which gave him control of mobilization and taxation and command in war. He made an alliance with the Aetolian League at this time. In the winter of 343–2 he arranged the affairs of Epirus, compelling some Greek cities in southern Epirus to submit themselves to the Molossian state and placing his brother-in-law Alexander on the Molossian throne. The displaced regent, Arybbas, fled to Athens and was given Athenian citizenship. These operations alarmed two Corinthian colonies in the vicinity, Ambracia and Leucas; they appealed to Corinth, and she asked Athens for help. This was Athens' chance to emerge from her comparative isolation, her only allies being her colleagues from the Sacred War, Sparta and Achaea. She sent citizen-troops to Acarnania, and when Philip withdrew from the vicinity of Ambracia she entered into alliance with Corinth, Ambracia, Leucas and Corcyra and established friendly relations with Cephallenia and the Argive group of states in the Peloponnese. In June 342 she made an alliance with Messenia, which upset her relations with Sparta.

In 342 Isocrates wrote a letter to Philip which has survived. He admitted the hostility of the masses at Athens to Philip but advised him still to cultivate the goodwill of Athens and the Greek states. To anyone who put the interest of Greece first in his scale of values it was obvious that Philip's initiative in 346 had replaced the previous years of carnage by four years of peace among the Greek states. But the success of Demosthenes and his supporters at Athens was now making the general peace precarious, and there were signs in the Peloponnese that each city-state was jockeying for position in case war should break out there. The position in Asia was also changing. After a long period of weakness when his western satraps were in revolt, Artaxerxes Ochus managed to recover Phoenicia in 345 and Egypt in 343. In these wars both sides employed Greek mercenaries to a total of at least 30,000, and a Rhodian captain of mercenaries, Mentor, was sent as viceroy to Asia Minor in 342, where he captured a local ruler, Hermias of Atarneus, who had been on friendly terms with Philip; Hermias was questioned about Philip's intentions before he was put to death by Artaxerxes. In this year Macedon and Persia became immediate neighbours, separated only by the waters of the Bosporus.

In Thrace Philip had always acted as the protector of the Greek city-states against the Thracian kings and had enjoyed the alliance of, for instance, Cardia, Perinthus and Byzantium, whereas Athens had sought alliance with the Thracian kings, alienated the Greek city-states by acts of andrapodismos and the planting of cleruchies, and relied on her sea-power to hold the Chersonese. In the summer and winter of 342 Philip completed the conquest and reorganization of Thrace, carrying his authority up to the coasts of the Black Sea and the Propontis where many Greek city-states became his allies, and making a pact of friendship with the king of the Getae on the left bank of the Danube, who gave his daughter and a very rich dowry to Philip. Military roads were built throughout Thrace, and military colonies were planted in new cities, for instance at Philippopolis (now Plovdiv) controlling the central plain, and at Cabyle on the route towards the Danube. On earlier campaigns Philip had extended his area of control in Illyria and Dardania so that his Balkan realm included most of the lands between the Danube and the Aegean Sea.

While Philip was busy in Thrace, Diopeithes, Athens' commander in the Chersonese, was not supplied with sufficient money to pay his mercenaries. He therefore exacted 'benevolences' from ships passing through the Hellespont; he now attacked Philip's ally Cardia, raided parts of Thrace, and held an envoy of Philip to ransom for a large sum. When Philip lodged a protest and offered to submit his differences with Athens to arbitration, Demosthenes delivered two speeches, *On the Chersonese* and *The Third Philippic*, in which he pressed for war in defence of the liberty of Greece. His arguments prevailed and his influence became paramount in the Assembly. Reinforcements were sent to Diopeithes, garrisons were landed on Proconnesos and Tenedos to control traffic through the Hellespont, and alliances were made with Byzantium, Abydus, Chios and Rhodes. Gold was sent to Diopeithes by Persia, probably in answer to an approach by Athens. Nearer home in 341, with the collusion of some Megarian democrats, an Athenian army entered Megara, installed a democratic government, and began to build long walls from the town to the coast. By similar intrigues and the use of troops democracies were installed in Chalcis and Eretria, and Euboea was won over from alliance with Philip to alliance with Athens. These actions were taken without denouncing the treaty with Philip, but it was clear that the 'general peace' inaugurated in 346 was drawing to an end. In March 340 the Assembly crowned Demosthenes with a golden crown for his services to the state.

CHAPTER 25

DECISION BY WAR AND THE ALLIANCE
OF MACEDONIA AND GREECE, 340–336

The premises upon which Demosthenes based his advice to the people were clearly stated in his speeches of 341, *On the Chersonese* and *The Third Philippic*. Referring only to the Treaty of Peace with Philip, he claimed that a state of war existed and indeed had existed since 346 between Macedon and Athens because Philip was constantly committing acts of aggression against Athens. Most of the examples of such aggression which he cited had happened either before 346 or in 346 and had taken place in Phocis, Macedonia, Chalcidice and Thrace; yet in Demosthenes' view they justified all the actions of Diopeithes and any further attacks on Philip's territory in Thrace. The fundamental premise was that Philip was planning to attack and 'destroy' Athens utterly because he was the implacable enemy of liberty and democracy and Athens was the champion of liberty and democracy, as she had been in the Persian Wars. The opponents of Demosthenes might have pointed out that Philip had supported liberty and democracy in Thessaly while Athens had supported the tyrants of Pherae and the Phocian oligarchs, and that, unlike Athens, Philip had not used andrapodismos and had not 'destroyed' Phocis at all. But Demosthenes did not engage in arguments. Anyone who argued against him was in his opinion a traitor to Athens and should be 'cudgelled to death'.

Demosthenes advocated acts of war without declaring war. He urged Athens to keep Philip far from Attica by raiding his coastal territories, to prepare her ships and raise money and soldiers, and to seek alliances throughout Greece. In these speeches there was no assessment of the military resources of Athens in comparison with those of Philip, or of the effectiveness of coastal raids on the economy of a continental power such as Macedonia, although Demosthenes had visited the country as an envoy; for such an assessment would have weakened Athens' appetite for war. The aim of Demosthenes was to commit Athens to war and to provoke war. By March 340 he had succeeded, and he had brought a number of states into alliance with Athens.

Philip had delayed long enough to see whether his policy of reconciliation would be acceptable to the Greek city-states, and the decision of Athens to receive aid for Diopeithes from Persia and to raise a coalition against Macedonia marked the end of the general peace. Just before the seasonal northerly winds were due, in July 340, Philip sailed a small fleet up the Hellespont, landing troops on the Chersonese to distract Diopeithes, and brought his siege-train by sea to Perinthus which, he claimed, had broken its alliance with him. He delivered attacks on the city with missile-firing catapults, battering-rams, scaling ladders and moving towers 120 feet high; and tunnels were driven under the walls. The Macedonians broke through the outer circuit, but the Perinthians fought from row after row of tall houses, the city being built like a theatre on the hillsides of a peninsula, and they received a constant flow of supplies, money and troops by sea from Byzantium and from the Persian satraps who were acting on the orders of Artaxerxes Ochus. When the siege became protracted, Philip, having raised his army to 30,000 men, opened an assault also on Byzantium which had been his ally but was now helping Perinthus.

During these operations Philip sent a letter to Athens in which he listed Athens' breaches of the treaty and her rejections of his offers to submit disputes to arbitration in accordance with the treaty. As Athens was now in league with Persia against Macedonia, Philip announced his intention to retaliate. In all this he showed respect for the oaths he had taken. At Athens the Assembly took the formal decision 'to man the fleet and hasten other measures' of war. Among these was to be the conclusion of an alliance with Persia.

Philip moved first. While the successor of Diopeithes, Chares, was at a conference of Persian commanders on the Asiatic coast, Philip captured a convoy of 230 merchantmen which had left the Black Sea ports and was waiting to be escorted by Athenian warships through the Bosporus and the Hellespont, no doubt on payment of 'benevolences' in appropriate cases. He retained all enemy vessels and let the rest go free. Enraged by Philip's action, Athens ordered Chares to relieve Byzantium; but the Byzantines would not admit Chares and his mercenaries, whom they distrusted. A citizen force, equipped with the help of the richest citizens – among them Demosthenes and his supporter Hyperides – reached Byzantium late in 340 and took part in the defence. Chios, Rhodes and Cos, which had helped Byzantium in the Social War, also came to her assistance. Persia sent troops as well as money to

Byzantium and landed troops somewhere in Thrace to create a distraction, and she concluded a formal alliance with Athens and sent her a large subsidy.

Late in the winter of 340 a final assault by moonlight on the walls of Byzantium was unsuccessful because the barking of the dogs roused the defenders in time and Philip broke off the siege. In order to extricate his fleet from the Black Sea, he made up a despatch which alleged a rising in Thrace and arranged for it to be intercepted by the enemy fleet. As a result the Athenians then sailed away to the Thracian coast; during their absence his fleet passed through the Bosporus and the Hellespont into the open sea and reached the Thermaic Gulf.

If Philip had succeeded in capturing Perinthus and Byzantium, he would have been in a position to control traffic passing to and from the Black Sea, because the northerly winds and the current flowing from the Black Sea often compelled ships under sail to put into the ports of the Propontis and the Bosporus. Once in that position he would have cut the corn supply from the Black Sea to the Peiraeus, on which Athens relied for feeding her very large population, and might have persuaded her to change her policy. Now that he could not do so, he prepared for the confrontation in war which he had hitherto avoided.

At Athens Philip's withdrawal from Perinthus and Byzantium caused great joy. Demosthenes persuaded the Assembly at last to divert the surplus revenue from the Theoric Fund to the Military Fund in mid-summer 339, and he himself was appointed 'Commissioner of the Fleet'. But by then it was clear that the campaign would be fought on land.

On leaving Byzantium Philip campaigned against Ateas, king of a group of migrating Scythian tribes which were crossing the Danube near its mouth. Philip claimed the right to dedicate a statue of Heracles at the mouth of the Danube, but Ateas refused to let Philip enter territory which Ateas now claimed was his own. On the campaign Philip took his eldest son Alexander, then sixteen years of age. The decisive battle was fought on the open plain where the hordes of Scythian cavalry might encircle the Macedonian army. Philip therefore placed his best cavalry to protect the rear and flanks of his infantry line and made a frontal attack with his infantry on the main Scythian host. His victory was complete. He took 20,000 captives including women and children, whom he planned to settle south of the Danube, and a great amount of stock including brood mares which he sent to Macedonia for breeding. On the way back he was attacked by the Triballi near the Danube and severely wounded in the thigh. Much of his booty was lost. He reached Pella in summer 339 to recover from his wound.

During his absence in Thrace a dispute developed at the Amphictyonic Council between the representatives of western Locris and those
of Athens. Thebes and Athens did not send representatives to the
meeting which declared a Sacred War on the Locrians of Amphissa for
an alleged act of sacrilege, and they sent no troops either, so that the
operations against Amphissa were abortive. At the next meeting, in
September 339, which was attended by the representatives of Thebes
and Athens and was presided over by a Thessalian friend of Philip, the
command in the Sacred War was offered to Philip. He accepted the
offer and marched south in November 339.

In the traditional alignment of powers Boeotia was an ally of the
western Locrians, in whose territory Amphissa lay. Although she had
been an ally of Macedon since 353, she resented Philip's lenient settlement of Phocis and the allocation of Nicaea and Echinus near Thermopylae not to her but to Thessaly. Recently Thebes had taken the law
into her own hands by expelling a Macedonian garrison from Nicaea
and placing one of her own there. These and other differences were
still under negotiation when Philip came south with his army; he
avoided Nicaea by going inland to Cytinium in Doris and sent envoys
to Thebes from his allies on the Amphictyonic Council asking that
Nicaea should be handed over to the eastern Locrians, in whose
territory it lay. Philip then moved his army through Phocis to Elatea
near the Boeotian frontier; he thus cut the communications between
Nicaea and Thebes. His presence was a threat to Thebes and, beyond
Thebes, to Athens.

The news of Philip's advance reached Athens in the evening. At
dawn the Assembly accepted Demosthenes' proposal to offer Boeotia
an alliance on generous terms, and he and others hastened to Thebes
where they found envoys from Philip and his allies asking the Boeotians
as allies of Philip and as members of the Amphictyony to act with his
army or at least to give his army free passage into Attica. The Athenian
envoys asked for alliance against Philip and offered to Boeotia the
command of both armies, a shared naval command, a contribution by
Athens of two-thirds of all expenses and the recognition of the Boeotian
League's authority over all cities in Boeotia. The Assembly of the
Boeotians voted in favour of alliance with Athens. It was a brave
decision because the campaign would be fought on Boeotian soil, and
Boeotia, in breaking her treaty of alliance with Philip, was exposing
herself to reprisals. It was a personal triumph for Demosthenes. At the
eleventh hour Athens was saved from invasion.

During the winter Philip restored the Phocian state with Amphictyonic approval and offered terms of peace to Boeotia and Athens. The offer was not even brought to the Assemblies of the two states but was rejected out of hand through the influence of Demosthenes. Meanwhile Boeotia and Athens made alliances with Achaea, Corinth, Megara, Euboea, Acarnania, Leucas and Corcyra. For six months or so the Macedonian forces held fortified positions at Thermopylae, Cytinium and Elatea, and the Greek allies held two widely separated positions covering Amphissa and Boeotia. Then in a well prepared night attack Philip destroyed a force of 10,000 mercenaries and captured Amphissa. He offered peace once again. The Beotarchs and the most experienced citizen general of Athens, Phocion, advised acceptance, but Demosthenes and his supporters persuaded both peoples to reject it. The Greek army fell back to a defensive position at Chaeronea and Philip delivered the attack on 2 August 338.

For twenty years the Macedonian army had fought against the most warlike peoples of the Balkans – Illyrians, Paeonians, Thracians, Triballians and Scythians – and at times against Greek mercenaries and citizen forces such as those of the Chalcidian League. It was superbly trained, each unit for its special purpose. The heavy cavalrymen, wearing protective armour and armed with lance, sword and shield, charged in close formation against the enemy cavalry or against the flank and rear of the infantry line, while the light cavalrymen, using javelins and a sword, skirmished and harassed the enemy and were deadly in pursuit. The cavalry were excellently mounted. Philip had developed in his Balkan warfare an infantryman of the line who was less heavily armoured than the Greek hoplite but had a superior weapon, namely a pike twice as long as the hoplite's spear, and he fought in a more flexible formation than the Greek hoplite. When the formation was contracted, three pike-heads could be presented by each file. There were many specialized units, recruited from other Balkan peoples and from Greek mercenaries, which acted as supporting troops for the cavalry and the infantry of the line and supplied special services such as commissariat and siege-train. The army had complete confidence in the king, who fought always at the head of the attacking forces, had been wounded several times and had rarely lost a battle and never a campaign.

The Greek armed forces were uneven. The Boeotian infantrymen had been hardened by continuous fighting in the Sacred War; the mercenaries were good professional soldiers; and the citizens of the other states were inexperienced, the Athenians, for instance, having had only a month's regular fighting since 362. The individual cavalry units were well trained, but they had never fought together, and had had no experience of the Macedonian cavalry. The Boeotian commanders were competent by Greek standards, but they had to control a large and varied team of contingent commanders.

The Greek army of 2,000 cavalry and 35,000 infantry held a strong defensive position in the plain, its left wing resting on the foothills east of Chaeronea, a walled city, and its right wing on the banks of the river Cephissus. The infantry line, two miles long, stood obliquely across the plain, eight men deep except on the extreme right where the Theban Sacred Band was in massed formation. The 12,000 Boeotians held the right, the 10,000 Athenians the left, and the others, stiffened by 5,000 mercenaries, the centre. The Greek cavalry was kept as a reserve behind the infantry line.

Map 11   The battle of Chaeronea, 338

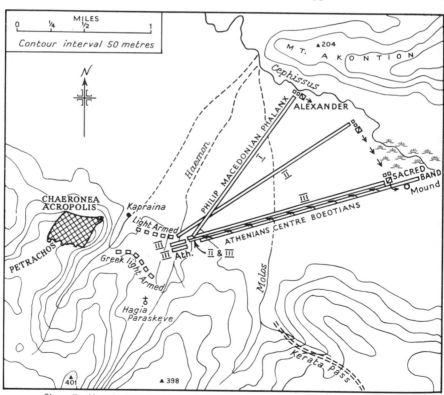

Phase I   *Macedonians advance; Greeks stationary*
Phase II *Philip retreats, his centre and left advancing; Athenians, Centre and Boeotians advance to left front, but the Sacred Band stands firm*
Phase III *Alexander charges, the centres engage, and Philip drives the Athenian wing up the Haemon valley*

Philip had 2,000 cavalry, Macedonian and Thessalian, and 30,000 infantry, all Macedonian, for this battle of prestige. He put Alexander in charge of all the cavalry on the left flank of his line, and he himself led the infantry line forward aslant so that the battalions would come into action one by one from right to left over a considerable time. Philip marched with the right-hand battalion and as it came up to the Athenians he ordered it to close ranks and to retire slowly to its right rear. As each of the other battalions came up, it did likewise. The Athenians advanced impetuously to their left front in pursuit but did not come to grips with the bristling line of Macedonian pike-points. Meanwhile the whole Greek line was moving to its left front to keep contact, except on the extreme right where the Sacred Band stood still and a gap opened up. Into this gap Alexander charged at the head of the heavy cavalry. At the same time Philip ordered his infantry to charge the Athenian line which broke in pieces, and the Macedonian infantry on the left wing, following the cavalry through the gap, swung right and rolled up the Greek line from the flank. The whole Greek line fled, leaving 1,000 Athenian dead and 2,000 captured, the Sacred Band annihilated and many Boeotian dead and captured. But there was no pursuit. Victory itself was enough for Philip.

Boeotia capitulated. Philip restored freedom to states which Thebes had subjugated or destroyed – Thespiae, Plataea and Orchomenus – and the Boeotian League was disbanded. Oligarchic exiles returned to Thebes and executed or banished the democratic leaders, and a Macedonian garrison occupied the citadel of Thebes. As a treacherous ally, Thebes was required to buy back her dead and her prisoners. Her fate was hard but less harsh than that which she had meted out to Coronea and Orchomenus. Philip made peace with the other states of central Greece which had opposed him. Some of their leaders were banished, and Philip placed garrisons at Ambracia and Chalcis.

At Athens preparations were made to man the walls. Of the three generals only one came home; he was condemned and executed. While Demosthenes sailed off to get supplies and money from Persia and other sources, Hyperides proposed to arm 150,000 tough male slaves. But wiser counsels prevailed when the Areopagus Council intervened in a debate of the Assembly. Phocion, Aeschines and Demades were appointed to negotiate with Philip. His terms were accepted. They were that he would not send troops into Athens or ships into the Peiraeus; Macedon and Athens would enter into alliance; Athens would retain Lemnos, Imbros, Scyros, Delos and Samos, but dissolve the rest of the Athenian Alliance and withdraw her other cleruchies;

and Thebes was to surrender a border town to Athens. The ashes of the Athenian dead were then brought to the city by a military escort headed by Alexander, and the 2,000 prisoners-of-war were restored without ransom. Such generosity was unprecedented in the whole history of Greek city-state warfare.

Megara and Corinth sued for peace, and Philip placed a garrison in the citadel of Acrocorinth, as he passed through into the Peloponnese. There he made peace with the Achaean League, reconstituted the Arcadian League and arbitrated in a number of territorial disputes. Sparta alone refused to admit him. Philip marched through Laconia to Gytheum unopposed and on his return gave to Messenia, Argos and the Arcadian League some territories which Sparta had recently annexed. The intention of Philip in making these arrangements was to reduce the capacity of Thebes, Athens and Sparta for upsetting any general settlement of Greek affairs.

Late in 338 at the invitation of Philip, all Greek states of the mainland except Sparta and many states in the Aegean basin sent delegates to a conference at which Philip announced his proposals for the Greek states. In spring 337 these proposals, having been considered by each state during the winter, were ratified at a conference held at Corinth. Greece now became a federal state called 'The Greeks' (known nowadays as 'The Greek League', or 'The League of Corinth').[1] Each member-state undertook to respect its own laws and neither to change its existing constitution by means of revolutionary violence and summary execution nor to redistribute landed property, except by legal decision; to respect the liberty and autonomy of the other member-states; and to submit any dispute with other member-states to arbitration. The states swore to preserve a general peace among themselves on the territorial basis of the status quo, to act collectively against any violator of the peace whether internal or external, and to suppress brigandage and piracy. The government of the federal state was vested in 'The Council of the Greeks', to which each constituent unit elected a member or members in proportion to its military or naval strength. The units were mostly city-states, either singly or grouped together, but some were made up of small tribal states grouped together. The size and the full membership of the Council are not known. 'The Council of the Greeks' dealt with all federal matters: declaring war and peace, raising taxes, requisitioning supplies, levying troops, appointing executive officers to safeguard internal arrangements, dealing with disputes by arbitration, trying offenders against federal laws and punishing those found guilty by sentences which included banishment from federal territory. The Council was to hold its meetings at the religious centres – Delphi, Olympia, Nemea and the Isthmus – and each meeting was to be presided over by a board of five, selected from the councillors by lot. The decisions taken by the Council on a majority vote in all matters were binding on the member-states. Thus the 'Council of the Greeks' was a sovereign body.

The first regular meeting of the newly-elected Council was held in summer 337. 'The Greeks' then made a treaty of offensive and defensive alliance with 'Philip and his descendants', that was, with the Macedonian state for all time, and went on to declare war jointly with Philip against Persia in order to avenge the sacrilege committed by Xerxes. For the conduct of the war Philip was elected unanimously commander-in-chief (*hegemon*) in view of his services 'as a benefactor of Greece'. It was also agreed that for the duration of the war Philip or his deputy should act as chairman at the meetings of the Council, and operations of war were to be conducted 'in accordance with the resolutions of the Council and the orders of the *hegemon*'. The presence of the Macedonian garrisons at Ambracia, Chalcis, Thebes and Corinth was approved as a measure of security in time of war, and arrangements were made for the Greek federal state to provide contingents, both military and naval, for the campaign of the ensuing year.

The position in Persia was favourable for an invasion. For Artaxerxes Ochus had been poisoned by the commander of the guard in 338, and his son Arses was killed early in 336. Mentor, the viceroy in Asia Minor, had died, and his brother Memnon succeeded to his military position only. In spring 336 an advance force of 10,000 men, supported by a fleet, established a bridgehead in Asia Minor, and the satrap of Caria, anticipating a successful advance, offered his daughter's hand to a Macedonian prince. Philip intended to bring the main army into Asia in autumn 336.

Meanwhile all had been quiet in Greece. At Athens, for instance, the people conferred citizenship on Philip and Alexander in a flush of gratitude for his leniency, and even resolved to erect a statue of Philip. Yet in 337 they elected Demosthenes Commissioner of the Theoric Fund, and early in 336 a proposal was made to crown him with a golden crown for his past services to the state. However, the proposal was held up when Aeschines indicted it as illegal; honours were accorded to a Macedonian general, and on Phocion's advice a force of cavalry and a flotilla of ships were provided for the invasion of Asia. Prevailing opinion was beginning to favour a more conciliatory attitude towards Macedon. In July 336 Athens sent a golden crown to Philip on the occasion of the wedding which was about to be celebrated at the Macedonian court.

The begetting of an heir is a vital matter in a hereditary monarchy. The ruling king in Macedonia normally took more than one wife in order to make sure of leaving sons behind him. Thus Amyntas had had six sons, Philip being one of them; Philip had had several sons but in 337 only two were alive: Alexander, son of Olympias, who was of the Molossian royal house, and Arrhidaeus, who was an epileptic son of a Thessalian lady. In 337 Philip married Cleopatra, the daughter of a Macedonian noble, in the hope probably of begetting another son who might be in the line of succession. This marriage caused a rift with Olympias and Alexander. But a reconciliation followed, and in confirmation of it a wedding was arranged between Olympias' daughter Cleopatra and the Molossian king Alexander. It was while this marriage was being celebrated in July 336 that Philip was assassinated by a young Macedonian noble, probably for personal, not political reasons.

The achievements of Philip by his forty-sixth year may be viewed from several angles. He greatly enlarged the Macedonian kingdom, carrying its frontiers to Lake Lychnitis (Ochrid) in the west and to the river Nestus (Mesta) in the east, and bringing under his rule a total population of at least two million souls. The social and economic revolution, which Philip had initiated in 359–4 (see pp. 247 f., above), was almost complete throughout the enlarged kingdom by the time of his death. The eastern territories brought him great mineral wealth and the Chalcidic peninsula was particularly rich in timber and olive oil. Agriculture flourished as a result of controlled irrigation and deforestation and stock was improved by careful breeding. For example, Philip sent 20,000 Scythian mares to Macedonia in 339. The extraordinary prosperity of the Macedonian kingdom was indicated by the vast circulation of Philip's gold and silver coinage in Europe. Within the kingdom the cities became economic and administrative centres linked by a road-system which was of commercial as well as military importance. The Macedonian citizenship was given by the king to an élite male section of the population, namely those of racial descent from the Macedonian tribes who were qualified and fit to serve in the army, and also to others whom he created 'Macedones' and incorporated in the army whatever their racial origins. We may number the citizens at not less than 50,000 since the field army at Chaeronea consisted of 30,000 men and some forces were no doubt retained in Macedonia and the Balkans. Thus Philip trebled the manpower of his kingdom between 358 and 338.

That this expanded national territorial state was so strong in contrast to the static city-state with its hereditary citizenship was due entirely to the genius of Philip, for it had never been so in the time of his predecessors. Philip attached the new citizens tightly to the state because he included every citizen alike within a graded system of military and social privilege and because he himself won their devoted affection by his magnetic personality and his example in war. At the top of the scale were the King's Own Bodyguard and King's Own Companions, themselves the cream of the élite Companion Cavalry, and at the foot of the scale were the infantry men of the Phalanx or of the Survey Company who were elevated above the unenfranchised population of the kingdom. Moreover, local patriotisms of long standing were harnessed to Philip's purpose because the squadrons and the regiments were recruited on a territorial basis, like those of the British Army. As the realm grew in prosperity, the King was able to grant more land to his soldiers, and it became possible to mount a standing professional army on the national revenue. At the same time there is no evidence of slavery. The unenfranchised element in Macedonia consisted of freemen who were citizens of their own community whether it was a tribe such as the Lyncestae or a town such as Dium or Pella. But they were not members of the armed forces of the state and so did not qualify for Macedonian citizenship.

The Balkan area outside Philip's enlarged Macedonia was peopled by innumerable warring tribes of Illyrians, Paeonians, Thracians and so on, each ruled by its own tribal monarchy and/or aristocracy. Their capacity for war was insatiable. The Thracians alone seemed to Herodotus 'the most populous nation after the Indians, and, if they could ever unite, potentially the most powerful'. These warring tribes threatened any Greek city-state in the vicinity and, when some of them combined, they invaded the frontier areas of northern Greece. The Illyrians, for instance, helped by Dionysius of Syracuse, killed 15,000 Molossians c. 384, and Illyrians and Dardanians overran Western Macedonia just before Philip came to power. As Herodotus said of the Thracians, 'a life of war and rapine was held in honour'.[2] Indeed, whole tribes preyed readily on one another; the Illyrian Autariatae for instance reduced neighbouring tribes to slavery, and the Thracians of one kingdom destroyed their fellow-countrymen of another Thracian kingdom. Philip made his attacks not upon the tribal communities but upon the tribal aristocrats who fought as cavalrymen. His own heavy-armed cavalry, especially when he led them himself, proved to be invincible; and he was able either to eliminate a tribal aristocracy or

275

to reduce it to vassal status. Early in his reign he had a buffer-ring of client kings but many of them disappeared from the scene later. He brought peace and not enslavement to the tribal communities, encouraged agriculture by flood-control and irrigation, built roads and cities and developed internal trade and maritime commerce. The Greek city-states on the coasts were always his allies at first because they profited by the development of the hinterland, and they joined him in resisting intervention by imperialistic Greek powers such as Athens. It was only later if they found themselves in danger of incorporation that they broke away, as Perinthus and Byzantium did in 340.

The aim of Philip in the Balkans was to create a Macedonian Empire bordered by the Adriatic, the Aegean, the Black Sea and the lower Danube. Its weakest points were in the north-western sector where the Autariatae were themselves pressed upon by the Gallic peoples, and in the north-eastern sector where the nomadic Scythian tribes were trying to migrate southwards. When he died, Philip was within an ace of success. Moreover, what he had built lasted; for he brought to the Balkan lands peace, security and economic development behind the shield of the Macedonian army and the auxiliary forces of Illyrians, Paeonians, Thracians and others who fought in the service of the Macedonian king. As Theopompus the contemporary Greek historian wrote, Europe had never produced such a man as Philip.

As a member of the Temenid dynasty Philip was Greek in blood. He was also Greek in culture and in outlook, for the Macedonian court had attracted the leading artists and poets of Greece for several generations and Philip employed large numbers of able Greeks and even made some of them 'Companions'. In 342, for example, he appointed Aristotle to teach his son and heir, Alexander, and he invited Theopompus to Pella. But to admire Greek culture was not to be uncritical of the Greek city-state. Thus within Macedonia the Greek city in the physical sense had a most important place. Dium or Pella or Aegae had its agora, theatre, temples, stadium and streets, and city life there was much the same as in any contemporary Greek city, except that the slave population was much smaller. These Greco-Macedonian cities, if we may call them so, were the centre from which the Greek way of life and Greek ideas spread into Upper Macedonia and the countries of the Macedonian Empire. But the city in Macedonia had no political independence: it was a privileged urban community like a Roman municipium, not a self-standing state. When a Greek city-state was an immediate neighbour of Macedon, it had either to fight for political independence, as Methone and Olynthus did, or surrender and become a city of the Greco-Macedonian type.

In his dealings with the Greeks of Thessaly Philip was the consistent champion of liberty against dictatorship, federalism against particularism and piety against sacrilege. He favoured economic progress; he brought the surrounding hill tribes under control and developed the country's communications and exports. There was certainly some truth in Isocrates' assertion that the Thessalians of the plain had more trust in him than in one another, and he repaid that trust when he made the Thessalian League a member of the Greek League in 337 on the same footing as Athens or the Arcadian League. A personal bond continued to exist between them because Philip the man had been elected President of the Thessalian League for life; but this was a token of gratitude and not a sign of bondage.

The policy of Philip towards city-states south of Thessaly and the Aegean coast of Thrace was one not of conquest, annexation and destruction, as Demosthenes and others claimed, but of control preferably without violence or occupation. In 352 Philip withdrew his army rather than clash with the forces of Athens, Sparta and Achaea at Thermopylae, and in 346 he brought the Sacred War to an end without bloodshed, annexation or destruction. The policy which he announced through the Amphictyonic Council in 346 gave to the Greek city-states the opportunity of maintaining a general peace within the status quo and without intervention by Philip. When it failed and Athens and Boeotia chose war, Philip imposed his control by force of arms; but he chose thereafter to create a Greek federal state, independent in its capacity to maintain a general peace within its own territory and to join in an invasion of Persia, but linked by a close alliance to Macedonia and accepting Philip the man as the commander of its armed forces against Persia. When he drew up the blue-print of the Greek League, he viewed the problems of the warring city-states of the fourth century from the same angle as Epaminondas, Timoleon and Isocrates. What the Greek states needed if they were to survive in health and power was a federal system designed to arrest the destructive cycle of internal revolutions and inter-state wars, and an outward-looking policy of expansion which could open new horizons, carry off a surplus population and ameliorate the over-crowded conditions of the Greek mainland.

Whenever a great state arises and traditional states become lesser in comparison, it is necessary to consider the advantages of a political reorientation. The first question is whether the great state will collapse or can be made to collapse. In his early speeches Demosthenes claimed that Macedonia would collapse, like a Greek dictatorship, under the strain of its internal stresses. But after 338, the truth lay rather with Phocion when he remarked, on hearing of the assassination of Philip, that the Macedonian army was reduced only by one man. Despite the new factor in international politics, Demosthenes and his supporters were determined to maintain the untrammelled liberty of Athens and to treat other states as she had done for the hundred years between 460 and 360: if they had had their way, she would have stood firm against the winds of change. There were two dangers in this course: that Athens would be subjugated and broken, and that, if she was left alone, she would be on the side-lines of historical development, as Sparta and the small states of Crete had been for many years and were to be in the future. The outlook of Isocrates, Phocion, Aeschines and others was more practical. They realized that if Athens and other city-states continued to play their self-contained game of internecine warfare and internal revolution, the springs of Greek life and culture would become embittered; the need was that the Greeks should be made to cease 'from their madness and their struggle for power'[3] and open up a new future by invading Asia. To enter the federal union of the Greeks was to limit one's own freedom of action, and this was a difficult step for a state such as Athens which had thought of herself as superior to her contemporaries. But if the outcome should prove to be a united Greece then there might be some truth in the claim made by Aristotle that if the Greek race should ever achieve political unity, it had the ability to rule the world – no longer in terms of imperial power but certainly in terms of cultural development and intellectual enlightenment.

CHAPTER 26

RETROSPECT AND PROSPECT

In this book we have concentrated on the Classical Age, whose hall-mark was the independent city-state, and on the cultural developments which took place within it. During most of the period the city-states differed one from another even more markedly than the national states of Europe differ one from another, and it was only in the fourth century that a tendency towards uniformity appeared in politics, buildings, literature and entertainments. In what sense then can we speak of 'Greek Civilization' before the fourth century as the common denominator in the outlooks, say, of Athens, Megara, Sparta, Syracuse and Miletus? The answer lies to some extent, in retrospect, in the traditions which were being transmitted in the pre-natal period before the birth of the city-state, traditions which reached back to the conditions of life in the last centuries of the Bronze Age.

The imprint of that 'Mycenaean world', as we call it, upon the Greek mind was indelible. Every Greek of the Classical Age knew that the leaders of the Mycenaean world had been Greeks and that their achievements had been recorded in epic songs in Greek before that world collapsed. The songs, it was then believed, had been composed close to the events. Thus the epic bard Phemius was represented by Homer as singing of the homecoming of the Greek from Troy while Odysseus was still only on his way homewards. When his song saddened Penelope in her longing for Odysseus, Telemachus tells her not to blame Phemius:

Begrudge it not that he sings of the evil lot of the Danaoi, for it is the song which is newest to their ears that men praise more.[1]

Thus the epic songs gave an entry into the world of the past which was, in Greek opinion, immediate and authentic. No one doubted the existence of those whom the singers extolled. They were 'a divine race of heroes', as Hesiod wrote, 'of whom a part were destroyed by evil war and dread battle, some beneath the walls of seven-gated Thebes in the land of Cadmus as they fought for the flocks of Oedipus, others at Troy whither they were brought on ships across the great gulf of the sea'.[2] Moreover, there was no lacuna, no break in the traditions. Naturally enough the Greeks of the early Classical Age believed that they were descended from the Greeks of that divine race in general, and they held that belief no less strongly than the Greeks of today hold the belief that they in turn are the descendants of the Greeks of the Byzantine Empire. Greek experience was seen as a continuum from the time of Hellen, son of Deucalion, to the dawn of the Classical Age, and there was nothing irrational in regarding the wars against Priam, Xerxes and Darius III as comparable instances of the clash between the Greeks of Greece and the barbarians of the East.

What the Greeks regarded as their common heritage was not the actual Mycenaean world as a modern archaeologist might reconstruct it but the image of that world as it was seen by the epic singers. It was a world of violence and strife on the divine level and on the human level, and the heroic figures on both levels were individuals who were able to uphold their honour and sometimes to enforce their will on a situation fraught with difficult circumstances. The call to heroism was very strong. It was thought right for Achilles to prefer a short life of martial glory to a long life of ease, and it was assumed that a man's finest qualities were brought to the surface in the heat of battle. Honour rarely admitted of compromise. Thus when Achilles thought he had been insulted by Agamemnon, he nursed his wrath until his closest friend, Patroclus, was killed in battle, and only then did he propose, though with great reluctance, to be reconciled with Agamemnon. His words, addressed to Agamemnon, reveal his embarrassment: 'Still, we will let all this be a thing of the past, though it hurts us, and beat down by constraint the anger that rises inside us. Now I am making an end of my anger. It does not become me unrelentingly to rage on.'[3] Oedipus never did relent. When his daughters obeyed the code of honour, he loved them deeply; but when his sons broke the code of honour and abused him, he cursed them even on the day of his death. Odysseus was heroic in his endurance of danger and distress. Quick-witted, he had a plan even in the most desperate situation and the courage to carry it through to the end.

The results of a hero's actions were not within his control. They were determined by those of the gods who concerned themselves with a particular situation. In the fighting for the corpse of Patroclus Ajax and Menelaus were unsurpassed in valour but their efforts were totally ineffective, and Ajax realized why as he called aloud: 'Shame on it! By now even one with a child's innocence could see how father Zeus himself is helping the Trojans. The weapons of each of these take hold, no matter who throws them, good fighter or bad, since Zeus is straightening all of them equally, while ours fall to the ground and are utterly useless.'⁴ The gods and goddesses were actuated primarily by caprice and favour towards individual men and women. Even Zeus, the king of the gods, although he may have demanded that men should practise justice, was very far from being an impartial dispenser of justice to men and women. And the final decision, the day of a man's death, lay not with Zeus but with an unpersonified power, *Moira* (Apportionment), which laid down not only the limit of a man's lifespan but also the limits of each god's sphere of power.

The order of society on the human and the divine stages was monarchical and aristocratic. There was a wide gulf between the gods and the warrior: 'And they were led by Ares and Pallas Athene, both golden (and golden was the dress they wore), both beautiful and tall in their armour, and as two gods conspicuous on all sides; and the people were small beside them'.⁵ There was a wide gulf too between the heroic champion and his retinue. The *Iliad* appealed most to aristocratic persons in the Classical Age who had the same sense of their own valour and the same scorn for the little man. The *Odyssey* was more compatible with democracy because during most of the poem Odysseus was unaligned politically and the aristocratic suitors behaved badly in the palace. Both of the great epics had a glamour and a scale which formed a contrast with the grim realities of everyday life in later centuries. Thus, one of the scenes engraved on Achilles' shield was 'a field of soft, rich soil, thrice turned over and extensive, and many ploughmen were in it, turning their teams as they drove the ploughs hither and thither'. But Hesiod's picture of a small-holder at his plough came closer to the conditions of life at Ascra in Boeotia: 'You hold the top of the plough-handle in your hand and put the goad into the backs of the oxen as they strain at the yoke-straps pegged to the pole; and the slave-boy with his mattock, a little behind, let him make trouble for the birds by burying the seed'.⁶

The vision of a glorious past in which warfare, brigandage and piracy played a dominant part was associated with a vast store of what we should call legend or myth. But most Greeks regarded such legend or myth as historical and didactic, as it contained a great deal of information on a variety of subjects such as we find in the fragments of epic poems attached to the name of Hesiod. This incomparable legacy was common to all Greek-speaking peoples of the Classical Age and it gave to them the background of belief and the standards of behaviour within which each city-state society played its historical part. What were the rights of suppliants or aged parents? What respect should be shown to the corpse of an enemy? What form of prayer is acceptable to a god? What omens or what day is favourable for doing this or that? The answers were to be found in the wisdom of a common past. To this extent Greek civilization was a meaningful term when the city-states began to expand and found themselves involved with peoples who had a totally different past and therefore a totally different outlook.

Some peoples were heirs in particular of the Mycenaean legacy. The Dorians and the speakers of West Greek who accompanied them, having destroyed the Mycenaean world, had merely taken over the physical remains in many parts of Greece at the end of the twelfth century BC, and a long time passed before they became capable of civilized existence. But their leaders in many cases were direct descendants of the greatest hero of the Mycenaean world, Heracles, and the 'Heraclidae', as they called themselves, established new kingdoms, in Argolis and Lacedaemonia for instance, on the Mycenaean model without a total break in the chain of tradition. On the other hand the Arcadians maintained themselves in their own homeland in the heart of the Peloponnese; and the line of continuity was felt to be so strong that in 479 they cited an historical event which had occurred some eight hundred years earlier, when the Arcadian king killed the Heraclid Hyllus in single combat. But the chief heirs were those who transmitted the epic songs from generation to generation, the Aeolians of central Greece (associated ultimately with the name of Hesiod), and the Ionians of the Peloponnese (especially in Messenia), who fled to Attica and from there migrated to the islands and the central part of the west coast of Asia Minor, where they were associated with the name of Homer. In the system of transmission, which was by word of mouth within social units, Athens and Attica occupied a key position. There, as in Arcadia, occupation was continuous from Mycenaean times and the kingdom created by Theseus stood firm against all attacks until the arrival of Xerxes. Religious cults and family worship were maintained there without a break for many centuries, and when Athens became strong in the sixth century she was the accepted centre of the Ionian peoples and the guardian of the greatest epic songs, the *Iliad* and the *Odyssey*.

In another respect too the survival of epic songs was very important.

They conserved the voice of poetry, both in epic and in lyric to which the *Iliad* refers, and they alone made possible the growth of Greek literature in the Classical Age. The first offshoots from epic songs – the elegiac and lyric poetry of the seventh century onwards – were steeped in the epic diction, which was the language of poetry, and drew freely on the store of Mycenaean myths. At the zenith of Greek poetry Pindar used the epic legends as the centrepiece of his epinician odes, and the Attic tragedians drew their themes almost entirely from the traditions of the Mycenaean period. And Aristophanes seemed to sympathize with the claim of Aeschylus that 'the divine Homer' won fame and honour by representing 'good things – stations in battle, martial valour, and the arming of men'. When poetry declined in the fourth century and Aristotle analysed the art of poetry, he saw Homer as the supreme poet 'whether because of technical mastery or natural genius'.[7] Another art which survived from Mycenaean times was that of painting pottery. Here Athens led the way forward from a decadent Mycenaean style to the austere Protogeometric style, which became widespread throughout the Aegean basin. In the ensuing period Athens lost her primacy when independent schools of Geometric style and then of Orientalizing style arose, particularly among the Dorian states.

The debt of the Classical Age to the past, great though it was in terms of religious and moral outlook and in concepts of art, must not be exaggerated. Its own initiative in creating the city-state, its vigour in so many fields of political and intellectual power and the great diversity in talent of the hundreds of city-states owed nothing at all to the Mycenaean world. And the re-creation of myth on Attic Black-Figure and Red-Figure pottery and the re-enactment of myth in the Attic theatre were new achievements which owed only a formal debt to the past. In the fifth century men were looking forwards: typical among them was Thucydides, who cut the past down to size and recognized in contemporary society the potential to conquer the world as it was then known.

The most potent force in the moulding of the post-classical outlook on life was Athens as we see her in the fourth century BC. Her pre-eminence then in the theatre, in philosophy, in oratory and in the Isocratean type of education (which came nearest to our concept of higher education) made her the centre of Greek culture to an extent unparalleled in the modern world if we look for a centre of European culture. It had not been so always. In the mid-sixth century Corinth and Laconia were still rivals of Athens in the art of vase-painting; in the fifth century Pindar of Thebes and Bacchylides of Ceos were as distinguished in the writing of choral lyric as the Attic tragedians; and after the Persian Wars some of the finest sculptures on the pediments of temples were the work of non-Athenians. But the second half of the fifth century saw a remarkable change. Athenian writers and artists were acclaimed throughout the Greek world as outstanding: Sophocles, Euripides and Agathon in tragedy; Aristophanes, Cratinus and Eupolis in comedy; Thucydides in history; Antiphon in oratory; Phidias in sculpture and Apollodorus in painting (the pioneer in the study of light and shade). Moreover, Athens attracted to herself writers and artists from other cities and in particular from the Ionian cities which were within her empire. Artists such as the painter Polygnotus of Thasos became citizens of Athens, and Socrates drew his pupils from many parts of the Greek world.

The invention of the book at Athens marked a new stage in the dissemination of knowledge, and books exported from Athens were reaching cities on the coasts of the Black Sea by the end of the fifth century. Thereafter the latest play, for instance, was being read, recited and perhaps produced in any Greek city from Spain to the Crimea. The broadcasting of Athenian literature led on to the development of a common form of Greek (*koine dialektos*) among educated persons, and its basis inevitably was formed by the Attic dialect. Again, in the fourth century, when prose took priority over poetry, the leading writers were Athenians such as Xenophon, Plato, Isocrates, Demosthenes and Aeschines; and men of learning and culture were attracted from all parts of the Greek world to settle at Athens. There the situation was summarized by Isocrates in his *Panegyricus*, written c. 380, as follows:

Our city has so far outstripped the rest of the world in intellectual insight and power of expression that her pupils have become the teachers of all others, and she has brought it about that the term 'Greek' has a connotation of outlook and not of race any longer, and that those who share our culture are called 'Greeks' rather than those who share a common blood.[8]

Athens led the way also in economics. In the fourth century she was the centre of banking, shipping, marine insurance, commercial exchange and financial speculation, and the whole system of commercial capitalism (more or less as we know it in Western Europe today) spread out from Athens into most parts of the Greek world. Her social system, involving a large slave basis, mobility of population and property and the breakdown of such racial and familial units as the tribe and the clan was adopted in most of the Greek states. Her form of democracy became the standard to which all types of constitutions were referred, and in the period c. 375–336 any other constitution was regarded as an aberration. Many Athenian philosophers acted as political consultants to other states, and political practice at Athens formed the essential background to political blue-prints, such as Plato's *Laws*. We have seen a similar development in modern times when the changes introduced into politics, economics and social systems by the politico-social revolution in France and the industrial revolution in England have affected the whole of Europe and produced a so-called 'European civilization' which has to some extent blurred the old national distinctions within Europe. Today 'social democracy', with all its rather vague implications about society and politics, is becoming the accepted norm within Europe and to a considerable extent outside Europe.

The standardization of so many city-states on the model of Athens had unfortunate consequences in the world of city-states. The new democracies proved to be aggressive for a variety of reasons. The change from an agricultural to a mixed economy made them more dependent on imported materials, and their policy was often directed towards imperialistic control of others. The growth of the capitalist system widened the monetary gap and increased the enmity between the rich and the poor (the latter in the sense of the class above the slave level) so that there was more sympathy between the rich of any two states than between the rich and the poor within any one state. Thus party-strife (stasis) arose frequently, and each side in the strife was quick to call upon the corresponding class in another state for help and even intervention. The half-century from 386 to 336 was a period of political instability, and the numbers of political refugees, mercenary soldiers and unemployed persons were constantly on the increase throughout the Greek world from Sicily to Ionia. These phenomena appeared at a time when material prosperity was advancing and large profits were being made by speculators and adventurers.

The old values were discarded as the outlook of the fourth century hardened towards individualistic materialism and realistic thinking. The plays of Aeschylus and Sophocles lost their appeal, and Euripides became the rage and those who followed his innovations in the art of tragedy. Comedy changed from the political scene at Athens to the realistic social setting of a cosmopolitan society, and much more attention was given to a parody of social manners. Communal religion played less part in life than the salvation of the individual through a mystery religion or a new philosophy. Personal integrity and attested patriotism carried less weight in city-state politics than the ability to sway large audiences by rhetorical displays, and a disillusionment with such politics set in among those who had received some higher education or believed in what they regarded as higher principles. The supporters of the extreme democracies naturally wanted a larger cut of the national wealth than they had enjoyed in the past, and there was some truth in the charge made by their critics[9] that they were more concerned with their share of any financial hand-out than with decisions of policy on matters of state.

The prospects of such a society of city-states achieving peace and avoiding disaster by its own unaided efforts were certainly grim by the middle of the fourth century. The fragmentation of political power, the distrust of political leaders, the split between classes in the franchised section of society, the struggle of the poor citizens to keep above the level of slave-labour occupations, the internecine wars between one city-state and another, and the decline in patriotic feeling and endeavour, except when service was necessary to avoid destruction – these were factors which made any return to the fifth-century balance of power almost impossible and any movement towards a union of Greek city-states unlikely. Attempts to break the cycle of political frustration had succeeded for a time and then withered away with the passing of an individual leader: the Second Athenian Alliance with the banishment of Callistratus, the Empire of Dionysius with his death, the Boeotian experiment in democratic federalism with the death of Epaminondas and the policy of reconciliation with the retirement of Timoleon. It seemed that only a brilliant individual – in Plato's ideal state a 'philosopher-king' – was capable of bringing the Greek city-states out of their troubles. The most influential and in many ways the most talented statesman of the city-states in the late 340s was Demosthenes, but he was a champion of fifth-century separatism and when opportunity offered, imperialism.

The decisive change in the direction of the city-states came about through two brilliant individuals, father and son, Philip and Alexander. Although historians write of them as Macedonians, the most important fact about them was that they were Greeks by descent on the male side and thought of themselves as Greeks ruling over Macedonians. In some respects they were primitive Greeks. They resembled the epic heroes Achilles and Ajax in their love of combat and in their personal prowess, and they believed, like them, that divine blood ran in their veins because they were descended from Zeus through Heracles. Indeed Alexander was doubly sure, for he was descended from the Nereid goddess Thetis, mother of Achilles, through his own mother Olympias. This does not mean that in the manner of some megalomaniac or religious fanatic they thought themselves to be 'gods'; rather, they knew that they had inherited an obligation to emulate their ancestors and serve their fellow-men. It was an attitude of mind which was best portrayed by Pindar in his epinician odes and which stemmed from the *Iliad*, the book which influenced Alexander most deeply. We see it at work when Alexander landed in Asia. He made sacrifices to Protesilaus (the first Greek casualty in the Trojan War), to the deities of the sea (Poseidon, Amphitrite and the Nereids), and to Athena and Priam at Troy; and he and his closest friend, Hephaestion, laid wreaths on the funerary mounds of Achilles and Patroclus in the plain below Troy. These were not acts of romantic sentimental posturing, but natural expressions of an outlook which had lasted into the archaic period of the Greek city-states and was still active in the court of the royal house of Macedon.

It lay within the power of Philip and again of Alexander to destroy the independence of the city-states on the Greek mainland and in the Aegean basin. That they did not do so has been explained in various ways. The fundamental reason is to be seen in a remark by Isocrates in 346, when he wrote to Philip and contrasted him as a Heraclid with the other Heraclidae (e.g. the kings of Sparta).

It is natural that the other descendants of Heracles do not look beyond the city-state in which they happen to live because they are tied to its legal and political framework, but that you, being as it were set apart, regard all Greece as your fatherland, as the founder of your race did, and take risks for the sake of Greece as readily as you do for your personal interests.[10]

There were two sides to their policies. The first was to preserve the independence of the city-states, but within the setting of a federal union which was designed to bring peace, stability and prosperity. It was a typically Greek decision in the manner of Callistratus, Epaminondas and Timoleon because it recognized the importance of independence to a Greek city-state if it was to maintain its self-respect and its creativity. The second was to provide an outlet for Greek culture in a wider world. What Philip initiated in Macedonia and the Balkans Alexander developed throughout Asia. They both attracted into their service individual Greeks of intelligence and reputation who shared in the counsels of the king and held high administrative posts. There were unparalleled opportunities for able and dependable Greeks to establish themselves and their families in profitable and exciting careers – unparalleled at any rate since the early days of Greek colonization. More valuable still was the welcoming of Greeks of whatever class or background into the new cities which were founded in the Balkans and in

Asia, and the assurance that they would hold a privileged position as citizens of these communities and as leaders in cultural and political activities.

It is customary to call the periods which followed after the Classical Age 'the Hellenistic Age' and 'the Roman Period'. In fact the stream of Hellenism ran through both periods and on into the Byzantine Empire. It would be more correct to speak of 'the Macedonian period' down to 167 and 'the Roman period' thereafter in lands where Greek was spoken. During the Macedonian period the policy of federal union succeeded only intermittently in old Greece, and the independence of the city-state proved to be precarious. There were faults on both sides, the Greek states being recklessly separatist and the Macedonians becoming impatient and domineering. But in cultural terms the merits were considerable. During the lifetime of Alexander and for some fifty years thereafter Athens produced literature, architecture and art of outstanding merit: the finest speeches of Greek antiquity, Demosthenes *On the Crown* and Aeschines *Against Ctesiphon*; the treatises of Aristotle as head of the Lyceum (analogous to a well-endowed research institute) and the establishment through him of scientific disciplines such as zoology, of libraries, museums and scholarly colloquia, and generally of the consolidation of learning; the growth of 'New Comedy' as a comedy of social manners – kindly, witty and cultivated – under the leadership and inspiration of the last Athenian poet-dramatist of distinction, Menander (342/1–293/89); and the building in stone of the theatre, the arsenal and the docks at Athens. Lysippus of Sicyon founded a school of sculpture, which had a new approach to portraiture and to proportion in marble and bronze statues, and Philoxenus of Eretria and Apelles of Colophon were remarkable painters, for instance of Alexander in battle-scenes, which were a model for later generations. Polybius of Achaea, growing to maturity in the last part of the Macedonian period, came close to Herodotus and Thucydides as an historian.

It was in New Greece, that was in the cities founded by Alexander and his successors overseas, that a city-life of a modern kind, without any striving for political separatism and independence, grew to maturity under the protection of the Macedonian rulers. Urban planners used the Greek grid-system, and the new cities incorporated from the outset such buildings as a theatre for large audiences (24,500 at Ephesus, for example), a council-house, a gymnasium, an odeon for musical performances, one or more temples, and a superb city-centre with colonnaded approaches such as one sees at Palmyra. Urban society was cosmopolitan, but urban life was in the Greek manner because the rulers fostered Hellenism and the native peoples adopted the Greek language and Greek ways readily. Capitalism and commerce flourished, and the upper and middle classes had plenty of leisure to enjoy tragedies and comedies, revues and mimes, athletic events and horse-races, club meetings and public lectures – indeed, all the pastimes of a modern European kind except cinema, radio and television. New forms of Greek art and literature arose, especially at Alexandria in Egypt, in response to the new conditions of life. Sculptors abandoned the traditions of idealism and restraint. They turned rather to sentimentality, Eros for instance becoming a playful Cupid, and to realism in all its forms from the sensuous Aphrodite of Melos (Venus of Milo) or the Cnidian Aphrodite crouching beside her bath, to a sleeping Satyr, a careworn old fisherman or a humpbacked beggar. Portrait sculpture became highly individualistic and remarkably indicative of mood and character. The same qualities and a superb mastery of technique were the marks of the paintings and the mosaics of the period, for instance the hunting-scene found recently at Pella in Macedonia. New forms of poetry showed meticulous scholarship, imaginative power and self-conscious perfectionism. Callimachus favoured the short poem, regarding 'a small draught from the sacred fount [of the Muses] as the highest flower of poesy'. His *Hymns*, for instance, were literary pieces, not intended for any religious service. Apollonius Rhodius composed the first literary epic, 'artificial' in the sense that, like Virgil's *Aeneid*, it was a piece of scholarly archaizing. Similarly Theocritus was the originator of 'pastoral' poetry in which realistic detail was illuminated by the playful humour and the awareness of beauty appropriate to a literary scholar. All three wrote at Alexandria in Egypt, which became the centre of learning in the third century. Pioneer work was carried out in mathematics and astronomy; specialists wrote on all branches of scholarship, and a few polymaths were famous. Eratosthenes, for instance, was known as a literary *pentathlos* (winner of an athletic competition which consisted of five events); for he wrote brilliantly on literary criticism, chronology, mathematics, astronomy, geography, history and philosophy, quite apart from composing a couple of short epics and a famous elegy.

Rome, Byzantium and Europe for many centuries were influenced more by the Hellenistic Age than by the Classical Age, partly through reasons of historical continuity but mainly because the conditions of urban life and scholarship were almost a replica of those of the Hellenistic Age. In recent centuries the significance of the Classical Age has been realized, not only as the *fons et origo* of western culture throughout the ages but as a period of unrivalled brilliance in its own right. Scholars of the Hellenistic Age were already aware of this. 'Longinus', writing *On the Sublime* (in literature), touched time and again on the qualities in the classical writers which made them capable of sublimity: their concern with practical life and with truth (to *praktikon* and *aletheia*) and their lack of sentimentality, wishful thinking and other forms of escapism. They possessed these qualities because they were so deeply and so widely involved in the day-to-day life of a relatively small and close-knit city-state community and because they insisted on the power of the human intellect to penetrate to the ultimate realities of human existence and face the facts of man's situation in the physical world.

NOTES

CHAPTER I

1 Aristotle, *Politica*, 1326b.
2 Plato, *Leges*, 737–8.
3 Thucydides, 2,40,2.
4 Herodotus, 9,26 ff.
5 Herodotus, 7,104,4.
6 Aristotle, *Politica*, 1327b; Plato, *Respublica*, 376, wishing to have these qualities in the rulers of his ideal state.
7 Pindar, *Nemean Odes*, 6,1 ff.
8 Aeschylus, *Eumenides*, 538 ff.
9 Isocrates, *Epistula*, 3,2, calling these forces *epithumia* and *mania*.

CHAPTER 2

1 Hesiod, *Opera et Dies*, 545.
2 Plutarch, *Quaestiones Graecae*, 17 (295b).
3 Aristotle, *Politica*, 1252b, 28.
4 Athenaeus, 695 ff.
5 Plato, *Leges*, 630.
6 Thucydides, 1,84,3.
7 Herodotus, 7,228,2.
8 Thucydides, 1,18,1.
9 Tyrtaeus, 6.
10 Tyrtaeus, 10,15 ff.
11 Theognis, 51–6; 1137–40.

CHAPTER 3

1 Plutarch, *Lycurgus*, 6,1; the charter is called 'The Great Rhetra'.
2 Alcman, 72.

CHAPTER 4

1 Aristotle, *Athenaion Politeia*, fragment 5.
2 Plutarch, *Solon*, 21,2.
3 F. Jacoby, *Fragmente der griechischen Historiker* (1923–), 328 (Philochorus), F, 35a.
4 R. Meiggs and D. Lewis, *A Selection of Greek Historical Inscriptions* (1969), no. 86.
5 Plutarch, *Solon*, 13,3.
6 Solon, 24, 5–10.
7 Solon, 24, 18–20.

CHAPTER 5

1 Solon, 1.
2 Solon, 3.
3 Solon, 4.

CHAPTER 6

1 Mimnermus, fragment 9.
2 Sappho, 27a.
3 Archilochus, 79.
4 See Herodotus, 4, 150–9.
5 *Supplementum epigraphicum Graecum* (1923), 9,3, translated in A.J. Graham, *Colony and Mother City in Ancient Greece* (1964), 225.

CHAPTER 7

1 Solon, 9.
2 Aristotle, *Athenaion Politeia*, 16,7.
3 Aristotle, *Athenaion Politeia*, 19,3.
4 Athenaeus, 695a.
5 M. Cary, *A History of Rome* (2nd edn, 1954), 322.

CHAPTER 8

1 Herodotus, 1,153.

CHAPTER 9

1 Aristotle, *Rhetorica*, 1411a; and Scholia to Demosthenes, *De Falsa Legatione*, 303.

2 *Suda* s.v. *khoris hippeis.*
3 Scholia to Aristides, edited by W. Dindorf (1829), 3, 566.
4 Herodotus, 7,145,2.
5 Herodotus, 7,141,3.
6 Meiggs and Lewis, op. cit., no. 23.
7 Herodotus, 8,143,2.
8 Thucydides, 1,95,7.
9 Aristotle, *Athenaion Politeia*, 23.5; Plutarch, *Aristides*, 25,1.

CHAPTER 10

1 M.N. Tod, *Greek Historical Inscriptions* (2nd edn, 1948), no. 204, 23 ff.
2 Pindar, *Pythian Odes*, 1,41–2; *Nemean Odes*, 3,40–2; 6,12–16.
3 Pindar, *Olympian Odes*, 1,71–4.
4 Pindar, *Olympian Odes*, 1,92–3.
5 Pindar, *Nemean Odes*, 6,47–9.
6 Aeschylus, *Septem contra Thebas*, 702–5.

CHAPTER 11

1 Plutarch, *Cimon*, 16,8.
2 Thucydides, 1,101,3.
3 Herodotus, 7,145,2.

CHAPTER 12

1 See Meiggs and Lewis, op. cit., nos. 40, 43, 47 and 52.
2 Ibid., no. 45.
3 Plutarch, *Pericles*, 17.
4 Plutarch, *Pericles*, 12,2.
5 Meiggs and Lewis, op. cit., no. 52.
6 Plutarch, *Pericles*, 26,4.
7 Thucydides, 1,23,6.
8 Thucydides, 1,140,1; 1,145.
9 Xenophon, *Hellenica*, 2,2,23.

CHAPTER 13

1 Hippocrates, *De Morbo Sacro*, 1,1.
2 F. Jacoby, *Fragmente der griechischen Historiker* (1923–), 1 (Hecataeus),
  F 1.
3 Cited in Plutarch, *Pericles*, 7,6.

4   Thucydides, 2,35–46.
5   Sophocles, *Oedipus Coloneus*, 1511–12.
6   Sophocles, *Ajax*, 967–8.
7   Aristotle, *Poetica*, 1450b,9.
8   Sophocles, *Antigone*, 332–71.
9   *Hamlet*, Act 2, Scene 2, 33 ff.
10 Sophocles, *Oedipus Coloneus*, 1224–38.
11 Sophocles, *Oedipus Coloneus*, 1240–8.
12 Sophocles, *Oedipus Coloneus*, 1615–17.
13 Thucydides, 1,8,3.
14 Thucydides, 2,62,2.
15 Thucydides, 1,70,2–9.
16 Thucydides, 2,63,2.

CHAPTER 14

1   Thucydides, 2,65,8–9.
2   Thucydides, 2,65,10.
3   Thucydides, 2,65, 7.
4   Thucydides, 5,85–113.
5   Thucydides, 6,18,3.
6   Thucydides, 6,24,3–4.
7   Thucydides, 2,65,11.

CHAPTER 15

1   Thucydides, 8,68.
2   Thucydides, 8,97,2.
3   Andocides, 1,97.
4   Xenophon, *Hellenica*, 1,7,3–34.
5   Xenophon, *Hellenica*, 2,2,3.

CHAPTER 16

1   [Xenophon] *Respublica Atheniensium*, 1,12.
2   [Xenophon] *Respublica Atheniensium*, 1,2.
3   Thucydides, 2,52–3.
4   Thucydides, 3,82,8.
5   Thucydides, 3,82,2.
6   Thucydides, 3,82,2.
7   Euripides, *Hecuba*, 864.
8   Aristophanes, *Ranae*, 1053; 1500–4.

CHAPTER 17

1   Thucydides, 5,79.
2   Xenophon, *Hellenica*, 1,1,23.
3   H. Macmillan, *Tides of Fortune* (1969), xviii–xix; his words apply equally well to the traditional concept of order in the world of city-states.

CHAPTER 18

1   M.N. Tod, *Greek Historical Inscriptions* (2nd edn, 1948), no. 95.
2   Xenophon, *Hellenica*, 2,3,32, 34.
3   Xenophon, *Hellenica*, 5,1,31.
4   Plutarch, *Lysander*, 8,4.

CHAPTER 19

1   M.N. Tod, *Greek Historical Inscriptions* (2nd edn, 1948), no. 123.
2   Xenophon, *Hellenica*, 6,3,19.

CHAPTER 20

1   Meiggs and Lewis, op. cit., no. 92.
2   Plato, *Epistula*, 8,353 d.

CHAPTER 21

1   Isocrates, *Panegyricus*, 18.
2   Xenophon, *Hellenica*, 7,5,10.
3   M.N. Tod, *Greek Historical Inscriptions* (2nd edn, 1948), no. 145.
4   Xenophon, *Hellenica*, 7,5,27.

CHAPTER 22

1   Thucydides, 1,141,6.
2   Aristotle, *Politica*, 1310a,9.
3   Isocrates, *Philippus*, 96.
4   Plato, *Apologia*, 32a.
5   Aristotle, *Politica*, 1291b, 17–28.
6   Plato, *Leges*, 744d.
7   Aristotle, *Athenaion Politeia*, 41,2.
8   Aristophanes, *Ecclesiazusae*, 197.

CHAPTER 23

1 Justin, 8,5.
2 Arrian, *Anabasis*, 7,9,2.
3 Diodorus Siculus, 16,60,3.

CHAPTER 24

1 Isocrates, *Philippus*, 154.

CHAPTER 25

1 M.N. Tod, *Greek Historical Inscriptions* (2nd edn, 1948), nos. 177, 179, 183, 192.
2 Herodotus, 5,6,2.
3 Isocrates, *Epistula*, 3,2.

CHAPTER 26

1   Homer, *Odyssey*, 1,350–1.
2   Hesiod, *Opera et Dies*, 159–64.
3   Homer, *Iliad*, 19,65–8.
4   Homer, *Iliad*, 17,629–30.
5   Homer, *Iliad*, 18,516–19.
6   Homer, *Iliad*, 18,541–3; Hesiod, *Opera et Dies*, 467–71.
7   Aristophanes, *Ranae*, 1034–6; Aristotle, *Poetica*, 1551a,24.
8   Isocrates, *Panegyricus*, 50.
9   For instance, Aeschines, *In Ctesiphontem*, 251.
10 Isocrates, *Philippus*, 127.

NOTES FOR FURTHER READING

Among general histories N.G.L. Hammond, *A History of Greece to 322 B.C.* (2nd edn, 1967) contains detailed references to the ancient sources, is up to date and is complemented by a volume of *Studies in Greek History* (1973); J.B. Bury, *A History of Greece to the Death of Alexander the Great* (4th edn, 1975) has been expanded since the original edition of 1900, and the text has been revised and the notes and references enlarged by R. Meiggs; and *The Cambridge Ancient History, III–VI* (1925–7) was written by the leading scholars of the 1920s and has full bibliographies up to that time. The most readable account of the Greek outlook is that of H.D.F. Kitto, *The Greeks* (revised edn, 1957). The most convenient reference book, which has up-to-date bibliographies, is *The Oxford Classical Dictionary* (2nd edn, edited by N.G.L. Hammond and H.H. Scullard, 1970). The following recommended books are categorized by the Parts to which they are relevant in the present work; many of them overlap two or more Parts, but they are usually mentioned in one Part only.

PART I (800–546): W. Jaeger, *Paideia I* (translated by G. Highett, 1939) shows the relationship between the political and cultural development for this and the next period. The origins and the development of the Greek city-state are treated by V. Ehrenberg, *The Greek State* (1960); G. Glotz, *The Greek City and its Institutions* (1929); and V. Martin, *La vie internationale dans la Grèce des cités* (1940). Special studies of individual states and topics are as follows: R.F. Willets, *Aristocratic Society in Ancient Crete* (1955); P. Oliva, *Sparta and her Social Problems* (1971); W.G. Forrest, *A History of Sparta* (1968); W. den Boer, *Laconian Studies* (1954); A.J. Graham, *Colony and Mother City in Ancient Greece* (1964); T.J. Dunbabin, *The Western Greeks* (1948); J. Boardman, *The Greeks Overseas* (1962); J.M. Cook, *The Greeks in Ionia and the East* (1962); A. Andrewes,

The Greek Tyrants (1956); C. Hignett, *A History of the Athenian Constitution* (1952). For thought, literature and art: G.S. Kirk and J.E. Raven, *The Presocratic Philosophers* (1962); E.R. Dodds, *The Greeks and the Irrational* (1951); W.K.C. Guthrie, *The Greeks and their Gods* (1954); A.W.H. Adkins, *Merit and Responsibility* (1960); C.M. Bowra, *Greek Lyric Poetry from Alcman to Simonides* (1961); R.M. Cook, *Greek Painted Pottery* (1960); A.W. Lawrence, *Greek Architecture* (1957); G.M.A. Richter, *Archaic Greek Art* (1949). A good general book on the period is A.R. Burn, *The Lyric Age of Greece* (1960).

PART II (546–466): In general, W. Jaeger, as above; A.R. Burn, *Persia and the Greeks, 546–478 B.C.* (1962); C. Hignett, *Xerxes' Invasion of Greece* (1963); P. Green, *The Year of Salamis* (1970). For political ideas see M. Ostwald, *Nomos and the Beginning of the Athenian Democracy* (1969); W.G. Forrest, *The Emergence of Greek Democracy* (1966). The battles of Marathon and Salamis are treated in N.G.L. Hammond, *Studies in Greek History* (1973). For literature, see C.M. Bowra, *Pindar* (1964); A.W. Pickard-Cambridge, *Dithyramb, Tragedy and Comedy* (2nd edn, revised by T.B.L. Webster, 1962); D.W. Lucas, *The Greek Tragic Poets* (2nd edn, 1959); G. Murray, *Aeschylus, the Creator of Tragedy* (1940); H. Lloyd-Jones, *The Justice of Zeus* (1971); F. Solmsen, *Hesiod and Aeschylus* (1949); and for art, J. Charbonneaux, *Greek Bronzes* (1961); C.T. Seltman, *Greek Coins* (1955); C.M. Robertson, *Greek Painting* (1959); W.B. Dinsmoor, *The Architecture of Ancient Greece* (1950); J. Boardman, *Archaic Greek Gems* (1968); *Pre-Classical from Crete to Archaic Greece* (1967).

PART III (464–404): R. Meiggs, *The Athenian Empire* (1972) and J. de Romilly, *Thucydides and Athenian Imperialism* (1963) are concerned with the central feature of the period. For Herodotus, see J.L. Myres, *Herodotus, Father of History* (1953); H.R. Immerwahr, *Form and Thought in Herodotus* (1966); C.W. Fornara, *Herodotus* (1971); and for Thucydides, J.H. Finley, *Thucydides* (2nd edn, 1947); H.D. Westlake, *Individuals in Thucydides* (1968); J. Fleiss, *Thucydides and the Politics of Bipolarity* (1966); A.G. Woodhead, *Thucydides on the Nature of Power* (1970); P.A. Stadter (ed.), *The Speeches in Thucydides* (1973), with a full bibliography; G. Kennedy, *The Art of Persuasion in Greece* (1963). For Attic drama, H.D.F. Kitto, *Greek Tragedy* (3rd edn, 1961); A. Lesky, *Greek Tragedy* (1965); C.M. Bowra, *Sophoclean Tragedy* (1944); G.M. Kirkwood, *Sophoclean Drama* (1957); B.M.W. Knox, *The Heroic Temper* (1964); D.P. Conacher, *Euripidean Drama* (1967); G.M.A. Grube, *The Drama of Euripides* (1961);

G. Murray, *Euripides and his Age* (2nd edn, 1946); T.B.L. Webster, *The Tragedies of Euripides* (1968); G. Murray, *Aristophanes* (1933); V. Ehrenberg, *The People of Aristophanes* (2nd edn, 1951). On social conditions, G. Glotz, *Ancient Greece at Work* (1926); A. W. Gomme, *The Population of Athens in the Fifth and Fourth Centuries B.C.* (1933); J.K. Davies, *Athenian Propertied Families, 600–300 B.C.* (1971); A. Fuks, *The Ancestral Constitution* (1953). On Socrates, F.M. Cornford, *Before and After Socrates* (1950); W.K.C. Guthrie, *Socrates* (1971). On architecture and sculpture, R. Carpenter, *The Architects of the Parthenon* (1970); P.E. Corbett, *The Sculpture of the Parthenon* (1959); J.D. Beazley and B. Ashmole, *Greek Sculpture and Painting* (2nd edn, 1966); G.M.A. Richter, *The Sculpture and Sculptors of the Greeks* (1950).

PART IV (404–336): For political developments, J.A.O. Larsen, *Greek Federal States* (1968); F.H. Marshall, *The Second Athenian Confederacy* (1905); T.T.B. Ryder, *Koine Eirene: General Peace and Local Independence in Ancient Greece* (1965); A.H.M. Jones, *The Athens of Demosthenes* (1952); H.D. Westlake, *Timoleon and his Relations with Tyrants* (1952); A.W. Pickard-Cambridge, *Demosthenes and the Last Days of Greek Freedom* (1914). For events in Sicily, see A.G. Woodhead, *The Greeks in the West* (1962). For regional studies, H.D. Westlake, *Thessaly in the Fourth Century B.C.* (1935); N.G.L. Hammond, *Epirus* (1967); G.T. Griffith and N.G.L. Hammond, *A History of Macedonia* (vol. I, 1972; vol. II, forthcoming). For philosophy and science, W.K.C. Guthrie, *A History of Greek Philosophy* (1962–); A.E. Taylor, *Plato: the Man and his Work* (2nd edn, 1966); W.D. Ross, *Aristotle* (6th edn, 1955); G.E.R. Lloyd, *Aristotle: the Growth and Structure of his Thought* (1968); O. Neugebauer, *The Exact Sciences in Antiquity* (2nd edn, 1959); L. Edelstein, *Ancient Medicine* (1967). Also, R.E. Wycherley, *How the Greeks Built Cities* (1962); F.E. Adcock, *The Greek and Macedonian Art of War* (1957) and F. Heichelheim, *An Ancient Economic History*, vol. 2 (1964).

INDEX

For five hundred years the Greek city-states
achieved a civilisation which has been an
inspiration and an ideal ever since. No
society has ever been so inventive and
original. Its political thought, its literary
forms, its commercial capitalism, its artistic
insight, and its approach to science and
philosophy have formed the basis of
Western civilisation.

The Classical Age of Greece is both an
introduction to, and an interpretation of, the
experience of the Greek city-states in their
finest period, from the eighth to the fourth
century BC. The author analyses the
sources of their creativity and illuminates
the intellectual clarity of their political and
artistic concepts. He examines the conflict
between religion and humanism, and the
social and economic developments which led
to a fragmentation of power. He investigates
particularly the city-state as a political unit;
and he shows how, suffering a loss of
confidence, the world of the city-states in the
end turned in upon itself, At times we see the
reflection of our own problems in the
history of the greatest of our predecessors.

Jacket illustration: Red-figure vase showing
Hercules and Apollo fighting for the sacred
tripod (*Photo:* Ronald Sheridan).

With 16pp of illustrations